FROM ANGEL TO OFFICE WORKER

THE MEXICAN EXPERIENCE

William H. Beezley, series editor

FROM ANGEL TO OFFICE WORKER

Middle-Class Identity and Female

Consciousness in Mexico, 1890–1950

SUSIE S. PORTER

UNIVERSITY OF NEBRASKA PRESS   LINCOLN AND LONDON

Library of Congress Cataloging-in-Publication Data
Names: Porter, Susie S., 1965–author.
Title: From angel to office worker: middle-class identity and
female consciousness in Mexico, 1890–1950 / Susie S. Porter.
Description: Lincoln: University of Nebraska
Press, 2018. | Series: The Mexican experience
Identifiers: LCCN 2017052150
ISBN 9781496204219 (hardback)
ISBN 9781496205780 (paper)
ISBN 9781496206497 (epub)
ISBN 9781496206503 (mobi)
ISBN 9781496206510 (pdf)
Subjects: LCSH: Women—Employment—
Mexico—History—20th century. | Women
clerks—Mexico—History—20th century. | Middle class
women—Mexico—History—20th century. | BISAC:
HISTORY / Latin America / Mexico. |
SOCIAL SCIENCE / Women's Studies.
Classification: LCC HD6101 .P67 2018 | DDC
331.40972/09041–DC23 LC record available
at https://lccn.loc.gov/2017052150

Set in Garamond Premer by E. Cuddy.
Designed by N. Putens.

CONTENTS

ILLUSTRATIONS

GRAPHS AND TABLES

ACKNOWLEDGMENTS

The most important acknowledgments I have to make are in the footnotes of this book and attest to the rich scholarship produced by my colleagues. The history that I have been able to piece together from newspapers, novels, and archives from across Mexico City is meaningful inasmuch as it builds upon and is in dialogue with the work of those scholars.

I have been fortunate to enjoy the camaraderie of scholars of Mexican and women's history, and I thank Mary Kay Vaughan for drawing me into those circles. I have benefited enormously from her support, from the first invitation to give a talk at a university, to connecting me to young scholars in the United States and in Mexico. She has always generously shared her vast knowledge and appreciation for Mexican history and taught me things not published in books.

My work has been inspired by the intellectual exchange with my colleagues, especially María Teresa Fernández Aceves, Ana Lau, Gabriela Cano, Mílada Bazant, Heather Fowler-Salamini, Francie Chassen-López, John Lear, Eddie Wright-Ríos, Nichole Sanders, Víctor Macías-González, and Anne Rubenstein. I have been fortunate to receive invitations to share my work with a broad audience, and I thank the following individuals: Ana Lau, who organized a series of conferences, including one on biography of women, at the Universidad Autónoma Metropolitana, Xochimilco; Gail Mummert at El Colegio de Michoacán; Mario Barbosa Cruz, Clara E. Lida, and María Dolores Lorenzo Río with the Seminario Permanente de Historia Social at El Colegio de México; Alicia Civera Cerecedo at El Colegio Mexiquense; and, Cecilia Bautista García and Ana Cristina Ramírez Barreto at the Universidad Michoacana de San Nicolás Hidalgo. Gabriela Cano and Aurora Gómez-Galvarriato at El Colegio de México, María Teresa Fernández Aceves at the Centro de Investigaciones y

Estudios Superiores en Antropología Social-Occidente, Gail Mummert at El Colegio de Michoacán, and Ann Rubenstein at York University have enriched my work both through their own engagement and by inviting me to work with their students. I am grateful to Bill Beezley for his constant support. From the time when I was a graduate student he has shared his enthusiasm and excitement for Mexican history with me and served as an important sounding board. Mary Kay Vaughan and Robert Alegre read the manuscript and offered important insights that helped me refine my argument and better present my evidence. Jerry Root read every word of this manuscript. I am grateful for his skills as a writer and deep commitment to me as a scholar. I could not have finished this book without Jerry's profound commitment to our raising a family together, as partners, sharing equally in the emotional, mental, and physical labor that family entails.

I began the research for this book during a seven-month research stay in Mexico City when my children were two and five. From that time, my children, Charlie and Cecilia Root, have accompanied me while I brought the project to conclusion. This book would not have been possible if not for the help of colleagues who helped me raise my children. Those same people—Janet Theiss, Bradley Parker, and Beth Clement—read multiple versions of the manuscript and helped me to consider an audience beyond historians of Mexico. I am grateful for the camaraderie and hospitality of Andrea Barrios Nogueira and Patricio Cháves Zaldumbide, and their children Manuela, Julia, and Emiliano. My dear friend Tanya Huntington, in Mexico City, has shared her creativity and, during earthquakes, the small space under her dining room table.

I would also like to acknowledge my mother, who is in part an inspiration for this project. When I was young she worked at home and did part-time dictation in a medical office. By the time I was in high school she was a single mother and worked as a secretary for a newspaper agency. I was in awe of the little notes written in shorthand that she tucked away in her purse along with train tickets, lipstick, and cinnamon gum. I never learned to type as fast as she does, and my spelling and grammar skills do not compare.

I would also like to thank Bridget Barry, Ann Baker, Sabrina Stellrecht, Emily Wendell, and Jonathan Lawrence with the University of Nebraska Press for their professionalism and generosity as editors.

The research for this book was supported by a García Robles Fulbright fellowship.

ABBREVIATIONS

AMEO   Asociación Mexicana de Empleados Oficiales
(Mexican Association of Official Employees)

CFM   Consejo Feminista Mexicana (Mexican
Feminist Commission)

CNAP   Confederación Nacional de la Administración Pública
(National Confederation of Public Administration)

CNC   Confederación Nacional Campesina
(National Peasant Confederation)

CNOP   Confederación Nacional de Organizaciones Populares
(National Confederation of Popular Organizations)

CROM   Confederación Regional Obrera Mexicana
(Mexican Regional Labor Confederation)

CTM   Confederación de Trabajadores de México
(Confederation of Mexican Workers)

DETIC   Departamento de Enseñanza Técnica, Industrial y Comercial
(Department of Technical, Industrial, and Commercial Education)

EPN   Escuela Politécnico Nacional (National Polytechnic School)

ESAP   Escuela Superior de Administración Pública
(School for Advanced Study of Public Administration)

ESCA   Escuela Superior de Comercio y Administración
(Business and Administration School for Advanced Study)

ETIC   Escuela Técnica, Industrial y Comercial para Señoritas
(Technical, Industrial, and Commercial School for
Young Ladies)

FRITI	Frente Revolucionario de Trabajadores Intelectuales (Revolutionary Front of Intellectual Workers)
FSTSE	Federación de Sindicatos de Trabajadores al Servicio del Estado (Federation of State Workers Unions)
FUPDM	Frente Único pro Derechos de la Mujer (Sole Front for Women's Rights)
IPN	Instituto Politécnico Nacional (National Polytechnic Institute)
MLT	Escuela Comercial "Miguel Lerdo de Tejada" para Señoritas ("Miguel Lerdo de Tejada" Commercial School for Young Ladies)
NDR	Nacional Distribuidora y Reguladora (National Distributor and Regulator)
PJMM	Partido José María Morelos (José María Morelos Party)
PNF	Partido Nacional Feminista (National Feminist Party)
PNR	Partido Nacional Revolucionario (National Revolutionary Party)
PRM	Partido de la Revolución Mexicana (Party of the Mexican Revolution)
SEP	Secretaría de Educación Pública (Ministry of Public Education)
SNTE	Sindicato Nacional de Trabajadores de la Educación (National Union of Education Workers)
STERM	Sindicato de Trabajadores de la Enseñanza de la República Mexicana (Union of Education Workers of the Mexican Republic)
TFCA	Tribunal Federal de Conciliación y Arbitraje (Federal Conciliation and Arbitration Tribunal)

FROM ANGEL TO OFFICE WORKER

Introduction

Inquiries into Mexican middle-class identity cannot avoid images of women who work outside the home, yet the history of such women remains largely unwritten.[1] Historians of Mexico and of Latin America have focused on middle-class women in the domestic sphere—*angel de hogar*, angel of the home and have also explored women's roles as teachers and professional reformers, though often without paying explicit, sustained attention to class.[2] *From Angel to Office Worker* centers on a quintessential middle-class occupation, office work, the changes that work brought in women's individual lives, and the societal change they drove based on that work experience. The book examines the material conditions of *empleadas públicas* (women who worked in government offices) and considers how debates over the shift in women's employment and public presence shaped middle-class identities in Mexico. Women played an integral role in shaping middle-class identity as they mobilized with pen, petition, and in the streets. As activists in organizations both independent and tied to the state, government office workers forged new ways of thinking about women's rights in Mexico.

The Angel of the Home Goes to Work

When women took to office work in the 1890s, their experiences were informed by prevailing gender and class norms. In nineteenth-century Mexico, as Silvia Arrom, William French, Sonya Lipsett-Rivera, and others show, people understood a woman's presence in the home as key to middle-class identity.[3] Respectability, a key component of that identity, depended on a woman's presence in the home, celebrated the "angel of the home," and questioned the morality of women outside its confines. Such conceptions of gender and class had a long history. Fray Luis de León in *La perfecta casada* (*The Perfect Wife*, 1583), for example, envisioned female respectability as women's physical seclusion. Although *La perfecta casada* was published in the sixteenth century, variations on this theme persisted for centuries. The phrase "angel of the home" was used throughout Europe in the 1850s and was most likely spread to Latin America by María del Pilar Sinués de Marco's 1859 advice manual *El ángel del hogar*.[4] During the late nineteenth century the phrase "angel del hogar" circulated in Mexico as the name of a women's periodical (1891–93) and as a descriptive phrase in articles, essays, and novels.[5] Among the generation that came of age in the early 1900s, however, fewer and fewer people relied on the presence of an "angel of the home" as a requirement of middle-class respectability. The ideal dissipated in the face of the changing realities of women's work.

Transnational shifts in women's role within production played out according to local contexts and affected women's role in middle- and working-class households alike. In the United States, for example, by the mid-nineteenth century the economic value of women's work within the household economy declined, as more and more consumer goods were purchased rather than made at home. Declining working conditions led the daughters and sons of artisans to turn to clerical work. A small number of women who claimed middle-class status entered the workforce, impelled varyingly by economic need and social or intellectual interest.[6] In Mexico, the women who first knocked on office doors seeking employment did so within a specific labor market that shaped the jobs they took, the wages they were paid, and the professional opportunities that work might have offered. This study focuses on Mexico City as a specific labor market where economic change in the mid- to late nineteenth century had a significant impact on the middle class, artisans, and factory workers alike.

Throughout the Americas, class and ethnic identities shaped women's workforce participation. Middle-class conceptions of respectability were defined by a woman's presence in the home and delimited women's workforce participation. Women's choices were informed by conceptions of female respectability that construed work in the public sphere—street vendor, factory worker, and work that required transiting the streets, such as domestic work—as a marker of lesser social status. In early nineteenth-century Mexico City, caste and Indian women were more likely than those who identified as Spanish to engage in work that drew them into public spaces. Some women, loath to work in public, devised strategies to generate an income nonetheless. Those with sufficient means to produce goods at home (clothing or food, for example) hired other women to sell in public markets and on the streets. Others might work from home, selling their services as a seamstress or by setting up a cigar dispensary (*estanquillo*), which allowed them to generate an income while remaining at home. To emphasize their distance from the public, women who set up cigar dispensaries positioned themselves behind a counter to separate themselves from customers coming in from the street. Additional strategies for generating income while limiting one's public presence included running a small tavern (half of which in Mexico City were owned by women), pawning personal items, and sending a servant to gather laundry to be washed at home.[7]

The ideal of female seclusion began to decline in mid-nineteenth-century Mexico City in response to economic recession and high levels of male mortality, opening the way for middle-class women to seek employment. According to Silvia Arrom, a limited number of "respectable" occupations opened to women midcentury, primarily in welfare institutions and teaching. Some 150 women worked as teachers in Mexico City in the mid-nineteenth century. The National Teacher Training School for Women did not open until 1889. Part of what characterized these occupations as respectable, Arrom notes, is that the women were employed to provide services to other women. Women also worked within the walls of monasteries in a wide range of occupations of varying social status such as accountant, teacher, cook, or maid. While physically secluded, they played an integral role in the economy. Women were barred from working for the government bureaucracy throughout the nineteenth century until they were first hired in the 1890s.[8]

Mexico experienced rapid economic growth between 1884 and 1900, the period during which women first began to work in government offices. By 1884 President Porfirio Díaz (1876–1911) had consolidated a particularly effective government, facilitated a flood of foreign investment, and shepherded in a gross national product that rose at a rate of 8 percent annually. The flood of foreign investment, a series of poor harvest years, and a sharp rise in prices led to inflation and a decline in real wages between 1900 and 1910. Between 1906 and 1908 an economic crisis led to layoffs, which, combined with the return of thousands of laborers from the United States, contributed to rising unemployment. Wage-earning women had access to a limited range of jobs. Nationwide, as much as a third of working women labored in domestic service. Women, whom one landowner described as "cheaper than machines," worked in agricultural production as well. According to economist Teresa Rendón Gan, women were 0.4 percent of agricultural workers nationwide in 1895 and 2 percent in 1910. Faced with limited opportunities at the turn of the century, women migrated to urban centers in search of work. Indeed, 67 percent of Mexico City residents were immigrants in 1900, and the Federal District had the highest percentage of women of any state in the country between 1895 and 1921.[9]

The Mexico City labor market differed from that of most regions of the country due to the robust manufactory sector and the jobs generated by urban services. According to an 1879 census, women constituted 37 percent of the Mexico City industrial workforce. While women made up a significant percentage of workers in industry, their employment was restricted to twelve of the thirty-eight occupations included in the census, with 70 percent of all women working in the female-dominated industries of tobacco products (85 percent female) and ready-made clothing (100 percent female). Women also worked alongside men in the production of matches and paper (50 percent of the workforce), cotton textiles (31 percent), chocolate (24 percent), shoes (23 percent), and hats (16 percent).[10] Those women who sought the respectability of non-manual work found opportunities in the expansion of the education system between 1895 and 1910, during which time the number of teachers increased from 12,748 to 21,017. The growth in the number of teachers, however, was accompanied by declining working conditions for women who frequently worked as low-wage primary school teacher aids.[11] The economic crisis between 1906 and 1908 saw a notable decline in women's employment in textile and clothing production, as well as in domestic labor.[12] Women from a wide range of occupations, working-class and middle-class alike, looked for new work opportunities. For some, that opportunity appeared with the expansion of government bureaucracy.

Bureaucracy, Lutz Raphael writes, is profoundly implicated in modernization. Public administration can be seen as a form of social control, a catalyst for the formation of categories of understanding, and as the generator of a significant portion of the archives that form the basis of the historian's craft. Napoleonic public administration, from which the Mexican state originates, cultivated the collection, generation, and communication of information.[13] The long process of development of an administrative culture based on writing has had many stages, timed according to national specificity, with an important expansion occurring in Mexico in the late nineteenth and early twentieth centuries. With the expansion of paperwork (and the implementation of new technologies like the typewriter, telephone, and telegraph) the labor required to study, count, inspect, license, communicate, and file required specialization that was implemented based on the gendered division of labor.

The feminization of bureaucracy was a transnational phenomenon that played out according to local context. The British government began hiring women to work in the Postmaster General's office in the 1850s.[14] In the United States, the federal government first hired women in 1861, part of a wave of government employment growth between 1859 and 1903. In 1860 most women who identified as middle class had grown up influenced by the domestic ideal, which held that respectable women should not, unless absolutely necessary, work outside the home. The exceptions were teachers, who replicated the role of mothers. Over the course of the next thirty years an important transformation in middle-class work occurred, with growing numbers employed in salaried white-collar occupations. In 1903 women were just under 27 percent of U. S. government employees. Different histories of national economic growth meant that the Mexican government did not hire women to meet the needs of an expanding bureaucracy until the 1890s; however, by the turn of the century women were 7 percent of government employees, growing to 13 percent in 1910.[15]

In Mexico, as elsewhere in Latin America, historians and historical actors have closely associated government work with the middle class. José Tomás Cuéllar, in *La linterna mágica* (The magic lantern, 1889–92), refers to a government job as turning a no-good into part of the respectable class. In 1900, Justo Sierra, in *Evolución política del pueblo mexicano* (*The Political Evolution of the Mexican People*), identified the growth of a middle class in Mexico with, among other factors, the expansion of the state's payroll, an argument repeated fifty years later by sociologist José E. Iturriaga. The Mexican middle class (8.3 percent of the population in 1900 and 15.5 percent in 1950), Iturriaga found, was primarily an urban phenomenon based on the expansion of the federal bureaucracy, as well as industrial development and internal migration. As evidence of the growth of the middle class, he noted that over a thirty-year period the number of government employees in the country grew 296.36 percent: in 1921 Mexico had 63,074 government employees (federal, state, and municipal); in 1930, 153,343; in 1940, 191,588; and in 1950, 247,000.[16] Sociologists writing during the 1970s so closely identified the middle class with government employment as to establish "bureaucratic bourgeoisie" as a necessary category for understanding class relations and the exercise of political power in Mexico.[17] The degree and nature of that political power has been debated extensively.

Mexican economists and political scientists writing since the 1950s have fretted over the limited size of the Mexican middle class because they believed in its progressive and democratic potential. Soledad Loaeza's groundbreaking work on the Mexican middle class challenged rosy characterizations of the middle class and argues that despite traditional demands for political participation, post-war economic growth and the promise of social mobility led the middle class to tacit acceptance of authoritarian political rule. Tiziana

Bertaccini argues that the Mexican middle class has not been associated consistently with a given ideological position, while Louise Walker's study of post-1968 Mexico argues the middle class pursued centrist politics and the ushering in of neoliberalism. Andrés Reyes Rodríguez, in his study of political culture in Aguascalientes during the 1940s and 1950s, demonstrates how the middle class sought incorporation into official party politics in order to claim privileges granted to industrial and agricultural workers during the 1930s. The aforementioned studies have, by and large, captured a broad range of people as middle class, some defined by occupation—artisans, bank employees, and professionals—others defined by demographic group, such as women or youth.[18] These studies include government workers but the specific conditions and politics of that group are often subsumed in a more general discussion of the middle class.[19]

Historians of class relations in post-revolutionary Mexico have focused primarily on the rural and urban working classes and have referred only in passing to the concomitant ascendancy of the middle class. Historiographical debates over whether the state imposed itself on workers and peasants or if the subaltern gave shape to the state have largely sidestepped the role of the middle class in those processes.[20] Although it would be an oversimplification to say that the state is the sum of its parts, most of which are middle-class employees, it is worth examining the class status and political role of the people who filled government offices and made the state function. Recent studies provide some insight on these processes during the 1920s. Susanne Eineigel shows how people mobilized as neighborhood residents and public service users, making claims on political promises made by revolutionary leaders. Some of these self-identified middle-class residents worked as government employees. Mario Barbosa Cruz provides the most sustained analysis of government workers with his essay on Department of the Federal District employees. Both Eineigel and Barbosa Cruz show that during the 1920s government workers mobilized, on an individual basis and sometimes collectively, for better working conditions, for material resources, and improved urban services.[21]

Though largely excluded from labor studies, government employees played an integral role in the Mexican labor movement.[22] The government-employee labor movement follows a trajectory similar to that of the working class more generally, though the dates of that mobilization are later than those for artisans and workers. Whereas Mexico City artisans established mutual aid societies in the 1840s, government employees did not do so until a short-lived effort in 1875.[23] In 1919, teachers, themselves government employees, went on strike and quickly learned they could not claim the rights conceded to *obreros* (workers) in Article 123 of the Constitution of 1917, including the right to strike. The state (*estado patrón*), the courts argued, was by nature a different sort of employer than the private sector. The courts, politicians, and public employees all debated the legal and administrative rights of public employees throughout the 1920s. The Federal Arbitration Board (Junta Federal de Conciliación y Arbitraje), established in 1927, would not hear complaints filed by government workers. While worker mobilization reached an all-time high in the 1920s, due to the different legal status of public employees, their organizing did not peak until a decade later. When the Federal Labor Law was proposed in the late 1920s, debated in 1929, and made law in 1931, public employees lobbied to be included but were unsuccessful. To appease public employees, the government promised a future civil service law, which, though introduced in the early 1920s, did not come to fruition until nearly forty years later.[24]

During the 1930s, state efforts to draw unions into its orbit of influence led to the consolidation of the labor movement and to a relationship that in subsequent decades limited the independence of organized labor.[25] Just as this was true for obreros, it was also true for government employees. The official history of the Federation of State Workers Unions (Federación de Sindicatos de Trabajadores al Servicio del Estado) credits women in the Ministry of National Economy with establishing the first employee union (1934), leading to a proliferation of ministry-based unions. Ministry of National Economy employees demanded enforcement of Articles 37 and 60 of the proposed civil service law, which established severance pay and overtime. The mobilization of working-class government workers (mechanics, printers, and sanitation workers, for example) formed unions that came together as the Alliance of State Workers Organizations (Alianza de Organizaciones de Trabajadores del Estado) in December 1935. Less than a year later, on

September 4, 1936, the Pro-Unity Congress of the National Federation of State Workers (Congreso Pro-Unidad de la Federación Nacional de Trabajadores del Estado) convened at Bolívar Theater. In efforts to contain the public-employee movement, President Lázaro Cárdenas sponsored the establishment of the Federation of State Workers Unions in November 1938, the Statute for Government Workers (Estatuto de los trabajadores al servicio de los poderes de la unión) on December 5, 1938, and the Federal Conciliation and Arbitration Tribunal (April 1, 1939), which would mediate conflict between public employees and their employer, the state.[26]

Labor Feminism

Feminism has most frequently been associated with middle-class women and demands disassociated from labor. The "other women's movement," as it is termed by Dorothy Sue Cobble in her book by the same name on working-class feminism, was made up of women who, based on work experiences, pushed for reforms with wide-ranging impact.[27] Middle- and working-class feminism should not, however, be considered as separate movements or even as distinct influences in the life of an individual. Daniel Horowitz has argued that to appreciate fully Betty Friedan's feminism, we have to understand her labor activism in the United Electrical, Radio, and Machine Workers (UE) during the 1940s and 1950s. Friedan's experiences in the labor movement informed her feminism, which, as it was construed in the 1950s, seemed to have little to do with labor and everything to do with domesticity. As a labor journalist, Friedan wrote about workplace gender discrimination, equal pay for equal work, racial discrimination, the need for day care to support working mothers, and corporate misconstrual of women as consumers rather than producers. These concerns, Horowitz argues, informed Friedan's analysis of suburban womanhood and middle-class liberal feminism in the 1960s.[28] While periodization appropriate for the United States should not be applied to Mexican history, the labor experiences of clerical workers served as a vital source of Mexican feminism. The 1940s maternalism, which some scholars have criticized for its limited political potential, in fact emerged as a labor demand during the

1920s as women articulated their struggles to balance motherhood and work as government employees.

Scholars frequently use the word feminism to describe a social movement or critical analysis, regardless of whether the historical actors themselves employed the word. In the Latin American context, some caution is necessary. First, feminism is a word with a fraught history. It has been characterized as a concept imposed from outside Latin American realities as a way to discredit women's activism as non-native. Second, whether or not historical actors themselves described a given idea or social movement as "feminist" should be considered integral to our investigation of the history of feminism. In response to such cautions, I examine the way historical actors employed the word feminism. Karen Offen identifies Hubertine Auclert (1848–1914) as the first self-proclaimed feminist in France and argues that the word *féminisme* began to circulate widely in France in the 1890s, where it was synonymous with women's emancipation. Offen writes that the word "jumped" from France over the Atlantic to the United States and Latin America in the late 1890s, although she also notes that Auclert used the word feminist in an open letter to Susan B. Anthony in 1888. Asunción Lavrin dates the use of the word *feminista* in the Southern Cone to the period between 1895 and 1905.[29]

While the word feminist may have come to Mexico from France, the United States, Spain, or perhaps Argentina, women in Mexico would have taken up the word in ways that made sense to local circumstances. The meaning attributed to the word feminism varied not only from country to country, shaped by the historical specificity of place and time, but also within the same society. As Gabriela Cano and Lucrecia Infante Vargas show, government functionaries and journalists used the word feminism to describe changes in women's social roles, regardless of any call for political change. This study argues that by the turn-of-the-century, one use of the word feminism in Mexico was to describe middle-class women's changing workforce participation.[30] By the 1920s, use of the word feminism shifted from a description of women's workforce participation to a way of describing the origins of a movement for social change.

Late nineteenth- and early twentieth-century feminism in Mexico has multiple roots in women's intellectual, political, and cultural life. The intellectual roots of feminism can be traced to a generation of women with access to written culture, both through formal education and through the appearance of periodicals by and for women in the last third of the nineteenth century. The first periodical produced by women appeared in Mérida in 1870, followed in 1873 by *Las Hijas del Anáhuac* (Daughters of Anáhuac) in Mexico City, where women's press flourished throughout the 1880s and 1890s. Women who came of age at the turn of the century were inspired by transnational anticlericalism, the masonic movement, and spiritism María Teresa Fernández Aceves argues that these cultural and intellectual traditions allowed for women to question their subjugation and facilitated a critique of the institutions they identified with that subjugation, especially the Roman Catholic Church. Women born into families that adhered to a liberal tradition often found support to pursue their beliefs and aspirations during a time when many questioned them. Women's empowerment within the Catholic tradition took on a very different trajectory, and Catholic women did not for the most part refer to themselves as feminists.[31]

The history of Mexican feminism has also been told as political and organizational history, particularly with regard to suffrage. Francisco I. Madero's call for "effective suffrage, no re-election" made women's political disenfranchisement all the more evident. Delegates to the constitutional convention (1916–17), however, sidestepped granting women the right to vote and left ambiguous language that would be debated in the following decades. Ana Lau, Gabriela Cano, and Carmen Ramos Escandón, in separate studies, have documented the rich organizational history of women's activism during the 1920s.[32] In addition to the growing number of professional women these scholars identify as feminist, a good number of office workers also gave voice to a range of concerns about self-determination and equal access to education, work, and political participation. Esperanza Tuñón Pablos shows in her pioneering study that the 1930s saw women mobilize en masse. While it is clear from its name that working women participated in the pivotal National Congress of Women Workers and Peasants (Congreso Nacional de Obreras y Campesinas, 1931, 1933, 1934), government employees played an important role as well. The current study highlights the role of women who worked in government offices in organizing and shaping the direction of those congresses and the subsequent founding of the Sole Front for Women's Rights (Frente Único Pro Derechos de la Mujer, 1935), which quickly came to claim more than fifty thousand members nationwide. Through this activism, government office workers contributed to a definition of Mexican feminism as the right to work, equal wages, and full citizenship. The public-employee movement was central to gaining suffrage; office workers—from professional women to rank-and-file clerical workers— pushed for the right to vote within the political party that dominated their workplace. These efforts built momentum toward full suffrage in 1953.[33]

In both the United States and Mexico, the women who gained access to government jobs played a crucial role in advancing the cause of working women. These women facilitated conversations within an institutional space that also gave them access to resources and influence. They also served as a conduit between rank-and-file and professional women who themselves also experienced discrimination. In the United States, by the late 1910s professional women moved into government bureaucracy. We see this most notably in the Women in Industry Service Agency opened by the Department of Labor in 1918, a precursor to the Women's Bureau, established in 1920. Mexican women did not gain access to similar levels of influence until the early 1930s, but when they did their influence was formidable, in part due to their numbers and in part due to their role within union and party politics. In Mexico both professional women and women who had worked their way up the ranks as office workers had, by the 1930s, made their voices heard and gained access to power.[34]

Women's position within the Mexican public-employee workforce informed their activism. Occupational segregation meant that women worked in low-wage jobs and had fewer opportunities for professionalization, especially prior to the 1930s. Nevertheless, women who had begun working in government offices in the 1910s, gained work experience and advanced to positions of some standing that empowered them to mobilize in the 1920s. Empleadas fought for the rights granted to obreras in the Constitution of 1917, including maternity leave and access to day-care facilities so as to make motherhood compatible with work outside the home. They also rallied around the issues of equal pay for equal work and respect for seniority in hiring and promotion. The structure of public-sector employment gave women leverage to argue for equality at work (job categories came with a standard salary), thereby fortifying the power of the equal rights argument within the Mexican women's movement. Empleadas also fought for safeguards for female autonomy and dignity inside and outside the workplace. These experiences served as the basis of their labor activism and the demands they made within the women's movement, as evidenced in the National Congress of Women Workers and Peasants in the 1930s and in women's union activism as government employees during the 1940s.

Empleada activism relied significantly on the power of the printed word. Work, writing, and activism blend in this history and are explored from the perspective of the concept of "cultura escrita" (culture based in the written word), developed by Carmen Castañeda. Castañeda takes up Renee Hobbs's work on "effective literacy . . . that allows one to enact personal and societal change."[35] In the specific case of young women in early twentieth-century Mexico City, writing, participation in the educational system, and work experiences empowered women, individually and collectively, to make changes in their lives. For many office workers, written culture was integral to their activism as they developed their ideas in published essays, engaged in the margins of literary culture, and employed their words to mobilize others at meetings and demonstrations. As a collective movement, the arguments and ideas developed by office workers who published and spoke to the press advanced the cause for those who did not have such access. And the printed word had all the more power because of the mobilization of rank-and-file clerical workers.

Expansion of the education system, a pivotal moment in women's history, supported women's effective literacy and an administrative culture based in writing. The efficiency of the state depended on the capacity of its employees to read and to write. In the mid-nineteenth century, governments established national administration schools, in France in 1848, and in Mexico shortly thereafter.[36] As was the case more generally with educational opportunities, access for women came later than for men. The vocational education system, established by Benito Juárez, opened its doors to men in Mexico City in 1856. Fifteen years later the School for Manual Arts and Trades for

Women (Escuela de Artes y Oficios para Mujeres) opened and eventually offered classes in clerical skills. In 1880 the school offered accounting, and by 1891 typing, stenography, and telegraphy were added to the curriculum. Young women of middle- and working-class backgrounds quickly filled the classrooms. The Advanced School for Business and Administration (Escuela Superior de Comercio y Administración), established in 1868, began to offer classes to women in 1894.[37] Women flocked to the school, and in 1900 they petitioned Doña Carmen Romero Rubio de Díaz, the wife of President Díaz, for more opportunities for women's commercial education. The word comercial was used to describe both business schools for men and secretarial schools for women. The next year a presidential decree called for the establishment of the "Miguel Lerdo de Tejada" Commercial School for Young Ladies (Escuela Comercial "Miguel Lerdo de Tejada" para Señoritas), which opened in 1903.[38] This school quickly became a vibrant cultural center in the city and served as an important space where women developed literacy skills and found their own voice.

Gendered Dimensions of Class Identities

This book suggests a different way for historians of Latin America and the Americas to approach class identity. Without always making their criteria explicit, historians have used objective criteria such as occupation, income, and place of residence as indicators of class status. They have examined political agenda or consumer habits to ascribe class status. Scholars have also enriched the study of social class with discourse analysis, particularly within the context of political struggle.[39] Many historical conceptions of class have been formulated while leaving women, roughly half of the population, out of the equation. To be sure, for decades labor historians have included women and have highlighted some of the ways women experience work differently than men. By and large, women have been disadvantageously positioned within a gender-segregated workforce, have been paid lower wages than men, and have had mixed success within the labor movement. Employers, co-workers, and social commentators have made sexual morality relevant to women's workforce experience. Some historians have argued that women's motivations for labor protest have differed from men's due to their responsibilities in the home. Women have also had a different relationship to consumer culture than men.[40] While we now have a fuller understanding of women's work experiences, our conceptions of class have not significantly altered. In part this is because we have applied definitions of class using models based on the experiences of men. This exclusion matters because women have had a different relationship than men to work, socioeconomic status, and other criteria used to define class.

The study of female office workers provides an ideal case to open a new dimension in the study of social class, because neither objective nor discursive configurations of class remained stable for women, and indeed were often seemingly contradictory. In a given historical moment people spoke in conflicting ways about the class status of female office workers. Contradictory class positions appeared within the same text or conversation. How do we understand how a typist or secretary could be construed as both working class and as middle class? Instead of asking which socioeconomic class these women belonged to, my work asks how and why multiple class identities adhered to women who worked outside the home. In this sense, I expand on the approach taken by historians who have questioned the way consumer habits have blurred class identity. Barbara Weinstein shows how working-class women's consumer habits confused middle-class observers and allowed some working women to "pass" as middle class in early twentieth-century Brazil. Nan Enstad demonstrates that working-class women's consumer habits in the United States in the first decade of the twentieth century, led middle-class observers to dismiss working-class women's capacity for political engagement.[41] While the present study takes consumer habits into consideration, it does so as part of a larger discussion of the ways gender norms, especially those related to domesticity, work, and motherhood, contribute to class identity.

The lives of women who worked in offices were also different from those of male office workers in material terms. The "salaried masses," as Siegfried Kracauer called office workers in 1920s Germany, were a heterogeneous group.[42] But there is something more going on when we talk about female office workers. To put it in Marxian terms, women's relationship to "the means of production" has often been mediated by a dependent relationship on men.

And, to draw from Pierre Bourdieu, women's access to capital (economic, social, cultural, and, symbolic), their habitus (dispositions), and practices of cultural distinction can all differ from that of men who might otherwise share their class identity. It is therefore problematic to define women's class status based on the men they are seen (sometimes mistakenly) to depend upon, for in doing so we miss the more complex relationship women have had to class. In many circumstances, women have had a changing and fluid class status, as Jane Eyre, Lily Bart, and Ifigenia (of Venezuela) would tell us. All of these women had, throughout their lives, multiple relationships to class identity. Women's social mobility and their class identity are contingent upon gender-specific circumstances including civil status (married, widowed, divorced, single), property ownership, parental responsibilities, and their position within a gendered labor force. Women took to office work under radically different circumstances than men. If a woman divorced, her class status was likely to change much more than that of a man. A single man had more likelihood of gaining respectability at work than a woman. As Cindy Sondik Aron shows in her study of government employees in the turn-of-the-century United States, men came to the work reluctantly and as downwardly mobile members of the middle class, while women jumped at the opportunity for relatively good wages in work that conformed to conceptions of middle-class female respectability.[43]

The fluid relationship some women have had with class identity leads us to question whether class identity is as fixed as we have assumed it to be. Both objective and discursive approaches have led scholars to study a single class (*the* middle class, *the* working class, even *the* lower middle class). And, in all instances, class is apparently a hermetic category. While individuals might strive to ascend (or avoid descent) in class status, the class identity itself is fixed. As in much feminist scholarship, my work does not search out rigid subject positions (e.g., "worker"). It does, however, explore the variable rhetoric of class invoked over the course of shifts in women's employment. When, with Ezequiel Adamovsky, we ask how middle-class identity serves as a metaphor, we open up more fluid and contingent notions of social class.[44]

This study also acknowledges the ways class formations are interdependent. Middle-class identity evolved in a dynamic relationship to working-class identity. In Mexico, social commentators drew on conceptions of women and work that were formulated as women entered into factory work prior to the 1880s. And, in order to justify their participation in the labor force, female office workers refashioned arguments utilized by working-class women of previous generations into a new language of middle-class identity. Just as working-class women had done, office workers claimed that "respectable" work would protect female sexual morality. Women who identified as middle class also borrowed arguments from working-class women regarding the propriety of new forms of female mobility and the rights of single mothers. By showing how middle-class subjectivity drew on the rhetoric of working-class femininity, my research emphasizes the relationship between class-based identities, rather than on class identities as discrete categories.[45]

Chapter Organization

Chapter 1 examines the material and discursive conditions of class in turn-of-the-century Mexico City as the setting for women's first forays into work in government offices in the 1890s. From 1890 through the Mexican Revolution (1910–17), growing numbers of women sought ways to support themselves and their families. The boundaries of middle-class identity became porous, and women stepped into new roles that questioned female dependency and opened the possibility of work outside the home. This shift in middle-class women's employment was called feminism. Chapter 2 examines the boom in women's public-sector employment and in commercial schooling during the 1920s. Chapter 3 shows how female office workers drew on their work and school experiences to formulate a critique of gender and class relations in and beyond the workplace. This critique resulted in a work-based strand of feminism. During the 1920s empleadas found more space to make their voices heard within the women's movement than in the public-employee associations that men established during the decade.

Chapters 4, 5, and 6 show how the 1930s marked a pivotal moment when the number of female government employees surpassed the number of female teachers and women in the public sector made vital contributions to both the labor and women's rights movements. Within the context of the political populism that celebrated workers, and a public-sector labor movement that sought gains made by workers, women continued to struggle to define middle-class status as inclusive of motherhood and work outside the home. Chapter 7 explores 1940s political culture with a focus on the empleada demand for day care, as it was represented in newspapers, sociological literature, and film. Each of these media presented a conservative vision of day care as necessary to keep women relegated to the home and in the role of mother. However, as the chapter shows, day care was vitally important to women who worked in government offices, and the gains they made in this respect were the result of decades of struggle and the growing power of women within the federal bureaucracy.

1 "Women of the Middle Class, More Than Others, Need to Work"

This proclamation, printed in *La Convención Radical Obrera* in 1894, may seem surprising.[1] With the important exception of teachers, public commentary had associated middle-class identity with women who remained in the private sphere. And yet, both artisans and the middle class engaged in a vigorous conversation over women and work in the mid-1890s. Economic growth during the Porfiriato (1876–1911) was marked by shifts in the labor market and inflation, with profound implications for women. Though household-level studies for the period are lacking, we do know that the mid-1880s were characterized by inflation that put pressure on artisan and middle-class households alike. Artisan households suffered to such a degree that people took to the streets in 1883, 1884, and 1892.[2] The years 1900 to 1910 were also marked by inflation, compounded in 1907 and 1908 by rising unemployment. In response, people began to rethink the role of women within the middle-class household economy and to question cultural restrictions on women working outside the home. For those women already employed outside the home, working conditions declined in the industries that hired primarily women, especially sewing and cigar and cigarette production.[3] Women, from seamstress to teacher, needed work, and that need would be answered, in Mexico City, with the opening of government office work to women.

Shifts in women's workforce participation led to new ways of speaking about women, class, and feminism. This chapter examines the public conversations in Mexico City regarding women and work that appeared in a variety of media—newspapers, journals, and public speeches—between 1884 and the mid-1910s. Public commentary about working women was nothing new in the 1880s. Commentators had for decades expressed concern over "mixing the sexes" when women entered into work spaces conceived of as male, factories primarily. Women's interaction with men outside the domestic sphere posed a danger, they argued, to female sexual morality. Politicians, labor activists, journalists, and intellectuals simultaneously drew on these conceptions of women and work, and on conceptions of class identities, to produce new ways of talking about female office workers. What was new about these conversations was the ways of marking middle-class identity. Education, work, and the capacity to choose when to marry began to eclipse the ideal of the "angel of the home" as foundational components of middle-class identity.

Commercial education played an important role in training women for office work and in defining that work as middle class. In efforts to meet the need for office workers to fill an expanding bureaucracy, in 1903 the federal government opened a new school for commercial education specifically for women, the "Miguel Lerdo de Tejada" Commercial School for Young Ladies. President Díaz, officials in the Ministry of Justice and Public Education (1891–1905), and teachers hoped the school would serve as a conduit to new professional and cultural opportunities for women. And it did. The female-centered school culture, the curriculum, and the public rituals to which women gained access contributed to expand public roles for women. Commentators identified the growing number of female office workers as middle class and associated them with feminism, despite the lack of a robust social movement that identified itself as such prior to the 1910s.[4]

Women and Work

Whereas the year 1879 had seen a series of articles asserting the primary role of women within the home, by the early 1880s articles ran on the topic "women and work."[5] By the 1890s a combination of social and economic factors led labor and middle-class newspapers alike to debate not whether women should work but rather how to support their move into new white-collar occupations and the consequences of this trend.[6] Commentators questioned traditional middle-class gender norms and lamented women's lack of options for work outside the home. For their part, women sought wage-earning opportunities that offered good conditions and reflected positively on their class identity. The possibility, and increasing reality, of women working outside the home contributed to shifts in class identities. The domestic ideal was decentered. The angel of the home continued to serve as a reference point but was no longer the pivot around which middle-class identity revolved. Middle-class identity came to include women working outside the home in "respectable" occupations. The respectability of that work was characterized by the education required to obtain it, by the condition that it be considered non-manual labor, and by the appearance of female sexual propriety. Nineteenth-century liberal reform, which included a reconceptualization of the legal status of women within the family and marriage, served as context for women's changing relationship to work, marriage, and family, and thus to class identity.

In the last quarter of the nineteenth century, important changes occurred in the Mexico City economy and workforce. The city's economy shifted toward machine manufacturing, with a significant impact on artisans, workers, and the middle class. Following the devaluation of silver in 1883 and financial crisis from 1891 to 1894, the government stabilized the foreign debt and successfully encouraged foreign investment. Some 70 percent of the Mexico City population was, in the late nineteenth century, composed of artisans, factory workers, small business owners, and unskilled labor.[7] From 1895 to 1900 the expansion of factory production outweighed the decline in artisan production. However, between 1900 and 1910 artisans were displaced more quickly than industry could absorb them.[8] This, coupled with growing inflation—at a rate of 2.1 percent between 1894 and 1904 and nearly 5 percent between 1904 and 1910—likely led to a decrease in the living standards for the average working- and middle-class household. Hyperinflation between 1914 and 1917 compounded the challenges people faced in making ends meet.[9] In response to economic pressures on households, women sought work outside the home.

Of course, women had a long history of work outside the home, as laundress, seamstress, cook, child-minder, and in artisanal production. Throughout the colonial period guild rules had not allowed women anything but temporary membership, in the case of the death of a spouse who was a guild member, and then only for one year. Despite the 1799 decree abolishing such barriers, Silvia Arrom found that women's workforce participation shifted only slightly.[10] From 1753 to 1854 women remained approximately one-third of the Mexico City workforce, concentrated primarily in paid domestic work. Sonia Pérez Toledo's in-depth study of Mexico City found 17 percent of women worked in artisanal trades—in order of significance, textiles, clothing production, tobacco, leather, and food preparation.[11] Women also worked in commerce (9 percent), in the home (5 percent), and in professions (3 percent) such as teacher and nurse.[12] Since the early years of the Mexican Republic women made cigars and cigarettes in large manufactories, while some women, seeking "respectability," sold cigars and cigarettes from behind a counter in a shop attached to their home, thus avoiding association with work outside the home.[13]

During the last quarter of the nineteenth century, women constituted more than one-third of the Mexico City industrial workforce, yet the nature of women's workforce participation was in flux. Census data for Mexico City note a modest decline (4 percent) in female employment between 1895 and 1910.[14] Several of the occupations that were considered "women's work"—cigarrera (cigarette worker) and seamstress, for example—saw increasingly difficult working conditions. Cigarette factory owners increased piecework allotments for rollers, who went on strike numerous times throughout the 1880s, with particularly significant mobilization in 1881, 1885, and 1887. *La Convención Radical Obrera*, official paper of the artisan group the Workers Congress (Congreso Obrero), was a vocal supporter of the cigarreras. By the

1890s the paper was calling for more respectable work options for middle-class women and may have had these same cigarreras in mind. Contractors for the ready-made-clothing industry raised production quotas as a way to reduce labor costs, and as a result, seamstresses also struggled to earn a living wage. A journalist for *El Imparcial*, a Mexico City daily, reported in 1897 that a seamstress who worked ten to twelve hours a day might earn 25 to 37 cents.[15] *La Convención Radical Obrera* characterized such women as "typical of the middle class" and as a "martyr without a palm frond."[16]

Teaching, one of the few "respectable" occupations open to women, initially represented an opportunity for intellectual life and an entrée to professional identity, but by the turn of the century it had become less attractive. In 1869 the Juárez government, as a part of its initiative to expand the Mexican education system, opened the Secondary School for Girls (Escuela Secundaria para Niñas) in Mexico City. Under President Díaz, in 1889 the Secondary School for Girls became the Normal School for Women (Escuela Normal para Mujeres).[17] Teaching became associated with traditionally feminine roles which bolstered women's growing authority and presence in elementary school education.[18] Between 1875 and 1905 women went from 57 to 76 percent of primary school teachers. In separate studies, Mílada Bazant and María Eugenia Chaoul Pereyra found that when the Mexican government reclassified teachers as public employees in 1896, a growing number of women worked as primary school teacher aides. Those positions, however, did not require a degree and were low paid. Occupational segregation placed a downward pressure on salaries, which remained stagnant between 1867 and 1903. Meanwhile, the cost of living increased.[19] Teachers petitioned the federal government, complaining of stagnant wages and a long workday accentuated by the commute to and from work.[20] *La Convención Radical Obrera* ran an article in 1894 that, after considering all work options for women, made financial calculations that were not encouraging:

> The education crisis takes its victims from our most honorable and hardworking families. Take, for example, the young teacher (*preceptora*) who earns her degree thanks to thousands of sacrifices and privations. It has

cost her family more than 2,600 pesos to support her studies and at the end of six years she has earned her degree, only to find a position that pays an annual salary of 300 pesos.[21]

The social status of teachers fell into such decline that one woman declared, "A teaching degree? Impossible! It has become so ordinary that even the daughters of doormen and women who iron get this degree."[22]

Women's need for work occurred within the context of a movement throughout Latin America that threw into question women's dependent legal status.[23] Liberal reforms swept the continent in the mid-nineteenth century, resulting in the increased rights of individuals (at least for some) and the establishment of civil marriage. The adoption of civil marriage raised questions as to its dissolution. During the 1860s and 1870s, jurists revamped civil codes and women exercised increased individuality within marriage and the process of its dissolution, as Ana Lidia García Peña argues.[24] And the conversation was not confined to the courtroom, jurists, or educated elite. In 1880 the newspaper *La Mujer* (Woman), published by the School for Manual Arts and Trades for Young Ladies, reported news of changing laws to allow for divorce in France.[25]

Long-standing concern about female dependency, both material and moral, framed discussions about women's need for work. In 1884, Concepción Gimeno de Flaquer, a Spanish women's rights advocate who resided in Mexico City and was director of *El Álbum de la Mujer*, wrote an article calling for more work options for women. If women were allowed the means to achieve economic independence, they could exercise their agency in a way that would safeguard their morality. "Allow a woman to support herself," she wrote, "and then she will marry only for love, and will not sell her heart for a crust of bread."[26] Work, in other words, provided women with a means to choose marriage rather than pursue it out of necessity or blind habit. Drawing on the middle-class rhetoric of choice, she validated women's capacity to work outside of the home because it allowed her to choose marriage and thus "guaranteed" female virtue. Gimeno de Flaquer participated in pushing the boundaries of female respectability to include work outside the home, as long as domesticity remained a reference point.

For some commentators, such as the pro-labor paper *El Hijo del Trabajo*, the problem of female dependency manifested itself as public handwringing over a perceived "surplus of women." A supposed demographic imbalance left women disadvantaged within the marriage market. Women could no longer depend on getting married and therefore posed a burden on society. The same concern had shaped English debates over the role of women in economic development as early as 1850.[27] Development in the Mexican countryside pushed men and women out of rural communities and toward metropolitan industrial centers like Mexico City. In 1900 only one-third of Federal District residents had been born there, while the remaining two-thirds had migrated from surrounding states.[28] As a result, between 1895 and 1921 the Federal District had the largest concentration of women across the country (roughly 53 percent of the population). The majority of these women, like men, were migrants to the city. One journalist drew attention to similar gender imbalances in Ireland and other countries around the globe.[29]

As in England, however, it seems that the primary concern was not a demographic imbalance but the inability of middle-class women to earn a living. Whereas poor women had long labored to support themselves and their families, discussions of a female surplus were either implicitly or explicitly about middle-class women who faced a restricted labor market. *El Hijo del Trabajo* lamented: "Overburdened by their excessive numbers, a woman has to choose between being independent and not being a burden to community, or being a dependent and humiliated slave. There can be no doubt as to the choice."[30] Such arguments set the stage for growing public opinion in favor of middle-class women's employment outside the home as a solution for those who might otherwise remain dependent or destitute.

Between 1884 and 1888, the press, concerned about a surfeit of women in need and the problem of limited work options, called for the hiring of women in government offices, frequently pointing out that this was the practice in other countries. In the United States and France women already worked in government offices. The U.S. government first hired women to work in the Treasury Department in 1861.[31] Rumors circulated in the press that the Mexican government might follow suit. In 1884, Concepción Gimeno de Flaquer made the case for women's employment in offices by identifying specific occupations appropriate for women: "A woman can be a lithographer, telegraph operator, book-binder, stenographer, and cashier."[32] An 1885 article questioned why the federal government, in need of office workers, did not employ women who had been trained for such work at the government-run School for Manual Arts and Trades for Young Ladies.[33]

Labor newspapers also weighed in on the prospect of women working in offices. "Elisa," likely a pseudonym, published an 1886 article in *El Socialista* that exemplifies how some observers struggled with what they construed as the problem of female dependency and yet resisted changes in gender relations. Elisa advocated for women's education so that a woman, if she were to find herself in adverse circumstances, might become the "arbiter" of her own future. Even "daughters of well-to-do families" ought to adopt a profession, Elisa wrote. Which professions the author had in mind is less clear. The article mentions "artistic" careers, like copying paintings, a skill that had been taught in schools since the colonial era but that as an occupation did not appear in censuses. While Elisa supported women's education, she raised concerns about the impact of new work and educational opportunities on gender relations, both between individuals and in the public sphere:

> I am not a partisan of those, fed by self-interested concerns, who deny the vast capacity of woman. Her quick understanding and clear intelligence give her an excellent capacity to fill positions in desk work, administration, business, etc., as she is allowed to do in other countries. I agree that her education should be as comprehensive as that which she receives today, but I hope that men will find in her a docile and sweet companion, not a rival. She should be amiable, not someone who wants to take the podium and show off her eloquence in public assemblies, not someone who wants to argue with distinguished orators and men of science, nor someone who aspires to become a dictator in skirts.[34]

Though Elisa begrudgingly approved of a woman pursuing limited kinds of work, the passage expresses concern over the threat to women's "docile and sweet" disposition toward men. Elisa's concern about the potential disruption of women's domestic roles was also a concern about emotional labor. Such disruptions within the private sphere, according to Elisa, might manifest in the public sphere as well. The image of a "dictator in skirts" drove home the point by drawing on the idea of gender inversion. A dictator (presumably male) was made ridiculous when dressed in a skirt (female). The metaphor had the effect of ridiculing the idea of women in positions of authority. Elisa supported abstract ideas of work and education for women, while at the same time she (or perhaps he) resisted women's claims for autonomy and their intrusion in masculine spaces of rhetoric, oratory, and politics.

Commentators often drew on earlier conversations about working-class women to express their ambivalence. During the 1870s and early 1880s public commentators had expressed fear that when a woman left the home to work in a factory or workshop, she inevitably suffered moral taint. To these critics, work outside the home brought women and men into close interaction, violating the cultural norm of separate spheres and suggesting sexual transgression.[35] Observers raised similar concerns with regard to office work. Federico Gamboa, writer, diplomat, and government employee, was deeply concerned about shifts in the moral fabric of Mexican society, especially as it related to women. Gamboa is well known for his novel *Santa* (1903), the tale of a young girl from the countryside who, deceived by her suitor, ends up working in a Mexico City brothel. The novel employs gender relations and female sexual morality as a means to express anxieties about modernization. Fifteen years earlier, Gamboa had written the short story "El primer caso" (The first time, 1888), when the press first voiced support for hiring women in government offices. In commentary on the story, Gamboa wrote:

> Making known to the public the misery in which a woman struggles when there is no man that helps her or supports her . . . this is how it is in Europe and in the United States. . . . At first I found all this perfectly fine as, in effect, it is. However, just because it is acceptable does it mean that dangers cease to exist when the two sexes are in proximity? . . . Whenever a man inhabits close spaces with a woman there will always be desire and temptation.[36]

While Gamboa acknowledged the problem of women's economic dependency, his reference to "desire and temptation" gave rhetorical force to warnings against women working outside the home. His concerns were informed by the idea that when a woman "left" the protection of a man, she entered into the public sphere from a position of weakness—socioeconomic and moral—that made her vulnerable and morally suspect. Whether office work was "respectable" was a key question for a woman's honor and for middle-class identity (see fig. 1).[37]

Middle-class identity formation occurred within a specific national context and as part of a transnational conversation. Some commentators defined "honorable" work as intellectual, not manual, a distinction marked by access to formal education. In an article from the French paper *L'Estafille* that was reprinted as "El trabajo de las mujeres" in *La Convención Radical Obrera*, A. Debarle reported that in France and the United States schooling prepared women for "honorable work" in offices.[38] Others defined "honorable" work according to the pay or by simply asserting that the work was "middle class." An 1885 article by the German women's rights advocate Lois Büchner appeared in *El Socialista* and celebrated the idea of work for middle-class women: "We congratulate you, above all, women of the middle class, because your birth bestows upon you the best position from which to develop all of your efforts. From your ranks, women of the best quality ought to emerge."[39] Both Debarle's and Büchner's articles gave validity to debates in Mexico about middle-class women's employment by situating them within the context of similar trends in Europe.

Instead of a smooth progression to new forms of middle-class identity, the boundaries of class remained in flux. In 1894 the newspapers took up the topic of limited work options for women in such a way that did not make hard and fast distinctions between artisan, working-, and middle-class occupations. One such newspaper, *La Convención Radical Obrera*, represented a voice from the Mexico City artisan class, a sector of the workforce that faced deteriorating working conditions.[40] The Workers Congress hoped not only to improve working conditions but also to increase workers' access to education and cultural opportunities. The Workers Congress closely allied itself with the Díaz government, as scholar Florencia Gútierrez shows, and, in consonance with their class aspirations, engaged in the politics of respectability.[41] The Workers Congress included

FIG. 1. Secretary working alongside Archibaldo Eloy Pedraza, 1918. SINAFO #14436.
Reproduction authorized by the National Institute of Anthropology and History.

a significant number of women, some as wives of artisans and others as workers themselves. For example, the Workers Congress represented seamstress and cigarrera mutual aid societies, as well as the Sociedad Leona Vicario and the Sociedad Josefa Ortíz de Domínguez.[42]

Given the material realities and class aspirations of Workers Congress members, class appeared as a more fluid identity than gender. The article "Women's Work" considered a range of options limited by poor working conditions and social constraints that did not permit women to advance:

> If we turn to the middle class, we will find numerous, profound defects in the manner of educating women. Women of the middle class, more than others, need to work. But, in what—they will ask—and with good reason. What options are available for a woman who needs to support herself, who does not have parents, brothers, or relatives who can provide for her? Teaching? Only a small portion of the women who seek this work can be accommodated. In a dress shop? There they are made to work all day without rest

and paid such a miserable wage that they barely earn enough to season their meager food, which is not enough to satisfy their hunger (this is what is heartbreaking) and merely keeps them from dying. . . . Textile factory, thread factory, tobacco factory? The same. . . . Scholar, engineer? Impossible.[43]

While historians have associated the occupations of seamstress, cigarrera, and obrera with the working class, this observer was less categorical in his or her consideration of work options for "middle class" women. The article seeks to distance women from these occupations, however they are nevertheless a reference point. What does this mean?

Dependency and the threat of poverty affected both poor and middle-class women. Some commentators conflated work options for women regardless of the class identity ascribed to the occupation. Writing for *La Convención Radical Obrera* in 1901, one author put it this way: "We see in our cities the effects of this sort of education that places women of the middle class and of *el pueblo* in circumstances of having to confront every type of unfortunate emergency that might present itself in life."[44] In this passage gender emerged as an identity that could supersede that of class. Within public commentary, women, regardless of class status, shared a common situation: dependency and a lack of occupations that paid a living wage. Discursively, office work was presented as something that could solve "gender" problems, regardless of class.

Though not always explicitly about women of the middle class, the critique of women's economic dependency threw into question central aspects of middle-class identity, especially domesticity and marriage. A shift had begun from an emphasis on women's role as consumers to that of producers. As an anonymous contributor to *La Convención Radical Obrera* wrote in 1903:

A woman who does not work, above all if she belongs to a poor family, is continually exposed to the imminent dangers that are necessarily a part of the misery in which she struggles, owed simply to the fact that she always consumes something and does not produce anything. The first problem that results for women when they do not work, that is to say, when they are not accustomed to satisfying their needs on their own, is that of acquiring the habit of turning to men as a superior being to whom they must subject themselves as if he were the arbiter of her destiny; the second, when they try to resolve their problems and find no other means to satisfy their needs, is to come quickly to a fatal conclusion, to turn to a man for protection. For women thus educated, marriage is an overwhelming need, and a thousand times they enter into marriage, less for love or for convenience, than for the sole reason of finding in their husband a man who will take on the responsibility of maintaining them. . . . By inculcating the ideas of work as a new source of sustenance for women, we would see a notable decline in imperfect marriages and victims of human perversity.[45]

As this writer suggests, work could also enable women to free themselves from male dominance. Domesticity may still have figured centrally in middle-class identity, but it was a domesticity construed in the context of work.

Women in Government Office Work

As people debated female dependency and sought to come to terms with shifting gender relations, women went to work in federal offices. The state needed workers. During the Porfiriato the Mexican government expanded to accommodate economic and demographic growth. Economic production grew at a rate of 2.7 percent and exports 6.1 percent per annum. By the 1890s, Minister of Finance José Yves Limantour oversaw resolution of the federal bankruptcy and a new era of growth. Solvency allowed for the expansion of social programs associated with a growing population (1.4 percent per annum) and business sector.[46] The government also oversaw expansion of the education and judicial systems and new infrastructural projects like the drainage of the Valley of Mexico, railroad expansion, mail delivery, clean water, and electricity. In order to plan, carry out, document, and communicate about these projects, the government needed more personnel.

It is not clear who hired the first women to work in government offices, or when, although there are several early, notable names. It may have been Justo Sierra, who hired a woman secretary and is purported to have first hired women to work in the Ministry of Education or in the Central Telegraph Office.[47] Firsts aside, the 1895 census registered 118 women out of a total of 3,616 government employees in the Federal District (3 percent). Between 1895 and 1900 the number of women employed in government doubled to become 7 percent (see table 1). In 1901, a contributor to *La Convención Radical Obrera* declared: "Men are not needed in offices and other establishments in which the careful attention of a woman brings order and makes possible the application of systems that result in stunning economic and financial results."[48] An even more dramatic increase came between 1900 and 1910, when the government tripled their numbers and hired 538 additional women. This increase made women 13 percent of government employees.

Women's rights advocate María Ríos Cárdenas claimed that it was the Post Office that first hired women, and whether this is true or not, the Post Office is a good example of transformations in the organization of office work.[49] Following transnational trends, in the late nineteenth century the Mexican Post Office expanded services to support a growing economy and population. Minister of the Interior Manuel Aguirre Berlanga, in his introduction to the 1905 federal budget, made special note of the Post Office expansion and the important role it played in facilitating economic growth. In 1884 mail delivery had been made a public service, and the following year the government opened three offices to provide delivery service in Mexico City. Mail delivery was expanded again in 1891, 1895, 1897, and so on such that by 1901 the Postmaster General office was upgraded to section status. The Post Office earned income for the federal government, which for Minister Aguirre Berlanga justified hiring a growing number of employees. In 1880 the Post Office had employed 60 people in Mexico City (to meet both federal and city services), and by 1914 it employed 1,570.[50]

While the federal budget lists employee occupations and salaries, it does not distinguish between men and women. Informed by anecdotal evidence and a Department of Labor 1914 report on women's employment, we can nevertheless make a reasonable guess as to women's role in the expansion of federal bureaucracy. A portion of hiring growth in the Post Office was in jobs occupied by men: drivers (motorcycle and car), inspectors, and mail carriers. A parallel expansion occurred in the occupations in which women were most likely to have been employed: clerk (from level 1 descending through

TABLE 1. Public- and private-sector employees and professionals by gender, Federal District, 1895, 1900, and 1910

	1895	1900	1910
	TOTAL / MEN / WOMEN	TOTAL / MEN / WOMEN	TOTAL / MEN / WOMEN
Public-sector employees	3,616 / 3,498 / 118	3,398 / 3,155 / 243	6,184 / 5,403 / 781
Private-sector employees	7,021 / 6,169 / 852	12,040 / 11,068 / 972	25,826 / 21,219 / 4,607
Professionals*	18,334 / 7,814 / 10,520	17,827 / 7,017 / 10,810	25,296 / 11,231 / 14,065

*The category "professionals" (profesionistas y sirvientes) encompasses a wide range of service providers, including "office workers" and "shorthand typists" as well as lawyers, acrobats, veterinarians, and prostitutes. Other office occupations, such as telephone and telegraph operators, were accounted for in "transportation and communication"; sales clerks and accountants were included in the category "business service providers."

Sources: Colegio de México, *Estadísticas económicas del Porfiriato*, Fuerza de trabajo y actividad económica por sectores (Mexico City: El Colegio de México, 1965), 54, 57; Dirección General de Estadística a cargo del Dr. Antonio Peñafiel, *Resúmen general del censo de la República Mexicana (verificado el 28 de octubre de 1900)* (Mexico City, Imprenta de la Secretaría de Fomento, 1905), 56–57.

level 6), scribe, and apprentice. In 1890 the junior clerk positions expanded significantly in relation to levels 1 and 2. Between 1890 and 1905 only levels 5 and 6 declined, while all other positions saw an increase. Between 1905 and 1909 clerk employment was erratic in most categories with the notable exception of clerk level 5, which grew. The number of low-level clerks grew significantly between 1905 and 1920. The positions of scribe levels 1 and 2 grew significantly between 1884 and 1890. Subsequently, there was a slow decline in the number of scribe level 1, while level 2 increased dramatically. There was also a dramatic increase in the number of apprentices, which peaked in 1914. By 1905 an apprentice usually earned one peso a day.[51]

Many female office workers were hired into entry-level unpaid positions or into positions categorized, sometimes for years, as "temporary." For example, in 1912 the High Commission on Health hired Señorita Esther C. Quijas as an apprentice, a position she worked in for five months without pay. Quijas's own labor trajectory explains why a woman might have done such a thing. In 1914 she was promoted to a temporary position as scribe level 2, and shortly thereafter she became a permanent, paid employee.[52] Some women trained for specific occupations that they were able to secure, as was the case for Emmy Ibáñez, an early government telegraph employee. Others found paid positions that did not correspond to their training or that required them to combine multiple tasks. The Department of Health, for example, hired women with secretarial training to administer vaccines and keep records for the yellow fever campaigns (1911, 1912) and the anti-typhus campaign (1914). Adela de Galván Viuda de Gastellum was first hired as a nurse in the public baths and then into a position that combined work as a stenographer and administering vaccinations.[53]

Public-sector employment provided a wide range of earning possibilities. Raquel Santoyo, director of the "Miguel Lerdo de Tejada" Commercial School for Young Ladies (MLT), estimated that in 1909 graduates from her school earned from 30 to 200 pesos a month, most earning an average of 80 pesos a month.[54] The lower end of that range provided wages similar to those of unskilled laborers and left many women in dire straits, especially when they were head of household.[55] In 1911 Carmen Gonzalez petitioned to be promoted from apprentice to the head of accounting, arguing, "I am in a very critical situation. I have to support my elderly mother and I have nothing more than my measly wages of 30 pesos [a month] as an apprentice. [With this] we pay rent, food, and clothing. As you can see, we are in dire need."[56] The office also hired stenographers, like nineteen-year-old Elena Larios from Guadalajara, who worked to become, in 1916, scribe level 2 in the High Commission on Health, earning 3.12 pesos a day.[57] An individual who managed to obtain a position for which he or she had been trained in a specific skill, like telegraphy, might have earned two to six times as much as an apprentice. By contrast, telephone operators, depending on the office

GRAPH 1. Post Office clerks, levels 1–6, 1880–1932.

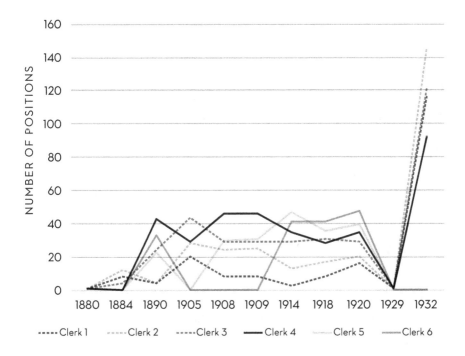

Sources: México, Secretaría de Hacienda y Crédito Público, *Ley de ingresos y presupuesto de egresos del tesoro federal, 1880, 1884* (Mexico City: Imprenta de I. Cumplido, 1880, 1884); *Ley de ingresos y presupuesto de egresos del tesoro federal* (Mexico City: Imprenta del Gobierno Federal en el Ex-Arzobispado, 1891); *Ley de egresos y presupuesto de egresos del erario federal* (Mexico City: Imprenta del Gobierno Federal, 1905); *Ley de egresos y presupuesto de egresos del erario federal* (Mexico City: Tipografía de la Oficina Impresora de Estampillas, Palacio Nacional, 1904, 1907, 1906, 1908, 1909, 1910, 1911, 1913, 1914); *Presupuesto de egresos de la federación* (Mexico City: Talleres Gráficos de la Nación, 1928); Poder Ejecutivo Federal Departamento de Aprovisionamientos Generales, *Ley de ingresos y presupuesto de egresos del erario federal, 1920* (Mexico City: Dirección de Talleres Gráficos, 1919); and Dirección de Pensiones Civiles de Retiro, Departamento de Estadística, *Segundo censo de empleados sujetos a la ley general de pensiones civiles de retiro, 1932* (Mexico City: Imprenta Franco Elizondo Hermanos, 1933).

GRAPH 2. Post Office scribes, levels 1 and 2, 1880–1932.

Sources: México, Secretaría de Hacienda y Crédito Público, *Ley de ingresos y presupuesto de egresos del tesoro federal, 1880, 1884* (Mexico City: Imprenta de I. Cumplido, 1880, 1884); *Ley de ingresos y presupuesto de egresos del tesoro federal* (Mexico City: Imprenta del Gobierno Federal en el Ex-Arzobispado, 1891); *Ley de egresos y presupuesto de egresos del erario federal* (Mexico City: Imprenta del Gobierno Federal, 1905); *Ley de egresos y presupuesto de egresos del erario federal* (Mexico City: Tipografía de la Oficina Impresora de Estampillas, Palacio Nacional, 1904, 1907, 1906, 1908, 1909, 1910, 1911, 1913, 1914); *Presupuesto de egresos de la federación* (Mexico City: Talleres Gráficos de la Nación, 1928); Poder Ejecutivo Federal Departamento de Aprovision-amientos Generales, *Ley de ingresos y presupuesto de egresos del erario federal, 1920* (Mexico City: Dirección de Talleres Gráficos, 1919); and Dirección de Pensiones Civiles de Retiro, Departamento de Estadística, *Segundo censo de empleados sujetos a la ley general de pensiones civiles de retiro, 1932* (Mexico City: Imprenta Franco Elizondo Hermanos, 1933).

GRAPH 3. Post Office apprentices, 1880–1929.

Sources: México, Secretaría de Hacienda y Crédito Público, *Ley de ingresos y presupuesto de egresos del tesoro federal, 1880, 1884* (Mexico City: Imprenta de I. Cumplido, 1880, 1884); *Ley de ingresos y presupuesto de egresos del tesoro federal* (Mexico City: Imprenta del Gobierno Federal en el Ex-Arzobispado, 1891); *Ley de egresos y presupuesto de egresos del erario federal* (Mexico City: Imprenta del Gobierno Federal, 1905); *Ley de egresos y presupuesto de egresos del erario federal* (Mexico City: Tipografía de la Oficina Impresora de Estampillas, Palacio Nacional, 1904, 1907, 1906, 1908, 1909, 1910, 1911, 1913, 1914); *Presupuesto de egresos de la federación* (Mexico City: Talleres Gráficos de la Nación, 1928); and Poder Ejecutivo Federal Departamento de Aprovisionamientos Generales, *Ley de ingresos y presupuesto de egresos del erario federal, 1920* (Mexico City: Dirección de Talleres Gráficos, 1919).

TABLE 2. Daily wages for selected occupations, Mexico City, 1914

Occupation	Daily Wage
School director, MLT	6.60
Secretary, MLT	2.20
Teacher, MLT	1.35, 1.65, 2.00, 2.75
Clerk, level 6	3.20
Scribe, level 1	2.50
Scribe, levels 2 and 3	2.00
Telephone operator	1.00, 1.50, 2.50
Telegraph operator	2.00–6.00
Apprentice	1.00
Mail carrier	.60–4.00
Seamstress, apprentice to master	.75–3.00
Knitwear factory worker	.88–1.50
Cigarette worker, apprentice to master	.75–3.00

Sources: For office wages see México, *Ley de ingresos y presupuesto de egresos del erario federal para el año fiscal que comienza el 1 de julio de 1914 y termina el 30 de junio de 1915* (Mexico City: Tipográfica de la Oficina Impresora de Estampillas, 1914), 233. Wages for scribe level 1 are for those employed in the Post Office, Interior, and Tribunals. Telephone operator wages are for the Chamber of Deputies. Some unranked operators worked for 1.50. Additional wage information is contained in reports filed by female inspectors for the Department for the Protection of Women and Children during 1914. Archivo General de la Nación, Deparamento del Trabajo, caja 90, exp. 4–35, and caja 91, exp. 1–2.

in which they were employed, earned between 1 and 2.5 pesos a day. Most of these office jobs paid better than sewing and factory work (see table 2).

Women who worked in low-level positions earned little, and during times of inflation earned less. As Aurora Gómez-Galvarriato and Aldo Mucsachio find, inflation was high in 1907 and again in war years of the mid-1910s. The overall decline in real wages from 1898 to 1911 was 26 percent, and data suggest that public employees' purchasing power declined as well.[58] In 1914 a kilo of beans and a kilo of tortillas would have cost half a day's wages; adding a kilo of meat would have required spending the entire day's earnings.[59] If a woman hoped to purchase shoes at El Palacio de Hierro department store, she would have had to come up with 7–10 pesos, and so more likely shopped at open-air and covered markets like La Lagunilla.[60] Despite inflation, some families managed to feed their daughters a cup of atole in the morning and send them off in worn heels to make their way to school.

Commercial Education, 1894–1910

The opening of commercial education for young women in Mexico formed part of a transnational shift in ways of thinking about middle-class women's wage-earning potential. The shift had begun in Spain in the late eighteenth century and in England in the 1830s.[61] During the second phase of Spanish Enlightenment during the reign of Charles III (1759–88), Count Campomanes had proposed vocational education for middle-class girls. José Joaquín Fernández de Lizardi, in *La Quijotita y su prima* (1818), portrayed training in arts such as painting, watchmaking, and silverwork as appropriate work for middle-class women. As Silvia Arrom points out, in nineteenth-century Mexico those who advocated for women's education did so in the name of "enlightened motherhood," especially as a counter to women's political mobilization during independence.[62] Women's publications like *Semanario de las Señoritas Mejicanas* (1841–42) attest both to the increase in women's literacy and to the importance of debates regarding appropriate education for young women.[63] By the late nineteenth century, some educators encouraged middle-class girls to pursue schooling that would prepare them, in some way, for work.

Commercial education for women began as ad hoc courses offered at primary and vocational schools.[64] The audience for these course offerings varied. The School for Manual Arts and Trades for Young Ladies (est. 1871) originally sought to serve the working class, and administrators expressed surprise when classes quickly filled with middle-class girls.[65] Administrators were also surprised that many of the students were teachers looking to change career. By the 1880s, the School for Manual Arts and Trades for Young Ladies had on average 210 female students.[66] According to Mílada Bazant, educators considered several professions as appropriate for women, including pharmacy. None would prove so popular, however, as commercial education. Indeed, by the turn of the century commercial classes filled to capacity with young women seeking work in public and private offices. Their middle-class parents, the Ministry of Public Instruction and Fine Arts reported, sought a free education for their daughters, one that would lead them to non-manual labor. In 1907, 20 women attended classes in pharmacy, while typing enrolled 364 and telegraphy enrolled 318. Students also studied stenography.[67]

One of the teachers at the school, Lucía Tagle Meza, may have been the first woman to earn a commercial degree. Born in Toluca in 1854, Tagle Meza was the daughter of a politically engaged family of artisans. She attended the Lancasterian Society "Libertad" School in Mexico City and earned a teaching degree in 1872.[68] Tagle Meza founded and directed the Benito Juárez School (est. 1878), later referred to as Academy for Secondary Education and Languages Night School. The school offered accounting classes. Like many teachers, she taught several subjects (math, bookkeeping) and occupied several positions. While she ran her own school, Tagle Meza also taught at the School for Manual Arts and Trades for Young Ladies.[69]

The Business and Administration School for Advanced Study (Escuela Superior de Comercio y Administración, ESCA), established in 1868, began to offer classes to women in 1894. Mílada Bazant notes that at its founding, ESCA offered courses free of charge, had no minimum requirements for admission, and did not offer diplomas or certificates. Under the direction of Alfredo Chavero, in 1897 more than a thousand students took classes at the ESCA that prepared them to work in banks and in public and private offices. By 1900, 255 women attended classes, alongside 1,225 men, receiving instruction from distinguished instructors like Professor Rafael Lozada, who for many years worked as a stenographer for the Chamber of Deputies, and José García Clavellina, a stenographer in the Ministry of Finance.[70] Classes offered by Professors Lozada and García Clavellina were very popular with women.[71]

The expansion of commercial education came in part from demands made by women. In January 1900 a group of young women in the beginning stenography class petitioned Doña Carmen Romero Rubio de Díaz, the wife of President Porfirio Díaz, for her support in securing a female assistant for the class.[72] As the young women explained, Professor Lozado had more than six hundred students in two classes, and if the school were to assign a second assistant, they hoped it would be a woman. The letter to Señora Carmen Romero Rubio de Díaz was an expression of women's organizational culture of the era. Following the rhetorical forms of such petitions, the letter praises Señora Romero Rubio de Díaz: "You are well known for your good deeds in favor of Mexican women: the 'Casa Amiga de la Obrera' and other charitable works, tell us that not only are you the First Lady of Mexico because you are the wife of the President, but you also occupy this position because of the good that you do."[73] The letter is also evidence of a culture of women-centered patronage. Seamstresses in particular had for decades established ties with society women who supported their organizational efforts, established sewing cooperatives, and held charitable events at downtown theaters.

The young women at the commercial school considered their socioeconomic status and occupations as relevant to their petition and simultaneously self-identified as working and middle class. The petitioners refer to themselves as "poor" and as seamstresses, cigarette makers, ironers, and washerwomen. They also refer to themselves using the words "señorita" and "honorable," which, along with reference to their education, served as markers of middle-class identity. The petition reads:

> In the constant struggle for survival that we poor engage in, we turn to the most effective means available to us: the thankless work of sewing, ironing, washing, cigar making, and other industries in which women are employed and which have taken the lives of innumerable victims, who have fallen prostrate in a hospital bed, and only upon ending up in the grave do they finally find rest.

Modern life in Mexico requires new conditions in the struggle to survive. For this reason, we have dedicated ourselves to our studies and to learning skills that we can employ. And that is why so many señoritas of different social conditions are in classes for shorthand, telegraphy, medicine, and even law. In the Commercial School last year shorthand classes were first offered as another honorable means of making a living, and a good number of students attended. That year 200 students enrolled and the Ministry of Justice and Education thought it important to provide Professor Lozada with an assistant. Now there are more than 600 students in the two classes, so that the last to arrive have to remain standing. Among these students there are more than 100 señoritas and niñas who seek new horizons and new weapons in the struggle for survival. The current Professor and only one Assistant are not enough.

Although they were enrolled in a new educational space, a mixed-sex environment, the women sought to retain something of the female-specific spaces they found familiar and claimed as culturally appropriate.[74] "Our request," they wrote, "is that you plead our case so that if the position opens, it be given to a señorita. . . . It would benefit us to be able to confide in a person of our same sex, to consult as well as to receive criticisms."[75] Later that year the ESCA named María Macaria teaching assistant for stenography and typing. Over the course of the following years, women's enrollments increased and ESCA hired a growing number of women instructors.[76] And in 1901, the year following the women's petition, a presidential decree called for the establishment of the MLT, a new commercial school for señoritas.

All across town, young women filled to bursting classrooms where they learned shorthand, typing, telegraphy, accounting, and other commercial and administrative subjects.[77] When the MLT opened in 1903, in downtown Mexico City at #4 Carmen Street, it marked a new era for women.[78] Federal investment in education increased between 1901 and 1911. The Ministry of Justice and Public Instruction endeavored to bring order to offerings and supported plans for expansion. A January 1905 law divided commercial education into two levels, primary and junior high school.[79] Primary education offered a two-year program that conferred a diploma as *dependiente de comercio*

FIG. 2. Inauguration of the "Miguel Lerdo de Tejada" Commercial School for Young Ladies with President Porfirio Díaz and Raquel Santoyo in attendance, 1903. SIN-AFO #5692. Reproduction authorized by the National Institute of Anthropology and History.

(sales clerk). Joaquín Casasús took over direction of the ESCA in 1903 and introduced advanced degrees, three-year programs of study that conferred a diploma in business accounting and bookkeeping for public administration.[80]

In the first decade of the twentieth century, the development of commercial education reinforced gender segregation. The MLT, led by Director Raquel Santoyo (1904–14, 1926–33), had an all-female student body, staff, and faculty, with the exception of Manuel Berrueco, the music instructor (*solfeo*).[81] The majority of teachers had received their degree from the Normal School for Women. As early as 1910 the school employed one of its own graduates, Ana Carbajal, as secretary to the director. The "Doctor Mora" Commercial School enrolled boys only and employed an all-male faculty and staff, with the exception of Señorita Guadalupe Gómez, the secretary.[82]

The MLT attracted a vibrant group of women who ran the school and played a significant role in the cultural life of the city. Like many others, Director Santoyo had worked her way up through the ranks of the teaching profession. Santoyo began her career in 1888 as a physical sciences teacher. After several years working as an assistant at the preschool annexed to the Normal School for Women, a position for which she was paid $500.05 a month, she took a position as a full-time teacher. In 1896 Santoyo became the director of the National Primary School #25, and in 1903 she was named director of the MLT. Her annual salary combined $1,500.15 for her work as director and $1,000.10 for teaching accounting. The federal government commissioned Santoyo to study commercial education in the United States (1904) and Europe (1906).[83]

School and work drew women into new spaces, physical and rhetorical, that stretched the boundaries of gendered spheres. On the occasion of the first anniversary celebration in 1904, Director Santoyo reported on the goals and progress of the school. As she began her remarks, she acknowledged the masculine space that she entered, one of "such distinguished men," and apologized for her words, which she characterized as "so inadequate and lacking in oratory style" (see fig. 2). Santoyo praised the school as "born in the heat of the highest patriotic ideals and eminently philanthropic sentiments." By referring to "philanthropic sentiments," Santoyo participated in the conversation about women, economic insecurity, and dependency. She thanked the dignitaries in attendance for remembering "this interesting part of humanity called 'woman'" and for having "thought to give her a great gift, a lifesaver in the struggle to survive, by facilitating appropriate and well-paid work."[84]

Some scholars have argued that vocational education was meant to reinforce women's labor within the domestic sphere.[85] Santoyo's words, and the history of her work at the school, suggest otherwise. In her remarks, Santoyo praised efforts to "open the sphere of action for women, to redeem her from perdition and to give life to a precious trinket and convert her into an effective ally of the family and a productive member of the fatherland." The school administration hoped to cultivate in students qualities more associated with labor discipline than domestic rhythms. As Santoyo remarked, "Students must not only acquire a commercial education; they must also cultivate other qualities, especially an entrepreneurial spirit, industrial values, and persistence." To reinforce such character traits, teachers took students on excursions like the one to the San Rafael Paper Company where they studied industrial production and business organization.[86] All classrooms had electric clocks to regiment students' use of time, and the latest equipment on which to learn their future profession. Considered a modern building for the time, the school had a laboratory, water filtration system, and a telephone. The school also opened a store where students could practice their skills by providing services to the public. Announcements appeared in newspapers like *La Clase Media* (newspaper for the mutual aid society Gran Círculo de Obreros from 1907 to 1909).[87] For Santoyo, a worthy education was that which promoted action: "Learn in order to work" ("Saber para obrar").[88]

Santoyo commented on the close association between women, work, and feminism, but she was careful to acknowledge the limits to which feminists should push for the expansion of women's sphere.

> We live in an era in which we breathe in an atmosphere of conviction that woman can and ought to take part in the universal and harmonious concert of human effort and, without falling into ridiculous feminist exaggerations that convert her into a hybrid being, carry out with dignity the sainted mission that the wisdom of nature has reserved for her.[89]

Santoyo's reference to a "hybrid being" echoed the characterization of middle-class women who worked outside the home as masculine. Her description of the physical organization of the school was careful to characterize the space into which these young women moved as an all-female—and therefore appropriate—space. The MLT, she noted, included a department of "domestic arts" with forty work tables and thirty sewing machines.

The Ministry of Public Education, through its *Boletín*, expressed excitement over the popularity of the MLT:

> The growth of commercial education classes coincides with the ever-growing need to channel feminine activity in new directions and as the demand of young ladies that have the aptitude to do accounting or desk

FIG. 3. Adela Garduño, graduate of the "Miguel Lerdo de Tejada" Commercial School for Young Ladies, 1908. *Libro de diplomas*, Archivo Histórico de la Secretaría de Educación Pública, with permission from the Archivo General de la Nación, México.

FIG. 4. Concepción Álvarez, graduate of the "Miguel Lerdo de Tejada" Commercial School for Young Ladies, 1908. *Libro de diplomas*, Archivo Histórico de la Secretaría de Educación Pública, with permission from the Archivo General de la Nación, México.

work increases daily. The creation of commercial departments was received with real enthusiasm, above all, night classes, which notably have a high number of teachers enrolled.[90]

Scattered evidence suggests that MLT students were older during the 1910s—from nineteen to twenty, and as old as thirty—than they would be during the 1920s. If this is true, it might be explained by the number of women who already had studied for a career like teaching and who went to school to change occupation. Night classes were popular with students already in the workforce. The 1906 register of diplomas shows photographs of girls in pretty dresses who wore their hair in bouclé or tied up with ribbon in a bow on the top of the head. Other graduates looked more mature, wearing their hair pulled back in generous folds akin to the Gibson girl hairstyle (see figs. 3 and 4). Students came from Puebla, Monterrey, Parral, and Chihuahua, although the majority were from Mexico City. While some students could easily afford the cost of school, others complained about the burden of purchasing supplies.[91] Graduates went on to a range of careers, working in shops and offices in both the public and private sectors. Beginning in 1911 the MLT expanded the number of degrees it granted. That year women graduated with degrees in shorthand and in business employee.[92] At least one graduate, María de los Dolores Rivero Fuentes, went on to study at the National Preparatory School and the National School of Medicine and became a doctor.[93]

The MLT quickly came to figure as an important institution in the cultural life of the city. Office girls, first as students and then as employees, drew on a series of skills cultivated at the school that allowed them to appear in public in new ways. Young women used a series of rhetorical styles to slip out of silence and into words and physical prominence.[94] The MLT curriculum included classes in public speaking and singing. End-of-year school ceremonies provided the opportunity for women to highlight such skills. Ceremonies featured young women, elegantly dressed, who made speeches, recited poetry and prose, and staged allegorical tableau (see fig. 5).[95] On the occasion of the MLT year-end festivities in 1908, *La Clase Media* gave the event front-page coverage.[96] Editors for *La Clase Media* were at pains to confirm the respectability of office work for women. After describing a speech made by the "beautiful orator, María Corona," the article noted that the editor of *La Clase Media* introduced Corona to the minister of finance, Yves Limantour, who offered her a position in one of the offices under his purview. The editor positioned himself as facilitator of the young woman's entrance into the new space of work and portrayed Minister Limantour as a benefactor as much as an employer. The reporter noted that the intention was not that the young woman work for "luxuries or conveniences, but to help her honorable father raise his other children, which are numerous."[97] The rhetorical distancing from the individualistic pursuit of luxury and the tie to working in order to sustain the domestic order conferred virtue on Señorita Corona, and it also marked her as middle class.

Director Santoyo, in her speech at the 1908 graduation, was more direct in her explanation for why women needed an education to work. Santoyo also seems to have gained more confidence since her speech in 1904. Women must not exist in a parasitical relationship with men, she argued. They must be allowed the capacity to work so as not to be subject to the whims of men, or fall victim to the "veritable plague" of female neurasthenia, or emotional instability caused by inactivity. Santoyo drew on statistics and observations gathered on her trips to the United States and Europe. In the United States, Santoyo claimed, 4.5 percent of married women worked independently of their husbands, while in France some 35 percent of women did so. Her words must have resonated with young women as daily enrollments continued to grow, from approximately 158 students (1910) to 500 in 1914.[98]

Women in education leadership positions were visible public figures. Director Santoyo and news of her activities related to the school appeared in city newspapers. The Mexico City daily *Diario del Hogar* reported on Santoyo's travels to Europe in 1906 to study commercial, industrial, and primary education.[99] In 1910, *La Clase Media* celebrated Santoyo's saint's day and praised her work at the school, which had led to magnificent results for "the daughters of the suffering middle class."[100] Alongside the article Santoyo appeared in a photograph, seated in a chair, with her head lightly resting on her hand. The photograph echoed the feminine gentility expressed in the text and the editor's praise for Professor Santoyo as exemplary of the

El Concurso de las Artes.—Alegoría.—Uno de los números más bellos de la fiesta habida en la escuela «Miguel Lerdo», la semana pasada

El viernes de la semana pasada tuvo efecto, en la escuela «Miguel Lerdo de Tejada», una hermosa fiesta con que la directora y profesores de dicho plantel dieron una cariñosa despedida á las alumnas que acaban de terminar sus estudios.

El patio de la escuela estaba para este día de fiesta significativa, adornado de manera artística y alegre, tal como era menester para dar adiós á ese enjambre de laboriosas muchachas que acaban sus estudios.

El programa, que fué cumplido en todas sus partes, era el siguiente:

I. Obertura. Orquesta de alumnos del Conservatorio Nacional.

II. Alocución Señorita Raquel Santoyo, directora del plantel.

III. «Los Sembradores», Luis G. Urbina.— Poesía recitada por la

La Srita. Margarita Ruiz Sandoval, recitando una poesía de Luis G. Urbina, llamada «Los Sembradores», durante la fiesta (Fot. Sem. Ilus.)

profesora señorita Margarita Ruiz Sandoval.

IV. Entrega de títulos, diplomas y certificados.

V. Discurso pronunciado por la alumna señorita Concepción Echeverría, secretaria de la sociedad de alumnas y exalumnas de la escuela.

VI. «El Concurso de las Artes». Alegoría.

VII. Himno Nacional.

El señor ministro de Instrucción Pública y Bellas Artes, licenciado don Justo Sierra; el señor subsecretario del mismo ramo, licenciado Ezequiel Chávez, y el señor ingeniero Miguel F. Martínez, director general de Educación Primaria, ocuparon los asientos de honor, sentándose á los lados la señorita Raquel Santoyo, directora del plantel, la señorita directora de la escuela industrial «La Corregidora».

FIG. 5. Graduation ceremonies included tableaux and public speaking, 1910. *La Semana Ilustrada*, April 20, 1910. Courtesy of HathiTrust.

quality of teachers who had come to lead the nation's commercial schools for girls. Santoyo also led charitable activities, which offered students the possibility to engage in public activity in a way that positioned them as middle class, as when MLT teachers and students took up a collection to purchase presents for poor children at Christmas.[101]

Feminism

The flurry of newspaper articles that had appeared in the 1890s with titles like "Women and Work" gave way to essays and commentary in the first decade of the twentieth century on "Feminism." Explicit use of the word feminism (as opposed to historians ascribing the word to the behavior or intellectual thought of historical actors) has its own history. Gabriela Cano dates public use of the word in Mexico to a 1903 speech Justo Sierra gave to women newly licensed as teachers.[102] Lucrecia Infante Vargas notes that Concepción Gimeno de Fláquer employed the word feminist in a Mexican women's periodical in 1904.[103] Secretaries, typists, and shorthand secretaries contributed to the growing use of the word feminism, though in a somewhat unexpected way. Both women themselves and observers of social change used the word feminism to describe women's move into office work—a shift, that is, in workforce participation. In this context use of the word feminist did not refer to women's mobilization for political change.

One opportunity to use the word *feminist* was in reference to typing contests. In March 1905 the newspaper *El Imparcial*, directed by Don Rafael Reyes Spíndola, announced a typing and stenography contest as the "Concurso feminista" (see fig. 6). In subsequent articles, *El Imparcial* identified the goals of the competition as "to stimulate efforts in favor of Mexican feminism." The newspaper and contest sponsors hoped "to encourage jobs appropriate for women and the adaptation of women to the practical life, and so decided to hold a typing and stenography contest, for these two new classes of profession, already widespread and sought after throughout the country, in commercial and bureaucratic environments, where Mexican women have distinguished themselves and have come to stay."[104] The feminism in evidence was not women who came together to make demands, political or otherwise. Rather, the newspaper used the word feminist to

FIG. 6. Standing-room only at the *concurso feminista* held by *El Imparcial*, March 1911. SINAFO #64465. Reproduction authorized by the National Institute of Anthropology and History.

describe an event sponsored by a newspaper and typewriter companies, with the support of the MLT, to promote women's professional advancement. The significance and visibility of this group of women was such that the reporter referred to female typists and stenographers as a trade group (*gremio*). So many women sought to participate in the contest that the sponsors extended the registration deadline.

The day of the event was standing-room only, and people were turned away at the door of the *El Imparcial* building. Sponsors moved the competition from the designated room to the central patio of the building in order to accommodate the unexpectedly large number of participants, family, and curious observers. Typewriter companies Oliver, Remington, Underwood, and Smith Premier sponsored the contest. Each woman would type on the machine of her choice. The first-place winner in each category (defined by company sponsor and skill) won a typewriter and a medal. Second place won 100 pesos. Señorita Raquel Santoyo, director of the MLT, presided over the judges, many of whom were MLT instructors. *El Imparcial* declared, "A Happy Week of Tickity-Tack" and reported that the festive event demonstrated that "'feminism,' properly understood, is a powerful force in the progress and well-being of society."[105] The newspaper published the names and photographs of the winners, who received a complimentary copy of that day's edition. In 1913 the same photographs appeared on the cover of sheet music titled "Beautiful Typists: A Slow Waltz" (see fig. 7).[106] The contest was so successful that several more were held in subsequent years, and in 1913 the Ministry of the Interior used a contest to hire women to fill vacancies for jobs that paid 150 pesos a month.[107]

The author, literature professor, diplomat, and Mexico City resident Julio Sesto also wrote about the contest. As a contributor to various newspapers, including *El Imparcial*, Sesto observed: "In business and in government offices Mexican women have a space where they are reaching the same levels of employment as men. The occupations of typist and stenographer have been turned over to women almost completely." Sesto gave a vivid description of the event. "The office filled with girls. When they took their places in that grand crystal atrium and the shout rang out 'attack,' the typewriters slammed out letters beneath beautiful and agile little hands. It was a contrast of an infernal noise produced by an angelic crowd: the dissonance of lyricism and iron, soft hands that slammed against hard keys. Feeling my heart swell with pride, I could not help but exclaim: sublime!" Sesto's pleasure in contrasts echoed a rhetorical device he employed to describe female factory workers filling male spaces of work. His discussion of typists fit into the narrative between his description of women transiting the streets to and from factories and a description of teachers, thus expressing a continuum of female employment that placed office workers in the middle. For Sesto, all these changes in women's workforce participation were indications of "feminism."[108]

In 1908 *El Imparcial* newspaper ran a three-part front-page series on feminism. The article also constructed a continuum of women's class positions that placed office workers in the middle, thus contributing to the identification of office work with middle-class status. *El Imparcial* had used the word *feminism* as early as 1897 to describe women's changing workforce

Vencedoras en el Concurso Feminista de "El Imparcial"
Triunfo de la "OLIVER"

SRITA. RUPERTA CERDAN.—1er. premio de Taquigrafía y Mecanografía. Después de cinco minutos de dictado taquigráfico, empleó 10 minutos y 30 segundos en la traducción y escritura de 373 palabras y tuvo cinco faltas.

SRITA. MARGARITA L. CARDENAS —Premio extra de copiar ofrecido por el Lic. Moguel, Director de "El Imparcial." Esta señorita alcanzó el premio porque su trabaj comparado con los demás resultó contener mayor número de palabras y mer os errores

El Jurado Calificador nombrado por la Secretaría de Instrucción Pública y presidido por el Subsecretario del ramo para juzgar de las pruebas de Taquigrafía y Mecanografía organizada por nuestro apreciable colega "El Imparcial" ha dictado ya su fallo en acta que publicó la prensa diaria. Este documento nos informa de que en el concurso tomaron parte cerca de doscientas competidoras, que en él se usaron 189 máquinas de escribir, siendo 116 de ellas "Oliver" y que se hicieron acreedoras á los primeros premios por la exactitud y rapidez de sus trabajos, las señoritas cuyos retratos aparecen en esta página usando todas ellas máquinas "Oliver."

SRITA. ESTHER BOCANEGRA.—3er. premio de Taquigrafía y Mecanografía. Tomó 399 palabras de 400 que le fueron dictadas y empleó en descifrarlas y pasarlas en máquina 11 minutos, teniendo 33 faltas.

SRITA. MICAELA RAMIREZ DE ARELLANO.—2o. premio de Taquigrafía y Mecanografía. 1er. premio de copia y 1o. de tacto. De 403 palabras que le fueron dictadas en 5 minutos tomó 401 invirtiendo en descifraarlas y escribirlas 9 minutos 30 segundos.

FOTS. URIBE.

FIG. 7. Winners of the *concurso feminista*, an image that later circulated on sheet music for a song titled "Beautiful Typists: A Slow Waltz." *La Semana Ilustrada*, April 20, 1911. Courtesy of HathiTrust.

participation when the newspaper first hired women in its offices.[109] The 1908 series echoed Sesto's conceptions of a class continuum of occupations in which women were employed, with the first installment interviews with women "intellectuals" (lawyers and doctors), the second "the vast middle sector" that consisted of office workers, and the third working-class women (a cigar worker, a seamstress, and a salesgirl). Women from all three sectors defined feminism as women's workforce participation. Doctor Señora María Montoya explained that feminism "aspires only to grant women the means to support herself in the face of misery and vice, which this, I defend with all my might." Emmy Ibáñez, employed in the Ministry of the Interior (and therefore representative of the middle sector), expressed her delight that the newspaper would take the topic seriously. "I understand feminism," she said, "to be the entrance of the weaker sex, as men sarcastically refer to us, into the struggle to make a living as long as her objectives are noble." The unidentified journalist expressed particular delight over the fact that a cigar worker, Señorita C. F., had no idea what feminism was and so supposedly could provide an unbiased response to the question whether women should "abandon the home" for work. "Well," she answered, "if there is no one at home who can bring in money, then the woman has to leave home to find work." Señorita N. de la R. (a seamstress) had read about feminism in the newspaper articles published days earlier and preferred the idea of staying home to care for a husband, children, and family, because "I have never liked all this going to work, arriving at a fixed time, being scolded by 'la Señora, and having to make an extra trip to get paid."[110] Not surprisingly, the journalist concluded that the more educated a woman, the more likely she was to want economic and familial independence and therefore to support feminism.

Horacio Barreda, contributor to *Revista Positiva* and son of the pre-eminent educator Doctor Gabino Barreda, also characterized women's entrance into office work as "feminism."[111] Barreda published a series of articles titled "Studies on Feminism" in *Revista Positiva* in 1909 where he identified feminists' primary goal as that of employment. "Feminist tendencies are the necessary result of the moral and intellectual chaos inherent to the revolutionary situation societies are experiencing." The "revolutionary situation" was not the mobilization of feminists but rather the growing visibility of women's workforce participation. Like the factory, the office also drew women out of the home and into mixed company with men:

> If we turn from our consideration of the industrial sphere to examine what happens if the doors to professional and political life were opened to women, we would soon see the same results, though the details vary. It is the fruit of the rivalry against nature that some propose between the feminine and masculine sex. . . . To see, as we do these days, a woman running after a man of industry, looking for work, to see her abandon the home only for her existence to be consumed behind a counter in a department store, registering sales; to contemplate her in front of a typewriter, working as a scribe in an office, turning her eyes with anguish towards the home she has lost, her ears morally offended by the crude masculine conversations that surround her, withstanding impertinences, gallantries, or harsh reprimands from superiors or employers; to see her fight shoulder to shoulder with man in order to be able to survive, in a spectacle that, without wanting to, brings to mind those barbarous times when women, exhausted and panting, in mixed company with men, suffered the fatigues of the hunt that were necessary in order to calm their hunger.[112]

By the 1910s, secretaries and typists made more frequent and wide-ranging appearances in Mexico City print media, including *Semana Ilustrada*, which highlighted the recently popularized photography.[113] In this periodical, directed at an urban readership, women appeared throughout reports on politics, social life, and theater.[114] Graduation announcements of women teachers, dentists, and lawyers included official identification photographs, focusing on the face. In reports on public ceremonies, teachers appeared alongside government officials dressed in somber and professional black dress that echoed men's suits. Young women and girls appeared at formal ceremonies dressed in white. At such ceremonies women read poetry and prose or recited speeches.[115] *Semana Ilustrada* also reported on a typing contest conducted by *El Imparcial* in 1911 and 1912.[116] The same year Señorita Rosario Lerma appeared photographed on the occasion of her being named typist for the private secretary for the minister of public instruction.[117] Secretaries were everywhere—an "American typist" appeared to the medium Doña Rosalinda Metate, who, while calling on spirits from the other world for those around the table, learned of her husband's dalliances with said typist.[118]

Both working- and middle-class women were already in the midst of a revolution when Francisco I. Madero made his call to arms in 1910. With their move into commercial education and government employment, women had initiated changes in their role in the workforce, family, and society. As the revolutionary conflict caught up Mexico City residents, some women engaged in political protest. One daring young government employee wrote to the wife of the president, asking that she use her influence to convince him to step down. In the Post Office seventy-nine women wanting to support the revolutionary cause petitioned the postmaster general to receive training to work in hospitals. Students at the MLT organized their own "feminist mutual aid society."[119] Drawing on their leadership, teaching, and public speaking skills, commercial school teachers took to political organizing and protest. María Arias Bernal, who had taught at the MLT for several years, established the Club Feminil "Lealtad" to protest Victoriano Huerta's assassination of President Madero and Vice President Pino Suarez in February 1913.[120] Bernal, joined by more than 350 other women, including teachers like Eulalia Guzmán, who taught geography at the MLT, made weekly visits to Madero's grave to make speeches, read poems, and engage in other forms of public protest.[121] Huerta jailed many protesters, young women of fifteen to sixteen years of age among them, and fired teachers who stood against his government.[122] Office workers were also present at the graveside protests, including Soledad González who had worked as Madero's secretary and purportedly typed *La sucesión presidencial* (1910). She later went on to work for Presidents Obregón and Calles. Hermila Galindo participated in the protests at the same time she taught typing at the MLT.[123] Galindo had moved from her native Durango in 1911, worked as a secretary for General Eduardo Hay, and once identified the Revolution and women's move into government office jobs as the two most important changes of the era.[124] All of these teachers served as mentors to the students who filled their classrooms. The office workers, who because of their clerical skills became involved in politics, served as models for a new generation of women.

Throughout the 1910s, observers continued to conflate the increasing visibility of women in office work with feminism. In 1914 the worker newspaper *Alianza* reported on the thousands of government office positions filled by women and declared "Feminism Is on the Rise."[125] The anonymous journalist described office workers with the words "honorable" and "capable" that connoted middle-class status. That women worked outside the home was not cause for consternation unless those women were middle class. The distinguished teacher Laura Méndez de Cuenca, in a 1907 article published in *El Imparcial*, put it this way: "Now what motivates the ugly sex is that the female rebellion is not coming from the lower classes, but rather from the middle class. The girls in factories and workshops, the old ladies plowing the fields ... middle-aged women, mostly working as sales clerks, even when they suffer a bitter existence, don't complain ... but middle-class women, raised like delicate hothouse flowers, and in leisure, are the ones who have called out: rebel! And they rebelled."[126]

General Venustiano Carranza's 1914 reform of the divorce laws, passage of the Family Relations Law (1917), and even much of the early feminist organizing all followed on the heels of change that had begun nearly two decades earlier.[127] Such political and legal change was preceded by shifts in women's workforce participation, including the 562 percent increase in office workers in Mexico City between 1895 and 1910. Though the number of women who worked in government offices remained relatively small compared to other occupations, an important shift in women's employment had begun. As working conditions declined in the primary occupations open to women, such as teacher, seamstress, and cigar worker, growing numbers of women sought ways to support themselves and their families. Middle-class identity, which had been defined by women's presence in the home, became porous enough to allow women to step into new roles outside the home. Domesticity continued to figure centrally in middle-class identity, but it was now a domesticity postponed. The productive role of women, be they dutiful daughters or sacrificing mothers, was now publicly acknowledged alongside the ever-venerated angel of the home.

Women who studied at commercial schools like the MLT and who worked in government offices accrued economic, symbolic, and cultural capital that allowed them to claim middle-class status. Young women were ushered into middle-class respectability by a formal education in an all-girls school where, in addition to acquiring professional skills, they studied history, geography, singing, and languages. They were trained in respectable ways to enter into public spaces and participated in an expanding repertoire of female words and gestures at official public ceremonies. In the absence of a public, politically engaged suffrage movement, the changes in women's workforce participation constituted a socioeconomic and cultural transformation that journalists, politicians, and women themselves called "feminism." The association of feminism with middle-class women was, in and of itself, a way of marking office workers as middle class.

2 Office Work and Commercial Education during the 1920s

Women, seeing themselves forced to work, and as a logical consequence, becoming independent both morally and economically, have not obeyed this or that feminist doctrine. Feminism emerged when women had already taken concrete steps on the path to work. Thus, women have not usurped professions, or jobs. They have demanded what they rightly deserve—equal rights in the various spheres of life.

—MARÍA RÍOS CÁRDENAS, "La mujer en la lucha," *Mujer*, February 1, 1927

María Ríos Cárdenas, writing for *Mujer*, the magazine she founded, acknowledged the association between work and feminism. However, she countered the notion that feminism had led women to demand new rights and, subsequently, to work outside the home. Economic need had forced women to seek work outside the home, Ríos Cárdenas argued, and this experience led them to make demands characterized as feminist. Her argument that women's work gave impetus to new ideas about women's role in society is the subject of this and the subsequent chapter. Chapter 2 explores women's work and school experiences, and chapter 3 explores how women's work experiences informed changing ideas about women, which they expressed in writing and through activism.

During the 1920s, more and more women donned their best dress, the hem of which crept ever upward, and made their way through Mexico City streets on their way to work in government offices. Depending on the path they took to work, the young typists, for example, may have passed by striking operators at Ericsson Telephone Company or seen the black and red anarchist flag draped across the entrance to their favorite movie theater. The 1920s was a decade of heightened labor protest.[1] But not for women who worked in government offices. Empleadas spent their days typing memorandums, processing correspondence, and filing reams of paper. Office work, like some industries, was transformed by a new wave of mechanization and rationalization of production.[2] Faced with a growing bureaucracy, many ministries reorganized and professionalized their offices. Hierarchy and obedience, the routinization of work and production (of written documents), and other forms of organization and workforce discipline were deeply gendered. Occupational segregation facilitated workflow, but it also laid the foundation for women's subordination to men. Although wages were standardized across government job categories, occupational segregation meant women earned lower wages than their male co-workers. Still, office work offered better pay than many occupations and had the advantage of being associated with middle-class status. Office workers accrued the capital that marked their work as middle class through education, social and cultural practices, and civic engagement.

Commercial education played an important role in the association of office work with middle-class status. Families had to have a certain level of resources in order to send their daughters to commercial schools like the MLT. At schools like the "Miguel Lerdo de Tejada" Commercial School for Young Ladies, students gained a skill set that prepared them for office work and provided the cultural capital necessary to be able to move in that world. Students studied music, history, literature, and geography, for example, all accoutrements of a middle-class lifestyle. Public schools also initiated students into the world of politics. Students earned political capital through school governance and the formation of professional networks with women of influence. As an all-female space, the school was associated with older conceptions of middle-class culture that segregated women from men. The all-female space also allowed teachers to carry out their shared mission of mentoring and supporting young women at a time when they were moving into an integrated workforce. Throughout the 1920s, the MLT served as an important space for women to teach and mentor each other, form networks, and engage in conversations about women's changing roles.

Women in Government Office Work

The 1920s saw what journalist Alicia Alva described in an article for *El Nacional* as an "explosion of women" in government employment.[3] ("Alva" was an alias for the journalist Elvira Vargas, who at one time worked in the General Office for Statistics.) The Mexico City daily reported that between 1921 and 1930 the number of female government employees increased 2,000 percent. Once the violent phase of the Mexican Revolution subsided, Presidents Álvaro Obregón (1920–24) and Plutarco Elías Calles (1924–28) committed themselves to the institutionalization of the revolution. Politicians and statesmen set to work passing laws and opening offices to carry out the reforms revolutionary leaders had promised in the Constitution of 1917. They sought to create a strong state to support economic growth, mediate class conflict, and impose political consensus. These initiatives required an enormous amount of paperwork. One individual, the private secretary to the comptroller general, oversaw the monthly production of 200–300 contractual agreements, 80–100 memorandums, 600–700 letters, and 200–250 telegrams.[4] More people needed to be hired. Women took entry-level jobs as clerks, secretaries, typists, and shorthand typists to process land petitions, record labor conflicts, and coordinate efforts to educate and inoculate the masses.

During the 1920s the federal government revised and updated the legal framework that regulated bureaucracy and set about to professionalize its workforce. The 1922 New Law of Ministries of State (Nueva Ley de Secretarías de Estado) confirmed the existing seven ministries and five departments and added the National Statistics Office.[5] The increased workload led ministries to reorganize and professionalize the workplace, and during the mid-1920s several prominent government employees published books on office organization. By the end of the decade some ministries and departments had implemented reforms, as was the case for example with the Ministry of Finance in 1927 and the Department of the Federal District in 1929.[6] Ministries evaluated and reconfigured the organization of work within their offices, thus streamlining workflow and creating more jobs. Between 1920 and 1924, according to Mercedes Blanco, the federal government grew at an annual rate of 11.50 percent.[7] Even with the rapid growth in the number of women in government offices, men continued to dominate government employment (making up 87 percent of the workforce).[8]

The "old guard," women who by 1920 had worked in government offices for almost ten years, was joined by a rush of young women who had recently graduated from a commercial school or who had been certified at a private commercial academy. Occupational segregation of the office workforce concentrated women in specific jobs and physical spaces. For the most part, they continued to report to men. Male *licenciados* (a title indicating a college education) dictated correspondence to female secretaries, and male chiefs of staff directed the work of female clerks, filers, and telephone operators. By the early 1920s, however, a shift had occurred in the gendered spatial organization of work. Whereas during the 1910s one or two typists or apprentices might have worked alongside a dozen or so men, by the early 1920s it was common for large numbers of women to occupy entire offices such as the typing pool or the office of administrative records (see fig. 8). Dozens of women were either positioned in the corner of a large office or had a room all to themselves. In some offices women were separated from the rest of the office by a desk or wooden banister. The increased number and concentration of women transformed work culture.

Women's sheer numbers, concentration in physical spaces, dress, and habits of social interaction filled the room, as one journalist commented, like "cheap perfume."[9] As they arrived at work, women took off the hat and overcoat that they, like men, wore as they transited to and from work. In the office, men continued to wear suits that marked them as professionals. Women secretaries, typists, telephone operators, and office assistants wore

FIG. 8. Central Department, 1925. SINAFO #607. Reproduction authorized by the National Institute of Anthropology and History.

dresses and heels that emphasized femininity as integral to their professional identity. Some allowed themselves the luxury of silk stockings and a well-fitted dress, while others contented themselves with dresses made at home using sewing skills learned in elementary school and based on a pattern printed in the newspaper. Late for work, a typist might slip into the bathroom to powder her face and add the last touches of lipstick. Attractiveness was a part of her uniform.[10]

Once settled in behind a desk, a woman might open a ledger or check the ribbon on her typewriter, readying herself for the day's work. Over the course of the 1920s that work became increasingly regimented. Women received praise when they were as quiet and productive as the "Remington Noiseless" typewriter advertised in *El Universal Ilustrado*.[11] All the young women who worked in government offices, remarked one journalist, were "capable, hard-working, and intelligent."[12] The public seemed to take note. The "Most Capable Employee" contest run by *El Mundo* in 1923 focused primarily on women's professional skills, such as dictation, English translation, and accounting. A highly skilled secretary took dictation at one hundred words per minute.[13] Increasingly, employees were hired based on examinations and not through personal connections. They were asked to sign time cards. The increased volume of correspondence needed to be registered as it moved into and out of the office. Managers hoped to improve work-space lighting so that employees' eyes would not tire from the piles of work that passed over their desks in the course of a day. Memorandums circulated admonishing employees to clean up their desks at the end of the day, file away papers, and put away piles that might otherwise have been left out. They were also urged of take good care of their typewriters and other office machinery.[14]

As women worked diligently at their jobs, eager to advance, they also socialized with co-workers. Some might have dreamed of becoming a movie star despite having been forced to take a job as a typist in a government office, like the young woman in Julio Jiménez Rueda's play *Cándido cordero, empleado público* (Simple lamb, public employee, 1925).[15] Some may have acted on their dreams and heeded the call of the newspaper *El Demócrata*, in partnership with AMEX Film Corporation, for a competition for the role of "a typist who chews gum."[16] A few women who worked in government offices went on to star in films, as was the case for Adela Sequeyro and Otilia Zambrano.[17] There was no shortage of newspaper-sponsored events for readers to follow: typing contests held by *Excélsior* and dance contests sponsored by *El Demócrata* and *El Universal Gráfico*.[18] As women socialized at work, the way they spoke to each other, what they said, and how they laughed was noteworthy to male observers. Journalist Gastón Roger, writing for *El Mundo*, reported that secretaries in government offices, gathered in groups here and there, spent more time gossiping and laughing than they did engaged in their duties.[19]

Observers also mused about how men and women interacted at the office. Coquettishness was often integral to work relationships. So was sexual harassment. Some men and women clearly established friendships, as was the case of a young woman who, when her boss told her she should show up at a local hotel to take dictation, consulted with her male co-worker to get his advice.[20] He advised her against it and stood by her when her boss threatened to fire her for insubordination. Observers, at one and the same time, celebrated women's beauty and admonished them not to be a "Señorita Flirt" at work. As the women in the "Most Capable Employee" contest earned more and more votes from their co-workers and the reading public, *El Mundo* reported on how a "tall, vivacious, and pretty" young woman was worthy of the votes she had received because she avoided spending her time flirting with men in the office.[21]

Expansion of the federal bureaucracy created growing demand for employees, and women were integrated into the workforce according to preestablished patterns of occupational segregation. Archival data suggest that across the wide range of government offices, women continued to work as apprentices, shorthand typists, low-ranking clerks and scribes. At the Post Office, which continued to expand during the 1920s, women sorted letters and worked as clerks and apprentices.[22] The number of entry-level positions at the Post Office, which had declined between 1914 and 1918, began to rise. Wages for these positions, however, had stagnated. Apprentice wages stagnated as early as 1905 and remained at 1 peso a day for more than two decades (1908–30). Wages for clerks of all ranks had increased steadily from 1880 to 1920 but then began to decline. Post Office salaries were characterized by a slowly expanding gap in earnings between junior and high-level positions. Whereas in 1890 the lowest-level clerk earned 39 percent of that earned by the highest-level clerk, in 1920 that gap was 41 percent. The growing wage gap and the decline in real wages led Post Office workers to send numerous petitions to the Chamber of Deputies requesting raises.[23]

What did these wages allow government employees to purchase, whether individually or as a part of a household? And how did those purchases relate to available class identities? Economist and historian Jesús Silva Herzog asked these same questions.[24] Silva Herzog, director of the Office for Economic Research for the Mexican National Railroad Reorganization Committee (1930–31), was charged with conducting a study of government employees' real wages and living standards. Government employees were an ideal group to study, Silva Herzog claimed, because they "represent the whole range of the Mexican middle class, from the most modest to those who blend in with the upper bourgeoisie."[25] He also noted that government employees were an easy group to study. They were centrally located and more easily cajoled into participating in such a study than obreros, whom government inspectors had found hesitant to respond to probing questions about their home life and personal finances.

In his study, Silva Herzog drew on research conducted in 1924–25 by the Department of National Statistics which found that government employees' living standards included a wide range of circumstances (see table 3). Although Silva Herzog did not take gender into account, his data suggest that women's wages were generally closer to wages in working-class occupations than to those of middle-class government employees. The study classified public employees into four groups: teachers and three other categories of government employee (A, B, C).[26] According to the Silva Herzog study, government employees in category C earned 75 pesos a month, slightly more than low-level employees in the private sector. Low-level employees, according to the study, earned less than half of that earned by carpenters and mechanics and had a standard of living similar to that of bricklayers, shoemakers, and obreros. They earned more than workers in rural settings such as miners, peasants, and agricultural day labor (*campesinos* and *jornaleros*).[27] Budget data and newspaper reports suggest that women who worked in government offices during the mid-1920s fell within or below the lowest category (C). A government office apprentice, for example, earned 72 pesos a month. Women's rights activist Sofía Villa de Buentello estimated that women office workers earned 50 pesos a month.[28] When compared to women in other sectors of the economy, some office workers might earn wages similar to those of factory workers (see table 4). The wages were attractive nevertheless because of the potential for mobility within the workplace and the promise of higher wages. Individual employment records show that while some women did not earn significantly more at the end of their career, others moved slowly up the employment ladder.[29]

Silva Herzog's study also gave a picture of how government employees spent their money. Food costs totaled 56 percent of monthly income (42 pesos), and housing took up another 13 percent (10 pesos a month). By contrast, obreros in Mexico City, according to another study, spent up to 25 percent of their wages on housing that frequently consisted of a one-room unit shared by more than five people.[30] The columnist for *El Universal*

TABLE 3. Average monthly salaries, Mexico City, 1924–1925

Occupation	Monthly Salary (pesos)
GOVERNMENT EMPLOYEES:	
Teacher	225
Government employee, category A	300
Government employee, category B	105
Government employee, category C	75
PRIVATE EMPLOYEES	
Private employee, category A	210
Private employee, category B	80
Private employee, category C	60
WORKERS:	
Mechanics	156
Carpenters	104
Brick workers	72
Shoemakers	84
Workers (obreros)	80
Agricultural day workers (jornaleros)	36
Miner (peones)	42

Source: Jesús Silva Herzog, *Un estudio del costo de vida en México* (Mexico City: Editorial Cvltura, 1931), 27.

TABLE 4. Gendered composition of the workforce and wage differentials, Federal District, 1927

Industry	Wages, Men (pesos)	Wages, Women (pesos)	Women's Wages as a Percentage of Men's
Clerk	4.00–9.00	4.00–9.00	100
Typist	4.00	4.00	100
Telephone operator	4.00	4.00	100
Office apprentice	1.00–3.00	1.00–3.00	100
Matches	2.33	2.07	89
Cigarettes	3.90	2.60	67
Men's shirts and intimate apparel	2.92	1.93	66
Sweets	2.31	1.37	60
Stockings/socks	2.75	2.00	73
Textiles/wool	3.37	2.50	74
Textiles/cotton	2.75	2.44	89
Preserved food	2.29	1.16	51
Yarn	2.16	2.00	92
Shoes	2.42	1.83	76
Sweaters	2.56	1.87	73

Source: México, Secretaría de Comerico, Industria y Trabajo, *Monografía sobre el estado actual de la industria en México* (Mexico City: Talleres Gráficos de la Nación, 1929); México, Secretaría de Hacienda y Crédito Público, *Presupuesto de egresos del erario federal* (Mexico City: Talleras Gráficos de la Nacion, 1927), 160–67.

Gráfico, Loreley, wrote that 10 pesos a month "would not get a family much more than a pigsty to live in."[31] While Silva Herzog's study did not specify the kind of housing government employees occupied, earning disparities shaped residential patterns, as Mario Barbosa Cruz shows in his study of employees in city government (Federal District Department). More modestly paid employees lived in working- and lower-middle-class neighborhoods like Guerrero, Peralvillo, and Santa María de la Ribera and in rented rooms in the area surrounding the Zócalo. Newspapers advertised rented rooms for employees wishing to live near offices where they worked, such as the Department of Public Health. Susanne Eineigel describes Santa María de la Ribera as a mix of artisans, military and religious personnel, and middle-class families. The mixed-class makeup of Santa María de la Ribera stood in contrast to newer neighborhoods like Roma, Condesa, and Cuauhtémoc, where more-costly real estate placed a higher bar on the class status of residents.[32]

A woman's standard of living was significantly shaped by whether she was part of a household of multiple income earners or not and by how much those individuals earned. Women who were head of household were likely to live in less expensive neighborhoods, spend less on food, and cut corners on the quality of clothing they purchased. Evidence suggests that many women who worked for the federal government were single heads of household. The impact of civil war, and the loss of life and economic turmoil it caused, contributed to precarious family life. Mexico City still, in 1920, had the largest percentage of women of any state in the nation. The 1920s was a decade during which the federal government, health professionals, and popular culture celebrated middle-class conceptions of childhood protected from labor, as Ann Blum shows.[33] Someone had to work in order that small children could remain at home under their mother's care. Eighteen-year-old Guadalupe Zamudio was one such individual. Zamudio worked in an entry-level position at the Post Office in order to support her mother who stayed home to care for siblings.[34] It is unclear if it was the pressure of supporting family or a broken promise of marriage that led her to decide she could not face another year. On New Year's Eve in 1919, Zamudio took a handful of mercury chloride pills and, after hours of agony, ended the day at

Juárez Hospital, her lifeless body laid out on the autopsy table. Most single-female heads of household did not take such drastic steps, but the tragic end of Guadalupe Zamudio highlights that while office workers might claim middle-class identity, their living standards could often be quite precarious.

Commercial Education and Middle-Class Identity

During the 1920s, both government-sponsored and private commercial education spread like wildfire, and most schools nearly overflowed with students. Beginning with President Obregón, the federal government made education a centerpiece of revolutionary reform. The federal government reasserted control of education (which had been shifted to municipalities under Carranza) and increased the budget dedicated to its expansion.[35] President Obregón established the Ministry of Public Education (Secretaría de Educatión Publíca, SEP) in July 1921 and named José Vasconcelos as minister (1921–24). Vasconcelos, perhaps best known for his contributions to a renaissance in rural education and the arts and for the creation of a public library system, also oversaw the reform of technical and commercial education. In 1924 President Obregón, in an oblique critique of Vasconcelos, publicly declared the importance of shifting away from what he termed a "literary" education to focus on skill-based education that prepared students for the workforce.[36] In this spirit, the minister of public education, Doctor J. M. Puig Casauranc (1924–28) established the Department of Technical, Industrial, and Commercial Education (Departamento de Enseñanza Técnica, Industrial y Comercial, DETIC) in 1925.[37] From its inception in 1921 the Ministry of Public Education faced significant challenges, including a diversion of funds in 1923 to fight the De la Huerta rebellion, and budget cuts in 1925. Administrators stretched resources in order to broaden course offerings to respond to a rapidly changing work environment. Schools were understaffed and teachers overworked. Some schools were overenrolled, while others suffered from uneven attendance. And yet with all these challenges, commercial schools served as vibrant spaces for young women to engage in social, cultural, and political activities that prepared them for the workforce and contributed to the association of office work with middle-class identity.

The 1920s was a decade of transition for women. As Mary Kay Vaughan has shown, vocational training prepared women for occupations that could combine with housework, textbooks affirmed the importance of women's contributions to the home, and a romanticized discourse of hierarchy within families infused educational texts.[38] Gabriela Mistral's *Lecturas para mujeres* (Readings for women, 1924), for example, celebrated women's domain as one rooted in the domestic sphere, and lamented the possible loss of associated values if women were to abandon the home completely for public activity.[39] Mistral celebrated those qualities she identified with women's domain, such as mothering, sweetness, and self-sacrifice, while she herself charted new professional territory for women outside the home. At the school named for her, home economics classes were interspersed with lessons in boundary-pushing topics like birth control and the benefits of divorce.[40] Federal commercial education maintained some emphasis on women's domestic responsibilities, but it was primarily designed to prepare women for the workplace. And these women learned more than professional skills. Commercial schools provided a space of socialization, where women acquired a professional identity and the cultural capital that allowed for the association of office work with middle-class culture.

As a decade of transition, the 1920s also saw the rapid growth of commercial and technical education nationwide and of women's enrollment in commercial schools specifically. DETIC oversaw thirty schools throughout the country and nine in Mexico City. Between 1921 and 1929 the number of students enrolled in government-sponsored technical schools, which included commercial schools, increased nearly 45 percent, from 7,550 to 10,919.[41] Of the total school population in Mexico City, from kindergarten through university, 10 percent attended technical schools (by comparison, 1 percent enrolled in Normal School and 3 in university).[42] High enrollments at the MLT (see table 5) made news. In January 1922, *El Universal* reported that a thousand women enrolled for classes that were about to commence, a clear indication for this journalist of "a radical transformation in norms regarding women's education and therefore in women's lives."[43]

Booming enrollments and national efforts to improve commercial education had an important impact on the direction of the MLT. Roberto

TABLE 5. Student enrollment at selected schools, Mexico City, 1921, 1923, 1927

School	1921	1923	1927
"Miguel Lerdo de Tejada" Commercial School for Young Ladies	1,250	1,163	991
Corregidora de Queretaro	2,665	1,789	1,344
Home Economics	1,710	1,702	1,085
Business and Administration School for Advanced Study	1,648	1,648	1,439
Manual Arts and Trades for Young Ladies	770	1,129	1,062
Doctor Mora Commercial School	839	2,924	—
Gabriela Mistral	—	1,611	1,014
School for Shorthand Typists	—	736	—
Dr. Balmis	—	281	1,404
Technical, Industrial, and Commercial School for Young Ladies	—	—	1,162

Source for 1921: Archivo Histórico de la Secretaría de Educación Pública, Departamento de Escuelas Técnicas, Industriales y Comerciales, caja 9, exp. 10, 1921.

Source for 1923: México, *Memoria de la Secretaría de Educación Pública, 1928, presentada al honorable Congreso de la Unión por el secretario del ramo doctor José Manuel Puig Casauranc* (Mexico City: Talleres Gráficos de la Nación, 1928), 504–7.

Sources for 1927: México, *Noticia estadística sobre la educación pública en México correspondiente al año de 1927* (Mexico City: Talleres Gráficos de la Nación, 1929), 682–83; José Manuel Puig Casauranc, *El esfuerzo educativo en México: La obra del gobierno federal en el Ramo de Educación Pública durante al administración del Presidente Plutarco Elías Calles (1924–1928). Memoria analítico-crítica de la organización actual de la Secretaría de Educación Pública, sus éxitos, sus fracasos, los derroteros que la experiencia señala* (Mexico City: Secretaría de Educación Pública, 1928), 1:504–7.

Medellín, head of the Department of Schools, oversaw the reform of commercial education, and it would fall to the new director, Dolores Salcedo, to carry out that reform. In 1920, Dolores Salcedo was named director, marking a new era in the history of the school.[44] Upon her arrival at the MLT she was feted by the students with theater, singing, piano music, and dance performed on the patio of the school. Young girls congratulated Miss Salcedo in French and English, showing off their skills learned in class. Salcedo quickly became well loved, increased the prestige of the school, and would have a lasting impact on the school and generations of students.[45]

Director Salcedo immediately set to work reforming the school curriculum, which made news. She called on teachers to create uniformity across the curriculum and in teaching methods. All teachers would, for example, now teach typing the same way. In 1921 Salcedo created two degree tracks, each with the option of two or three years of study, to respond to the needs of students from more modest socioeconomic backgrounds. A degree as shorthand typist consisted of two tracks: two years of study prepared the student for commercial and office work (*certificado de taquigrafía corresponsal y oficinista*), or three years of study prepared the student to become an executive secretary.[46] The school offered a similar set of accounting degrees: two years of study for assistant bookkeeper, or three years of study for bookkeeper.[47] Thus students, who for economic reasons were unable to study for three years, would nevertheless be prepared for employment at an early age. Whereas the first generations of MLT students came from a broad range of age groups, including women in their twenties, by the 1920s the average student age had fallen more in line with typical secondary school enrollment. Students began school at age thirteen, the minimum age required to enroll, after six years of elementary school (although only two years of elementary school were required). Depending on the degree the student pursued, she would enter the workforce at age fifteen or sixteen.

Salcedo's curriculum reform sought to accommodate young women from different socioeconomic circumstances and with different career objectives. Nevertheless, those who attended had to have some economic means in order to do so, not only because they spent time studying when they could be working but because commercial school was not free. Article 3 of the

Constitution of 1917 provided free education for all Mexicans, but only for primary school. In 1923 the initial cost of enrollment at the MLT was 5 pesos, and students made additional payments that added up to a total of 29 pesos a year. Elective courses cost between 1.50 and 3 pesos per course. Students were also required to purchase some of the materials needed for classes.[48] In addition, students who lived across town had to pay for transportation. The school offered scholarships and served breakfast for those who needed it.[49] Regardless of the socioeconomic status of the families from which students came, the SEP characterized clerical work as intellectual and not manual labor, and many aspects of the MLT educational experience contributed to student acquisition of middle-class cultural capital.

In accordance with the *callista* educational reform and the direction taken by DETIC, Salcedo stepped up efforts to guide students toward practical employment skills while at the same time maintaining instruction that provided the cultural background necessary to function within an office.[50] The MLT curriculum included lessons in technical skills, legal code, and general knowledge of commercial subjects. Students also studied modern history, geography, singing, music reading, and languages (Spanish, English, and French), all considered essential to be able to excel as clerical and administrative workers.[51] Teachers also revised instructional materials used to teach dictation, for example, so that at the same time students learned technical skills they also acquired the "culture" needed to obtain a position in an office. The arts and humanities also contributed to the patina of middle-class identity.

Although the federal government sought to expand and exert influence over education, as Patience Schell shows, the SEP had insufficient resources to supplant private schools. American businesses that manufactured and sold modern office machines like typewriters established commercial schools where girls learned typewriting, stenography, and other office skills free of charge. Private Mexican interests also set up shorthand and secretarial academies. For example, women took classes at the Pitman Academy of Mexico and the Pitman Acuña Institute.[52] Mexican private interests also offered commercial education classes, as was the case at the British School for Young Ladies (Inglesa para Señoritas) and at Catholic schools, though the latter were threatened with being closed down by the government. Manuel Gómez Morín, president of the board for the Banco de México, and Alberto Mascareñas, the bank's general manager, founded the School for Banking and Commerce (Escuela Bancaria y Comercial) in 1929 and named Agustín Loera y Chávez as president. The school closed in 1932 but later reopened as a private institution.[53]

The federal government struggled to dedicate funds to expand school infrastructure to meet growing enrollments. In 1922 SEP officials considered building an annex to the MLT and eventually added a third floor, but then opted to decentralize commercial education and build new schools.[54] The SEP established the School for Shorthand Typists (Técnica de Taquimecanógrafos) at 281 Chapultepec Avenue explicitly to compete with private schools. The school tended to serve older students who were already employed. Classes focused on training in shorthand and typing, without the additional subjects taught at schools like the MLT.[55] The same year (1922) the government invited public employees to attend commercial and administration classes offered at the Normal School. Five hundred people signed up, and four hundred attended classes in accounting, inspection, customs, taxes, memorandum and exegesis, accounts payable, military notation, and filing.[56] Building on the success of this initiative, in 1925 the newly formed School for Advanced Study of Public Administration (Escuela Superior de Administración Pública, ESAP) began to offer courses and degrees not available to students at the MLT, including sociology and railroad accounting, industrial organization, fiscal auditor, and public accountant.[57] The ESAP tended to enroll students who on average were thirty years old and already a part of the workforce. In order to meet growing demand for commercial education, in 1923 the SEP also expanded night-class offerings. The School for Manual Arts and Trades for Young Ladies and the Industrial Night School Centers for Popular Culture had for some time offered classes in shorthand, typesetting, bookbinding, cooking, sewing, and shoe and parasol manufacture.[58]

Manuel Puig Casauranc (1888–1939), named minister of education in 1924, continued much of the Vasconcelos project, with an increased emphasis on workforce preparation. During his tenure (1924–28, 1930–31), Puig Casauranc expanded urban vocational and commercial education. In 1925 the SEP created the category of advanced secondary education (*educación secundaria superior*), distinct from higher education (*educación superior*), to focus on providing technical education for workers and administrative and commercial training for government employees.[59] As education officials expanded commercial education they were very aware of the mix of class backgrounds of the young women who sought clerical training.

In 1925 the SEP opened new commercial schools in locations that might better serve a diverse population. With the assistance of the Huasteca Petroleum Company and of Señor Abel R. Pérez, who donated 20,000 pesos to the project, the SEP built the Technical, Industrial, and Commercial School for Young Ladies (Escuela Técnica, Industrial y Comercial para Señoritas, ETIC). Built on the grounds of Lira Park in Tacubaya, ETIC was designed "to train young ladies of the middle and poor classes that live in the areas of Roma, Condesa, Del Valle, Tacubaya, Mixcoac, San Angel, and San Pedro de los Pinos, with the means to earn a living."[60] New classrooms and workshops, spacious patios, and gardens created an attractive and "hygienic" atmosphere. The curriculum consisted of office skills, a smattering of home economics, and housekeeping. With the goal of improving the general education of the students, the school offered film screenings, talks, and literary and musical events. Within four days of opening, 150 students had enrolled.[61]

On opening day, Director Carmen Kraus de Alvarez de la Rosa (sister-in-law to revolutionary hero General Felipe Angeles) asked those in attendance for their support to ensure the school's success in providing "upstanding morality, discipline, and positive educational results."[62] DETIC identified the purpose of the school as allowing "thousands of young ladies, deprived until now of education, to contribute to the well-being of their families with the application of what they learn, so that they become productive and useful to society."[63] By academic year 1928–29, ETIC enrolled 584 students in the Commercial Section and 577 in the Industrial Section. In the Commercial Section students studied for the careers of shorthand secretary and of bookkeeper, both of which were three-year degrees. In the Industrial Section, students studied cooking and fashion. Students also chose from a wide range of electives including poultry husbandry, hair styling, machine embroidery, hat making, toy making, and sewing women's undergarments.[64]

Within this expanding system of commercial education for women, the MLT remained a leading school. It had consistently high enrollments for most of the 1920s, and was the largest commercial school specifically for women.[65] Of all DETIC schools, the MLT had the largest concentration of women teachers and staff (see table 6). While enrollments remained high, a lower percentage of students graduated from the MLT than from other schools, though the reasons are unclear. The School for Manual Arts and Trades for Young Ladies, the Gabriela Mistral, and the Sor Juana Inés de la Cruz all had graduation rates between 94 and 100 percent. The lower graduation rates at MLT may have been due to students having secured a job before completing their degree, as MLT administrators argued. For example, a candidate for the degree in shorthand secretary could take an exam given by a potential employer and did not need a certificate in order to find a position in private business or government offices.[66]

The speed with which commercial education grew, along with the impact of an economy still recovering from war, took its toll on the school system, its teachers, and its students. Budget cuts led to the closure of the School for Shorthand Typists (1925), the Dr. Mora Commercial School (1927), and fifteen night schools (between 1924 and 1928).[67] Overall demand for commercial education was not the problem. Even with the increased number of commercial schools, enrollments remained high. Administrators attributed the closure of the Dr. Mora Commercial School to poor student performance. They explained the poor quality and inconsistency of education at the school as due to the socioeconomic heterogeneity of students, or in their own words, there were "too many poor children mixed in with middle-class children."[68] The SEP also called for the closure of the Public Administration School (Escuela de Administración Pública). In response, students and their parents wrote in protest to President Calles, arguing for the importance of the school for the future of the nation, which they hoped to serve as government employees. The petitioners also attested to the dedication of teachers who taught classes for free. One hundred and twenty students signed the petition, and of the legible signatures, forty-eight were women and thirty were men.[69]

Through the ups and downs, the MLT offered a rich cultural and political space that contributed to the association of commercial education

TABLE 6. Ratio of students to teachers and staff at selected schools, Mexico City, 1927

School	Students	Teachers and Staff
"Miguel Lerdo de Tejada" Commercial School	1,163	153
School for Manual Arts and Trades for Young Ladies	1,129	91
Business and Administration School for Advanced Study	1,648	172
Corregidora de Querétaro	1,789	153
Home Economics	1,702	92
Gabriela Mistral	1,611	89
Dr. Mora	2,924	127
School for Shorthand Typists	736	62
Dr. Balmis	281	27

Source: México, *Noticia estadística sobre la educación pública en México correspondiente al año de 1927* (Mexico City: Talleres Gráficos de la Nación, 1929), 682–83.

with middle-class identity. The government relied on women's volunteer labor to carry out official programming that, while associated with the revolutionary project, dovetailed with middle-class reform culture. The Department of Schools, which oversaw commercial education, also led the urban literacy campaign. Students and faculty at the MLT took advantage of their own education to be able to participate in the campaign led by Eulalia Guzmán (1890–1985), who herself had briefly taught at the school.[70] In 1922, after taking classes in a building with crumbling walls, broken windows, and doors hanging from their hinges, students joined the 3,022 teachers and went, on a voluntary basis, out into neighborhoods to teach people how to read and write. Like teachers in rural Mexico, MLT teachers and students encountered fellow Mexicans less privileged than themselves. While engaging in the important work of teaching reading and writing, the young women reinforced their conceptions of themselves as literate and socially privileged.[71]

Women's participation in President Emilio Portes Gil's 1929 anti-alcohol campaign also built on women's history of reform activity. Women had engaged in anti-alcohol reform movements since the late nineteenth century when they published in women's journals like *Las Hijas del Anáhuac*, petitioned government representatives, and established reform societies.[72] As in many countries, the assertion of women's moral authority served as the basis for middle-class women to mobilize outside the home and create networks of influence. Many women understood alcoholism as a condition that afflicted men, especially working-class men, and for which women paid the price. Reformers' defense of women was often directed at working-class men, further contributing to class distinction. The issue continued to resonate with women in the 1920s when, throughout Mexico, Jacobin governors like Emilio Portes Gil, Adalberto Tejeda, Francisco Múgica, and Tomás Garrido Canabal sponsored women's anti-alcohol brigades. María Ríos Cárdenas's newspaper *Mujer* frequently published articles on the anti-alcohol effort.[73] The SEP published anti-alcohol pamphlets in 1927 and 1929. President Portes Gil's National Anti-Alcohol Committee provided yet another opportunity for young women to engage in reform efforts, this time tied to a national campaign and in association with women working in the Department of Public Health.[74]

The MLT also encouraged physical education. School-based physical fitness for women had its roots in the performance of tableau that had been so popular during the first decade of the twentieth century. Educational officials expressed a strong commitment to exercise, so much so that even though space was limited, students rotated use of the central patio for exercise. Students took classes in *gimnasia plástica*, a regimented and choreographed form of exercise, and showed off their skills at official events. School-sponsored exercise contributed to women's physical well-being, collective identity, and ties to revolutionary culture and gave them entrée into new public spaces. In May students might compete in the government-sponsored student athletic meets and in September march in a regimented Independence Day parade at the National Stadium. Volleyball and basketball tournaments were especially popular with women (see fig. 9). Schools also held dances where young women could enjoy the pleasures of moving their bodies to the sound of music. While a 1921 dance to celebrate the centenary of Mexican independence was a special event, over the years the MLT school hosted dances for students from other schools and for visiting students from other countries.[75]

Fashion also reflected women's changing roles in ways that supported their professional goals and at the same time reinforced their association with the home. The SEP reported proudly on the "Economical Dress and Design Competition," sponsored by *El Universal*.[76] The contest distributed various awards, with first place given to a student at the Home Economics School for a "modern style, just the right geometrical combination . . . distinctive, discreet, and [at 14.50 pesos] economical." The dress was described as ideal for the office, the street, a visit, for every occasion in which working women and women of the home need to appear appropriately dressed."[77] A dress with wide appeal, then, served a dual purpose (work and home) in a way consonant with women's dual identity. The feminist women's magazine *Mujer* offered advice on diet, exercise, and aging as well as changing fashion. Contributors warned a female readership, increasingly on the move, against the adverse health effects of using a corset and high heels.[78]

Young women enrolled in commercial school were introduced to the world of politics through student body government, and despite their exclusion from national suffrage, exercised their voice and vote at school. Each DETIC school had a student government and representatives on the Student Federation. While MLT students were usually active in school governance, in 1922 they refused to participate in Student Federation elections. In an effort to curry the favor of the MLT students, Francisco del Río went to the school to persuade the young ladies to vote for Raúl Pons. Quite to the surprise of del Río and the *Excélsior* journalist who reported on the gathering, the young women questioned the candidate and his motives. With "measured and energetic words, indicative of talent and character," student Irene Montes explained she did not believe in their promises. Though not fully explained by the journalist, Montes pointed out that in the past these men had used the Student Federation against MLT students and had publicly and unfairly

FIG. 9. Basketball team, Ministry of Agriculture, 1922. SINAFO #105596. Reproduction authorized by the National Institute of Anthropology and History.

criticized Director Salcedo. When another student, Miss Lara, was more "violent" in her reaction, Otilia Zambrano, a third-year student, stepped in and calmly pointed out that the MLT students would not dignify the Student Federation by participating in elections that involved people who had offended them. Thus informed, del Río could not but acknowledge the young women's protest and commend them for their eloquence and solidarity. That these and similar gatherings were reported in the press contributed to legitimating women's political engagement. As word of the dispute spread, DETIC authorities sought to calm the students and encouraged them to focus on their studies. Despite official reprimand, women gained political skills that informed their move into the world of office work.[79]

The MLT cultivated work skills through contests, professional development activities, and school-based cooperatives that gave women entrée into the world of business and public activity. Students from the MLT and

ETIC participated in contests to prove their skills in typing, shorthand, and handwriting. The MLT also collaborated with organizations like the National Board of Commerce to sponsor an annual contest on business topics. Business representatives served on examining boards, allowing students to make connections with potential employers. Students attended talks at National University (Universidad Nacional Autónoma de México) to practice their dictations skills. At the ESCA, the Women's Society "Fraternity" participated in a public-speaking contest. A month later in the same room used for the forward-thinking public-speaking contest, a screening of the film *Falso pudor* (False modesty) may have been meant to provide a counterbalance.[80] A 1924 regulation provided the framework for school-based cooperatives that the SEP hoped would instruct the students in collaborative work at the same time they earned money for the school. At the MLT cooperative, students could sell their services as typists. The profits were used to pay for scholarships, class materials, and the repair of school equipment. Each of these activities represented parts of a larger shift in the infrastructure of women's education and professional engagement.

The shift in women's roles was fostered by a generation of teachers and professional women who circulated through the MLT. In addition to its curriculum, course content, and extracurricular activities, the school served as a transformative space for mentoring and professional networking. Professional women with social connections and growing influence frequented the school as teachers, students, and invited speakers. The journalist, suffragist, and educator Margarita Robles de Mendoza, for example, made a presentation to the MLT on children's education in the United States (1928).[81] In 1922 Robles de Mendoza published the pamphlet "The Political Rights of Mexican Women" and in 1931 she published interviews with President Portes Gil on the status of women. Other professional women participated in the school's monthly lectures on morality and home economics.[82] Teachers and students alike engaged in vibrant intellectual exchange at the school and in SEP publications, all of which contributed to the growing visibility of professional women. Director Salcedo and the teachers under her guidance promoted the visibility and celebration of women. An event to honor the Argentine actress Camila Passera de Quiroga featured a dance performance by MLT students, known for their professionalism, and was, according to *El Universal*, yet another example of the importance of celebrating women's successes.[83]

During the 1920s the MLT was an all-female space.[84] Increasingly, however, people began to discuss the benefits of coeducation. These conversations were provoked, no doubt in part, by the realities of the workplace into which graduates entered. In 1923 Director Salcedo, in an internal memorandum, explained to her superiors the importance of coeducation. The young women at her school, she pointed out, required a full understanding of civics in order to succeed in the world of office work. A course she implemented taught students their "obligations . . . first, as daughters, second as students, third as members of society, and fourth, as capable employees who are dignified and conscientious in their work." Salcedo took care that students graduated from the MLT with "a well-formed character so that they do not run into problems in the government, business, and private offices where they work."[85] Salcedo was not alone in her concerns. In 1927 Rafael Zubarán Capmany, who had served as the minister of industry, commerce, and labor from 1920 to 1922, wrote an article in *Coopera* (published by the SEP) calling for coeducation, which he described as "closely tied with modern industry and the growing rights of women, who are transformed by social change and the evolution of collective life."[86] Both the shifting gender dynamics of work and the "difficulties" that Salcedo referenced were more fully discussed in newspaper articles, short fiction, essays, and novels, many of them written by women who themselves had attended the MLT.

Whereas the women who took office jobs in the 1890s did so accompanied by commentary that construed their employment outside the home as exceptional, by the 1920s women's presence in government offices had become well established. Employment growth contributed to occupational segregation that concentrated women at the lower levels of the wage scale. Women also tended to work in positions subordinate to men. Men certainly occupied low-wage positions, but women were virtually always positioned to report to male authority. In this regard, women's work experiences in offices shared something in common with those of women who worked in factories (also marked by occupational segregation), where they were subject to overseers and mechanics who determined their capacity to earn a living.[87] In contrast to factory work, however, the cultural attainments of office work, and sometimes the salaries, allowed empleadas to claim a middle-class identity.

Women who came of age during the 1920s had been raised in a milieu that anchored middle-class female identity within the domestic realm, celebrated romantic love, and considered women's primary vocation to be that of mother. They were also part of a generation of change. As Mary Kay Vaughan argues, the social history of education shows how teachers and students interpret and appropriate educational directives.[88] At the MLT, teachers pursued a commitment to women's education and professional advancement well beyond the romanticized ideals of domesticity and traditional gender norms that continued to pervade textbooks. Young women who attended commercial schools entered into networks that included teachers who had fought for women's rights before, during, and following the Revolution, had protested against undemocratic practices in national politics, and had struggled for better working conditions. The school provided training in a professional skill set and middle-class culture. Literacy and anti-alcohol campaigns, sport and cultural events, and attendance in all-female federal schools contributed to the association of office work with middle-class identity and gave students entrée into official culture. Despite the fact that women did not have the right to vote in national elections, they exercised their voice and vote within the political culture of the educational system.

Young women in commercial schools and women who worked in federal offices filled the imagination of city residents. Increasingly it was a young woman who might help someone fill out paperwork in a government office, who appeared in the pages of the morning newspaper, and who filled the streets of downtown Mexico City. Employing their typing and literacy skills, office workers themselves contributed to transforming those images. Work and educational experiences served as the basis for a rich *cultura escrita* that informed the content of women's activism, as we will explore in the following chapter.

3 Writing and Activism in 1920s Mexico City

During the 1920s many young Mexican women lived with one foot in the past and one in the future. Tension over tradition and modernity manifested in civil rights, culture, and class relations. Between 1923 and 1925 the states of Yucatán, Chiapas, and San Luís Potosí allowed women limited suffrage.[1] In response to these and other advances for women, the *Excélsior* initiated the celebration of Mother's Day in 1922 as a way to emphasize women's domesticity, self-sacrificing, and sweetness.[2] Older conceptions of middle-class femininity continued to shape women's education, work experiences, and public discussions about women office workers. Those same workers gave voice to new ideas about work, female autonomy, motherhood, and other markers of middle-class identity. Literacy and writing were essential skills for office workers at the same time that they were fundamental to middle-class culture. Drawing on Carmen Castañeda's use of the concept of *cultura escrita*, this chapter examines women's "effective literacy," the way they converted reading and writing skills into the capacity to enact personal and societal change.[3] A vibrant female-centered professional culture flourished in government offices and in the classrooms of the "Miguel Lerdo de Tejada" Commercial School. That culture echoed throughout Mexico City—in commercial culture, popular press, and literature. For many office workers, written culture was integral to their activism as they developed their ideas in published essays, engaged on the margins of literary culture, and spoke out at meetings and demonstrations. The societal change they advocated was far-reaching and included suffrage, civil code reform, and birth control.[4] Women who worked as typists, secretaries, and clerks found little space to make their voices heard within the male-dominated public employee movement and so filled the ranks of the women's movement. Office workers' experiences informed their critique of working conditions and of women's status more generally and gave shape to the women's movement.

Domesticity continued to frame middle-class female identity. Critics of women working outside the home sought to hem them in with reminders of their obligations to motherhood. In response, women defended their right, as mothers, to work outside the home. They also advocated for maternity leave, a right recently granted to obreras in the Constitution of 1917. Having made significant advances in office employment during the late 1910s and early 1920s, women expanded their arguments beyond simply justifying a working life to formulate specific work demands, especially equal pay for equal work and elimination of the glass ceiling. Office workers also developed a critique of gender relations within and beyond the workplace. Women's lower earning capacity, some argued, subordinated women to men socioeconomically and reinforced women's cultural, psychological, and sexual subordination to men. Office workers contributed to a more capacious middle-class identity for women, one that included work, and to a definition of feminism that tied inequality at work to social inequality.

Echoes of the Past and Visions of the Future

Women who came of age in the 1920s had been raised on a hearty dose of melodramatic narratives that reified traditional gender norms and hierarchical relations within the home. Short stories, novels, and the press celebrated romantic love, which placed women firmly within the domestic realm. Forward-thinking literary groups such as the Stridentists or those writers associated with the novel of the Revolution did not create any significant space either for women writers or about women's issues in urban Mexico. As Elissa Rashkin has argued, "Señorita Etcétera" and "Mabelina" may have been modern women, but in Arquela Vela's novella they are primarily a projection of unfulfilled male sexual desire. Salvador Novo and other *contemporáneos* sprinkled their prose with modern female characters like "Miss Remington," identified only by the brand name of the typewriter she used, who exercised little agency. Even with significant shifts in women's employment, domesticity continued to serve as a pillar of literary depictions of middle-class identity.[5]

At the same time, another kind of writing culture began to flourish, this one produced by office workers. Inspired by work-related experiences, occupational segregation, salary disparities, and subordination to male co-workers, individual women and networks of women posed new questions about their role in society and women's rights. María Ríos Cárdenas and Leonor Llach Trevoux were two such individuals. Both attended or were tied to the MLT and went on to work for the federal government, Ríos Cárdenas intermittently and Llach continuously for more than fifty years. Both women were also at the forefront of the feminization of the School for Advanced Studies (which became the School for Philosophy and Literature in 1924), when women's enrollments went from 15 percent in 1910 to 78 percent in 1926.[6] This shift in women's enrollment has been associated with growing numbers of women who had been trained as teachers and who sought to expand their intellectual horizons. Some women who had studied at commercial school or were headed for careers in public administration joined them at university. Both Ríos Cárdenas and Llach were prolific writers and central figures within women's networks of cultural, social, and political influence. Taken together, their thinking about women's roles is indicative of widespread discussions about women and middle-class identity.

María Ríos Cárdenas

María Ríos Cárdenas, born in Sabinas, Coahuila, in the late 1890s, graduated as a nurse in 1917 and went on to study at the national School for Advanced Studies, where she obtained a degree in Spanish literature and language. She became a prominent writer, publisher, and feminist who worked for decades to advance women's inclusion in Mexican political life. She also briefly taught at the MLT. In 1922 she published *Atavismo* (Atavism), a novella that explored how the unequal relationship between men and women in the workplace formed the basis for gender inequality in society at large. She went on to publish the self-proclaimed "feminist" newspaper *Mujer* (*Woman*, 1926–29) and wrote a women's column for *El Nacional* from 1929 to 1934. These publications and her activism in the suffrage movement informed the publication for which she is perhaps best known, *La mujer mexicana es ciudadana: Historia, con fisonomía de novela de costumbres* (Mexican women are citizens: A novelistic history, 1942). Ríos Cárdenas's opus weaves together critiques of gender inequality in the home, at work, and in politics. Moreover, she helped to advance conversations about the balance between women's rights and responsibilities in these different spaces.[7]

Ríos Cárdenas's early publications challenged prevailing ideas about the rights of mothers to work outside of the home. The 1920s' focus on puericulture (the science of hygiene and raising children) and eugenics were both movements that frequently focused on women as mothers. The violence of civil war and the loss of an estimated 1 to 2 million lives were still fresh in people's minds, and professionals and average citizens alike concerned themselves with raising healthy children. From inoculation campaigns to puppet theater, the government expanded programming and heightened rhetoric that emphasized the importance of healthy children. Ríos Cárdenas was also influenced in her writing by women's mobilization in the early 1920s to reform the civil code, achieved in 1928, and to establish a civil service law.[8] In many of her publications, Ríos Cárdenas wrote about subjects distant from her own life and social class. This distance permitted her to write about sexual exploitation with no threat to her own reputation. By writing on behalf of those who had no real forum where they could speak for themselves, Ríos Cárdenas positioned herself as a reformer exercising her middle-class privilege.[9]

Ríos Cárdenas's 1922 novella, *Atavismo*, is framed by the idea of a transitional moment in women's social roles, specifically the move of middle-class women into the workforce. The title of the book evokes the idea of both generational change and the heavy weight of the past. The word *atavism*, from the Latin *atăvus*, which means "ancestor," refers to the expression of archaic customs and behavior inherited from prior generations.[10] In the novella, atavism expresses itself as actions that tarnish a woman's sexual reputation and therefore her middle-class identity. The protagonist, eighteen-year-old Antonina, needs to earn an income, but by entering into the workforce she jeopardizes her respectability and social worth. She relives the moral struggle faced by women of generations past whose respectability was defined by their presence in the home. Employed as a shorthand typist in the offices of a shoe factory, Antonina is one of a sad lot of employees, "all of them more or less screwed."[11] While the male employees suffer poor working conditions, unpaid overtime, and a lack of independence, Antonina's travails begin when she meets Luis del Real, the factory owner's son. The relationship that evolves is embedded in class inequalities and sexual exploitation that played out inside the office and beyond.

The complexities of Antonina's class identity sit at the heart of the story. Ríos Cárdenas describes Antonina as of "simple and distinguished behavior appropriate for the middle-class young lady that she was." Ríos Cárdenas writes that Antonina was "of a routine character . . . and a middling intellectual level." Antonina's education, however, was more closely associated with popular literature than a formal education. Ríos Cárdenas deems novels a questionable influence on the young girl: "romance novels sparked misguided desires in a young virgin, victim to her passions."[12] Whereas a formal education would have taught appropriate sexual morality, Ríos Cárdenas implies, an education rooted in popular novels leaves her ill-prepared for the workplace. Such an education feeds Antonina's downfall, and that downfall threatens her middle-class identity.

The novella is more than a story of sexual harassment at work. It describes how women's position within the workforce lays the basis for their economic subordination to men. Indeed, while Antonina initially meets Luis at work, the story takes place outside the office. And while work is not the location of the transgression, the need to work establishes the basis for the exploitation of the office girl. Antonina is invited to a party hosted by people of a social standing superior to her own, where she reencounters Luis. The overlap of social worlds and the potential thrills and dangers in such a space are palpable from the start.[13] Luis shares his lofty ideals of romantic love. His words sound not unlike those one might find in the novels Ríos Cárdenas disparages. Antonina responds to him with a clear vision of the implications of such love for a young woman of her socioeconomic class. "For men, women like us who work out of necessity are a well-known entity and thus, easily seduced, and therefore without merit. The love they give us is fragile and passing, and in light of this, the best that we can do is keep our hearts virgin." Despite such clarity, Antonina gives herself to Luis.

Some months later, Antonina, now pregnant, confronts Luis in his office and begs him to marry her in order to give the child his last name. She promises that if he marries her, he can do as he wishes with his time and other women. He refuses her offer, and Antonina falls to the floor in a flood of tears. As the story culminates, the precariousness of middle-class status for women who work outside the home becomes all the more apparent. Antonina's out-of-wedlock pregnancy threatens to tip the balance and place her outside middle-class respectability. The possibility of recovering middle-class respectability comes to her in the form of an offer for marriage. Señor Calderón, himself an employee, offers Antonina his name and to live as "husband and wife" in a comfortable apartment in Colonia Roma (a middle-class neighborhood), a step up from both the stain of illegitimacy that marked her own birth and the "marginal neighborhood" (unidentified) from which she hailed. Ríos Cárdenas ends on what is meant to be a hopeful note: "Antonina, with her marriage, had initiated an upward movement . . . and the examples that she would encounter in her new life, along with education, would refine her sentiments and perhaps her children would leave their pathological inheritances behind."[14] *Atavismo* thus instructed its readers that marriage, a formal education, and middle-class consumption (a house in Colonia Roma) continue to serve as markers of middle-class identity for working women. It would seem that, Ríos Cárdenas engaged in her own atavistic behavior, recycling a definition of middle-class identity for women that hinged on sexual morality and domesticity, even within the context of new roles for women in the workplace.

In 1923, Ríos Cárdenas established the newspaper *Mujer*, a self-declared feminist publication that was informed by women's workforce participation in at least two ways.[15] First of all, Ríos Cárdenas drew on a network of professional women who worked in government offices to contribute to the paper. Amalia de Castillo Ledón, for example, promoted theater and puppet shows for the Department of the Federal District and wrote a column for *Mujer* that highlighted women in theater.[16] Esperanza Velázquez Bringas, just embarking on what would be a prestigious career as a government employee, reported on women's labor rights and Guillermina Llach, employed in the Department of Health, contributed recipes and literary reviews.[17] *Mujer* also published articles that drew on the expertise of the many women employed in the Department of Health, covering topics such as alcoholism, abandoned youth, eugenics, and the health effects of makeup and using public telephones.[18] Women's publications like *Mujer* served as a venue for office workers to develop expertise that, as Nichole Sanders shows, played a central role in policy formation.[19]

While drawing on the expertise of women who worked in government offices for content, *Mujer* also addressed issues important to working women, including when to marry and whether mothers should work outside the home. While in the 1910s women's middle-class identity had idealized a seamless move from the paternal to the marital household, during the 1920s women began to imagine a significant number of years in the workforce between those two spaces. There was also a shift in which women in the household would work. If before it was daughters who worked to support a mother to stay home and care for small children, now women began to advocate for the right of mothers to work outside of the home. Ríos Cárdenas also participated in a growing conversation about the ideal age at which to get married, which she identified as twenty-five.[20] Although she did not state so explicitly, this would have meant a woman might work for eight to ten years before having children. Ríos Cárdenas took children as a given aspect of marriage, which meant that a woman would need to make a choice about how to balance children and work. She wrote: "If she does not need to work, she should stay home and care for her children and husband. If she needs to work she should, and her children will thank her for it."[21]

Ríos Cárdenas's arguments in favor of women's right to work informed her writing about concrete threats to women's employment. The 2,000 percent increase in the number of women working in government offices had not gone unnoticed. Some commentators worried about entrusting women with government work. Others argued that women tended to be Catholic and therefore necessarily conservative, thus positioning them as enemies of the revolutionary project. In response, Ríos Cárdenas argued that women had a civilizing effect on the world of office work: "With so much effort made by talented functionaries to ensure that the federal administration provides satisfactory service to the public, we need to purge government offices of undesirable employees. This would, in general, improve the service offered by the government and benefit women in particular."[22] The pages of *Mujer* filled with international news of women's successes working in offices and of advances made by feminists in favor of women's right to work.[23]

During the 1920s, threats to women's employment, and to their independence more generally, frequently played out as cultural conflict. In 1923 a series of newspaper articles appeared with headlines criticizing "Necklines at Work." A journalist for *El Mundo* claimed a campaign for more discreet attire had been initiated not by the archbishop or a priest but rather by empleadas themselves. The article, playing on class prejudice, went on to say that even the doorman was overheard asking, "Is this the Statistics Department or a cabaret?" The secretaries simply laughed, their grating voices drowning out the strident clacking of fingers on the typewriter. Laughter is lovely, the journalist remarked, but when the office workers did so their sensual mouths opened wide, and so too did the neckline of their dress. Journalists, while critical of women, did not want to appear completely against them. The *El Mundo* journalist reminded his audience that serious empleadas were never "flappers and fly-by-night girls."[24] A follow-up article a few days later asking for "More Discretion at Work" commented that debates over women's dress should be expected, as this was always the case when women shift from being "an object of entertainment to productive members of society."[25] The following year observers criticized the modern woman, female athletic bodies, the "bob" haircut, and new trends in makeup. In 1928 the archbishop of Mexico City weighed in, and a group of male students physically attacked women who had bobbed their hair (*pelonas*).[26]

That same year, Deputy Sotelo proposed that women who worked in government offices wear a uniform. Rumors of flirtations and indecencies circulated in the halls of government. Some rumors may not have been unfounded. The former minister of public education himself, José Vasconcelos, described his amorous desire for two women who worked in government offices, noting that they were, "without exaggeration, gorgeous empleadas, timid and silky-soft, like doves lost in a storm."[27] The practice of calling on female secretaries to pose for artists creating Mexican calendar girls drew on and contributed to the objectification of women.[28] The debate over the introduction of uniforms as a way to address sexual impropriety spilled out from the halls of government and into the pages of newspapers. In *Mujer*, Ríos Cárdenas supported uniforms as an economical solution to "provocative dress."[29] As always, however, she advocated absolute equality between the sexes and asked why uniforms had not been proposed for male employees. Some women may have found the uniforms degrading because service workers (*servidumbre*) wore uniforms. Mainstream newspapers like *Rotafolio* weighed in as well, with articles like Juan Zaravé's "Women Office Workers Say."[30] While some women interviewed for the article mused that the uniform might help them save money, others felt the initiative was misguided. Otilia Zambrano, who worked in the Ministry of Public Education, opined that women would always be a temptation to men and that male government employees would need to get used to the presence of beautiful young women in the halls of government. She asserted women's right to autonomous behavior and placed the onus of self-regulation on men—an argument that while immediately relevant to debate over dress also spoke to the fight for women's agency more generally.

To reinforce her defense of office workers' rights, Ríos Cárdenas drew on revolutionary rhetoric that privileged obreros and campesinos. The Constitution of 1917 had established categories that throughout the following years gained increasing political currency. As Christopher Boyer shows, individuals who claimed campesino identity did something more than simply point out that they worked the land.[31] During the 1920s people from a wide-range of labor experiences mobilized around campesino identity to gain access to material and political resources promised in the constitution. The same was the case for obreros. While empleados públicos were excluded *de jure* from constitutional protections afforded to obreros, in her writing Ríos Cárdenas included the empleada alongside the obrera and the campesina, implicitly asserting that the plight of female office workers also merited public attention. In 1929 she wrote, "Do women office workers [empleadas], factory workers [obreras], and rural workers [campesinas], just because they are workers, have to serve the double role of worker and lover?"[32] In this statement Ríos Cárdenas brought together different occupations in a way that rhetorically created a shared condition among women, across class and occupational differences. By continually including the empleada alongside the obrera and campesina, feminists acknowledged the growing importance of office workers and sought to protect their labor rights at a time when other workers had been granted significant protections.

Toward the close of the decade, public debate over the proposed federal labor law created an opening for government employees to make claims for rights already granted to workers. Women who worked in government offices mobilized in hopes they too would be included in the final version of the law. In 1928, as the government prepared draft proposals, Ríos Cárdenas and others advocated for the rights of women who worked in offices, factories, and the countryside. After all, she insisted, the constitution stated that "work is a legal obligation for all Mexicans," which, she reasoned, included women.[33] In 1929, *Mujer* reported that Ríos Cárdenas typed the draft of article 90 of the proposed federal labor law. It was reported that several articles of the proposed law allowed women to take a paid day off from work, in addition to regular holidays. The federal labor law proposal reaffirmed the constitutional right to maternity leave for obreras. Office workers wanted the same. Furthermore, Ríos Cárdenas claimed, the law stated that "when a woman is fired as a result of an attempt against her honor she will have the right to three month's salary."[34] No doubt concerned about the obvious victim blaming, Ríos Cárdenas's responded to the proposal with "No comment." Consistent with her belief in equality between men and women, her silence implied that she questioned why a woman would lose her job when a man was the aggressor. As the debates dragged on, *Mujer* was happy to identify allies. The Ministry of the Interior, for example, asked for several modifications to the law to benefit obreras, empleadas, and campesinas.[35] However, when the final version of the labor law was passed in 1931, public employees were explicitly excluded. As state employees, the argument went, they did not work for an employer whose motive was profit, and therefore did not require protection. Politicians promised that in the future they would work on a civil service law to address the concerns of government employees.

Leonor Llach Trevoux

As the number of women in office work ballooned, women writers who had access to publication venues questioned gender relations within the family and at work. One such writer and lifelong government employee was Leonor Llach Trevoux. Born in Barcelona, Llach migrated with her family to Mexico in 1918.[36] Her father, Jaime Llach Llagostera, a carpenter, had arrived the year prior. Leonor arrived on the steamship *Montevideo* with her mother María Trevoux Sendros, an office worker, and her sister, Guillermina, a typist. The Llach family lived in Santa María de la Ribera.[37] Both sisters attended the MLT. Leonor Llach also studied law for a year and then spent two years earning a master's degree in history at National Autonomous University of Mexico (Universidad Nacional Autónoma de México). During the 1920s she worked in the SEP, including as chief administrative officer for the Department of Child Welfare, and in the Department of Health.[38]

A keen observer of her surroundings, Llach was particularly articulate in defending the rights of female office employees. Llach published widely. During the late 1920s her articles appeared in Mexico City and regional newspapers: in Mexico City, *Elegancias, La Prensa, El Nacional, El Universal Gráfico, El Universal Ilustrado, Crisol,* and *Horizontes*; in Veracruz, *Alborada*; and in San Luis Potosí, *Alas*.[39] All of the venues in which she published were directed at a literate, middle-class audience. While most of the outlets had a mixed (male and female) audience, she also published in magazines specifically for women, as was the case with *Elegancias* and, in the 1930s, *El Hogar, Ideas,* and the Argentine *Vida Femenina*.

Llach wrote frequently of the changing balance of work, love, and domesticity for women. Her 1926 essay "La femeninidad y la cultura" in *Elegancias* is a good example of her concern about how the reality or mere invocation of motherhood restricted women. *Elegancias* was written for a well-educated female public interested in essays, poetry, fashion, and social commentary. Llach's essay sought to expand the boundaries of femininity to include a life of the mind and professional identity: "For a cultivated woman, love is a secondary concern, the home a refuge, at times very agreeable, but not so much so as to isolate her from the world. Maternity is a masterly work of art, to which she can dedicate all of her inspiration, but not an absolute and definitive objective in life, a sentence without appeal, that separates her from all material or intellectual work." She agreed that invocations of maternity were as nothing more than an excuse to limit women: "It is comical, the argument that men make when they want to prove women wrong, and when they have no logical argument to put forth: maternity, the home. In other words, fantasy."[40] Certain stereotypes of middle-class femininity had become a fantasy, no longer applicable to women's lives, except when invoked to limit their action.

Rather than celebrate the home as the ideal space for women, Llach saw it as the place where women learned their subordination. That subordination played out in interpersonal family relations and had both economic and psychological components. Gender relations within families, Llach pointed out, had not caught up with the new realities of women's wage earning. Specifically, families treated daughters and sons differently:

> Family discipline is often more severe on daughters than on sons. That is why women learn to lie. At times, without even realizing it, a desire for freedom that she cannot even put her finger on pushes her to do the same as her brother. Such enthusiasm is seen, above all, among women who work, often to support their brother, and they want to spend the money that they themselves earn and yet have to obey those who live off their earnings.[41]

Llach went on to condemn mothers who perpetuated discrimination within the home: "When young women pursue the freedom to which young men easily have access, they are dealt with a severity which would never be used with men, even in similar circumstances. When a man transgresses, the first one to defend him is his mother. I would call this stupidity."[42] To use the word "stupidity" in the same breath as "mother," needless to say, went against the idealization of motherhood to which most readers would have been accustomed. Llach's criticism chipped away at what had been a pillar of middle-class female identity: the moral authority of mothers.

Llach, like Ríos Cárdenas, countered the public discussion that blamed feminism for what was construed as a societal wrong: women working outside the home. Llach highlighted the cynicism and hypocrisy of anti-feminists in an essay on the causes of prostitution:

> Those who fret over the growth of feminism and want to free women from having to work by running them out of offices are not going to liberate women from the fields, women who harvest crops and push a plow during the most difficult months of pregnancy. Women should be given preference in jobs that do not require physical exertion. Education, a propensity for work, and good pay for it are the only means by which to resolve such problems.[43]

Llach, like Ríos Cárdenas, made a nod to the growing political power of the identities of field and factory workers.

Llach was particularly persuasive when it came to the politics of dress at work. Women, Llach argued, were caught in a bind, because their appearance was widely promoted as essential to workplace success. Women themselves cultivated such practices, as when *Mujer* published articles that encouraged exercise to retain a svelte body type and offered fashion advice.[44] Llach herself acknowledged that physical beauty and attractive clothing were requirements for employment, since women received attention and often respect based on appearances. Respectable people (*gente decente*), she wrote, only paid attention to those who dressed well. Thus for her "it makes sense that women who want to be well received pull out all the stops to achieve that indispensable, good appearance." While Llach recognized the demands of the work place on women's dress, she took pains to ensure that this focus on appearance not restrict women's autonomy. In a 1929 article, Llach wrote: "In order to achieve dominance of the spirit, freedom of the body must be secured."[45] She frequently used clothing as a metaphor for habits that restricted women's freedom of expression.[46]

Fashion was a battlefield for women's rights. In 1925 Llach wrote in defense of women's right to make decisions about their own bodies in an article that appeared in *Elegancias*. Whereas Ernestine Calles, the daughter of President

Calles, sported a bobbed haircut and wanted the world to know that Mexico had flappers too, Llach was no fan of such styles. She was appalled by actress-inspired fashions: the powdered white complexion and penciled-in, high-arching eyebrows inspired by Mae Murray, and the exaggerated facial expressions of Gloria Swanson were no more than "grotesque gringo" adoptions, she lamented. Nevertheless, Llach defended women's right to adopt whatever fashion she chose. Llach also made sure that such debates not distract people from what was really important: "Those who attack women's fashion bring out their best arguments: tradition, feminine beauty, and the masculinization of women. Not so fast, mister! The real issue, and what is important to us, is the vote!"[47] Although the battle over women's rights was fought through debates over women's fashion, feminists worked to put that battle in its place.

Both Llach and Ríos Cárdenas were prolific writers, and through their essays and newspaper articles they contributed to conceptualizing new roles for women. They were instrumental in shifting conversations that had primarily associated middle-class women with the home to acceptance of women combining domesticity and work. The nineteenth-century emphasis on domesticity gave way, during the 1920s, to conversations about women's capacity to choose when to marry. Conversations about *whether* women should work outside the home expanded to the articulation of specific labor demands. Furthermore, feminists denounced male privilege within the home and at work. Conversations about women's dress, haircut, or other aspects of the physical body served as a mechanism to delimit and defend women's autonomy over their own body. It was a challenge to keep labor demands and suffrage at the forefront of their agenda, but through publication in women's journals and the general press alike, Llach and Ríos Cárdenas did keep that conversation going by combining writing and activism. Clearly, they had access to print culture as authors in a way that most office workers did not, but what about those women who did not? The public sphere of activism would serve as a space for other women to shape the conditions of their work.

Building a Multi-class Women's Movement

Empleada activism was informed by a rich culture of writing (*cultura escrita*) and framed by a lack of clarity about the legal status of public employees.

When teachers, classified as public employees, went on strike in 1919 they were told that it was illegal to do so.[48] Public employees did not have the right to strike against the state (*estado patrón*). Then, in 1926, the Supreme Court found that "as the aforementioned constitutional article [123] does not in any way limit the definition of employee, nor does said article express that it might only refer to private employees, public employees must be included as well."[49] In 1929 the Supreme Court reversed itself, arguing that the Constitution sought "to create a balance between capital and labor, as elements of production, circumstances not applicable to the relationship that governs public power and the employees that serve it."[50] The decision reinforced restrictions on public employees' right to organize.

Denied the right to organize and strike, public employees sought other ways to improve working conditions. Initiatives came from different quarters, including professionals who proposed reforms to improve government service and working conditions for public employees. In 1921 engineer and civil servant Modesto C. Rolland made a series of proposals that included a civil service law, tax reform, and professionalization of the public-sector workforce, all meant to bring order and transparency to city government, and eliminate corruption.[51] Rolland's civil service proposal was concerned specifically with municipal employees and would have provided for a thirty-nine-hour workweek, overtime pay, paid vacation, hiring based on an examination system, and a depoliticized workplace. The law would also have provided for savings banks, employee housing, and training schools. Rolland's proposal did not specifically address women's concerns, such as maternity leave, although he advocated for benefits included in article 123 of the Constitution, such as workers' compensation for injuries. Nothing came of Rolland's initiative. In 1925 Pedro C. Solís Cámara proposed a civil service law and a cooperative bank.[52] Growing awareness of the need for some employee benefits led the government to enact the General Law of Civil Service Retirement Pension in August 1925, which provided a pension at age sixty and money for the family of deceased employees.[53]

Employees also used petitions to try and make changes in the workplace, or to at least improve their own personal circumstances. Based on personnel files and employment records from the Department of the Federal District,

Mario Barbosa Cruz finds employees expressed their concerns in petitions over insufficient salaries, deferred payment of wages, and the managerial demand for professionalization.[54] Evidence of women's petitioning is sparse, though it does exist. In late December 1920, for example, a group of nearly two dozen employees, including women, wrote to their superior asking that they receive a year-end bonus of half a week's pay.[55] The petitioners noted that head of the Ministry of Finance and Public Credit, Adolfo de la Huerta, had done so for his employees and that the private sector also had the "lovely tradition" of giving employees a month's pay as an end-of-year bonus. In 1922 a group of women teachers wrote a letter denouncing unequal wages. They pointed out that the male instructors at ESCA were paid more than the women who taught at the MLT and asked that the budget for the following year rectify such inequities. ESCA paid instructors 5.00, 4.00, and 3.30 pesos per day, while MLT did not pay instructors more than 4.00. The SEP did not agree to the salary request and argued that MLT teachers only provided an hour of instruction. MLT instructors also complained about the reduction in the number of instructors, from 102 to 84, despite the positive results produced by the school and reported on in the city newspapers.[56]

The impetus for organizing may have been different for men than for women due to their different positions within the workforce. Between 1921 and 1925 the federal government, faced with financial crisis and the need to make payment on the foreign debt, looked to public-sector employees' salaries to economize, and thousands of women lost their jobs to budget cuts.[57] In 1922 President Obregón implemented a sliding scale of pay cuts so that employees earning less than 5 pesos a day had their salary cut by 5 percent, while those earning more had their salaries cut by 5 to 15 percent.[58] While both men and women faced salary cuts, the cuts affected men in higher-paid positions differently than women and men in lower-paid positions. And, mid- to high-level male government workers had already begun organizing as early as 1920. Faced with job insecurity and salary reductions, high-level employees established the National Confederation of Public Administration (Confederación Nacional de la Administración Pública, CNAP), a self-described mutual aid society. Such claims distinguished the organization from a union, which was not permitted, and carried the connotation of a conciliatory approach to change. Antonio Caso, rector of the National University, served as president of the CNAP board of directors, and honorary members included Minister of Public Education José Vasconcelos, Minister of Industry, Commerce, and Labor Miguel Alessio Robles, and President Obregón. The association's central demands included job security, a savings bank, and affordable housing for public employees. As a part of their membership campaign the CNAP promised that those who joined the organization would be guaranteed not to lose their jobs at the end of the year. Many of the offices involved in forming the CNAP employed large numbers of women, but it is not clear to what degree women were active in the organization. In any case, the CNAP was dissolved a year later.[59]

In response to growing complaints from public employees, President Obregón declared "Employee Day" in October 1922 as a holiday. Department heads wrote to the president expressing their concern that they did not have money to pay for celebrations or to allow employees a paid day off. Obregón also received dozens of telegrams from men and women, some praising the idea and others complaining that it was all fine and good to have a holiday but that without sufficient salaries that would allow them to celebrate a day off, it did not mean much.[60]

President Obregón, unable to pay the country's foreign debt in 1924, again turned to government jobs and salaries to economize. The *New York Times* reported that the government was as much as two months behind in paying employees' salaries.[61] In 1924 Licenciado A. Cruz formed the Mexican Association of Official Employees (Asociación Mexicana de Empleados Oficiales, AMEO). Rather than using CNAP language of mutual aid and professional association, Cruz, in an editorial that appeared in the government newspaper *El Demócrata*, used the language of class. He identified AMEO members as "the proletariat of the office" and construed their history as emerging out of working-class mobilization, indicating that their organization "rested on the giant shoulders of organized labor."[62] In a meeting in May 1924 some 350 employees attended to elect a governing board. Although Ministry of Finance employees were at the forefront of AMEO, employees from many government offices participated. Ministers and other high-level functionaries began to talk and circulated memorandums about employee organizing. In

November 1924 Francisco Valdés, director of the National Mint, indicated to the Department of Labor that he had no problem with the workers in his unit drawing up internal regulations that supported employees, or to their establishing a union.[63]

Government employees whose work put them in close contact with the working class also organized as a part of the broader labor movement. In 1922 federal sanitation workers organized. Between 1925 and 1928, four groups of government employees joined the Mexican Regional Labor Confederation (Confederación Regional Obrera Mexicana; CROM), including the Worker and Employee Union of Graphic Arts and the Government Press Union in 1926. As a part of the broader crisis that the CROM experienced between 1929 and 1933, several government employee unions split from the organization. *Revista CROM* did not report specifically on female office workers or their concerns. Although the CROM had made declarations in favor of working women at the time of its founding, in the early 1920s it engaged in several campaigns to push women out of jobs. The teacher and prominent women's right activist Elena Torres split with the CROM over its lack of concern for women.[64]

Secretaries, typists, and other female office workers turned to Mexico's burgeoning women's movement to express their labor concerns. Over the course of the decade, as their numbers grew and opportunities for a collective conversation increased, women who worked in government offices developed a sense of themselves as a group (see fig. 10). The women's movement, composed of diverse players and a wide range of philosophies, concerns, and methods, served as a vital space for office workers to become active in public life and bring their labor demands to the table. As historians Ana Lau and Gabriela Cano have shown, the 1920s women's movement was primarily concerned with civil code reform, child welfare, and suffrage.[65] Professional women played a growing role in child welfare congresses and international women's conferences focused on suffrage.[66] Office workers filled auditoriums and debated these issues with fervor, thus making up the rank and file of the women's movement. They also brought their own agenda to the women's movement, especially between 1919 and 1924, pushing the movement in the direction of labor demands.

FIG. 10. Group photograph on the patio of government offices, 1928. SINAFO #602. Reproduction authorized by the National Institute of Anthropology and History.

The women's movement can trace its roots to synergy between teachers, office workers, and working-class mobilization. Women activists, when they did not find full support in labor organizations, established feminist organizations in order to be able to determine their own priorities and strategies. Elena Torres and expatriate Evelyn Trent Roy established the Mexican Feminist Commission (Consejo Feminista Mexicano; CFM) on October 31, 1919, and on November 24 they participated in the formation of the Mexican Communist Party.[67] (Torres later worked as a secretary for the government secret service, reporting to General José Domingo Ramírez Garrido, general inspector for the Mexico City Police.) The CFM sought to provide women with more opportunities to organize and to share a commitment to socialism. Its broad agenda, which included support for a commercial education center for young women, a sewing cooperative, and a day-care center, attracted women from diverse backgrounds and would have been particularly attractive to office workers and working mothers. The CFM also held events—announced in the social section of *El Demócrata*—that combined music, poetry, and speeches given by members and invited guests. The CFM was an attractive space for many women who worked as government employees, including María del Refugio (Cuca) García and teacher Estela Carrasco, and brought members into closer interaction with the labor cause as when the CFM joined the May Day parade in 1925.[68]

The CFM published a magazine, *La Mujer* (not the same one published by María Ríos Cárdenas), which made the case for "feminism," a word that included a wide range of positions and concerns. Articles in *La Mujer* made general statements such as "feminism will transform society and has no boundaries." *La Mujer* also made specific statements that connected working conditions and feminism. In a 1921 editorial, the staff (perhaps Julia Nava de Ruisánchez, the newspaper's editor) wrote that the undeniable proof of the existence of feminism in Mexico was "the existence of a broad number of obreras, empleadas, profesoras, etc., who with the fruits of their labor support their households."[69] The CFM's concern about women's working conditions shaped many of their activities. In 1921 it sponsored a talk given by Señor Duplán, who reported that women supported more than half of Mexican households, and many of the other 50 percent included women who worked outside the home. When the CFM established its platform, labor demands figured centrally: "equal pay for equal work," "limits to the work day and allowance for days of rest," "salaries based on the principle of women as heads of household and that take into account the cost of living," the abolishment of the glass ceiling, and maternity leave "as stipulated by law." Labor demands were integral to CFM social and political demands.[70]

In 1922 CFM members attended the Pan-American Conference of Women, organized by the U.S.-based League of Women Voters Congress in Baltimore (April 20–29). Teachers Elena Torres, Eulalia Gumán, Luz Vera, and Julia Ruisánchez attended. Ana Lau argues that the CFM agenda evolved into something less "radical"—that is, less closely associated with labor—and more broadly concerned with issues of education, sexuality, and legal status. At the Baltimore meeting, Mexican delegates spoke on issues such as birth control, sex education, marriage and divorce, the white slave trade, access to higher education, and suffrage. Even given the shift in emphasis, office workers continued to play a significant role in women's congresses, attracted by the range of issues being discussed relevant to their lives.[71]

With government support, the following year the CFM convened the First Feminist Congress of the Pan-American League, held at the Business and Administration School at the National University of Mexico (May 20–30, 1923). The location signaled ties between the feminist movement and the large number of women office workers who attended the congress. The government gave its female office workers the day off to attend. Congress participants developed a program that included support for a federal labor law, agrarian reform, social security, and civil code reform. They also proposed to form a government employee union and establish day care for the children of working women. Such was the enthusiasm for some of the speakers, including Sofía Villa de Buentello, a central figure in civil code reform movement, that the text of her speech was printed as a pamphlet to be distributed among the public.[72]

Sofía Villa de Buentello is known for her activism for legal reform, thus forming a part of the liberal feminist tradition in Mexico. She also played an important role in organizing office workers. Villa de Buentello's business card presented her as an educator and shorthand instructor. In 1921 she published *La mujer y la ley* (Woman and the law), analyzing the legal status of women. She also addressed women's economic status and wrote that it was "economic factors that really determine the lamentable dependency of women."[73] Villa de Buentello sent a copy of the book to President Obregón, asking that he read it and offer his opinion. She hoped the government would pay for copies of the book that she could then distribute to women employed in government offices.[74] Although the president responded politely, it is unclear whether the government ever purchased the books. Villa de Buentello sent her next book, *La verdad sobre el matrimonio* (The truth about marriage), to Señora Obregón, and again asked that the president pay for its distribution.[75] Clearly, Villa de Buentello considered female clerical workers as a target audience and felt that her ideas would resonate with them. "It is from these professional women and office workers," Villa de Buentello told the *New York Times*, "that feminists are recruiting their forces."[76] Two organizations—Free Women (Mujeres Libres), established by María Casas y Miramón in 1922, and the Cooperative Women's Union of Racial Pride (Unión Cooperativa de Mujeres de la Raza), established by Villa de Buentello in 1923—brought together large numbers of office workers, which the *New York Times* described as "feminists, largely middle class."[77] The feminist conferences of the 1920s served as the proving ground for women who would go on to be organizers in the government employee unionization movement in the 1930s.[78]

In 1924 the Cooperative Women's Union of Racial Pride united with Free Women, claiming more than fifteen hundred members.[79] According to Villa de Buentello and Casas y Miramón, more than 90 percent of their membership was office workers and professional women, many of whom had participated in the urban literacy campaign led by Eulalia Guzmán. Together, the two groups called on presidential candidates in the 1924 election cycle to formulate a platform on women's issues. In return, they would consider an endorsement. The group hoped for an end to bloodshed and war and denounced Presidents de la Huerta and Calles, whose warmongering, they argued, got in the way of women's efforts to reform divorce laws and the progress of the country. Villa de Buentello informed the *New York Times* that they were not impressed with the presidential candidates' sweet-tongued, vacuous pronouncements.[80]

The Cooperative Women's Union and Free Women gathered statistics on women's employment as a way to bolster their call for taking office workers demands seriously. Villa de Buentello provided those statistics to the *New York Times*, which reported that in 1910 Mexico had 13 typists and 1,962 women office workers, and that in 1921 there were 23,457 office workers, of which 18,750 were typists. In the private sector, women's numbers grew from 21 percent of all merchants, salespeople, and clerks in 1910 to 26 percent in 1921.[81] The article also reported that stenographers were paid 50 to 150 pesos a month. The women argued that these statistics justified their demand for equal pay for equal work.

Office workers continued to fill the seats at women's conferences. The International League of Iberian and Hispanic-American Women held the Racial Uplift Congress on July 5 and 6, 1925. Sofía Villa de Buentello was elected president of the congress, which was held at the Palace of Mines and attracted more than two hundred attendees.[82] *El Demócrata* reported on the congress and the significant participation of stenographers, typists, and other office workers, especially from the Ministry of the Interior, the Ministry of Public Education, and the Ministry of Industry, Commerce, and Labor. Several of the more visible participants identified themselves to the newspaper either as commercial education teachers or as office workers. It is worth noting these specific women and their varied backgrounds. María Angulo came from the ESCA, where she had begun in a temporary position in 1905 and took a permanent position in 1915. Rosario Ochoa de Palacios identified with El Colegio Teresiano, known for offering commercial education for women. Sara Pérez represented the Mexican Society of Women Shorthand Typists. Yet others identified themselves to the press by their work-based affiliation: Refugio Garcia, Department of Indigenous Affairs; Doctor Antonia L. Ursúa, Department of Health; Fidelia Brindis, Teachers Union; María Luisa Ross, Ministry of Public Education; Reinera Penagos and Rosa Narváez, Teachers Union.[83] Congress participants, in identifying themselves to the press by the government office where they were employed, gave their own professional credentials and claimed some of the political legitimacy of those offices. The identification was also strategic and made known that the government had, in its very own offices, women who demanded change.

As Ana Lau points out in her rich study of women's congresses during the 1920s, the objective of the event was "to discuss and to implement as practice, all of the ideals of the modern woman, to bring dignity to women and children as much as possible."[84] At the heart of such complex issues was the fight for better working conditions for women. One of the initiatives that emerged from the congress was a petition to President Calles asking that "reactionary" employees be fired and that women be given those jobs.[85] That many of the participants were women who worked in federal offices may have facilitated their efforts to lobby government. The next day a group of women went to Luis Morones, head of the Ministry of Industry, Commerce, and Labor (1924–28), to ask for his support, which he reportedly gave.[86]

It is likely that sometime in 1928 a young woman employed in a federal office typed up the early drafts of the federal labor law. She would not be covered by this law, because it built on constitutional article 123, which the courts had concluded did not apply to government employees. That typist, if she wanted to improve her circumstances, might petition her superior or join a government employee organization. There is little evidence to show that during the 1920s women made their voices heard in the public employee movement, and abundant evidence that they did so in the women's movement. Typists, secretaries, and clerks filled the auditoriums of feminist congresses and in so doing shaped the movements' agenda. Rank-and-file office workers, along with women who gained some standing and were able to publish, crystallized arguments in favor of equal access to jobs and salaries. They also made the circumstances of working mothers more visible. Observers identified office workers who engaged the women's movement as middle-class. Women themselves contributed to the meaning of middle-class identity by introducing new ideas about the balance between domesticity and work outside of the home. Historians have often tried to distinguish between women's arguments for special protections based on difference, often associated with their domestic roles, and demands for equality.[87] When in 1920s Mexico City office workers wanted both recognition of their domestic roles and equality at work there was no contradiction, because both demands stemmed from central components of middle-class identity. It was, however, also strategic to associate empleadas with obreras who could claim constitutional protections denied to empleadas. Ríos Cárdenas and Llach drew on the political rhetoric of the era that privileged obreros and campesinos to argue that empleadas also deserved legal protection.

Women's organizational experiences and the rich *cultura escrita* that informed the content of their activism in the 1920s laid the foundation for the labor and women's movements of the 1930s.

4   Women at Work in Government Offices in 1930s Mexico City

A 1935 newspaper article published in *Excélsior* noted that the government had opened its office doors, and women rushed in. True, the journalist remarked, this is a good thing, but "do they think that just because of this, women find themselves in a bed of roses?"[1] In the period from 1932 to 1938 women increased from 18 to 24 percent of government employees.[2] In the process, female office workers came to outnumber teachers. Government jobs promised equal wages without regard to sex. However, as in industry, sex-typing of occupations, occupational segregation, and seniority violations all contributed to continued wage disparities. In the 1930s workers consolidated gains made over the course of the 1920s. Some of those gains were codified in the Federal Labor Law (1931).[3] But government employees were excluded from that law. Nevertheless, the law served as a reference point for both upper-level administrators regulating office work and office workers themselves. This chapter examines the ways professionalization, battles over the definition of seniority, and politics shaped women's work experiences.

Beginning in 1932, Congress passed a rapid-fire succession of laws that reorganized and increased the number of federal offices. A 1932 law eliminated the Ministry of Industry, Commerce, and Labor and created the Department of Labor and the Ministry of National Economy. The Ministry of National Economy subsumed the work of the Department of National Statistics, which was eliminated. A 1934 law reflected the increased emphasis on the rural sector, with the establishment of the Department of Agrarian Reform, and on the growth in legal oversight, with the Federal Attorney General's Office and the Attorney General for the Federal District. The 1934 law also eliminated the Department of Procurement and Accounting. The year 1936 ushered in yet additional offices and reorganized the division of duties between ministry offices and departments. The Office of Indigenous Affairs was established in 1936 and the Department of National Marine in 1939. In addition to the creation of new offices, the function of many offices shifted to include increased responsibilities for research and planning for federal projects.[4]

The legal framework for the reorganization of government offices was accompanied by the continued expansion in the number of personnel. Public-sector employment continued to grow, according to Mercedes Blanco, at a rate of 3 percent between 1925 and 1934 and of 6 percent between 1935 and 1940.[5] The shift away from the military phase of the revolution toward the implementation of social programs was reflected in the fact that the number of civilian employees surpassed the number of military employees. Significant growth occurred in areas that supported revolutionary programs, especially health, education, and agrarian reform, as well as in offices necessary for national development, such as the Ministry of Finance and the Ministry of Communications and Public Works. President Cárdenas (1934–40) expanded health and human services significantly and opened the Ministry of Public Assistance (1937), which led to an increase of more than eight thousand employees on top of the almost four thousand already employed in this area. More than 76 percent of all central administration public employees worked in the Ministry of Public Education, the Ministry of Communications, and

FIG. 11. Typist, workers, and bureaucrats produce a labor agreement, 1930. SINAFO #83442. Reproduction authorized by the National Institute of Anthropology and History.

the Ministry of Finance. Along with the expansion of offices so obviously tied to the revolutionary project, in 1933 the government created the Office of Stenographers to address the increase in paperwork.[6]

In 1930 the two offices with the largest number of women were also those with the largest percentage of women, thus to some degree repeating patterns of occupational segregation seen in other sectors of the workforce (see table 7). The Ministry of Public Education employed 3,720 women, who represented 41 percent of employees in that office, many of whom were likely teachers (the 1930 federal employee census did not distinguish between teachers and other government employees). The Department of Health employed 659 women, 35 percent of that workforce. An uncertain number of these women may not have been considered office workers per se, such as nurses, social workers, vaccine campaign workers, and other health-related employees.[7] The Ministry of the Interior employed 100 women, 32 percent of employees in that office. Archival records, while not systematic,

TABLE 7. Number and percentage of employees by government office, 1930

Office	Total Number of Employees in Office	Women as a Percentage of Employees in Office	Number of Women in Office	Women in Office as Percentage of All Female Government Employees
Ministry of Public Education	2,553*	38*	971*	14*
Department of National Statistics	809	38	212	3
Department of Health	1,872	35	659	8
Ministry of the Interior	315	32	100	1
National Supreme Court	387	29	111	1
Federal Attorney General	185	28	51	< 1
Ministry of Agriculture and Development	1,229	24	293	4
Ministry of Finance and Public Credit	2,876	23	655	8
National Graphic Workshops	316	22	69	< 1
Ministry of Industry, Commerce, and Labor	1,300	22	281	3
Ministry of Foreign Relations	457	20	93	1
Department of the Comptroller	1,097	16	170	2
Ministry of Communication and Public Works	2,737	15	414	5
Military Industrial Production	1,563	14	215	3

Chamber of Deputies	457	13	60	< 1
Department of the Federal District	14, 859	12	1,214	15
Office of the President	212	6	12	< 1
Senate	135	2	3	< 1
Total**	37,148	22	8,332	–
Executive Branch	36,289	23	8,154	98

*Numbers given for 1932.

**Includes data not shown in the table.

Source: México, Dirección General de Estadísticas, *Censo de funcionarios y empleados públicos, 30 de noviembre de 1930* (Mexico City: Talleres Gráficos de la Nación, 1934), 58; México, Dirección de Pensiones Civiles de Retiro, Departamento de Estadística. *Segundo censo de empleados sujetos a la ley general de pensiones civiles de retiro, 1932*. Mexico City: Imprenta Franco Elizondo hermanos, 1933), 36. According to the authors, only 5–6 percent of employees did not fill out the 1930 census.

show that women in the Ministry of the Interior worked largely as typists, stenographers, filing secretaries, and low-ranking clerks.[8]

During the 1930s several important shifts occurred in women's employment that resulted in an increased association of women with office work. By 1938 the number of female government employees (12,838) surpassed the number of female teachers (12,126).[9] The hiring of typists, secretaries, and filing secretaries, for example, had continued apace, while the number of female teachers had declined slightly. The shift in which ministries employed the largest number of women also contributed to the increasing association of women with the modern office. By 1938, the Ministry of Public Assistance employed the largest number of women (2,982), followed by Communications and Public Works (1,837), Finance and Public Credit (1,863), and Public Education (1,306) (see table 8).[10] Specific offices that hired a large percentage of women came to be identified with the new face of government workers. By 1938 the offices with the largest percentage of women were the Ministry of Public Assistance (57 percent), Public Education (40 percent office workers, not including teachers, versus 38 percent in 1932), and Public Health (34 percent versus 35 percent in 1930). By and large the work women did in these government offices was classified as "administrative," "specialist," and "service" (see table 9).

As the number of women working in government offices grew, they also experienced job mobility. Over the course of the decade a growing percentage of women occupied professional positions, increasing from .8 percent (1932) to 2 percent (1938). Specialists (called sub-professionals in 1932) grew from 12 percent (1932) to 24 percent (1938). The percentage of women in administrative positions decreased from 76 percent (1932) to 58 percent (1938). Although the percentage of women in administrative positions declined over the decade, it is important to remember that the majority of women continued to occupy such positions.[11]

According to journalist Alicia Alva, the continued growth in the number of women in office work was due to their economic need (*vulnerabilidad*) and acceptance of lower salaries than men for the same work. Many women, she explained, were the sole breadwinner for their family or provided vital

TABLE 8. Women's employment in government offices, 1930 and 1938

Office	1930	1938	Percent Change
Ministry of Communications and Public Works	414	1,837	+344
Ministry of Finance and Public Credit	655	1,863	+184
Ministry of National Economy (Department of National Statistics in 1930)	212	522	+146
Department of Health (Public Health, 1938)	659	1,221	+85
Ministry of Public Assistance (est. 1937)	—	2,982	not calculated
Ministry of Foreign Relations	93	143	+54
Ministry of the Interior	100	152	+52
Ministry of Agriculture and Development	293	348	+19
Ministry of Public Education	971*	1,306	-35
Department of the Federal District	1,214	1,170	-4
Department of Labor (Ministry of Industry, Commerce, and Labor in 1930)	281	147	-48
Total**	8,332	12,838	54

*Numbers are for 1932, which is the first year that teachers and other government employees were counted separately.

**Includes data not shown in the table.

Sources: México, Dirección de Estadísticas, *Censo de funcionarios y empleados públicos, 30 de noviembre de 1930* (Mexico City: Talleres Gráficos de la Nación, 1934), 58; México, Dirección de Pensiones Civiles, *Segundo censo de empleados federales*, 37; México, Dirección de Pensiones Civiles, *Tercer censo de empleados federales sujetos a la ley general de México* (Mexico City: Imprenta M. L. Sánchez, 1938), 36.

TABLE 9. Female government employees, 1938

Office	Number of Women	Women as a Percentage of Employees of Office	Women as a Percentage of Total Government Workforce
Ministry of Public Assistance	2,982	57	23
Ministry of Finance and Public Credit	1,863	17	15
Ministry of Communication and Public Works	1,837	14	14
Ministry of Public Education	1,306	40	10
Ministry of Foreign Relations	143	23	1
Ministry of the Interior	152	25	1
Ministry of National Economy	522	29	4
Department of Public Health	1,221	34	10
Agrarian Department	348	21	3
Department of Labor	147	26	1
Department of Forestry, Hunting, and Fishing	96	11	>1
Department of the Federal District	1,170	20	9
Total*	12,838	–	23

*Includes data not shown in the table.

Source: México, Dirección de Pensiones Civiles, *Tercer censo de empleados federales sujetos a la ley general de México* (Mexico City: Imprenta M. L. Sánchez, 1938), 50.

contributions to the household economy. Women also worked, Alva continued, out of "a desire for liberation, liberation which, considered from a certain vantage point, is in itself a need."[12] While "liberation" was a word people used to describe the so-called modern woman, Alva also tapped into a use of the word that had emerged in the 1890s that associated economic self-sufficiency with women's autonomy. The modern woman might be characterized by social behaviors, certain hairstyles, and fashion, but for Alva it was important to emphasize that the basis of such cultural change was the capacity to earn money.

The story of Carolina Escudero, executive secretary to General Francisco Múgica in the Ministry of Communications and Public Works, is illustrative of how many women worked to support family and in the process exercised their autonomy. After her mother died and her father remarried and formed a new family, Escudero supported several of her siblings on her own.[13] That she would do so was not unusual. The 1930 public employee census found that in Mexico City 10,013 women supported 37,816 dependents, or an average of 3.8 dependents per woman. This compared to 31,408 men who supported 143,631 dependents, or an average of 4.7 dependents per man.[14] The Mexico City population depended on the income of government employees to a greater degree than any other region of the country. Eighteen percent of Mexico City government employees supported dependents, compared to just under 5 percent nationwide.[15]

Compared to female public employees nationwide, in 1930 women in the Federal District tended to begin work at a younger age and to continue to work to an older age. While the majority of women employed were between twenty and twenty-nine, in the Federal District women were more likely to be working both under the age of twenty and well over thirty. By 1930 a generation of women was well established in office work. Eighty-nine women were over sixty-five years of age and had worked for decades in government offices. The hiring boom of the 1920s, however, meant that almost half of the women working in government offices in Mexico City had five years or less on the job. Marital status followed similar patterns in the Federal District compared to the nation as a whole: men were more likely to be married, women were more likely to be single, and women were more likely to be divorced or widowed than men. Some offices may have been either more attractive or more receptive to women who were widowed or divorced. The highest percentage of divorced women worked in the Ministry of the Interior (2 percent), followed by the Ministry of Communications and Public Works.[16]

While the majority of female public employees were single, they did not, as some implied, work in order to purchase frivolities. Throughout the 1930s, those who sought to disparage women's public-sector employment accused empleadas of spending their earnings on unnecessary luxuries. Office girls, they lamented, spent their money on the movies, dances, and shows. Some smoked cigarettes and "even drank." Critics and defenders alike seemed to assume that women worked to purchase "mysterious cosmetic potions" and the latest shade of nail polish. "How many times have we seen women who come to work dressed to the nines," lamented an editorial for *El Nacional*, "as if going to a party or a beauty competition, while other families starve?"[17] Such concerns were premised on the idea that women should be supported by men and only work out of necessity. Throughout the decade, women's rights advocates drew on the 1930 and 1938 census numbers to counter such arguments. In June 1936 a *La Prensa* article declared that "more than half a million women are heads of household in the country."[18] The article drew on 1930 census data and sought to reassure the public that while the number of working women was on the rise, family was still the basis of Mexican society. The 1938 census showed that empleadas were, by and large, either female heads of household or significant contributors to their household.[19]

Although the majority of women working in public administration were a vital if not the sole contributor to the household economy, this was not reflected in their wages. As in other fields of work, men might well earn as little as women, but they were more likely to earn more, primarily the result of occupational segregation of women into lower-paying positions.[20] Drawing conclusions about salaries is difficult. Little research has been done on wages in general for the 1930s. Evidence for public-employee wages ranges from surveys conducted in that decade to scattered archival evidence. We also have the federal budgets, which itemized salaries per position; however, both work practices and the structure of the workforce shaped wage earnings in ways that make that data difficult to interpret. Many employees filed complaints about individuals who collected wages for more than one position, something that, according to a 1932 study, men were more likely to do than women.[21] Nevertheless, we can discern some aspects of wage earnings for public employees for the 1930s. Typists, shorthand typists, and low-level clerks earned between 1,536 and 1,656 pesos a year. An archivist could earn 2,400 and a mid-range controller (financial oversight) as much as 2,400 a year. Wages, according to the Ministry of National Economy, remained static from 1931 to 1934.[22] The Department of Labor claimed that in 1934 the cost of living in the Federal District was 2.24 pesos a day, and that the average wage was 2.30 pesos a day. The federally mandated minimum daily wage for Mexico City workers, established in 1934, was 1.50 pesos.[23]

The shift from the gold standard to the silver standard in Mexico had a negative impact on middle-class purchasing power. As one woman complained to President Ortiz Rubio in April 1931, "all the poor of the middle class are suffering a terrible crisis."[24] In 1931, in response to the implementation of the Monetary Law (July 25, 1931) and the subsequent decline in the exchange rate (from 2.50 to 4.00 pesos per dollar), merchants who sold imported goods raised prices, which had an impact on the prices of nationally produced goods as well. The cost of canned fruit at the Piggly Wiggly grocery store may have always been beyond the means of the average secretary, but now even the cost of food produced in Mexico had increased 25 percent. Prices of drugstore goods increased 42 percent, although even before inflation a jar of Pond's Cold Cream at 1.50 pesos would have been a luxury. According to a U.S. Department of State report, middle-class Mexicans, who made up the majority of urban employees, relied on the purchase of imported goods. Mexican clothing was poorly made, one report stated, and so middle-class Mexicans were more likely to invest in the higher-quality imported goods that they hoped would last longer.[25] The price study was based on the high-end department stores La Perfeccionada and El Palacio de Hierro. The average secretary was more likely to shop at open markets like La Lagunilla, where she could have a dress made from Mexican-produced cloth (the cost of dry goods, including textiles, had declined 25 percent). During the summer and fall of 1931, a young woman working in an office might have read in the paper about a smuggler bringing silk stockings into the country, but she herself was more likely to purchase synthetic or cotton stockings.[26]

For the vast majority of government-employee households, like most of the Mexican middle class, expenditures outweighed income even before the inflation that hit hard in 1931 and again in 1936–37. Silva Herzog concluded that only households with an annual income above 6,000 pesos were likely to avoid going into debt. The only explanation for why families that outspent their income from 5 to 30 percent survived at all was that they borrowed money from a relative or better-off acquaintance, avoided paying the rent some months, and accumulated debt at department stores and shops that sold clothing on layaway. "Living not only day to day," Silva Herzog wrote, "but spending more than one has, aspiring to the lifestyle of higher social classes, is the age-old tragedy of the middle class, not only in Mexico but in all countries in Western culture." He also discussed the role that family size played in the balance between income and expenditures, noting that larger families tended to outspend household income by lower percentages: "Such social phenomena are extremely complex. It would be foolhardy to try to explain them with logic and simple mathematics."[27] Silva Herzog concluded that the labor of children and women must explain how larger families managed to make ends meet. The 6,000-pesos-a-year income necessary to remain out of debt would have been difficult for women who were heads of households.[28]

The vastly different incomes earned by employees in the Silva Herzog study show that the average clerical worker, government workers engaged in the cultural life of Mexico City in quite different ways. Carolina Escudero described a class-based cultural landscape of the city. By the mid-1930s, Escudero, a single head of household, worked in a well-placed job in a government office that earned her more than she had in the private sector. Money was tight, but the city offered different opportunities according to income. While individuals from better-off families attended dances held at the University Club and took weekend outings to a country club, many public employees rubbed elbows with taxi drivers at El Salón México dance hall or downtown cabarets. Escudero and her colleagues played sports and organized activities at work. Occasionally, they treated themselves to lunch at Sanborns or Lady Baltimore, while employees of more modest means would have frequented small restaurants or purchased food on the street.[29]

In Silva Herzog's cost-of-living study, employees also listed among their expenses the contributions they were required to make to the political party.[30] Shortly after the founding of the National Revolutionary Party (Partido Nacional Revolucionario, PNR) in 1929, public employees were asked to make monthly contributions of one day's pay to the party. The January 1931 policy reinforced the power of the party over government employees, politicized the workplace, and reduced take home pay. The government also ran campaigns to gather funds for various causes, such as a village affected by a storm. Some employees complained—both as individuals and as groups—that the various "voluntary contributions" reduced their wages by 20 percent.[31] The Union of Federal Employees sent a telegram to President Ortiz Rubio, to say that with the salary reductions they could not support their households. Others complained that the mandatory contributions were yet another example of the "administrative machine" and compromised democratic practices, stating that "the practice necessarily robs the people of any desire to exercise their rights, and little by little kills the ideals for which so much Mexican blood has been shed." The political party to which public employees paid a part of their salary did not give women the same rights as men. One woman wrote President Abelardo Rodríguez:

> This order only serves to take the bread from one's mouth each 31st day of the month. Thousands of families literally live from day to day. He who does not work, or in this case is not paid, does not eat. Not even women were exempted from this order. Women are required to pay to support the Party, and yet in exchange the Party does not concede them any rights.[32]

This injustice fueled women's demand for full rights within the party, including the right to vote in party elections.

It is worth noting that income is not determined solely by wages. Job stability also has an impact on earning capacity. The Great Depression decreased state funding, and during the early 1930s, especially from 1931 to 1933, government employees faced uncertainty due to budget cuts. Each December they quivered in fear of the "Sword of Damocles" that swung down to lay off hundreds of employees. The intertwined nature of hiring and politics meant that as high-level functionaries transitioned out of power at the end of each presidential administration, their followers lost the job gained through patronage. Critics pointed out that constant layoffs were inefficient and left low-level bureaucrats in precarious circumstances, and that private businesses knew how to retain employees and thus benefit from their expertise.

But how did someone get a government job in the first place, and what was that experience like for women? Some women from working-class occupations, through their activism, moved into government office work. Such was the case for Gudelia Gómez Rangel and Elvira Trueba Coronel. Gómez was born in Oaxaca in 1905, attended Protestant schools, and arrived in Mexico City in 1919. She worked at the Streetcar Company, in the publications department where, according to labor activist Luis Araiza, "she showed herself to be an able organizer and agitator."[33] In 1921 Gómez began work as an operator for Ericsson telephone company, where she helped to lead the unionization efforts throughout the 1920s. When Ericsson operators and telephone workers went on strike, Gómez served as the union representative to present their case before the Conciliation and Arbitration Board. Through the Ericsson conflict she came to play a central role in the CGT as well. It was her persistence, wrote women's rights activist Adelina Zendejas in a 1947 article for *El Nacional*, that led to enforcement of the constitutional guarantee to maternity leave. Gómez left Ericsson in 1931 and lived in poverty from 1933 until 1935, when, helped by her experience as a labor organizer, she secured a position as an Inspector in the Department of Labor. Having secured that job, and building on her union experience, she gradually moved up within the bureaucracy. Gómez was named to serve on the Toluca Conciliation and Arbitration Board. In 1936, under the auspices of the Department of Labor and at the insistence of the distinguished lawyer Genaro Vásquez, Gómez established the Office for the Investigation of Working Women and Minors. Gómez served as office chief in the 1940s. During her time in the office, she served as an inspector and conducted studies on women who worked as piecework seamstresses, cardboard factory workers, mica workers, and in the sugar industry. She later worked in the Ministry of National Economy. Thus

Gómez, through the hard work of labor activism in the 1920s, gained a skill set and political allegiances that served her professional advancement in the 1930s and beyond.[34]

Elvira Trueba Coronel (1899–1993), born in Nanacamilpa, Tlaxcala, may have come from a family of some means, for her father sent her to Mexico City when she was ten to attend the English School for Young Ladies. After graduating in 1916, Trueba worked as a secretary for the National Railroad offices in Puebla, where in 1919 she organized her co-workers. She then played a leadership role when railroad workers went on strike in 1921. Trueba worked in the Department of the Federal District, where she was active in the Union of Government Employees (Unión de Empleados del Gobierno), which fought for severance pay. During the 1930s she worked as a shorthand typist in the legal department of the General Office of National Patrimony, Ministry of Finance.[35] Like Gómez, Trueba built on her experience in labor organizing and moved into a government job where she was able to increase her earnings and move into positions of influence both within the government-employee movement and the women's movement.

Many women obtained work in ways similar to most government employees, through connections made by family and friends, a practice documented by Maria Dolores Lorenzo.[36] One man who worked in a government office made connections with higher administration in Banamex, where he secured a secretarial position for his daughter, who, though fifteen, claimed to be sixteen in order to take the position. She worked at the bank for more than fifty years. Letters of recommendation also helped women get jobs. One woman wrote a desperate letter to the head of the Ministry of Health in which she accused the office of losing her letters of recommendation, which she referred to as her "WORK RECORD," the capitalization suggesting the anxiety she felt about potentially losing the documents. In her autobiography, office worker Alicia del Rosal described the importance of letters of recommendation for opening doors to influential individuals and potential employers.[37] However, as one journalist pointed out in 1935, women did not benefit from the revolutionary old-boys club that facilitated employment for men bound together by "fictive kinship, political (revolutionary) camaraderie of the battlefield and many other reasons of varying degrees of pliability."[38] In the absence of political networks, women drew on the networks they established at school and on the job.

Looks also mattered, so much so that at times it was a required job qualification. Throughout the 1930s, *El Nacional*, the official PNR newspaper, ran ads offering employment to "respectable young women of good appearance."[39] Of course, not all jobs were advertised in the newspaper. In the early 1930s, Ms. Galvarriato migrated from Sinaloa and arrived in Mexico City alone, eager to find employment. She hung around the offices of the Department of the Federal District day after day until someone gave her a job. The man who hired her said that she had caught his attention because she looked like the actress María Félix, who was herself purportedly discovered while transiting the Zócalo to and from work in a government office. Galvarriato worked for many years registering inmates at Lecumberri Prison. Her job provided connections that served her well in unexpected circumstances. One evening when she was out with friends, they were held up. One of the men, a former Lecumberri inmate, recognized her and told his partners in crime to leave her alone.[40]

The importance of physical appearance in women's employment is reinforced by stories of sexual harassment. Stories circulated about job interviews where physical appearance and being accessible for one's boss came into play. In "Crónicas de Lorely," an advice column, Lorely responded to a young woman who wrote in about her interview with a "gentleman in a well-known office." The man said that he would give her a job but that he needed "elegant young ladies" so that the office made a good impression. "Show me your garters," he demanded, "so I can tell how you will dress when you work for me." Loreley's response to the woman was emphatic and directed at all young women who found themselves in a similar situation:

> If you can, get married. [It is better to] prefer the rough hand of a worker, the modest house of a worker who calls you his wife, to the tempting silks that you see typists show off. Contemplate marriage with confidence. Do not fear the children that will come. Be the slave of your children and husband if necessary, and not the pastime of lecherous old men.[41]

While such articles appeared in the women's press and the women's column of mainstream newspapers, very few women ever filed a formal complaint within the workplace against their employer.

Journalists for Mexico City newspapers weighed in on how women should behave in the workplace. María Ríos Cárdenas warned that while camaraderie between women and men at the office was fine, women should not adopt the more vulgar aspects of male culture. Other observers discussed behaviors associated with female character and essential to work performance. A woman's subordination to the needs of men, at work and otherwise, was praised as a quality of a good office worker. The journalist Arlette (pseudonym for María Aurelia Reyes de Govea) joyfully discussed the increased efficiency and personal pleasure of the male employee whose secretary was always one step ahead of him, providing him with the appropriate papers for his meetings. According to the article, such efficiency on the part of his secretary would allow him time for personal pleasures like going to the movies. Women's columns gave advice to typists and secretaries on how to dress, what exercises to do to maintain an attractive body, and how to discipline "feminine traits," such as being chatty, to the demands of the workplace. Women were also counseled to be discreet, and to foresee when they should absent themselves from the room instead of eavesdropping to pick up tidbits of gossip. And while at work, secretaries should never, ever cry.[42]

Toward the second half of the 1930s observers expressed contradictory ideas about empleada class identity. The article "Busy Bees," which appeared in *Gráfico* in 1937, exemplifies how some observers considered women office workers as working- and middle-class at the same time. Arlette wrote, "The other category is that of middle-class girls who, due to a desire on the part of their parents to see them raise themselves up and earn a living in a decent manner, have completed high school, commercial school, and typing classes, and leave behind their somewhat inferior social status. This genre of 'empleadita' (little office girl) has become an obligatory fixture in every office." Though in some way conceding middle-class status to the empleada, the author questioned that standing by alluding to more modest origins. The use of the diminutive "ita" also threw her status into question. Another observer placed a question mark next to empleada class identity when he described them as having "acquired ambitions beyond their standing."[43] Yet another journalist qualified empleadas as having "no culture," and therefore lacking the qualities that had defined middle-class occupations since the Porfiriato. If public administration was coded middle class, and women of humble origins took these jobs, then those women were overstepping their bounds.

Within the logic of middle-class identity thus articulated, the supposed dissonance between class origins and aspirations led to the corruption of female honor. "Crónicas de Arlette" referred to office work as "street work" (*trabajo callejero*), echoing the way people spoke about prostitution. Arlette went on to say that such work "made women resent the home, leaving them ill-prepared, and neither resigned, selfless, nor submissive. They are presumptuous, and then they no longer conform to old customs. They take on independent ways of being, and aspire to a certain level of luxury, something that cinema aids in developing." Reference to the loss of feminine qualities like selflessness and submissiveness was meant to indicate the empleaditas' distance from middle-class norms. So while the journalist fretted that "feminine virtues like those of the past century have diminished to such a degree that there is a great abyss between a woman of then and of today," she was lamenting shifts in middle-class identity that had been anchored in domesticity and the idealized qualities that characterized women's role within the family.[44]

The Federal Conciliation and Arbitration Tribunal: Professionalization, Seniority, and Politics at Work

In 1937, on the centenary of Isaac Pitman's publication of the first manual on shorthand, *Stenographic Sound-Hand*, María Duarte asked, "What have women gained in the time since 1837?" For Duarte, women had gained an efficient means of preparing themselves for productive work, a means by which to contribute to the household, especially widowed mothers and siblings. In short, women had gained independence: "How many women, by virtue of this quick and accessible training, have escaped falling into an unhappy marriage or in with evil and cowardly forces or, out of desperation, succumbed to suicide!" While her article was celebratory in tone, Duarte pointed out that shorthand typist was often a dead-end job, as evidenced, she pointed out, by the women she knew who had worked ten or twenty years in the same job, earning the same insufficient salary, while the men around them quickly moved up the ladder. Duarte encouraged shorthand typists to take the occasion to recognize their shared situation and to unite in common cause for the benefit of this "important sector of workers, all-suffering (*abnegadas*), many blessed with talent, grace, and beauty."[45] So had office work, by the late 1930s, become a dead-end job? The archive for the Federal Conciliation and Arbitration Tribunal (Tribunal Federal de Conciliación y Arbitraje, TFCA), the board with administrative oversight of government-employee labor relations, helps answer the question.

The TFCA was established in 1939 to centralize public employee conflict arbitration. Whereas workers in the private sector had the right to present grievances before the Conciliation and Arbitration Board (Junta de Conciliación y Arbitraje, est. 1926), government employees did not. Throughout the 1920s and 1930s government workers took labor grievances to a ministry-level board, a system that functioned until 1941. Overlapping the ministry-based system for three years, in 1939 the government established the Federal Conciliation and Arbitration Tribunal. Three members represented different sectors: the state, public employees, and a legal representative. The initial board members were Lic. Manuel R. Palacios, representative for the state; Emiliano Navarro P., representative for public employees; and Lic. José G. Zuno as third arbiter.[46] Although the Supreme Court ruled in two separate cases that TFCA decisions were "purely administrative," it had a decisive impact on daily work relations and the development of labor practices within government offices.[47] Public employees categorized as rank and file (*de base*), including administrative, clerical, and service workers, could file a complaint or be brought before the TFCA. Employees classified as management (*de confianza*) could not appeal to the TFCA. The rights and protections provided for in the Statute for Government Workers of 1938 applied only to employees with membership in the Federation of State Workers Unions (Federación de Sindicatos de Trabajadores al Servicio del Estado). During the first year of its functioning, 1939–40, the TFCA saw 335 individual conflicts and 8 collective conflicts. The cases established a series of precedents: that a manager (*titular*) could not fire an employee without a hearing; that hiring must adhere to seniority (even in cases when seniority rules had not yet been written); and that hiring must give first priority to former employees. Managers could not fire anyone without first consulting with the union, though unions did have the right to hire or fire on their own.[48]

Women frequently appeared before the TFCA, as claimants, defendants, and third parties. Between 1939 and 1941 at least 570 women appeared before the TFCA, with the majority of cases filed by women themselves for seniority violations or unjustified firing. If for the most part women filed complaints about issues similar to men's, they were slightly more likely to seek respect for seniority. While there had been a vociferous public campaign against women's lack of work ethic and questionable morals, such issues only occasionally arose within TFCA proceedings. Women did not file sexual harassment complaints, because such abuses were not accounted for in the Statute for Government Workers. The majority of cases brought by women were in the ministries where they worked in greatest numbers: Public Education, Health, Finance and Public Credit, National Economy, and Communications and Public Works. Women also filed complaints from the offices of Indigenous Affairs and of Marines.

Professionalization of the government employee workforce during the 1930s may have benefited some women, but it caught others unprepared. Ana Maytorena Iñigo Viuda de Villaseñor (Señora Iñigo) began to work for the Department of Health as a permanent employee (*de planta*), inspector level 5, in the Public Baths and Disinfection Office. Never given a permanent position, she was moved around almost every year, her monthly salary rising and falling between 310 and 220 pesos a month, and in 1939, with the approval of the Seniority Board, she was classified as visiting nurse "C" in the Office of Food Hygiene at 180 pesos a month. Then she was fired. Iñigo was caught in a moment of flux. The government-employee workforce was increasingly professionalized, and women who had been hired into low-level positions were at risk. Social work and nursing increasingly required higher levels of education and certification.[49] Señora Iñigo had no formal training and her employer claimed he had given her a job as a favor so that she would not suffer financial hardship. That is, the job had been offered in the spirit of charity and, by implication, should not be judged as formal employment. He also pointed out that even though she had worked for the government since 1935, all of the positions given to her were provisional. Furthermore, the work she had performed was unrelated to the job positions she had held. In a Kafkaesque argument, TFCA officials asked Iñigo if she felt that by occupying the position of nurse she hindered service to the public. Iñigo acknowledged that she had no formal training and answered yes. Based on Iñigo's admission that she worked in a position for which she had no training, the TFCA found against her.[50]

Several cases show how initial terms of employment could impede professional advancement. During the 1930s positions increasingly required a degree that many women had not obtained. Josefina Poulat de Durán, Ana Mekler, and Humberto González Angulo, all economics interns, filed a claim against the Ministry of National Economy in a dispute over a recommendation made by the Seniority Board. The three economics interns were passed over for a permanent position as economist "D" in favor of a temporary employee, Luis Yáñez. The board declared that a degree was required for any technical position, including economist, economist intern, and practicing economist. A bachelor's degree in economics or other certification from the School of Economics would qualify. Poulat de Durán, though in her fourth year of study for a bachelor's degree in economics, did not yet have a degree and lost her case.[51]

Professional identity and credentials were also important for women in clerical positions such as typist, stenographer, and secretary. After six months of employment such as typist level 3, Carmen Aillaud Betanzos was named "mozo" (boy), which she considered an insult, surely because the term signified errand boy or unskilled male labor. Her position was given to Rosa Bandera, who, she claimed, had not done as well as herself on the entrance exam. The position in question, executive secretary, required more education and was more prestigious. To strengthen her case, Aillaud Betanzos self-identified as a "daughter of the revolution" and pointed out that she had attempted to join the union but, she claimed, they would not let her and in fact had tried to get her to quit her job. The TFCA decided to put her in a temporary positin as typist level 2, perhaps thus avoiding conflict. Other cases show women complaining that their training as shorthand typist prepared them to work for clerk positions to which they were never promoted.[52]

The distinction between "professional," "administrative," and "worker" became increasingly relevant and concise over the course of the 1940s. For example, in 1948 the SEP defined the division between technical and administrative personnel in its internal regulations. Administrative personnel (class III) included rank-and-file office workers for whom hire was "not predicated on a professional title or special studies in a given science or art, but rather on possession of the skills required to carry out the work determined by the budget designation."[53] Such class III administrative personnel included stenographers, operators, copy editors, office chiefs, messengers, and accounting assistants.

Perhaps the single most pressing issue women faced was respect for their seniority, the basis of the majority of cases that women brought before the TFCA. The definition of and process for respecting seniority was not always clear, but became increasingly codified over the course of the decade. The Statute for Government Workers allowed each bureaucratic unit to develop its own Seniority Board and regulations. However, in 1939, the first year of the TFCA, the statute had been unevenly implemented across government offices. Some offices had formulated their own regulations prior to the Statute for Government Workers, and for a time they adhered to those rules. Individual offices progressed at different rates in drawing up seniority guidelines for their specific units. Under such circumstances, various factors came into dispute: salary, which the TFCA sometimes used to determine rank; seniority, defined either by time working for the government within a specific office or in the position held immediately prior to the position in dispute; and, whether one was hired on a permanent or temporary basis.[54] The statute required that all personnel movements be published in the office bulletin. The bulletin identified vacated positions and the relevant seniority rankings to fill the position. An employee could not file a complaint against the Seniority Board, and its decisions were considered irrevocable. Julia Moreno Hurtado learned this in 1940 when she sought the position of clerk level 2 and based her case on the argument that the Seniority Board was mistaken as to who had the right to the position.[55]

The conditions of clerical work exposed women to complicated seniority disputes. Conflict emerged over whether to define seniority by years of service for the government, years of service within a designated office, or time in the position held immediately prior to the one to which an employee might aspire. Adding to the confusion, sometimes a position placed an individual physically in one office, while the budget for the position pertained to another office. Some office heads sought to diminish seniority calculations, or to fire individuals, by arguing that a position was not included in their budget but rather in that of another office.[56] The definition of seniority was particularly difficult to untangle in ministries like Finance, which was exceedingly large and contained a wide range of offices. Typists and stenographers were likely to be moved around from office to office according to workload demands, which could also jeopardize seniority. In 1939 María Luisa Miranda Fragoso had been working for the Ministry of Finance for nineteen years and considered herself a "career stenographer."[57] She had worked as stenographer level 3 in the Office for Correspondence and Archive, when she was then commissioned in the Office of the Quartermaster in the Ministry of Finance. In January 1939 she was named clerk level 5 with a monthly salary of 128 pesos, and in April of the same year she was demoted to clerk level 6, with a monthly salary of 102 pesos. Miranda Fragoso was then replaced by Señor Humberto Luna Alvarez.

The Miranda Fragoso case hinged on the definition of seniority and of what constituted administrative work. Luna Alvarez argued that while he had worked as mozo, watchman, and warehouse dispatcher, the work he performed made him an "office worker by virtue of the fact that he had been charged with the general management of gasoline vouchers, vehicle inspection and reports, drawing up weekly personnel lists, payroll, timecard verification, monthly summaries of gasoline usage, archive maintenance, and general correspondence with companies that did business with the Ministry of Finance." The 1939 budget created the position of clerk level 5, and Luna Alvarez petitioned the National Union of Workers in the Ministry of Finance (Sindicato Nacional de Trabajadores de la Secretaría de Hacienda) for the job. While he had worked for fourteen years, four months, and three days in the very same office, Miranda Fragoso, who had worked more than nineteen years for the government, had worked in the Office for the Quartermaster for only two months. The case first went to the ministry-based Junta, which had found in favor of Miranda Fragoso.[58]

The case then went to the TFCA, where the question of how to define the unit in which seniority was calculated continued to vex deliberations. A definition of seniority calculated based on total number of years of government service in any office would favor Miranda Fragoso, whereas a narrow definition of seniority as based on the specific unit in which an individual worked would favor Luna Alvarez. Article 41 of the statute maintained that seniority was to be defined by ministry, but Luna Alvarez claimed that the Ministry of Finance was so large that each branch, office, department, or section has its own seniority. In the final analysis, the TFCA clarified that statute defined seniority by ministry, not the specific office within a ministry. Such a division would be, in the words of the TFCA, "artificial" and prejudicial to the very employees it was meant to protect.[59] The Seniority Commission claimed that it followed practices "that custom has created."[60] An important precedent for calculating seniority had been set.

The Miranda Fragoso case, in conjunction with *C. Felicidad J. López v. Minister of Finance and Public Credit*, also established precedent regarding the relationship between the budget and seniority. Basing its findings on Article 41, Section 1 of the statute, the TFCA found that seniority should be calculated taking into consideration the personnel of the entire unit in which an individual worked, not by the unit that controlled the budget for the position. An individual could not be denied seniority due to the fact that his or her position pertained to the budget of a different administrative unit.[61] The finding informed statute revisions in the 1940s and protected those who might, after their initial hire, be moved from one office to another.

Women were often hired on a provisional basis (*internino*), sometimes working without pay until a permanent position (*de planta*) opened up. Hiring on such terms gave an employer access to low-wage labor. For the employee it was a way to get her foot in the door. The risk she took, however, was that she might work for years on a temporary basis. By taking a provisional position, the individual was disadvantaged when calculating seniority, as was the case for Sara Flores Olguín. Flores began working for the federal government in 1918 as a temporary, low-level clerk in the Department of the Comptroller and rose up through the ranks. She filed a complaint with the TFCA when she was passed over for promotion and

C. Sergio Salcedo was promoted to clerk level 1. Both Flores and Salcedo had worked for the government for twenty-three years. Unable to calculate seniority, Flores Olguín was passed over for promotion because of her problematic relationship with the Ministry of Finance union. Flores Olguín bitterly remarked, "having spent my life doing my job I'll end up practically dying of hunger."[62]

Party, union, and national politics played an important role in shaping working conditions. In August 1941, Carmen Orlaineta Badillo demanded that she be named clerk level 2 in the Department of Planning and Economic Research in National Economy. When the position had opened up, the head of the department named Beatríz Escobar García, a temporary employee, to the position. When questioned as to whether Orlaineta's seniority should have merited her the position, the minister stated he did not know how many years Orlaineta had worked for the government (already a violation, as superiors were required to know the seniority of each subordinate). He was sure, he stated, that she did not have seniority over Escobar. He was mistaken. Orlaineta described herself as a *trabajadora*, a worker, with more than twenty-seven years as an *empleada federal*, and she had been employed in the specific unit since 1934. Here, use of the terms "worker" and "federal employee" at the same time allowed her to invoke populist political rhetoric that identified her with left-leaning politics, and, without stating it explicitly, to the statute that protected employee rights. It seems that both Orlaineta and Escobar had begun work in the Department for Economic Studies on the same day in January 1939, however the two women did not have the same claim to the position immediately prior to the one in dispute. Escobar had begun to work as clerk level 3 in August 1937, and Orlaineta in January 1934. What seemed to be a case of favoring one woman over another was, however, considerably more complicated. The conflict, which dated back to 1938, shows the ways politics and accusations of improper sexual morality could come into play in labor disputes.[63]

The Orlaineta case is one of a handful infused with the sorts of rhetoric used against female government employees in the newspapers that maligned their sexual morality. In 1938 Carmen Orlaineta Badillo and her co-worker Emma Emilia Otero were both brought before the Ministry of National

Economy Arbitration Board for lacking "any inclination whatsoever for work, and for a lack of discipline." Orlaineta had begun in National Statistics in 1924 and continued there until 1932, when she took a position in the Ministry of Communications. According to her boss, Director General Emilio Alanís Patiño, when Orlaineta was first hired she "had proven to be efficient and of quite acceptable conduct." Two years later, however, when she returned to his offices "her general behavior was completely different." Alanís Patiño accused Orlaineta and Otero of spending their mornings at work reading novels and newspapers, and talking on the telephone with their numerous family members. The two women, he claimed, usually arrived late to work and frequently left the office for long stretches at a time. And, Otero conducted business—sales on credit (*abonos*)—in the office. Alanís argued that he offered the position to Beatríz Escobar García, because when she was given work, even though the work was not for her department, she always performed well and on time. That Escobar was, as a temporary employee, vulnerable to such demands seems to have escaped the minister.[64]

Political differences infused the workplace and this specific conflict. Orlaineta had offered her services as a typist to the ministry union and was accused of "labor agitation, without having any formal union position, thus contradicting the legal rules for State workers." Orlaineta, in her own defense, described herself as a leftist and as a supporter of the Cárdenas presidency.

I have clearly demonstrated my genuinely leftist revolutionary affiliation, and I have confronted each and every one of the employees in this Office who do not have any qualms against [yelling] "long-live Franco," and "death to General Cárdenas," and who by their actions repeatedly demonstrate the hatred they feel for everything that pertains to the social movement that, with nothing but patriotism, the President [is carrying out]. They never go to any events that we attend, those who feel the need to fight for the freedom of the People. They did not want to contribute even one cent to the Oil Expropriation Debt, and make a tremendous scandal when they are obliged to contribute one day's pay, like we all do, and with pleasure, those of us who know and understand our obligations as revolutionaries.[65]

The Orlaineta case, as well as others, was complicated by the passage of a new statute on April 16, 1941. Her case argued that the promotion occurred before passage of the new statute and so Section 1 of Article 41 of the older statute should apply. In its findings, however, the TFCA followed the new statute and concluded that Escobar had more seniority than Orlaineta. Contrary to the precedent set by the Fragoso case, mentioned above, in this case the TFCA defined seniority according to the specific office, and not the ministry, in which the employees worked. Escobar was given the position. In July 1941 Carmen Orlaineta found herself in Tapachula, Chiapas, working in the Agency for the Economy. Whether the post-election political climate had anything to do with the reversal is a question that the archive does not answer.

As for Otero, the accusation of "misconduct" was reinforced with insinuations about her sexual identity. Alanís Patiño, after criticizing her job performance, made a point to mention that in the paperwork filled out at the moment of hire, Otero had claimed to be male. Emma Emilia Otero Pablo had indicated at the moment of hire to be thirty-two years of age, born in Huatabampo, Sonora, and to have completed elementary but not high school. In the response to the question regarding sexual identity, "masculine" was typed, along with the other typed responses, and in pencil someone had written on top of that "female." The resolution of this case does not appear in the archives, but the purges of homosexuals in public office documented by Víctor Macías-González suggest that Otero was left vulnerable by a queer sexual identity.[66]

The TFCA decided increasingly in favor of competency over political allegiances, coinciding with both professionalization of the workforce and political shifts felt among the ranks of public employees. Historians have indicated that 1940 marked a governmental shift back to the center of the political spectrum. Some have even suggested that the shift occurred in the last months of the Cárdenas presidency, as a reaction against organized labor, the oil expropriation, and socialist education.[67] Within this context the TFCA began to support professional preparation and job efficiency over ideological and political commitments. The Seniority Board's *Bulletin* no. 4, published on August 29, 1939, stated that in equal circumstances, priority would be given to employees with seniority, first relative, and then absolute; and, second to "ideological position."[68] The President of the Republic circulated a memorandum stating the same. It posted throughout government offices. The transition was, however, accomplished in fits and starts.

Veteran status also shaped work relations. Though letters from women (and men) requesting work for themselves (or a family member) are scattered throughout the archive, we lack data on how many jobs were meted out or to whom based on claims of veteran status. It was not unusual for a woman to get a job by claiming to be the widow of a veteran. There were also cases when women informally claimed veteran status for themselves. Bertha Escorcia Valencia worked as stenographer level 1 (monthly salary 152 pesos) when in December 1940 she brought suit against the minister of National Economy for a seniority violation. Escorcia asked for the nullification of the promotion of the clerk Señora Josefa Alvarado. In her defense, Alvarado claimed seniority based on her current salary, competency, Article 41 of the statute, and the presidential memorandum. Escorcia pointed out that her studies qualified her for the clerk position, an administrative position, which was not the case for Alvarado, who, she claimed, did not perform "any sort of office work," but rather worked in service (*servidumbre*). The administrative job Alvarado was given, Escorcia argued, was assigned because she had argued that was due "privileges as a veteran." In another case a woman claimed that as the widow of veteran Florencio A. Rojo Cárdenas her seniority should be counted double. Referring to a presidential decree limiting the degrees of separation from a veteran necessary to claim privileges, the TFCA in 1941 declared that it was not the same to be a relative of a veteran as it was to be a veteran oneself, a rule that disproportionately privileged men.[69]

The criteria for promotion increasingly relied upon performance, efficiency, and a clean attendance and behavior record. These standards were written into by-laws drawn up during the 1940s. The 1948 SEP by-laws, for example, first considered efficiency and then demerits and performance reports. The by-laws defined efficiency as professional improvement through certification and continued study. Each employee kept a card that indicated years of service and any official sanctions or demerits.[70]

Women continued to make significant gains in government employment during the 1930s, both in terms of sheer numbers and as a percentage of the workforce. The generation that had entered the workforce in the 1920s had made progress, with some women rising to management positions. If professionalization is associated with middle-class status, then a growing number of female government employees were closely associated with middle-class identity. The wages paid to clerical workers tended to outstrip factory wages. Indeed, compared to other options, women fared relatively well in public-sector employment. But as one journalist noted, it was no bed of roses. To be sure, the categorization of government occupations ostensibly meant equal pay for equal work. However, women repeatedly saw their seniority rights ignored, which impeded professional advancement and contributed to women's claims that they suffered a wage gap. It is impossible to quantify how frequently this might have occurred, though the petition from the women in the SEP discussed in chapter 3 would suggest that it happened often enough for women to feel they were treated, as a group, unfairly. Women's concerns with regard to seniority, equal pay for equal work, and recognition of their role in supporting their families informed what they wrote about, the subject of chapter 5, and their activism, the subject of chapter 6.

5   Commercial Education and Writing during the 1930s

During the 1930s, female office workers, reflecting on work and living conditions, wrote about their experiences in ways that contributed to new ways of thinking about women. Commercial education provided young women with the tools to reflect on individual and generational transformation. Empleadas contributed to a rich *cultura escrita* that fostered notions of middle-class identity which included women's work outside of the home. The written (and typed) word empowered many women to express their views on work, marriage, family, and feminism. Female government employees engaged in conversations about new ways for men and women to relate to each other in the spaces where work and personal life overlapped, about new ways to value working mothers, and ways to question accepted norms of femininity. Shifts in middle-class identity occurred within the context of the Mexican government's response to the Great Depression and educational reform designed to prepare the population to contribute to economic development. While during the 1920s the SEP had expanded commercial education for women, during the 1930s system-wide reform of technical education transformed women's educational experience and opportunities. The decade opened with the "Miguel Lerdo de Tejada" Commercial School as a woman-centered educational space, and by the close of the decade the MLT was coeducational, and then integrated into the National Polytechnic Institute.

Commercial Schools

Commercial education for women continued to flourish in the early 1930s, but change was afoot. A constellation of factors converged that led to educational reform which, by mid-decade, transformed women's opportunities within the commercial educational system. In response to deepening economic crisis after 1929, education authorities formulated new goals, models, and practices.[1] The government needed well-trained professionals to engage in national development and technological modernization. Engineers, economists, agronomists, and scientists were needed to build roads and infrastructure, improve agricultural production, and to work in the petroleum and other industries. Economic development also required office workers, although that sector of the labor market had become saturated. Minister of Public Education Narciso Bassols (1931–34) oversaw significant reform of the Department for Technical, Industrial, and Commercial Education (Departamento de Enseñanza Técnica, Industrial y Comercial, DETIC). The campaign to improve technical education, framed by "preferential attention to proletarian youth of our country," sidelined commercial education for women.[2] The shift in emphasis and imperative to reduce budgets led the department to close almost all of its women's schools. By mid-decade overall women's enrollments declined. Female teachers and administrators faced barriers to access leadership positions within the new polytechnic. The establishment of the National Polytechnic School (Escuela Politécnico Nacional, EPN) in 1932 and the National Polytechnic Institute (Instituto Politécnico Nacional, IPN) in 1936 transformed the MLT.[3]

Named minister of education in 1931, Narciso Bassols embarked on a vigorous program to give new life to technical education while at the same time implementing economizing measures. The National Educators Assembly, held in 1930, had prioritized budget reform as one of three central goals for the coming years.[4] The assembly also prioritized reform of technical

FIG. 12. Secretary working with Juan de Dios Bátiz, chief of the DETIC, 1935. SIN-AFO #10471. Reproduction authorized by the National Institute of Anthropology and History.

education, which would affect the entire purview of DETIC: 28 schools, 1,192 employees, and 20,380 students. The EPN was a cornerstone of that reform. Chief of DETIC, Juan de Dios Bátiz (1929–31, 1935), completed the plan for the EPN in 1931, and the school began to function in 1932 as part of a coordinated program of technical education for boys. Students progressed from their early years of schooling through a sequential plan of study that led to the Technical Industrial Institute, the National School of Master Carpenters, or the Mechanical and Electrical Engineering School. At the same time, DETIC declared that commercial and technical education for women was in need of reform. A commission, with one woman out of the ten members, reviewed all DETIC school curricula. Minister Bassols informed directors of women's commercial and technical schools that they would need to reform instruction at their schools "or face consequences."[5]

The next year Bassols concluded that while the MLT had successfully implemented reforms, other schools had not. In the spring of 1932 Bassols dismissed two directors: Carmen Kraus de Alvarez de la Rosa, director of ETIC, and Elodia Chirón y Gómez, director of the Gabriela Mistral school. Angry students stormed Minister Bassols's office in protest. Bassols told the press that the women had started yelling so he kicked them out. He also gave a written statement to the press in which he pointed out that over the past several years the schools had become overrun with students and were no longer effective. Young women wasted their time making "ugly" decorative gifts for their boyfriend or father and left the school with little to no skills that prepared them to be successful in the labor market.[6] To bolster his case, in an article titled "Technical Schools and Not Community Centers for Coeds" in *El Universal* Bassols informed the public that the state had spent more than 700,000 pesos to fund ETIC over the course of four years, and the school had in the last five years granted only sixty-two diplomas and ninety-two certificates. He also pointed out that when required to make changes, some schools, such as the Sewing and Design Academy (formerly La Corregidora), had been able to do so, while others, like ETIC and the Gabriela Mistral school, had not.[7]

The reform of women's education was motivated by both ideological priorities and financial considerations. In 1934 the SEP suffered a 1.3 percent budget cut and DETIC an 8.3 percent budget cut.[8] Women's education represented 41 percent of the department's annual budget. SEP authorities argued that federal technical and commercial schools were inefficient and redundant and that they competed for the same students. In 1934 the department closed all but one school per specialization. As a result, three Mexico City schools for girls were closed and only seven of the eleven that had functioned in 1928 remained.[9] Women's enrollment in Mexico City's DETIC schools dropped drastically between 1932 and 1934, from 9,768 to 1,383 (see table 10).[10] Enrollment at the MLT, however, continued to grow, from 1,689 (1936) to 2,680 (1937).[11]

The SEP also eliminated elective course offerings (71 percent of all technical and commercial school enrollments in 1923), which took a toll on women's education.[12] Luis Enrique Erro Soler, chief of DETIC from 1931 to 1934, dismissed criticisms of the closures of women's schools and echoed justifications offered up earlier in the year by Minister Bassols.[13] The loss had

TABLE 10. Enrollment and average attendance, DETIC schools, Mexico City, 1933

School	Enrollment	Average Attendance
"Miguel Lerdo de Tejada" Commercial School	1,379	881
Business and Administration School for Advanced Study	1,085	523
Sewing and Design School	1,007	525
Commercial and Sewing Academy Number 2	303	215
Commercial and Sewing Academy Number 3	476	422
Commercial and Sewing Academy Number 4	985	477
National Home Economics School	190	154
Technical Preparatory, Mechanical and Electrical Division	518	473
Technical Preparatory, Construction Division	484	444
Advanced School for Mechanical and Electrical Engineering	182	145
Advanced School for Construction	44	19
Technical Institute, day school	757	242
Technical Institute, night school	185	72
School for Manual Arts and Trades, day school	184	83
School for Manual Arts and Trades, night school	185	72
School for Manual Arts and Trades, Annex to the Master Mechanics School of the Industrial Technical Institute	127	71
Industrial Technical Institute, Master Mechanics Night School	386	235
Total	8,477	5,053

Source: Enrollment and average attendance, Archivo Histórico de la Secretaría de Educación Pública, Departamento de Escuelas Técnicas, Industriales y Comerciales, caja 21, exp. 46.

not been in the number of serious students, Erro Soler told the press, but rather among those "middle-class girls and women who go to school, at the expense of the State, for personal and not professional goals."[14] Erro Soler, who played a fundamental role in the establishment of the IPN, characterized the young women enrolled in commercial schools as frivolous. His dismissal of the educational needs of middle-class women dovetailed with populist rhetoric that emphasized the centrality of the working class within national development. The market was saturated with clerical workers, according to the SEP, and young women should look elsewhere for work.[15]

Continued strong leadership ensured that the MLT thrived despite the attacks on women's commercial and technical education. Director Raquel Santoyo (1903–14, 1926–33) stepped down in 1933, and René Rodríguez de la Rosa was named director. Rodríguez de la Rosa brought with her a deep commitment to socialist education and the advancement of women.[16] Originally from San Luis Potosí, she began her career in 1925 as a primary school teacher. Like many other teachers, she held numerous positions. Indeed, she held no fewer than seven positions in her first two years of employment. In 1926 she was a rural school teacher, director of a suburban school in the Federal District, and an instructor at the Industrial Popular Culture Night School. In 1928 she traveled to the United States to study vocational schools, and upon her return she worked as a secretary at the MLT (1931); the same year she was an organizer of the National Congress of Women Workers and Peasants. Rodriguez was then named director of the Malinalxóchitl school (1932). After working at Malinalxóchitl, briefly as director of ETIC (1932), and director of the Business and Sewing Academy Number 2 (established in 1933), Rodríguez was named director of the MLT (1933–42).[17]

When Juan de Dios Bátiz returned to serve as chief of DETIC in 1935, he played an active role in the establishment of the IPN and in reform of women's education (see fig. 12). Under his direction, the MLT curriculum shifted away from the liberal arts education that had complemented commercial training since the school's founding.[18] Reform was carried out with an eye toward curriculum uniformity across schools, improved teaching methods, and an increased emphasis on testing.[19] The school continued to offer stenography, typing, bookkeeping, filing, correspondence, documentation, statistics, commercial law, English, commercial and administrative sciences, and office management. The MLT was the only women's commercial school to offer statistics, psychology and logic, publicity, organizational theory, and economics as fourth-year topics of study. The curriculum also included Spanish and calligraphy. Newspaper articles advertised MLT degree offerings and emphasized the quality of instruction and the success of the graduates from a school that offered so much for "middle-class women."[20] In the face of student activism in the early 1930s, DETIC also sought to improve classroom discipline and reduce class size.[21] Socialist education became a more integral part of commercial education and included support for cooperatives, scholarships for students, and heightened rhetoric on the social value of education.[22]

The MLT continued to serve as a vital intellectual space for young women who, in between lessons in taking dictation and studying English, learned the power of public speaking and the written word in ways that transformed lives. Professional women—public intellectuals, government employees, and activists—circulated through the school as teachers, students, and invited speakers. The distinguished doctor and women's rights advocate Mathilde Rodríguez Cabo, for example, gave a lecture at the school.[23] DETIC invited speakers, many of whom addressed topics that echoed middle-class cultural practices such as home economics, food preparation, industrial hygiene, the benefits of rest and of dreams, and the importance of bathing. The content of some talks may have missed the mark. For example, one speaker warned that "food preparation should not be entrusted to maids until one is absolutely sure that they know how to cook in hygienic conditions, because the majority of them are uneducated and they do not know even the most rudimentary rules of cleanliness."[24] While such a talk might suggest that MLT graduates could look forward to employing domestic labor, data on the student body do not indicate this was likely for a majority of graduates in the 1930s. School talks on how to supervise domestic labor and the science of housekeeping did nonetheless contribute to associating MLT students with the aspirations of a middle-class lifestyle.

The school also gave students a way to be civically engaged and participate in public events celebrating women's advancements. In 1935, for example, students were granted permission to put on a ceremony honoring Amelia Earhart, who had recently become the first person to fly from Hawaii to the mainland.[25] In 1938, SEP employees sponsored film screenings, theater productions, and kermesses, where students contributed funds to pay the oil expropriation debt.[26] The following year DETIC ordered classes canceled to allow students to attend demonstrations in favor of women's right to vote and against the high cost of living, thus facilitating women's political engagement.[27] Employees, teachers, and students also participated in a campaign to support national economic growth by buying Mexican-made products.[28] MLT students, like other public school students, also held membership on the DETIC Tuition Governance Board and served on the Honor Guard at the Angel of Independence Monument.[29] They were also invited to make "voluntary" contributions to the PRM.[30]

The MLT continued to figure within the cultural life of the city, in part thanks to the growing ranks of women journalists. María Ríos Cárdenas published a regular column directed at working women for *El Nacional* and occasionally wrote articles beyond her column. In 1932 she published an interview with Director Santoyo. Ríos Cárdenas asked Santoyo about the school, its successes, and the large number of women who were now employed in government offices. Santoyo commented, "As Nietzsche said, 'Women, not content with conquering us with their beauty, now surprise us with their talent.'"[31] Ríos Cárdenas concluded the article by reflecting on what the future might hold. If in prior decades journalists portrayed empleadas as new on the scene, in the 1930s Ríos Cárdenas aimed higher: "Empleadas, secretaries, managers, accountants and . . . why not ministers of State?"[32] The growing numbers of women in government offices encouraged women to contemplate greater political influence.

The MLT also had its own magazine, which served as a space for teachers and students to write about school activities and the challenges women faced in society. The Section for Special Education (also referred to as the Female Industrial Education Section), under the direction of Professor Isaura Castillo, published *Senda Nueva: Revista Popular de Orientación* (New path: Popular magazine of social engagement).[33] Castillo had served as director of some of the most important technical and commercial schools for women.

She was director and founder of the "Malinalxóchitl" school (1926–31) and director of the "Corregidora de Querétaro" School (1931), the School for Manual Arts and Trades for Women (1932), Toluca Normal School (1933), and the Home for Working Women (Casa Amiga de la Obrera) Number 1 (1934). In December 1934 she found herself unemployed and wrote to the SEP asking for a job, pointing to government claims to support women in leadership positions, her long history of supporting socialist education, and her dedication, "above all," to women.[34] Her petition was successful. For Castillo, *Senda Nueva* was an integral part of the school's efforts to promote its mission and socialist education.[35] Its circulation reportedly reached fifteen thousand, it was distributed free of charge in all women's commercial schools, and it could be purchased for ten cents.

The cover of the first issue showed a young women's sports team. Sports had become an important SEP initiative and was integral to official culture celebrating the revolution. Tournaments, national parades, and the photographs of such events published in magazines and newspapers offered women an avenue for public appearance that replaced the photographs of women in tableaux in the 1910s. First as students and then as public employees, women joined teams and participated in volleyball, basketball, and fron-tenis tournaments (see fig. 9). It was a point of pride for the school that, in 1935, the MLT team tied for fourth place with Academy Number 4 in the volleyball tournament.[36] After graduating from school, women continued to join teams and participate in tournaments when they went on to work as government employees. Offices across government supported teams, competitions, and the celebration of those activities as a way to improve employees' moral and physical condition.[37]

Senda Nueva offered women a space to read and to write about a wide range of topics. Articles appeared that resonated with government priorities, like the continued literacy campaign and anti-alcohol movement. For example, a reader might learn how to play an anti-alcohol hymn on the piano (with lyrics by Carmen G. Basurto and music by Francisco Aceves). Students could also participate in charitable activities that brought credit to both the school and the government, as when MLT students and teachers sent a special brigade with food, clothing, and financial aid to people affected by natural disaster.[38] Many *Senda Nueva* articles sought to raise women's consciousness about gender inequality, such as "Woman: Your Ignorance Has Placed Man on a Pedestal." Aurora Ursúa de Escobar made her views clear in "Women's Tribunal: Women, Wake Up!" And Delfina Huerta argued that commercial education empowered women, as she explained in "Vocational Schools and Women's Emancipation."[39] The magazine also publicized student organizations like the "Senda Nueva" Experimental Educational Theater Group.[40]

Senda Nueva also included more standard magazine fare like games, contests, advice, and recipes—from home remedies to whiten one's skin, to how to cook a chicken. The article "Calisthenics at Home to Maintain Your Figure" offered advice to office workers who might spend much of the day sitting. Some games tested women's professional skills, like deciphering messages written in shorthand. The magazine also sponsored contests "to promote the intense educational and cultural work, so deeply significant, that the Department carries out," as was the case with a 1937 Shorthand Typing Contest (see fig. 13).[41] Prizes included Remington typewriters, 100 pesos, and for the two winners, jobs in SEP offices.[42] Typewriter companies John Deere and Remington, among others, advertised within the pages of *Senda Nueva* regularly. Julia Nava de Ruisanchez advertised the children's books she wrote. The "Correspondence Club" urged readers to join and get involved in all the opportunities around them.[43]

The 1935 SEP end-of-year report stated that "the middle class, whose destiny is tied to that of the national proletariat, ought to be educated in technical schools . . . to better carry out its role in a new society."[44] The close relationship that the report drew between the middle class and the proletariat had multiple meanings. Political rhetoric continued to validate the central role of the working class in national development and politics, and the statement in part validated the middle class by the company it kept. The statement also oriented the middle-class toward technical education that would contribute to ecomonic development. The INP was the cornerstone of educational reform and was meant to counter the influence of the National Autonomous University of Mexico. While newspaper reports on technical education tended to emphasize the role of the proletariat or

FIG. 13. Professor Aurelio Manrique (*left*) participates in a typing competition, 1936. SINAFO #20760. Reproduction authorized by the National Institute of Anthropology and History.

el pueblo, SEP functionaries and administrators understood that students enrolled in the MLT, and DETIC schools more generally, came from a wide range of socioeconomic backgrounds and circumstances not easily categorized as working or middle class.

The SEP was interested in the socioeconomic status of its students. A DETIC study conducted in 1937 found that the majority of students enrolled in its schools came from "modest" circumstances. Department schools enrolled 17,563 students, of which 32 percent were the children of public- and private-sector employees, 22 percent were the children of artisans and industrial and agricultural workers, and 2 percent were the children of domestic workers and those defined as engaged in menial labor.[45] According to SEP officials, the statistics highlighted "the extremely modest circumstances of our students, and therefore the true social service that DETIC schools provide and in whose classrooms are gathered people of the most simple and noble origins."[46] With large numbers of students coming from the families of public employees, the school served an important government constituency.

Students at the MLT differed slightly from those enrolled in other DETIC schools.[47] The MLT enrolled the largest number of students in the department, with 2,542 students (see table 11). MLT students, compared to the entire DETIC student body, were more likely to be second-generation office workers (though whether it was the mother, father, or both who was the employee is not clear). The largest group of MLT students (38 percent) came from families where the head of household was an employee in the public or private sector, though the majority came from the public sector. The second-largest group (14 percent) came from families where the head of household was an artisan or industrial or agricultural worker.[48]

Behind the categories established by the 1937 study there were a wide range of living circumstances among MLT students. The "empleados" category included an accountant for the Ejido Bank who earned 600 pesos a month, while other employees earned 2.5 pesos a day, or approximately 60 pesos a month. While one student came from a family that owned a business generating between 1,000 and 5,000 pesos in capital per year, another student's father was categorized as a "businessman" (perhaps a market or street vendor) who earned 30 pesos a month and supported five people living under the same roof. A substantial portion of those listed as engaged in business sold goods and services in the city streets and markets, as was the case with a vendor at the Tacuba Market who took in between 30 and 50 pesos a month. Some parents claimed only a spotty income. Women heads of households also managed to send their daughters to commercial school, as was the case for a dressmaker who earned 2 pesos a day, or about 45 pesos a month.[49]

DETIC students in general, including those at the MLT, came from a variety of family arrangements. For all students, the average household was just under seven (6.71) members. While some MLT students came from families with two parents, many came from households headed by single women.[50] Nevertheless, the unidentified author of a 1939 DETIC report

TABLE 11. Enrollment at selected schools, National Polytechnic Institute, 1936

School	Enrollment
"Miguel Lerdo de Tejada" Commercial School	1,548
Advanced School for Economics, Administration, and Social Studies	1,092
School for Homeopathic Medicine	67
Federal School for Textile Industries Number 2	91
Advanced School for Construction	258
Advanced School for Mechanical and Electrical Engineering	346

Source: Instituto Politécnico Nacional enrollments, 1936, Archivo Histórico de la Secretaría de Educación Pública, Departamento de Escuelas Técnicas, Industriales y Comerciales, caja 2831, exp. 58.

assumed that the average household included a father, mother, two brothers, two sisters, and a relative or friend living in the home. The study was based on a scenario of two economically active family members. If everyone worked, the monthly household income would be 266.50 pesos. However, the author noted, given the reality that not everyone is able to work, the study estimated an average monthly income of 132.40 pesos. A separate study (1939) of all DETIC students found 91 percent of fathers were employed, most commonly and in order of likelihood as: worker, businessman, artisan, employee, unemployed, sub-professional, technician, chauffeur, professional, police, and industrialist. The occupations most common for the 6 percent of mothers of DETIC students who worked were, in descending order, housework, employee, businesswoman, and domestic worker. Nineteen percent of siblings worked, especially in more modest households made up of workers, technicians, domestic workers, and soldiers.[51]

The modest household income of DETIC student families shaped their living circumstances. The majority of DETIC families lived in rented homes for which they paid an average of 26 pesos a month. Those who could only afford more modest living arrangements paid 20 pesos a month. In the latter case, an employee who earned 2.50 a day paid 33–40 percent of his or her income toward rent. Some individuals came from families who lived with relatives and did not pay rent. While there is no systematic data on residential patterns for the 1930s, we know that some of the women who worked as typist, stenographer, or filing secretary in the Ministry of the Interior lived in Santa María de la Ribera, San Juan de los Pinos, Colonia del Valle, Colonia de los Alamos, and Tacubaya.[52]

A comparison of the monthly income of students' family of origin with that of female public employees shows that, over time, office work could lead to modest socioeconomic mobility during the 1930s. An MLT graduate who worked in an entry-level position such as an apprentice would not have earned more than 40 to 50 pesos a month, but might eventually, if she could advance to typist level 2, earn more than four times that of most female heads of household in the 1937 DETIC study of student household income. The same typist might earn double that of her two-parent household composed of some combination of market vendors, workers, and/or seamstresses.[53]

With family income and housing costs as noted above, we can conclude that students lived a modest lifestyle. Consistent with sociologists of the time, SEP officials associated household infrastructure and consumption of durable goods with socioeconomic status. Analysis of such markers of living standards led them to conclude that the student population "consists of poor people who, at best, rarely reach the level of the so-called 'middle class.'"[54] The author of the study assumed that better-off professionals and students attended private schools and therefore fell outside the study.[55] The study described most kitchens in DETIC student homes as "improvised." In most homes (85 percent) women shopped at markets for clay cookware and purchased coal for the brazier on which they prepared their meals. Smoke would have filtered through the majority of homes, for only a minority (13 percent) had a modern gas stove in their home.[56] Household furnishings were modest. On average, student homes had two beds, a dresser, a chest of drawers, a washbasin, a bureau, and a lamp.

The SEP study also examined the clothing used by DETIC students and their families, described as "the usual for the middle class, of run-of-the-mill quality," made from jean (31.48 percent) and common cloth (5.55 percent).[57] Department store goods would have been a luxury for these families: at El

Palacio de Hierro, "MAJESTIC" silk stockings cost 3.95 pesos, and an "As You Like It" garter belt cost 5.95 pesos.[58] Liverpool Department store advertised dresses at 5–9 pesos in 1939. Furniture represented a significant investment, if purchased new. The Palacio de Hierro department store sold beds for 59 pesos, cots for 54 pesos, and pure wool blankets for 18 pesos.[59] Most families likely shopped elsewhere.

What leisure time students might have had was often spent in school-sponsored activities. While there are no data for MLT students specifically, DETIC students as a whole were most likely to engage in sports, attend a popular fair, or go on an outing to the countryside. Entertainment expenditures went to sports (48 percent); fairs (28 percent); outings to the countryside (26 percent); movies (20 percent); the circus (19 percent); gambling (19 percent); theater (6 percent); and musical performances (2 percent).[60] Women participated in all of these activities, sometimes in all-female spaces and at other times in mixed company. As Ann Rubenstein shows, while men and women both attended the cinema, they often segregated themselves as an audience as they chose seats.[61] If only one-fifth of DETIC students went to the movies, how many, then, would have seen, for example, *Santa* (1932) or *Allá en el Rancho Grande* (1936)? If they did, it may have more likely been as a matinee or second-run showing. A show (in 1938) at the Cine Palacio cost 2 pesos, while the Cine Moderno offered showings at 1 peso and at 40 centavos. DETIC students may have been more likely to see a show at the Roxy, Principal, or Alarcón theaters, which specialized in matinee screenings of films like *Quesos y besos*, and *Mademoiselle Frou-Frou*. The government occasionally offered free tickets for shows.[62] SEP employees and teachers had access to discount tickets (50 percent off) for theater productions by the Gloria Iturbide Company at the Hidalgo Theater.[63] DETIC offered film screenings and highlighted European productions with the intention of countering the "pernicious" influences of films in English from the United States.[64]

Affiliation with a government entity, such as a government-sponsored school like the MLT, offered students (and government employees) access to consumer culture, including national tourism.[65] By the late 1920s the Mexican government had begun to invest in tourism as integral to state-led modernization. While a good portion of that investment focused on attracting a foreign market, Mexican citizens traveled in growing numbers around the country as well. The Mexican government supported travel for teachers and students, who could request discount tickets from the Streetcar Company to get around town, or train tickets to travel throughout the country at vacation time.[66] While some returned to the provinces to visit family, others took part in a growing trend of national tourism increasingly associated with a middle-class standard of living. Magazines featured articles on travel to nearby Taxco, Acapulco, and Hidalgo.[67]

Access to urban consumer culture had a significant impact on some students' lives. Such was the case for Leonor Yáñez Piedras, an MLT student whose enrollment records shed light on the way attendance at the MLT represented significant transitions in geography, class, and self-representation. By placing her within the context of the larger student body, we see the ways the MLT was a transformative space for some women. The majority of students (304 of 500, or 61 percent) were born and raised in Mexico City. The remaining students came from the provinces: Mexico state, 15 percent (77); Veracruz, under 2 percent (9); Guadalajara, 1 percent (6); and a handful from Puebla, Guanajuato, and Durango. For those who migrated from the provinces, like Leonor Yáñez Piedras, it was an impactful transition.[68] At fourteen years of age, Yáñez migrated from Puebla in 1935. In her MLT school identification photograph Yáñez appears in a simple white dress with long sleeves, her hair parted on the side and formed into braids that lay down the front of her shoulders. The following year her photograph shows her in a black dress, hair parted down the middle and cut in a bob. In 1938 her photograph shows her dressed in a short-sleeve print blouse, her bob slightly grown out and let loose in a soft wave.[69]

Yáñez, who began at the MLT in 1935 and most likely graduated in 1938, surely engaged in the activities listed above. While we do not know the cultural milieu of her youth or if she came from rural or urban Puebla, as she integrated herself into the MLT she would have been exposed to the vibrant cultural life offered by the school. Through her schooling, Yáñez would have been inculcated into a culture that valued the printed word, from typed memorandums to women's magazines and perhaps the stories and newspaper articles written by women who had also passed through the halls of the MLT. She also experienced a shift in the educational experience of students at the school. During this time the MLT transitioned from an all-female to a coeducational school. Each of these cultural adaptations, from how she dressed and cut her hair to a familiarity with working alongside male colleagues, would prepare her for the cultural milieu of office work.

The founding of the National Polytechnic Institute had a significant impact on women's commercial education. Building on technical and commercial school reform, initiated early in the 1930s, and the formation of the EPN, the plans for the IPN were laid out in 1933 and 1934.[70] In 1935, the head of DETIC, Francisco Vázquez del Mercado, formed three commissions, one to study commercial education, one to study women's industrial education, and one to study technical and industrial training for men.[71] The commercial education committee members, all men, came to the conclusion that the quality of those schools had declined and planned for major reform and school closures.[72] In 1935, Juan de Dios Bátiz returned to the position of chief of the department to lead the IPN project. The IPN included college-preparatory technical education, institutes for technical studies, and schools for advanced studies. Secondary schools were also integrated into the system, including the MLT, ESCA, the commercial education sectors of Academies 2, 3, and 4, and schools in Guadalajara and Hermosillo. The two former Business and Sewing Academies served as prevocational schools that fed into the MLT. The federal budget first allowed for IPN teaching positions in 1936, and an official inauguration was held in 1937 in the Palace of Fine Arts.[73]

Tensions between DETIC administrators and teachers arose. The MLT in 1936 was one of the IPN schools for advanced studies and had 1,548 students (see table 11). In 1937 the MLT was converted to a vocational school.[74] De Dios Bátiz reintroduced home economics into the MLT curriculum, which led to grumbling among the teachers. In October 1936 he wrote to the directors of women's schools under his charge, stating that he was disappointed

> upon hearing the comment of some young lady or one of the female directors of women's schools about the Department attempting to take the schools back

into the Dark Ages . . . by starting cooking and preserving classes. Individual and official opinion confirms that a woman will always be a woman, whatever the education to which she aspires and the social activities she develops. By establishing such classes, the school offers women the opportunity to prepare themselves in the area of domestic work, as well as in other aspects of social work. So, I will demand that, far from obstructing the work of the Department, you give all the support necessary so that these classes are carried out.[75]

While De Dios Bátiz stood by his decision to reemphasize domestic education for women, the women's school directors must have had some impact, as he closed his letter by remarking, "Note: These classes will be electives."

Some women teachers and SEP administrators saw the closure of technical and commercial schools as evidence of a lack of official support for women's education and employment in government offices. Female administrators documented the disproportionate support for male over female students, despite near parity in enrollment. A group of teachers took a stand and wrote to the department head. They asked him to provide equal training opportunities for women and men, given, as they said, "that women, like men, have entered fully into the struggle for life." They reminded their superior of the purported goals of the SEP and argued that

> by providing equal opportunities for women we will fulfill one of the most transcendental postulates of socialist education. Important data in this regard include: industrial schools for men (14), for women (6), for a difference of 8. Number of students in men's schools in the Federal District: 4,520; number of female students in the Federal District: 4,220, with a difference of 300. Department scholarships for men: 215; scholarships for women 10 (9 in commercial schools and 1 in an industrial school), for a difference of 205.[76]

To these SEP employees, the lack of gender equity in the distribution of resources was patently obvious and systematic. The data, they argued, justified their request for more women in leadership positions. They also argued that women's professional credentials be recognized in the hiring process, adding that directors of women's schools ought to be "distinguished teachers and of revolutionary ideology."[77] The archives do not reveal a response to the petition.

The MLT suffered radical transformation during the establishment of the IPN. The SEP changed the name of the school to Vocational School Number 4 in 1937 and subordinated it to the Institute of Political Science, Economics, Administration, and Social Sciences (Instituto de Ciencias Políticas, Económicas, Administrativas y Sociales).[78] Director René Rodríguez de la Rosa was dismissed and reassigned to direct a vocational school in Ciudad de León, Guanajuato. Rodríguez, however, resisted the reassignment and took her case to the Federal Conciliation and Arbitration Tribunal.[79] After taking her complaint all the way to the Supreme Court, in 1943 she was reinstalled as director of the Vocational School Number 4.[80] In 1944, Minister of Public Education Jamie Torres Bodet (1943–46) eliminated the position of director of Vocational School Number 4, and Rodríguez lost her position, though she remained a teacher at the school. She was later reassigned within SEP offices to conduct pedagogical research. She resigned from all assignments in 1947.[81] During her career, Rodríguez had seen significant change. The MLT as an all-women's commercial school had become the Vocational School Number 4, which began to accept male students, and in 1938 enrolled 1,080 women and 1,250 men.[82]

For scholars Federico Lazarín Miranda and Enrique León López, the IPN represented the welcome end of an era characterized by sexist education.[83] In this telling of history, the IPN put an end to schools that trained women in domestic activities and for what were at best dead-end careers. Separate, these scholars argue, is not equal. Such a perspective is understandable, especially when viewed through the lens of the present. When the IPN opened its doors, officials publicly announced that women were welcome into programs of study in engineering, bacteriology, and other fields. It is not clear, however, how much effort went into opening doors for women in new fields. In his report to Congress, Juan de Dios Bátiz asserted that it was unlikely that women would enroll in most of the degree tracks offered at the school. The pre-vocational system was therefore divided into those fields of study that administrators considered men and women were more likely to attend.[84] For men, pre-vocational schools offered physics, math, economics, and biology; for women, they offered biology and administrative sciences. The IPN did, eventually, open new opportunities for women, but to dismiss the history of the schools that the IPN replaced, namely the MLT, is to ignore the contributions the all-female space made to women's professional and social advancement.

A Typewriter of Her Own

While Virginia Woolf yearned for a room of her own in which to write, women who worked in offices in 1930s Mexico City were empowered to write by having access to a typewriter. Rather than "dark years" for women's literary production, the 1930s gave birth to a generation of female office workers who not only typed up memorandums to the sound of their boss's voice but also typed up their own thoughts and words.[85] Rubén Gallo argues that the typewriter transformed the noble occupation of author. If this was the case for men like José Vasconcelos or Salvador Novo, it was also the case for countless women who during the 1930s worked in offices.[86] Secretaries, typists, and mid-level functionaries all contributed to a *cultura escrita*, drawing on their capacity to read and write, and on work experiences, to create new identities and effect change.[87] Women who hoped to publish their work faced barriers, both professional and literary; however, they found their way into mainstream magazines and newspapers or came together to create their own publishing opportunities. In so doing, they transformed the ways people conceptualized women's social roles.

Leonor Llach sat at the heart of a generation of women immersed in literary production tied to personal and collective change. She was an early member of the Athenaeum of Mexican Women (est. 1934), for which she served as secretary during the 1930s and as president during the 1940s. The Athenaeum, as Ana Lau Jaiven notes, brought together women from across the professions to support women's writing, publication, and culture.[88] In addition to Llach's participation in women's literary circles, as a government employee she collaborated with men well known for their literary and artistic skills, such as José Vasconcelos, Jamie Torres Bodet, and Carlos Chávez.[89] Llach, who had begun publishing in the 1920s, published three books between 1933 and 1939: *Cuadros conocidos* (1933), *Motivos* (1936), and *Retratos de Almas* (1939). Her newspaper publications during the 1930s included pieces for *El Informador* in Guadalajara, *Alborada* in Veracruz, and

El Nacional, El Nacional Dominical, and *Sucesos para Todos* in Mexico City. She also published in *Vida Femenina* (Argentina) and *Américas* (Cuba).[90] The topics Llach addressed in her writing were wide ranging, but the situation of working women remained a passion throughout her life. Her defense of the right of women—including mothers—to work outside the home informed her activism throughout the decade. From shifting public discourse in newspapers to fighting for policy change and for programming to support working women, Llach challenged middle-class norms that restricted women.

Although office workers appeared with some frequency in print during the 1930s, traditional ideas about women, class identity, and work continued to prevail. Mariano Azuela, himself a government employee, set several novels in offices. In *Regina Landa* (1939) he characterized office work as "a well-organized farce" and degrading for men and women.[91] Azuela, in his effort to portray office work as unsuitable for women, compared it to factory work—the incessant, deafening sound of typewriters, the grim faces, and gray light—conditions inappropriate to the vivacity of middle-class girls like Regina Landa. The most significant danger, however, was the constant threat to women's sexual honor. Invitations to socialize with male superiors that "one cannot refuse" and the boss who publicly declares "in a week you will be mine" surround Regina Landa until she eventually quits.[92] Men can disdain social conventions, Azuela writes, but not women. "Marriage is no mere social convention," he warns, and Regina Landa leaves behind the government office workers, many of them described as single women and women of questionable morality, to find marriage and respectability.[93]

Llach countered depictions, like Azuela's, of marriage as the basis of middle-class respectability. In *Cuadros conocidos* (Familiar scenarios), a collection of short stories, Llach pointed to the role of marriage in defining social class when she wrote:

Woman, from the time she is a child, is spoken to of love, and when young, of marriage. If she cannot make the two coincide, too bad for her. And no young lady from a good family, at twenty years of age, could admit that in life there is any other option than marriage.[94]

Llach not only criticized thinking of marriage as a woman's only vocation, she also criticized the centrality of marriage in defining social status for a woman from a "good family." She also questioned the cultivation of certain qualities that since the nineteenth century had been associated with middle-class women's pursuit of marriage. In "The Decline of Don Juan," published in *Retratos de Almas* (Portraits of souls) the central character cultivates her own innocence and submissiveness in order to attract a husband, but these very qualities lead her to fall victim to sexual transgression: "They had taught her many things, but above all to obey, and they had tricked her by saying that it was enough in life simply to be good."[95] It was not enough. In several stories, the central character either loses her husband or never has one, and finds herself without a means to support herself and her children. In the end, abnegation, for Llach, is "no more than the bitter impotence of the nonconformist and the weak, a cover for hatred."[96] Llach thus turns normative middle-class femininity on its head.

Llach critiqued the ways middle-class gender norms of days gone by weighed on women. In the story "An Honorable Woman," Regina is deceived by a man, in part because of the faulty education she has received. She was taught to deny her own desires and to submit to the pursuit of marriage. The narrator of the story concludes, "it turned out that for her, life was not like what she read in stories."[97] For Llach, the culprits were "romantic novels, newspapers, parents, religion, society in general"—all sources of an inadequate moral compass for modern women. Llach wrote:

> Contemplating the pitfalls that times past have forced upon us—chivalry, poetry, and all those things that, passing from one hand to the next and shuffled around, have lost their luster and their original form—we are faced with this useless inheritance, which produces enormous distress, a fatigue that results from looking back in vain. As with a poorly written novel in which one encounters the description of a dress that is no longer in fashion, the reader is irritated with the author who did not know how to free his characters from the offense of such costume.[98]

The trope of the dress was fitting. Times had changed, but just as out-of-fashion dresses continued to haunt the female reader, society continued to impose an old-fashioned morality. The seclusion of women celebrated in poetry that might have been appropriate in another era was now irritating and confining. Outdated conceptions of morality not only restricted women's actions, they constituted a vice. Llach concludes, "there is nothing sadder than the lives of women for whom nothing ever happens. They have never faced temptation. And they reach old age without ever having sinned, with nothing to repent. Their lives are not even virtuous, because they docilely do what they are told."[99]

The idea that women should sacrifice economic well-being for female honor lay at the heart of the phrase "poor yet honorable" (pobre pero honorable), a phrase Llach would have found outmoded. In "A Question of Chance," Llach describes a scenario in which the opposite is true. Margarita knows how to cook and sew, while her sister, Lucrecia, who is described as neither intelligent nor beautiful, works in a risqué second-rate theater. Lucrecia occupies a questionable work space and her behavior borders on scandalous: "it is not her voice that the public applauds."[100] Following the lives of the two sisters, the reader finds that it is Lucrecia, not Margarita, who is the moral figure in the story. Not only is Lucrecia happy, she is financially successful and disproves the saying that praised women for being "poor but honorable."[101] Margarita, trapped in an unhappy marriage with a man who cannot support her, takes a lover to support her financially. Ironically, Margarita is not even in love with the man. At the close of the story, Margarita, who sought marriage and public respectability, is the hypocrite who has lied to herself and everyone around her. Domesticity is not, a priori, virtuous. In "A Taste of Life," Llach states bluntly that "a bad path can start anywhere, and always begins at home, even if no one is at fault, rather simply due to a desire to preserve innocence, which is, in itself, a fault."[102] In a time when family was upheld as at the heart of Mexican national identity, Llach had a very different take on the function of family: "In reality, family is no more than a conventional organization that is maintained by pretense."[103]

The danger of daily contact with men was central to discourses that criticized women who worked outside the home. Separate spheres had shaped middle-class education and social practices and had informed the idea that women working alongside men in government offices violated middle-class respectability. In both short stories and newspaper articles Llach countered such ideas and celebrated the possibility of *compañerismo*: non-sexual, friendly work relationships between men and women. In "To Give," Blanca, a secretary, and her boss, Alfonso, work together in an office. In surprisingly frank language, Llach describes the pleasure Alfonso feels in arriving at the office every day, where he can contemplate Blanca. Alfonso, a married man, falls in love with her: "he had to love her, for that is the only human way to deal with the admiration one feels for a person they see all the time." Contrary to older discourses of morality, which would have condemned Blanca, Llach describes the love Blanca feels for him. The love between Blanca and Alfonso does not lead to an affair, but their spiritual connection is profound. Llach values that intense spiritual connection and love as "important for her faith: friendship without commitments."[104] For Llach, it was a tragedy when women and men could not recognize their own humanity and take pleasure in each other's company.

Despite her criticisms of aspects of motherhood as it was traditionally practiced, Llach was an advocate for mothers. She criticized the image of the mother as a "decorative figure that inhabits useless daydreams, uninspired beauty that hangs on to a decaying prestige, unable to come to terms with reality."[105] At the same time, Llach defended actual mothers, both married and single. Her observations were informed by her work in the Child Welfare Office within the Ministry of Public Education and in the Department of Health. Her speeches at women's conferences on the subject appeared in newspapers. "Lyricisms aside," she wrote, "maternity is deeply problematic, physically, emotionally, and economically."[106] In an article that made the case for providing social security for mothers, Llach argued that society was obliged to look out for the well-being of mothers, pointing out that in other countries the state paid mothers for each child. "We are accustomed to appreciating only the poetic aspect of motherhood.... It has been easier to glorify maternity as something supernatural and marvelous though it is not, than to protect it in a rational way, to recognize in practice, not in public speeches, such enormous transcendence as simply human."[107] In other essays Llach called for maternity homes and dining halls for pregnant women.[108]

Llach thanked feminism for its powerful and positive influence on Mexican life. In 1939, in the Argentine magazine *Vida Femenina*, Llach wrote:

> What feminism has accomplished, as it develops and obtains protectionist laws or equal rights, has been to raise the level of women's work and provide her with better earnings, so that she is not ashamed of developing her abilities. Her opinion counts because she can write, and there is no power like that of the printed word.[109]

Llach joined an important conversation that stretched back to the turn of the century and associated women's work outside the home with feminism. While more conservative voices had lamented the impact of feminism on women, Llach joined those who praised the possibility of middle-class women working outside of the home.

Llach's faith in the power of the printed word reflected a privileged position. Her work in government offices brought her into contact with influential people, and her entry into circles of women with shared interests provided support and opportunity. As she ascended in bureaucratic rank and her culture capital increased, she worked alongside a generation of office workers who were less privileged. Most office workers typed the words of others rather than their own thoughts and words. Leonor Llach and Leonor Yáñez Piedras (whom DETIC officials would have described as "barely middle class"), both graduates of the MLT, lived very different lives, yet together they contributed to shifting middle-class identity for women. Together, their activism as government employees rocked Mexico City during the 1930s.

6 Office Workers Organize during the 1930s

During the 1930s, women activists wrote petitions, confronted high-level government officials, and filled the streets of Mexico City in their struggle for legal equality, suffrage, and sex education. There was also a labor movement at the heart of the women's movement. A generation of women who began working in government offices in the 1920s filled the ranks of the numerous organizations that made up the women's movement. Women who organized primarily around labor concerns overlapped with those who advocated for a broader set of goals. They brought workplace concerns into the national debate over women's rights, most visibly and early in the National Congress of Women Workers and Peasants in 1931, 1933, and 1934. During the second-half of the decade, clerical and administrative workers leveraged their position as government employees to the benefit of the women's movement more generally. Together, and sometimes apart, empleadas and allies built on their skills and networks to mobilize on three fronts. This chapter analyzes three intertwined histories that played out during the 1930s: the women's movement, the government-employee movement, and official party politics.

Women's activism of the 1930s was fueled by a generation that had at least a decade of experience working in government offices. This generation was joined by a continually expanding number of women. By mid-decade the number of office workers had outpaced the number of female teachers. At least three events related specifically to the conditions of working in government offices served as catalysts for women's mobilization. First, in January 1930 the National Revolutionary Party (Partido Nacional Revolucionario, PNR) required all federal employees to pay one day's wages per month to support the party, even though women could not vote in party or federal elections. Second, the passage of the Federal Labor Law in August 1931 excluded public employees. A forthcoming civil service law, President Ortiz Rubio promised, would attend to their specific working conditions. Throughout the decade, government workers advocated either to be included in the Federal Labor Law or for a civil service law to in fact be enacted. Finally, economic depression and unemployment hit Mexico hard in 1931 and again mid-decade. As in other countries, hostility against working women increased.[1] Faced with high unemployment, some groups conducted public campaigns in 1934 and 1935 calling for women to be fired from government jobs so that men could be given work. Empleadas organized to defend their jobs and reignited long-standing demands for respect for seniority, elimination of the glass ceiling, and equal pay for equal work.

Empleadas Make the Women's Movement

The National Congress of Women Workers and Peasants, held in Mexico City in 1931 and 1933 and in Guadalajara in 1934, brought together women from disparate experiences, perspectives, and political agendas. The name of the congress, and much of the discussion that occurred there, highlighted women who worked in factories and in agriculture. The women who organized the congress, and many who attended, were government employees: teachers and administrative and clerical workers. Many of these women would have known about, or perhaps attended, the women's conferences held in the mid- to late 1920s. Perhaps some of the women knew each other because they attended the same schools, participated in activities such as the urban literacy campaign, or engaged in work-sponsored sports, dances, and cultural events. Clerical workers also formed ties with each other as they moved from job to job within government offices. Some may have been drawn to the congress not knowing who or what they might encounter there. The national press highlighted the divisions among women, with PNR faithfuls on one side and Communist-influenced activists on the other.[2] Even with such differences the congresses served as a catalyst to advance women's causes. The issues that brought them together included suffrage, the broadening of women's social roles, schools for women in rural areas, social welfare, and women's workplace rights.

Some organizers of the first congress in 1931 were motivated by government-employee working conditions. As government employees, women paid a portion of their salary to support the PNR, but they did not have the right to vote in party, municipal, or federal elections. The contradictions for women between obligations and rights fueled a sharp critique of the government as employer and of the Revolution as the political project that politicians claimed to carry out. María Ríos Cárdenas, in her memoir of the first congress, wrote: "the government denies the majority (women) the right to citizenship, and in exchange requires us to comply with all obligations . . . supporting political parties, parading in political demonstrations, and the like."[3] Disgruntled that such obligations did not come with full rights, and faced with obstacles to professional advancement, empleadas filled the ranks of the six hundred women who attended the congress, shaped its platform, and drew on the energy generated by the event to further their agenda.

The congress platform, drawn up in June 1931, included the demands of office workers. The president of the Congress Commission had close ties to the world of clerical workers. René Rodriguez de la Rosa, trained as a teacher, worked temporarily as a secretary (1932), as a teacher, and then served as director of commercial and industrial schools for women, including (soon after the congress) the "Miguel Lerdo de Tejada" Commercial School for Young Ladies.[4] Members of the platform committee are not identified, but their demands suggest the influence of office workers. Among a wide range of points, the platform called for the establishment of cooperatives for "empleadas, obreras and campesinas, a minimum wage for obreras and empleadas, and an eight-hour maximum workday for empleadas, obreras, and domestic workers."[5] The sheer repetition of the word *empleadas* alongside *obreras* and *campesinas* reflected a political strategy. The authors tapped into politically privileged identities within populist rhetoric. Furthermore, obreras had rights that empleadas did not, which the committee pointed out.[6] One of those rights was maternity leave. At the congress in November, empleadas called for maternity leave—one month prior and two months following giving birth.[7] Government office workers were also concerned about the regular waves of layoffs that had occurred that year.[8] On the closing day of the congress, despite disagreements between women affiliated with the Communist Party and those affiliated with the PNR, all agreed that the government should fire government employees associated with the Knights of Columbus and limit the number of priests in the country. This demand stemmed from cultural conflict in the wake of the Cristero War (1926–29), but it was also a labor demand. Religious groups like the Knights of Columbus had sought to fire women from government offices. At the same time, some politicians who did not favor the presence of women in government offices accused women of being politically reactionary Catholics. When it was suggested that "reactionaries" be fired from government jobs, women defended themselves from such accusation and highlighted the threat to their jobs posed by conservative forces.

Following the 1931 congress at least three organizations continued to press for office worker labor demands. No sooner had the congress concluded than the National Feminist Party (Partido Nacional Femenista, PNF) initiated a campaign in favor of working women. Edelmira Rojas de Escudero led this PNR-affiliated group, which advocated for women's suffrage and also set its sights on passage of a law to regulate civil service employment.[9] When the final version of the Federal Labor Law had been approved in August, government representatives promised public employees that they would propose a civil service law. President Ortíz Rubio then submitted a revised proposal that had been written a year earlier by Amílcar Zetina.[10] The proposed civil service law would have granted female federal employees the constitutional rights granted to obreras in Article 123, including maternity leave. This proposal, however, barely saw the light of day. In addition to supporting the civil service law, the PNF called for respect for women's rights in government offices, job security, and equal treatment regardless of sex, especially for promotions, calculation of seniority, and salaries. The PNF targeted specific practices that favored men, such as the use of letters of recommendation in hiring. Entrance exams, women argued, would be more equitable and ensure that qualified individuals were hired, not those with connections and political influence, who tended to be men. The PNF also called for an end to the glass ceiling that kept women from moving up to the highest-level clerk positions. The move from typist to clerk level 1 was of particular concern, and the PNF asked for professional development classes to support women's advancement. In the case of layoffs, they demanded sixty days' notice. PNF members also wanted to enjoy life "despite meager salaries" and asked the state to fund sports and excursion clubs, recreation centers, a library, and a boardinghouse for office workers. They also planned to form a mutual aid cooperative. Women from both public- and private-sector offices signed the petition, which they then sent to government officials. The PNF sought to solidify alliances beyond a single workplace and claimed to support women working in private offices, factories, and agriculture. They called for an eight-hour workday for all women, a government ministry for women, and support for women's civil rights.[11]

The Mexican Women's Confederation (Confederación Femenina Mexicana) also emerged after the first congress and hoped to unify women "in the home, the field, the workshop, the factory, the office, and the clinic."[12] They asked for resources to help women balance work and home and to stretch their wages and planned to start "cafeterias for empleadas and obreras."[13] The confederation also sought to transform the PNR from the inside out. In the days following the congress, General Manuel Pérez Treviño, president of the PNR, promised modest financial support for the organization and proposed that the PNR's National Executive Committee discuss women's citizenship rights. At that committee's meeting, several women's groups spoke, and the first response came from Enrique Pérez Arce, who favored hiring women over the reactionaries, he pointed out, who were already employed by the government.[14]

The National Bloc of Revolutionary Women (Bloque Nacional de Mujeres Revolucionarias), many of whose members were longtime government employees, also emerged following the congress and publicly supported the National Congress of Women Workers and Peasants and the PNF platform.[15] Taking advantage of the twenty-first anniversary of the Revolution, the National Bloc presented the Chamber of Deputies with a formal petition requesting women's full inclusion in public administration. Despite strategic timing, according to Ríos Cárdenas there was no official response then, or subsequently, from the deputation. Remembering the event in her memoir, Ríos Cárdenas concluded, "the condition of obreras and empleadas is sad. Carrying a ray of hope for a better future, the abandoned woman, with her faulty skills, throws herself into the fray. Under such circumstances, she begins to live by her own means and is surrounded by a negative and hostile environment."[16]

Women's right to work in public administration was raised in Congress only a few weeks later, in December 1931. In a debate over the requirements to work as a notary public, Deputy Fausto Bojórquez Castillo, representing the state of Campeche, questioned women's qualifications to be employed in public administration. Bojórquez Castillo confused the requirements to work as a notary public (full citizenship rights) with public-sector employment. Because women did not have the right to full citizenship, he argued, they should not be employed in government offices. Deputy Wilfrido C. Cruz, representing the state of Oaxaca, accused Bojórquez Castillo of forgetting his school lessons, which should have taught him the distinction between a political appointment and a job in public administration.[17] Cruz further accused Bojórquez Castillo of waxing poetic: "I am by no means intending to take anything away from this poetic adoration that my colleague Bojórquez Castillo feels for women, but romantic arguments against feminism, especially those against women's labor rights, have already been dismantled and discredited."[18] Bojórquez had drawn on a decades-old association of shifts in women's employment with feminism. Cruz responded with a defense of women's right to work elaborated by women like Leonor Llach, who insisted on the contradiction between celebrating motherhood and yet invoking motherhood in order to deny women's rights. "When someone wants to attack women's rights, the first thing they do is invoke femininity, poetry, and romanticism about the home," Cruz told the Chamber of Deputies. Turning his attention to the entire chamber, Cruz challenged the very revolutionary project that the government purported to represent, asking, "What side is the Mexican Revolution on?" Cruz and his colleagues had recently passed the Federal Labor Law, conceding rights to the obreras. "Were they now scared," he asked, to extend those rights to government workers?[19] Some deputies may indeed have feared women's increased presence in government offices, which they associated with feminism. The legitimacy of the Revolution and the politicians who filled the chamber had been called into question.

Government representatives and PNR officials faced increasing pressure to clarify their position on women's suffrage. The month after the debate over women in public administration (and just three months after the National Congress of Women Workers and Peasants), the PNR made its first pronouncement on suffrage: "The Constitution does not deny women the vote, however, given that the state hopes to introduce women little by little into civic life, it is appropriate not to do so too quickly."[20] If PNR officials hoped to satisfy women with such explanations, they did not. Rather, women heard in the statement a concession that urged them to action.

Following the first National Congress, prominent government employees continued to speak of the shared condition of empleadas, obreras, and campesinas. In May, María Luisa Ocampo gave an address on XEO, the official government radio station. As secretary for the National Industrial and Agricultural Development Board, Ocampo discussed women's importance in the Mexican economy, grouping together the "bureaucratic, industrial, and agricultural proletariat." While the term "bureaucratic proletariat" suggested the association of public employees with the working class, Ocampo also equated such workers with the middle class:

> Women of the middle class, the majority of them a part of this bureaucratic proletariat that cram major cities and monopolize state funds, have or develop needs that the nature of their environment and the salaries they earn do not allow them to meet. As a result, they sometimes make a series of poor choices to reach their aspirations. . . . Due to a lack of education the empleada, except in some cases, is condemned to constant anguish.[21]

Ocampo had made an interesting commentary on women's relationship with class identity. She associated secretaries with middle-class status and with the inability to fully inhabit that status. She characterized the empleada as having "aspirations" that her wages did not allow her to fulfill. Ocampo also feared that office workers might not have the necessary education to guide them to make choices associated with middle-class respectability. Whether or not Ocampo's characterization of empleadas was accurate, the gap between material conditions and cultural aspirations may have spurred some empleadas to activism.

The National Bloc of Revolutionary Women organized the second National Congress of Women Workers and Peasants in Mexico City on November 27–30, 1933. From beginning to end, attendees took up government workers' labor concerns. The inaugural speaker, Blanca Lydia Trejo, representative from Durango and contributor to *Izquierdas* magazine, spoke out against women being fired from government jobs. Trejo characterized women as inherently more moral than men and therefore better suited for such work. Such characterizations were rooted in the middle-class assumption that women, relegated to the domestic sphere, were morally superior to men who occupied the public sphere of competition and egotism. Trejo played upon the assumption that the private morality of women would have a positive influence on the public morality of government. "We want morality in public services," and to accomplish this, she continued, women should be allowed to work in government offices.[22] Several other speakers addressed women's labor demands. Elvira Vargas, who wrote the column "Women at Work" for *El Nacional*, spoke about the working conditions of women in government offices and advocated for equal pay for equal work.[23] While Vargas called for reform of the Federal Labor Law, Consuelo Uranga questioned whether women's interests were best served by a law she characterized as ineffectual politicking on the part of a "bourgeois government."[24] The congress was an important space for empleadas, so much so that despite political differences, many traveled to Guadalajara in September 1934 for the third congress. In Guadalajara, Leonor Llach advocated for acknowledgment of women's reproductive labor when she spoke of the need for financial support for the work performed by mothers.[25] The congress was not the only venue where women made labor demands for empleadas. The National Women's League, part of the Union of Women of the Americas (Unión de Mujeres Americanas), held a National Women's Congress in 1934, with a platform that also called for respect for seniority in government offices.[26]

On April 9, 1934, President Abelardo L. Rodríguez announced an agreement regulating civil service work. It was, however, a temporary agreement that lasted less than a year and was never made into law.[27] Not knowing this would be the case, government employees celebrated what looked like progress. Empleadas in the Department of the Federal District demonstrated in the streets in support of President Rodríguez's declaration.[28] When in June 1934 the law had still not been put into effect, Ana María Hernández, as president of the National Bloc of Revolutionary Women, wrote to presidential candidate Cárdenas, requesting that the law be expedited so as to head off conservatives seeking to take government jobs away from women.[29] So while the civil service law was not explicitly designed with women in mind, many empleadas considered it protection against unfair labor practices. Women's fight for labor protections was not limited to congresses, and it spilled into public debates.

The increasing visibility of women secretaries, typists, and mid-level functionaries in the halls of government, newspaper headlines, and city streets met with a backlash. The economic depression hit Mexico hard, and in 1934 and 1935 organized groups engaged in public campaigns to fire women so that men could take their place. In a 1934 article in *La Prensa*, an anonymous journalist wrote: "Political work, political information, the power of knowledge, which are the basis of such work, and secrets of state, are all under the control of women, and the simple fact that women belong, body and soul, to the party which is not liberal, is all the evidence one needs to conclude that such circumstances are immoral, prejudicial, and dangerous."[30] The journalist characterized the Revolution as a masculine prerogative by identifying women with religion and conservative politics, both of which were qualities contemporaries considered antithetical to the Mexican Revolution.

In the late summer of 1934 the José María Morelos Party (Partido José María Morelos, PJMM), which did not identify its members but claimed to belong to the PNR, petitioned president-elect Cárdenas to fire all women who worked in government offices.[31] Not only would this help with the current economic crisis, they argued, women should return to the home and occupy themselves with being mothers. This antimodernist argument fed into an increasingly antiquated middle-class ideal that continued to relegate women to the domestic sphere. The PJMM sought to bolster their demands by claiming that women moved up the employment ladder through illicit sexual relations.

The petition set off a maelstrom of protest and commentary. María Ríos Cárdenas denounced the move against working women in *El Nacional*. She denied that hiring women had caused the current economic crisis, as the PJMM and others suggested, and countered that unemployed men should look deeper into the causes of the current economic situation. For her own part, Ríos Cárdenas explained that the economic downturn was caused by mechanization, overproduction, a lack of private initiative to create more jobs, and dependency on government jobs (*empleomanía*). In an article in *La Prensa*, Leonor Llach echoed Ríos Cárdenas's criticism of empleomanía and accused the PJMM of being hypocritical because they did not ask for land or industrial jobs, only for comfortable jobs as a form of government welfare. Llach also accused them of being disingenuous because they showed no concern for women exploited in private offices or shops, but only those who, if eliminated from government offices, might open up a job for one of themselves. To bolster the position of the Mexican Women's Confederation, Ríos Cárdenas invoked the support of Senator Carlos Rivas Palacio (president of the PNR), the PNR itself, society, the press, and "even men's organizations."[32]

Following on the heels of the articles by Llach and Ríos Cárdenas, journalist Gonzalo de la Parra published an article in *El Universal* criticizing the initiative to fire women from government offices. De la Parra described the PJMM's claims as outrageous and offered a sympathetic take on some stereotypes about the "humble female employee." Women's motivations for working, he pointed out, were not frivolous. He stated that women's "legitimate" reasons for work included not having a father who could work, and youthful desires for "silk stockings, though not quite as nice as those of other women, a permanent, gloves, and shoes that are not misshapen from wear."[33] At the same time de la Parra was sympathetic to the plight of the empleada, he also accepted the claim that it was precisely in government offices that many women began their slide toward immorality. Gonzalo de la Parra affirmed that this was true but lamented men's misbehavior as well. Even if a woman were her boss's lover, he wrote, that did not mean that she did not work hard and do her job. Indeed, it was often a typist or secretary in the office who kept things running smoothly. De la Parra described women as more punctual than men and better with money. The central concern that informed de la Parra's article was his hope for the elimination of corruption in all its forms, including among government employees. He pointed out the flaws of male empleados who only worked a few hours a day, created a web of dependents, and relied upon corruption to fill their pockets. De la Parra concluded that only after a thorough housecleaning—that is, eliminating the corruption perpetrated by men—could the thought be entertained of replacing women with men.

An unsigned editorial in *El Nacional* responded directly to "other newspapers," accusing them and the PJMM of taking exaggerated positions. At the same time that the unsigned editorial recognized the real need women had for work, whether as single mothers or as women in households where their earnings were essential, it also provided a luxurious litany of female consumption in such a manner as to throw into question office workers' middle-class status and therefore their right to government jobs:

Those of us who have worked in public offices have, on payday, witnessed the parade of street merchants who sell on installments, shoe salesmen, dressmakers' errand boys, et cetera, who come to collect their due. A good percentage of girls only need work to pay for clothes, adornments, all sorts of potions for their hair, skin, eyes, eyelashes, eyebrows, and lips, and a festive polychrome of tints, for twenty nails (fingers and toes) that go from cactus flower red to gold. And then there are the women who sign in for work and then go visit with friends, to the endless "dentist visit," or make salesmen sweat at the market clothing stalls by obliging them to show them everything, even their own conscience, to then, in mysterious whispers, do complicated mathematical calculations for the ten cents less a meter of cloth it will cost them in some stand in La Lagunilla. Or else they dedicate themselves to the prudent task of copying dress models, to later go and get a 'known' and inexpensive seamstress (on Guerrero and Santa María de la Ribera Streets) to make it for them. How many times have we seen women who come to work dressed to the nines, as if going to a party or a beauty competition, while other families starve?[34]

The editorial, in mapping out women's consumer habits in working-class neighborhoods like La Lagunilla and on the mixed middle- and working-class streets Guerrero and Santa María de la Ribera, implicitly discredited empleadas as having a tenuous claim to middle-class status. Critics and supporters alike portrayed empleadas as unsuccessful aspirants to the middle class and therefore undeserving of jobs that should have belonged exclusively to the middle class. Such descriptions also threw into question women's morality by describing their dress as seductive rather than professional. The idea that women would spend money on clothes and makeup "while other families starve" also insinuated that empleadas lacked a social conscience. The solution? Do not hire good-looking women, highflyers, or those with no skills, and replace married women with men. While the *El Nacional* editorial took an extreme position, even those who supported women engaged in similar stereotypes. When the petition that women be fired from their jobs was disregarded, a front-page piece ran in *La Prensa* that included photographs of empleadas reading the news. The journalist reported that "indeed, the little boxes of rouge and the lip pencils had been hidden for a long forty-eight hours and the color returned to the cheeks and lips of the lively typists."[35]

In 1935 the conflict over empleadas' right to work raged on. In the fall a group that called itself Revolutionary Youth (Unión de Jóvenes Revolucionarios) petitioned the Chamber of Deputies to authorize firing women and hiring men. The ensuing debates continued to hinge on women's consumption, morality, and economic need. Women, from the rank and file to the highest levels of public administration and across government offices, as well as feminists in other occupations, spoke out. The National Bloc of Revolutionary Women published a point-by-point refutation of the claims made by Revolutionary Youth.[36] The organization Feminist Action, which had been meeting since earlier in the year, also responded with a gathering in the offices of the Ministry of Public Education. Two distinguished government employees, Elvia Carrillo Puerto and Otilia Zambrano, made speeches to those gathered and to the press. Carrillo Puerto expressed her doubt that the men who had protested were heads of household, given the fact that women supported 72 percent of Mexican households. (Whether these were her words or those of the reporter, according to the 1931 census of public employees, this number refers specifically to public employees, not the general population.) She also stated that if there were immoral women, it was because of retrograde employers. In response to criticisms about how women spent their money, Carrillo Puerto concluded that as long as men spent their money in cantinas and other "unmentionable places," empleadas used their money well. Repeating popular conceptions regarding women and morality, Zambrano added that women were more honest than men and therefore better government employees.[37]

Joining in the denunciation of Revolutionary Youth, journalist Ana Salado Alvarez interviewed various well-placed women in public administration and within the PNR. She wrote that based on her interviews it was clear that the petition was made by men neither "young" nor "revolutionary." Amalia de Castillo Ledón, vice-president of Civic Action, expressed her shock that the "young" revolutionaries would propose such a foolish solution to such a serious problem as unemployment.[38] Caridad Bravo Adams, private secretary to the head of the Department of Popular Culture for the PNR, expressed her belief that if there was one area where there should be equality between men and women, it was in the workplace. By allowing competition between men and women, she continued, the government would be able to hire the best-qualified people available. Salado Alvarez also interviewed Leonor Llach, at the time employed in the Department of Health, who offered a redefinition of morality rooted in a feminist logic. Llach argued that while some may not have considered it advisable or proper for women to work outside the home, it was practical and appropriate. Women should be able to earn and spend money without having to keep accounts to anyone. "Women who don't have a way to earn a living," she pointed out, "may turn to marriage out of necessity. Would these young men like to feel that a woman was forced to marry them?"[39] Llach concluded by defining the issue in terms of workers' rights, suggesting that those unemployed men put forth proposals for a six-hour workday with pay for more than eight hours, or for a five-day work week.

Government representatives were under increasing pressure to define their position on women's right to work in government offices and to fuller party participation. The response of PNR leadership to the debate indicated women's growing importance in these spaces. A variety of well-placed articles—not only in the party newspaper, *El Nacional*, but also in *Excélsior*, *El Universal*, and *La Prensa*—declared PNR support.[40] Each article made clear that any group that organized against women working in government offices had no part in the ranks of the PNR. In response to news of Revolutionary Youth's petition, Deputy Luis Mora Tovar and José María Dávila, president of the PNR, made public speeches defending women's right to work in government offices.[41] The question of women's voting rights in both party and federal elections circulated among ministry heads, a clear indication that the government's position on suffrage was important for employee relations. Minister of the Interior Juan de Dios Bojórquez declared that there was no reason to deny women the vote. Other ministers, not named in the documents, joined in agreement.[42] In September 1935 the PNR adopted an "open-door" policy, inviting women to organize within its ranks, and shortly thereafter it granted women the right to vote, on a provisional basis, in party elections for senators who would be serving during the 1936–40 session.[43] The PNR's concessions were a reflection of the growing power of women who worked for the federal government and were a precursor to national suffrage.

In October 1935 women from a broad range of interests formed the Sole Front for Women's Rights (Frente Único pro Derechos de la Mujer; FUPDM). Public employees, feminists, professional women, workers, campesinas, housewives, Catholics, and atheists all found a place to make their needs heard (see fig. 14). Centered in Mexico City and with affiliates across the country, the FUPDM came to represent fifty thousand women and eighty-eight organizations.[44] Its platform was as wide ranging as its membership, uniting women who believed that with a broad platform they

FIG. 14. Members of the Sole Front for Women's Rights, 1939. SINAFO #230235. Reproduction authorized by the National Institute of Anthropology and History.

could mobilize enough women to be able to take advantage of the political moment. Many government workers joined the ranks of the FUPDM and shaped its agenda and organizational efforts. Some empleadas did not join and indeed sought to distance themselves from the combativeness of FUPDM members because their first allegiance was to the public-employee unionization movement.

Women at the Heart of the Public-Employee Labor Movement

Armed with voting rights within the PNR and faced with repeated attacks against their right to work, empleadas continued to focus on workplace demands. The generation of women that had entered the public-sector workforce in the 1920s had been active in different forms of organizing, from school politics and beauty contests to the labor and women's movements. By the 1930s they formed a critical mass of women who had worked in government offices for five, ten, or more years and who built on their skills and networks to mobilize around workplace issues. While some prioritized workplace rights, others allied with suffragists and combined labor demands with calls for women's right to vote. At the same time, some empleadas continued to organize with co-workers in the effervescent public-employee labor movement. The different threads of activism were interwoven.

The public-employee unionization movement has its origins in many different quarters of the workforce, from teachers who in the 1910s tested the limits of state employees' right to strike to the high-level functionaries who established short-lived mutual aid societies in the 1920s. In the 1930s, workers and employees in the Department of Munitions were among the earliest to organize. Some scholars credit the group Female Evolution in the Ministry of National Economy (Evolución Femenina de Economía Nacional) in 1935 with having begun the movement among women that spread to other ministries. According to Otilia Zambrano, women in the Ministries of Public Education, of Health, and of Finance were the earliest and most active union organizers. More important than firsts, changing political circumstances sparked women to build on their accumulated workplace experiences to organize in the offices where they were employed and across government.[45]

Empleadas shared similar goals, but they diverged in terms of strategy. Many women supported the retroactive inclusion of public employees in the Federal Labor Law, which would have given them the same rights as workers. Other women prioritized the passage of a civil service law. A government commission had been working on a proposal for nearly a decade. As we have seen, President Rodríguez had made a short-lived decree in 1934. In 1935, Rodríguez, now as PNR president, and Lucío Mendieta y Nuñez, head of the PNR Institute for Social, Political, and Economic Studies, produced a new civil service law proposal.[46] Given the delay in enacting the law, women continued to press for its passage, both at work and within the women's movement. Those who favored the civil service law had a variety of reasons for doing so. First, their employer, the government, supported a civil service law over the inclusion, retroactively, of public employees in the Federal Labor Law. Second, the civil service law proposal did not give public employees the right to strike, and while this might seem like a limitation, many employees thought that, strategically, it was therefore more likely to come to pass. Divergent positions over how best to regulate government work contributed to tensions among women as they organized.

On April 22, 1936, empleadas met in the offices of the Ministry of Public Education. Their plan was to draw up a list of demands to present to the president of the PNR's executive committee, Emilio Portes Gil. In an article in *La Prensa* titled "Empleadas Rebel over Wage Deductions," women told reporters they had been organizing across government offices for some time and that they were all waiting for the long-promised civil service law.[47] Because they paid into the political party, they insisted that their demands be heard. And while salary deductions had spurred them to action, their demands were based on working conditions that women had experienced for years, if not decades. They wanted respect for seniority at work, equal pay for equal work, and benefits like medical and dental care. And they wanted the vote. In preparation for the meeting the following day office workers secured permission from President Cárdenas to leave work in order to attend.

The next day over four hundred women filled the seats of Hidalgo Theater, eager to hear Portes Gil's response to their petition. But they were left waiting. A message arrived ordering them back to work. Upon hearing the news, *La Prensa* reported, women began to shout. Some expressed their dissatisfaction that Margarita Robles de Mendoza, who lived in the United States, had been selected to represent their interests. Others focused on the fact that women in the countryside continued to live in poverty, pointing to the widow of revolutionary leader Emiliano Zapata as an example. Some women became nervous about getting back to work and left. Others, instead of going back to work, headed off to the Presidential Palace.[48]

Nearly 250 women who identified themselves as "women who work in government offices" sought to enter the presidential offices. When they were not allowed to enter, they occupied the patio.[49] Luis L. Rodríguez, personal secretary to the president, let the women know that the president was in a meeting about agrarian reform and that they should return the following day. Then and there the women pulled out paper and pencil and wrote to the president to protest the sabotage of their meeting. The petition began by identifying themselves as "public employees in the various ministries of government." They wrote:

While seeking to create a proposal to the PNR regarding concrete demands for women, to which we believe we have a right as members of the party, Licenciado E. Portes Gil informed us that you had ordered that the meeting be stopped, something we do not believe represents a progressive revolutionary spirit in favor of women and we therefore respectfully request you clarify this version of the story for us.[50]

In signing the letter, women identified themselves by their office of employment. Legible signatories included Refugio Moreno Ruffo, Central Department; Ernestina E. María de M., Eva Rodríguez Cabo, and Luz Rondero, Public Education; Esperanza Balmaceda, Ministry of the Interior; and Guadalupe Vargas.[51] The letter closed with the slogan "FOR THE BETTERMENT OF THE MEXICAN WOMAN" by Ester Chapa, representing the FUPDM. The letter nicely expressed the two related agendas of the women who drew up the letter in the patio outside the president's office. They had organized as office workers and sought to put pressure on the government as such, including by pointed out that they were members of the PNR. The office workers had also allied with the FUPDM, which included government office workers in its ranks, and thus extended their coalition. While the FUPDM had a presence in the protest, it was but one of many women's organizations present. The majority of women signed as empleadas who represented offices across the government.

The next day President Cárdenas met with the protesters, a group of more than fifty women from across government offices, as well as representatives from the women's sector of Civic Action (Acción Cívica Femenina) and the FUPDM. Civic Action submitted a letter to the president, claiming to represent "obreras, empleadas, and private individuals" with approximately four thousand Mexico City members and two thousand affiliates in the provinces, and once again asked him to expedite the civil service law. They also underlined the urgency of providing maternity leave for women working in government offices. The women's sector of Civic Action, while careful to express support for the PNR, also reiterated its desire to stay independent of top-down direction on the part of the government.[52]

President Cárdenas expressed his support for women's full engagement in public life. He informed them, however, that although obreras and campesinas were covered by the Federal Labor Law, government employees would not be. Cárdenas then explained that he had canceled the meeting at Hidalgo Theater because he had heard that the women intended to make personal attacks. This was evidence, he added, that "women were not yet fully prepared for this sort of serious discussion."[53] The personal comments had apparently been made by Refugio García and were directed at Emilio Portes Gil, though what she said was not made clear. Another version of events circulated. *La Prensa* reported that when Portes Gil found out that more than four hundred women had filled the theater, he decided not to attend and had himself called off the meeting. Consuelo Uranga, Nita Rodriguez, Refugio García, Otilia Zambrano, and Lydia Cordero each spoke to reporters and made their case for women's right to organize in a democratic fashion and for electing their own leaders. This latter comment was in reference to the unpopular appointment of Robles de Mendoza, who, they pointed out, did not represent the interests of women who worked in government offices. Despite President Cárdenas's assurances that they had the right as women, and as public employees, to organize, rumors circulated that those who had taken part in the protests would be fired. *La Prensa* reported that women in the Ministry of Communications and Public Works had already been let go.[54]

Despite threats of losing their jobs, empleadas continued to press their demands. On April 30 they gained entrance to the inner offices of the PNR to meet with Emilio Portes Gil and Ignacio García Tellez, president and general secretary, respectively, of the PNR executive committee.[55] The empleadas demanded the vote and insisted that the proposed civil service law be published (and thus made official) as soon as possible. It was urgent, they argued, to "put an immediate end to the arbitrary actions of which empleadas are victims, those women who, with no regard for their years of service, skill, and political leanings, are frequently replaced with ill-prepared and inefficient individuals with no merit other than personal influence in obtaining a job."[56] While Portes Gil insisted on highlighting the benefits that the government had provided for office workers, such as sporting events, parades, and cultural programming, the women returned the focus of the conversation to the need for maternity insurance and pay increases. Portes Gil purportedly promised to initiate an investigation in response to women's demand for equal pay for equal work. The women also asked for a committee of empleadas specifically, one that would have five representatives, one from each of the largest ministries. In response, Portes Gil committed to support a convention for female public employees.[57]

The women who mobilized in the spring of 1936 represented different factions of the public-employee movement. Thaís Garcia, who worked in the Ministry of the Interior, represented those who supported the civil service law and distanced themselves, at times, from the FUPDM. García began her career as a government employee as a teacher in the Children's Hospice in July 1922. Three months later she shifted from teaching to administration and was promoted to a mid-level clerk position. García later moved to the Migration Office in the Ministry of the Interior, where she had a long career. Along with Esperanza Balmaceda and other women, García was an early activist in the public-employee movement in the Ministry of the Interior. Women played a central role in the unionization movement within this ministry for several reasons: large numbers of women worked there, many held leadership positions, and the Ministry of the Interior brought together women of varying levels of education. Many had ties to the labor movement.[58]

Thaís García's allegiances lay first with the public-employee union. García told the press that she and other empleadas had nothing to do with "political activities related to the vote."[59] She also distanced herself and her group from "feminist agitation," the FUPDM, and the conflict over who would represent women within the PNR.[60] Their primary concern, she told the press, was equality with their co-workers, equal pay for equal work, respect for seniority, the passage of the civil service law, and an end to the 20 percent deduction from their monthly wages. Accompanying García and Balmaceda at the meeting with the minister of the interior and president of the PNR were Leonor Llach, from the Department of Health, and Soledad Orozco, from the Ministry of Public Education. As many of these women had self-identified as feminists in the past, their distancing from the FUPDM appears to have been one of tactics rather than principles.[61]

A group met with Emilio Portes Gil and Minister of the Interior Silvestre Guerrero (1936–38) on May 7, 1936, to express their frustration with the roadblocks being thrown in their way. When they had tried to reschedule the April 23 meeting that had been called off, they were told that the space they requested was unavailable. Portes Gil proposed the formation of a women's committee within the PNR and urged them to choose their representatives then and there. His desire to impose leadership met with resistance, and the women pointed out that it would be undemocratic to select representatives at that moment, as not all the leaders were present at the meeting. Rather, they preferred to hold a congress to vote. The group also sought recognition of a federation of public-employee unions. At the meeting, tensions erupted. Soledad Orozco asked Esperanza Balmaceda to make her position clear, as she had been at events organized by both the group of empleadas and by the FUPDM and the women's sector of Civic Action.[62]

Two days later, on May 9, public employees held a meeting at the SEP offices. The purpose of the meeting was to elect representatives to the Women's Action Committee of the PNR. In a controversial move, Soledad Flores, who had been campaigning for herself, called a competing meeting for the same day in a different place (Orientación Theater). She managed to attract more than fifty attendees. The meeting turned chaotic as some participants accused Flores of self-promotion and political manipulation. The schism was in part rooted in class differences between clerical workers and teachers. While Flores put herself forward to represent all women working in the SEP, administrative worker Cholita Alvarez said that office workers and not teachers should be elected to leadership positions. Despite Alvarez's concerns, several days later Flores was elected in a contentious meeting.[63]

La Prensa interviewed several women about the elections. Esther Chapa expressed her fear that Flores represented a reactionary political faction and support for the civil service law. Chapa insisted that employees did not support a civil service law and wanted to be included in the Federal Labor Law. Chapa also raised the problem of the tension between teachers, like Flores, who saw themselves as superior to clerical workers. According to Chapa, Flores supporters "didn't mix with school administrative staff because they considered them an inferior social class."[64] Flores supporters preferred the company of the archbishop, Chapa declared, and not those in the pro-government camp. Chapa was concerned that the politicization of the workplace had worked against the election of a more progressive leadership. Many women said that they had been told by high-level functionaries that they should vote for Flores or risk losing their job. Of the nearly 472 women who worked in the SEP, only 57 had voted, and not all of them for Flores. She represented a minority.

On May 11, a group of empleadas met at Orientación Theater. "Employees Do Not Want a Civil Service Law," the newspaper headline read. Although earlier meetings had been organized and dominated by women, this meeting attracted a large number of men who must have been attracted by the power women seemed to be exercising. The meeting included representation from three left-leaning cardenista organizations from the SEP: Esther Chapa and Gustavo Best for the Alliance of Workers of the Ministry of Public Education; Armando List A. for the Left Wing; and José Vicente Quesada for the Action Group. They were joined by employees from the Ministry of Communications and Public Works, the Telegraph office, and a cross-ministry public-employee group. The meeting was a forum for those who opposed Soledad Flores, and they voted for Soledad Orozco to represent them. Those who voted Orozco into leadership included male public employees, who requested that if she were a SEP representative to the PNR that she represent men's interests as well.[65]

The government-sponsored meeting of empleada representatives met on May 14. The PNR executive committee presented its program to address work and living conditions for women in factories, agriculture, and government offices. The platform called for equal rights and opportunities for working women, equal civil rights, and equality in the home. It highlighted support for maternity insurance, day-care centers, and a promise to combat the exploitation of women wherever they were employed. The program also stated that public employees would be covered by a civil service law. Eva Rodríguez Cabo, representing National Economy, questioned how the party could advocate for the civil service law when she represented employees who supported inclusion in the Federal Labor Law. Portes Gil insisted again that public employees would not be included in the Federal Labor

Law. There was also a long discussion, initiated by Leonor Llach, about who should be able to represent empleadas. Portes Gil conceded that women who worked in government offices should elect their own representation to the women's committee of the PNR. With many issues unresolved, the meeting concluded at 12:30 a.m.[66]

On May 21, empleadas held a meeting—the one that Portes Gil had promised to support—to establish a women's public-employee organization, the National Women's Organization (Organización Nacional Femenina), affiliated with the PNR.[67] This organization consisted of seven representatives from different entities across government offices. The executive committee was elected and led by women active in the public-employee movement: Thaís García, secretary general; Gudelia Gómez, secretary of social action; Leonor Llach, press secretary; Soledad Flores, secretary of the interior; and Refugio Rangel, secretary of education.[68]

Women's interests as government workers continued to conflict with party efforts to contain their activism within Feminine Action (Acción Femenina). Organized women disagreed significantly with party officials over the purpose and functioning of the organization and protested what they saw as women's subordination to PNR priorities. In a letter of protest, they identified themselves specifically by union affiliation as a way to legitimate their demands as workers who supported the political party with a portion of their hard-earned wages. By identifying themselves by office affiliation they also indicated that although they might be a handful of signatories, they represented a growing number of government employees. Elvira Trueba, from the Ministry of Finance Employee and Worker Union, and two other signatories (names illegible) representing the Agrarian Department and the Ministry of Communications and Public Works "Revolutionary Action" group signed.

Writing as "Empleadas de la Federación," they protested that Feminine Action did not meet the needs for which it had been formed:

> Considering that the National Revolutionary Party is an eminently political party, in which only political issues are addressed and which at heart have no real social utility,

Considering that our participation ought to be based on demands organic to our own needs and our condition as women,

We appeal to you and seek to make clear our urgent need to exercise the right to work "as and for women" and therefore ask that you consider the justifiable request that a budget be designated for a Ministry of Feminine Action, a budget sufficient to support the entirety of its needs.

There are an infinite number of women who need work and who due to a lack of concrete support resort to prostitution. There are an infinite number of painful scenarios of miserable women, scenarios that could be remedied by means of the money paid by all the women who work for the government, or if not remedied, at least [we might] prepare those women culturally to elevate their status. . . .

In light of the points made above, we ask that you consider this request, based on the call that you constantly make for woman to take her place in the social struggle for the enrichment of our country.

We want part of the money that we women, who work for the government, contribute, to be: FOR THE IMPROVEMENT OF WOMEN THEMSELVES.[69]

Drawing on an argument that women had made since at least the beginning of the decade, as government employees who gave part of their wages to the party, they wanted that money to go to women. They also, strategically and due to practical experience working in offices like Social Welfare and the Department of Labor, invoked the needs of women who were not office workers. Women might avoid prostitution, they pointed out, if a women's ministry could provide jobs. Nominal party membership was not enough. Therefore, they threatened, "we refuse to lend our presence as public employees at events when called upon."[70] The following year the PNR integrated Feminine Action into the PNR Executive Committee and tasked them with overseeing women's activism in Mexico City.[71]

The cardenista government had, by late 1937, reached a point where it could, and needed to, corral growing political activism. Organized labor, agricultural workers, government workers, and women had coalesced into identity-based organizations of national reach. In December, in the midst of the oil conflict, President Cárdenas announced the reorganization of the PNR. When Cárdenas proposed the reorganization of what became the Party of the Mexican Revolution (Partido de la Revolución Mexicana, PRM), he laid out a new political framework that tied different sectors of workers to the state. Scholars have long considered this a pivotal moment in Mexican political and labor history for the way it established state control and kept different sectors of organized labor from joining forces. The National Peasant Confederation (Confederación Nacional Campesina, CNC) provided representation for agricultural workers, and the Confederation of Mexican Workers (Confederación de Trabajadores de México, CTM) became the most powerful industrial worker organization. There was also a sector for the military. In the face of the massive mobilization of government workers, Cárdenas was very concerned to keep the different sectors of organized labor from joining forces. The fourth sector, the National Confederation of Popular Organizations (Confederación Nacional de Organizaciones Populares, CNOP), brought government workers into the fold while drawing them away from organized labor in general and the CTM in particular. The CNOP, however, diluted the power of government workers, as it also included market vendors, small business owners, and neighborhood organizations.[72]

Kevin Middlebrook characterizes these sectors as the "symbolic commitment to the political inclusion of mass sectors."[73] Many Mexicans thought they heard Cárdenas extend that commitment to women when he laid out his vision in January 1938. In February 1938 women organized to demand the right to participate at the party convention, where the details of the proposal would be worked out. In March, organized women from across the country, including women who worked for the government, held a conference to formulate their demands. In May, women from a range of organizations attended the party meeting in Querétaro, where they argued that a fifth sector, to represent women, should be added. Some thought the fifth sector should be a Ministry of Feminine Action, which, supporters argued, worked with a wide swath of the women in public administration, neighborhood associations, and working-class women who had affiliated with the PNR.[74]

A large group of government workers—many of them women—had a different idea: to form a sector for "intellectual workers." The Revolutionary Front of Intellectual Workers (Frente Revolucionario de Trabajadores Intelectuales; FRITI) consisted of public employees of some stature who identified with Cárdenas's revolutionary project, including José Mancisidor Ortiz, Eugenio Mendez, Enrique Othón Díaz, Francisco Arellano Belloc, Mathilde Rodríguez Cabo, and Esperanza Balmaceda.[75] The FRITI claimed more than 82,000 members and represented a significant alliance between women, bureaucrats, and intellectuals. Their membership included the sixty thousand women the FUPDM claimed as members at the time. Many other FRITI member organizations were also dominated by women, including the School of Social Work, the Women's Social Studies Group, the Women's Revolutionary Institute, the Mexican Society of Women Lawyers, Mexican Women Doctors, the National Social Workers Union, and the Midwife and Nurses Union.[76] The Athenaeum of Mexican Women, Feminine Action, and the League of Iberian and Hispanic-American Women were also members. At a minimum, therefore, women made up two-thirds of the FRITI. Though the most significant representation was in Mexico City, the FRITI claimed members across the country.[77]

On February 12–14, 1938, the FRITI held a national convention to formulate a proposal to secure representation within the new party structure.[78] In a lengthy letter to President Cárdenas, arguing for a fifth sector, they stated that the PNR was not fully representative, especially when it came to women. Women's organizations in Mexico City, they pointed out, were not even taken into account. And rather than respect women's leadership and autonomy, the government had repeatedly attempted to impose leaders on them. The FRITI requested that the president convene a congress to form a fifth sector to represent intellectual workers, women, and organized youth, who should have "the same rights, voice, and vote as manual and agricultural workers, and soldiers."[79] At the congress, they drew up an action plan, statutes, and regulations. Their demands centered on women's labor rights and included the "fight for the improvement of women's salaries in offices, workshops, factories, schools, etc., in order to achieve the immediate improvement of their economic status."[80]

During the days of the FRITI convention, empleadas organized on several fronts. Some took to the streets hoping the government would pass the civil service law. *La Prensa* reported that groups of "empleaditas" put up fliers across town and demonstrated in the streets. While men were present at the demonstration, newspaper reporting and photographs reveal that women dominated the protests. Others called meetings to spread the word.[81] Women from the Federation of State Workers Unions, the CNC, and the National Alliance of Women met on February 12 to rally around women's demands and inclusion in the new party.[82] Esperanza Balmaceda, one of the organizers, requested permission to close down government offices so that women employed there could attend.[83] According to government security forces sent to report on their activities, some three hundred women "of all social classes" attended the "Special Meeting for Women" held at Hidalgo Theater.[84] Empleadas from more than a dozen offices across the government attended. Other organizations in attendance, which might also have included government employees, included the Women's Mid-Wife Union, the Association of Women Doctors, the FUPDM, the FUPDM Children's Assistance group, and a group of pharmacists. Some of the groups overlapped with FRITI membership.

As a first order of business, candidates were presented for election to hold office. María Rocha was elected president, and Carmen Meza and Elvira Trueba were elected as secretaries of proceedings. The congress then moved to speeches. Refugio García called for the "improvement of women's status in the home, office, countryside, and at school."[85] Speakers also called for day care in all government offices and in factories. Someone made a speech demanding raises for female government workers, bitterly pointing out that there were women who had worked in government offices for years without ever getting a raise. Some women spoke in favor of the civil service law, while others argued that a proposed statute to regulate public employees would better serve their interests.[86] As in prior years, labor demands and political representation were intertwined.

Meeting organizers hoped to garner more support for their demand for women's representation within the political process in general and the party in particular, but women continued to disagree over whether the PNR could be trusted. Esperanza Balmaceda, according to the government observer, advocated for women's representation within the new party, arguing that it was crucial that women be given an equitable number of delegates based on the number of organizations they represented. Balmaceda also called for the PNR, at every level, to include three representatives: an adult, a woman, and a youth. Though the government observer did not identify specific speakers, some women characterized the PNR as "crooked, authoritarian, and a fraud in everything it does and in all of its history."[87] Someone questioned Balmaceda's proposal to organize within party-sponsored unions. Despite disagreement, a vote resolved that they would seek the support of other government-allied organizations such as the CTM.

In April 1938, organized women, many of them public employees, met with representatives from the three sectors that had thus far been formed: the CRM, the CNC, and the CNOP. They sought to persuade leaders that women represented a unique class that merited, like the others, their own organization. In order to create a women's sector, each of the preexisting sectors would need to vote in favor of its creation. In a meeting of the CNOP on April 3, Vicente Lombardo Toledano sought to dissuade women from pushing for a vote, imploring that they have patience. They would not wait. Women forced a vote to create their own women's sector and won approval. The three other sectors voted it down.[88] The majority was able to accept work-based mass organizations but did not believe that women represented a distinct class that merited the level of party representation granted to others. In the days following the vote, the PNR made public statements that reiterated that women would not be allowed have their own organization.

The PNR, through an article by an unidentified author that appeared in *El Nacional*, stated that women did not form a class based on economic interests and that therefore to organize their own sector would contravene the objectives of the Revolution and break with the inherent logic of the party. "Sexual difference is not a difference based on economic activity," the writer stated, "nor is it a position within the class struggle. To differentiate, based on sex, among people who identify based on the nature of their economic activities, would be contrary to the ideas of the Revolution, and would work against the objective of leveling men and women in the exercise of their rights."[89] Women were directed to enroll in one of the four sectors that had been approved. In a document titled "Platform for the Inclusion of Women into the Party," women were urged to join the CNC, for example, as landowners, wives of landowners, and wives of rural wage workers, or to join the CTM as workers or as the wives of workers.[90] As historian Esperanza Tuñón Pablos recounts, in March 1939 the president imposed a leader on the women's section of each of the four sectors: Josefina Vicens for the CNC; Estela Marrín for the CTM; Lucina Villareal for the military; and Estela Jiménez Esponda for the CNOP. Tuñón Pablos concludes that from that moment on, each group focused on its sectoral constituency and no longer made a broad appeal to all women, thus marking a fatal blow to the FUPDM.[91]

Many of the women who had been leaders in organizing employees within the offices where they worked—while attending women's meetings, distributing fliers, and protesting on the steps of the Chamber of Deputies—had in 1938 continued to be active in public-employee unions. In response to this increased activism, President Cárdenas held a congress to form a state-sponsored federation of public-employee unions. Government employees amassed in more than thirty unions, each represented by five delegates, to meet at the Palace of Fine Arts from October 29 to November 1, 1938. The congress led to the formation of the Federation of State Workers Unions (FSTSE), which took as its slogan "For a State in Service to the People."[92] In the wake of the congress, new unions formed and allied themselves with FSTSE. On December 21, FSTSE wrote to confirm their loyalty to the PRM. Leadership in public-employee unions was quickly brought into the fold of the party, and most of that leadership was male. A FSTSE representative sat on the party advisory board, and one FSTSE member was designated as an official candidate for deputy. As Arturo Anguiano points out, union membership was virtually obligatory.[93]

Public discussion about women's labor activism and the vote continued to be intertwined. In the wake of the congress, *El Nacional* interviewed public employees about the formation of FSTSE and about women's right to vote. Equal numbers of prominent male functionaries and public-employee union organizers were quoted as favoring or opposing women's right to vote. Reporters framed their interviews in a way that continued to construe women as an uneven fit within office culture. At the same time, reporters were forced to recognize women's power within the unionization movement. "A beautiful and competent employee in the Judiciary, Miss Leonor Conde, politely answered our question, telling us 'This Congress has been a great education for me with regard to the union struggle.'"[94] Some women expressed concern. The "active and combative" Gudelia Gómez, described as occupying a "modest job" in the Department of Labor, declared:

> I believe that if indeed there has awoken among public employees a true class consciousness, it is likely that the Federation will serve as a real guarantee for all. I believe that those who are fighting for the formation of a Federation will be successful, because they come from the old guard—labor militants through and through—and I, who was and continue to be an *obrera*, have full faith in our *compañeros*. My only hope is that the path that the Federation follows is not centered in politics, for if this is the case the employment guarantees afforded to public employees will be no more than superficial.[95]

Gómez was one of several employees in the Department of Labor who, while they agreed not to form a competing union, did not join FSTSE.

The frustration some women felt with regard to the relationship between the party and women's unionization efforts came through in the interviews. "A beautiful and competent worker, Miss Gloria Barrena, who lends her services in the Ministry of the Interior, upon questioning declared, 'By suppressing all personal interests, we have to reach a true and effective unification to benefit the interests we represent.'" Barrena was not only "a beautiful and competent worker," she was a leading force within the union movement. While the article gave the impression of expressing the opinion of a run-of-the-mill employee, in fact the journalist had selected prominent women to interview.

Gloria Barrena Campuzano had begun working for the government in 1929 as a shorthand typist, and by 1937 she was working as clerk level 1 in the Department of Social Welfare in the Ministry of the Interior. In 1938 she was elected to serve as the women's representative on FSTSE's National Executive Committee. In January 1939 she was involved in brokering agreements between FSTSE and the National Confederation of Veterans over the allocation of jobs. Barrena also belonged to the women's section of the PRM, which in 1939 organized a demonstration against the high cost of living and in support of President Cárdenas. The protesters walked from the Juárez Hemicycle monument, along Madero Street, to the Plaza of the Constitution, stopping in front of the National Palace for a series of speeches. The demonstration continued on to the Chamber of Deputies, where Barrena, as a representative of FSTSE, demanded a voice in formulation of the budget within government offices. She could frequently be found on the steps of the Chamber of Deputies, protesting or representing the interests of FSTSE. Barrena, as FSTSE representative, joined the growing number of women, in leadership positions within the public-employee movement and the political party, who pressed the government for women's labor, political, and civil rights.[96]

As the end of the Cárdenas presidency came into sight, women pushed hard for the vote, and office workers continued to play an important role in this and other struggles. Barrena took a major role in rounding up some three thousand women who demonstrated on the steps of the Chamber of Deputies on May 19, 1939.[97] The next day the demonstrations continued. Women from the Union of Education Workers of the Mexican Republic (Sindicato de Trabajadores de la Enseñanza de la República Mexicana, STERM), FSTSE, and a host of other organizations marched, as they had many times before, from the Juárez Hemicycle monument, down Donceles Street, to the steps of the Chamber of Deputies, where Thaís Garcia (Ministry of the Interior) and Otilia Zambrano (Ministry of Public Education) spoke. They argued, as they had many times before, that true democracy would not exist until women had the vote.[98] A few days later, Barrena, in company with other FSTSE members, including Josefina Vicens, Estela Jiménez Esponda, Maria del Refugio García, and Francisca Zárate, wrote to Cárdenas, and their first demand was equality at work.[99] And in June they published a letter in *Tesis*, the FSTSE magazine, making the case first for women's equal rights at work, as well as for equal civil and political rights.[100] The article sought to emphasize the power of organized women, both through the title ("Organized Women and Citizenship Rights") and by signing with the name of the federal employee organization they represented. Over and over again, groups of office workers telegrammed the president, expressing their appreciation for his reform of Article 34, which would have granted women's suffrage. It was approved by both chambers of government and awaited publication to become official. The decade closed, however, without women achieving the vote. They had convinced very few that women constituted a class in ways analogous to industrial or agricultural workers, and they had failed in their efforts for an autonomous women's organization within the political party or the government. After nearly a decade of attempts to gain formal recognition for an independent national women's organization, many women must have concluded that their battles had to be fought elsewhere. From this perspective, the decision to refocus their energies toward the organizations to which they belonged—FSTSE, CTM, CNOP, or other organizations—was strategic.

From the first National Congress of Women Workers and Peasants in 1931 and throughout the 1930s, government employees gave form and content to the women's movement. Informed by their work experiences, government office workers mobilized at work, within the political party, and in the streets. A coalition of teachers, mid-level administrators, and clerical workers built on their shared experiences and drew on work-based networks to galvanize a movement. Their grievances dovetailed with suffragists' call for equal political and civil rights. Office workers leveraged their position as government employees and through membership in the political party that controlled their workplace. Their strategic position allowed office workers to access government officials where they pressed an intertwined set of labor, political, and civil rights demands. While empleadas and suffragists were sometimes one and the same, at times tensions emerged and groups of office workers prioritized labor organizing over collaboration with the FUPDM (which also included empleadas). While some historians have distinguished between suffragists and working women, the history of the women who worked in government offices is one of intertwined interests of a practical and political nature: they mobilized for their rights as workers, as party members, as women, and as citizens.[101]

7   Women, Work, and Middle-Class Identity during the 1940s

By the 1940s women's presence in public-sector employment was well established. For more than fifty years, women had worked in government offices alongside men. Even with a slight decline in the percentage of female government employees during the 1940s, working women had become a fixture of Mexican society, so much so that one sociologist identified the *burocracia femenina* (bureaucracy of women) as a social group with its own characteristics. What we understand about the *burocracia femenina* depends on where we look. This chapter examines representations of female office workers in four different genres: newspapers, sociological studies, film, and women's literary production. Each genre tells a very different story. Sociologists and journalists simultaneously celebrated modernity and fretted about the impact of women's growing workforce participation on the fabric of Mexican family and society.[1] Individual behavior seems to have been an easier target for criticism than declining wages and the challenges of maintaining a middle-class lifestyle. The pleasures of modernity played across the silver screen in the form of attractive women in dress suits and new refrigerators delivered to one's doorstep. However, when the film industry took up stories of women who worked outside of the home, those women invariably suffered for having done so. Film portrayals of women celebrated motherhood within marriage and the home. The sacrifices women made for their children tended to be existential or relational. Yet another picture of office workers, one much more critical of gender inequality, emerges in the literary production of these same women.

Certain themes had persisted since the 1920s: the balance between work and home, the possibility of companionate relationships between men and women within and outside work, and the reality and symbolic value of single motherhood. Domesticity continued to be a necessary component of middle-class identity for women who worked outisde the home. During the 1940s these discussions took on new meaning. The observations of women who had worked for the government exposed the ways women's subordination to men at work served as the basis of women's subordinate class position and their social and emotional subjugation to men. Whereas during the 1930s empleadas mobilized in women's organizations and took to the streets and halls of government to voice their demands, during the 1940s their activism shifted location. The politics of conciliation that characterized the 1940s did not, however, squelch women's activism. It was redirected from the street to union and party politics. Sources are difficult to come by. This chapter, therefore, tentatively explores women's fight for equal treatment at work and for day care within public-employee unions. With regard to day care in particular, we see that during the 1940s it was working women themselves who fought for resources tied to the identity of "mother," because the work struggles they faced were directly affected by their reproductive labor. Office workers' activism thus complemented what Nichole Sanders has shown for the 1940s, when the Ministry for Public Assistance acknowledged the single mother as an important beneficiary of state resources.[2] As Sanders shows, professional women played a crucial role in the design and implementation of state programming. With regard to day care in particular, we see that during the 1940s it was government office workers who fought both for themselves and for other women for resources tied to the identity of mother.

La burocracia femenina

Women's employment shifted dramatically between 1895 and 1950. Whereas at the close of the nineteenth century women were employed primarily in domestic work, sewing, food preparation, and the textile industry, in 1950 women's workforce participation had diversified. The majority of women who worked outside the home continued to do so in domestic work, but others worked in the expanding sectors of education, health services, banking, and commerce.[3] Women's national workforce participation, which had declined during the 1930s, began to grow again during the 1940s. Nationally, the percentage of women who worked increased between 1930 (4.6 percent) and 1950 (13.6 percent).[4] Such increases still referred to a small percentage of the national workforce as women went from 2.2 percent of the workforce in 1940 to 4.4 percent in 1950. Throughout the period, women continued to be just under a quarter of the federal bureaucracy.[5]

Just because women had long been employed in government offices did not mean that everyone thought it was a good idea. Many took the opportunity of the new presidential term of President Manuel Ávila Camacho (1940–46) to argue against employing women in government offices at all. In December 1940, for example, Francisco J. Ferrer, who had risen from the position of scribe to department head, wrote to the president calling for a total purge of the "female bureaucratic element."[6] Drawing on conceptions of government employment as a sort of charity for women, Ferrer claimed they constituted an enormous drag on the state: "It is a complete disaster to be supporting so many women," he lamented. His solution to these problems revealed his politics: fire all married women and Communists and revoke the public-employee statute. Ferrer argued that, based on his forty years of experience, the Ministries of Education, Finance, and Economy were perfect evidence of women's inefficiency. If there were thirty women in a given office, he wrote, five or six were working and the rest were talking, saying stupid things, smoking cigarettes, or sitting at their desk cross-legged and with their panties showing. Others, he claimed, spent the day knitting or reading movie magazines. Ferrer figured that 40 percent of them were probably prostitutes and therefore did not need the work anyway. In a separate letter, Carlos Garrido wrote to the president complaining about the number of women who, just to buy luxury items, worked in government offices, while many men could not support their families.[7] It was nothing new for individuals to write to the president to try to get women fired from government jobs; however, the transition to a new presidency seemed to provide an opening for a new flush of such letters.

The tension over who had the right to government jobs was shaped by rising inflation and a higher cost of living. Mexico City, while the seat of federal government, should also be thought of as a specific labor community. Migration, an increased cost of living, inflation, and new consumer goods shaped urban life. Mexico City was home to 1,448,422 inhabitants in 1940, nearly half of whom were immigrants to the city, and this trend intensified throughout the decade.[8] The price of basic goods increased significantly, in part due to the outbreak of World War II. Jorge Basurto calculates that, taking 1940 as baseline, prices increased from 100 to 135.5 in 1942–43, to 201.3 in 1944–45, and to 273.3 in 1946. The increase in the cost of living during the 1940s "wreaked havoc on the working class," he concluded.[9] Sociologists documented similar challenges for government employees. While the average government-employee salary had increased 18 percent between 1932 and 1950, the cost of living increased 589.72 percent.[10] As a result, the average employee lived twice as well in 1932 as in 1950. Put another way, government employees' purchasing power declined from a baseline of 100 in 1932 to 50.33 percent in 1950. Government dining halls across the city filled with middle-class government employees. Organized labor mobilized around cost-of-living issues, and the Confederation of Mexican Workers demanded a 50 percent raise in wages to account for declining real wages.[11] Public employees grumbled about the high cost of living, and the government implemented a series of programs.

Building on initiatives begun late in the 1930s, President Manuel Ávila Camacho sought to address the high cost of living by increasing state intervention to regulate food prices and distribution. In response to public-employee demands President Cárdenas had created the Commission for Commodity Regulation (Comité Regulador del Mercado de Subsistencias) in 1938. Ávila Camacho built on *cardenista* programs and regulation, framing them not in populist rhetoric but in the language of wartime exigencies. The June 1, 1942, "Suspension of Guarantees" facilitated the capacity of the federal government to respond to the state of war. Legislation included a rent freeze (July 24, 1942) and a wage increase for public employees (September 30, 1943).[12] While the salary increase applied to government employees throughout the nation, the rent freeze applied only to Mexico City. The government also declared a price freeze on selected basic goods. Such legislation was accompanied by increased penalties on strikes, which were declared illegal, and on other worker actions that interrupted industrial production or could be construed as inhibiting the capacity of the state to act quickly. President Ávila Camacho created the National Distributor and Regulator (Nacional Distribuidora y Reguladora, NDR) to regulate prices on basic foods, especially wheat, corn, beans, and rice. The government distributed price-controlled goods through community stores, which by 1945 numbered 688, of which 190 were located in Mexico City. Prices were regularly published in the paper.[13] Critics, however, described the NDR as having little impact on living standards. In August 1943 more than 800,000 people, many of them women, protested against the high cost of living.[14] Private business interests like the Confederation of Chambers of Commerce and the National Association of Food Product Merchants lobbied persistently against what they considered unfair state competition, and beginning in 1946 President Miguel Alemán Valdés (1946–52) began to pull back on the purview of NDR operations; after that, the price-controlled stores became privately owned.

Economic conditions chipped away at public employees' purchasing power, with a direct effect on women on the lower rungs of the employment ladder. While some women made significant professional gains during the 1930s, gendered segregation of the workforce persisted. In 1943 a journalist for *Excélsior* put it bluntly: "A woman should not even try to be a doctor, a lawyer, or involved in finance, because she will fail. Her consolation is that there are all sorts of jobs for her, namely housewife, secretary, or teacher."[15] While no aggregate data for public-employee wages exist that allow us to distinguish between men's and women's wages, there are indications that occupational segregation and wage differentials persisted.[16] Journalist, author, and women's advocate María Elena Sodi de Pallares said as much in a 1942 article titled "The Pittance That Is Women's Wages," published in *El Universal.* Prompted by a group of women who worked in government offices who had come to her and asked for her support, Sodi de Palleres seconded their call for an investigation of government corruption that affected women's earning capacity. In her investigation, Sodi de Pallares found women's earnings were one-third that of men's for the same work. While women's average daily earnings were 1.25 pesos a day, men's were 2.68 a day. Low wages hurt not only individual women, Sodi de Pallares argued, but the household as well. She estimated weekly household earnings, if the father and mother both worked, at 27.51 pesos, not nearly enough to make ends meet. A family of two parents, four children, and a grandmother, she calculated, would need 36.46 pesos a week. Sodi de Pallares did not do calculations for single female heads of household. The article criticized the NDR for not doing enough to reduce the high cost of basic foodstuffs.[17] In addition to taking their cause to sympathetic journalists, female government employees petitioned the president about the problem of low wages and the high cost of living.

Despite such economic difficulties, many observers continued to associate public employees with middle-class identity. Sociologists considered government employees not only as middle class but as a central component of that class. Many sociologists noted the prominent role of women in government offices and expressed concern about the impact that the integration of women into the workforce had on Mexican society. Examination of the work of two sociologists in the 1940s shows how scholars in the field worked with definitions of the middle class characterized by fluidity and emphasizing cultural practices as markers of class identity. Lucio Mendieta y Nuñez's *La administración pública en México* (Public administration in Mexico, 1942) and José I. Iturriaga's *La estructura social y cultural de México* (Social and cultural structure in Mexico, 1951) both celebrated economic development and the cultural trappings of modernity while simultaneously fretting over the impact of modernity by focusing on the changing role of women in the workforce and family.

Lucio Mendieta y Núñez, who coined the term *burocracia femenina,* was trained as a lawyer and is considered one of the early luminaries of Mexican sociology.[18] The list of his accomplishments and publications is extensive, and includes a significant focus on public employees. He was also concerned with questions of social class. Mendieta y Núñez worked with a conception of social class that combined objective and subjective factors, material conditions and cultural practices. He resisted the conception of social structure as something that trapped individuals within a certain set of circumstances. Class, for Mendieta y Núñez, was not fixed. Rather, he thought of it as circles that formed around individuals based on shared characteristics and through which individuals could travel. Government employees, with their varied relationship to class identity, proved a useful object of study for Mendieta y Núñez. He considered public employees as a central fixture of the Mexican middle class and offices as a space of acculturation. Accordingly, he argued that even women, who may have had modest earnings, acquired and required certain cultural capital necessary to carry out their jobs. "The work of the bureaucrat is never solely manual or mechanical," Mendieta y Núñez wrote, "rather it implies, always, discernment, good judgment, and a minimum of culture. Even the typist ought to be habituated to reading, have a certain level of education, for otherwise it will be impossible for her to write with good spelling and to understand the circuitousness of bureaucratic language."[19] His assessment of the requirements of the job also indicated his ambivalence as to whether a typist was necessarily cultured in the ways demanded by office work.

Mendieta y Núñez believed in social mobility, both up and down, and this had particular implications for how he thought of women and class identity. When discussing the possibility of an individual transiting from one socioeconomic status to another, he pointed to the way a woman ascended in class status through marriage: "For example, a middle-class woman marries a millionaire and thus she and her family become a part of the upper class." Men's class mobility, Mendieta y Núñez believed, was the result of work promotions. His ideas of how class mobility worked for women also played into decades-old stereotypes of the sexual promiscuity of female office workers. "The elegant and easy life of rich women encourages prostitution among women of the other social classes. The great majority give in to the constant proposals of men with money who seek a conquest by means of gallantry or insincere proposals of love, proposals that offer the illusion of what seems to these women, the ultimate goal in life."[20] While not wholly sympathetic to women who engaged in sex outside marriage, Núñez y Mendieta acknowledged the disadvantaged position women occupied within the workforce.

In 1951, José Iturriaga published *La estructura social y cultural de México*, which crystallized a constellation of ideas that came together during the late-1940s debate over women's employment in government offices. Iturriaga was a lawyer, sociologist, historian, and journalist who worked for nearly thirty years for the Mexican Development Bank (Nacional Financiera). He drew on a range of social theorists in his work and claimed "an eclectic set of criteria by which classes are distinguished by economic levels, levels of culture, and habits of comportment—all of these crisscrossing in different equations." In many ways, Iturriaga's definition of the middle class echoed those expressed in the first decade of the century, although Iturriaga claimed German sociologist and philosopher Georg Simmel as his inspiration. Iturriga, like Mendieta y Núñez, thought of the middle class as heterogeneous, as drawing in "people from above and below, resulting in a blurring of borders."[21] That blurring of borders between the classes was a quality inherent to what Iturriaga termed the dependent (as distinguished from the autonomous) middle class. The dependent middle class, which Iturriaga considered the truly modern middle class, consisted of public- and private-sector employees (whose work he defined as intellectual and not manual), some skilled laborers, professionals, and technicians. In 1940, according to Iturriaga, 83.08 percent of the Mexican population was popular class, 15.87 percent middle class, and 1.05 percent upper class. He differentiated the middle class from the popular class by its access to culture and consumer goods, due either to greater income or to education. Iturriaga pointed to Cárdenas's support of public employees, among other middle-class occupations, as explanation for the recent surge in the size of this class. Iturriaga also identified two organizations as having contributed to the growth of the middle class: the public-employee union FSTSE and the teachers union STERM.[22]

Although sociologists celebrated the growth of the middle class, many (Iturriaga among them) were concerned about how work had transformed the Mexican family. Iturriaga was particularly concerned with changes in the lives of middle-class women. Women had become, for Iturriaga, a worrisome percentage of the labor force by 1940. By his count, women represented 14.44 percent of industrial workers, 17.50 percent of banking and commerce employees, 22.04 percent of public employees, 9.39 percent of those employed in liberal professions, 12.52 percent of those in undefined occupations, and roughly 85 percent of domestic workers. As a result of women's workforce participation, he argued, families were falling apart. Mexico had paid for modernization, he believed, with the declining size and cohesion of the family. In 1895, he found, the average family size was 6.0 members, and had declined to 4.5 in 1940, with smaller families in urban areas, where they averaged 4.0 members. Divorce and other forms of "family disintegration" were on the rise. Between 1936 and 1945 the divorce rate rose 161 percent, and the number of people cohabiting grew from 1.36 to 1.61 million people, according to Iturriaga. Iturriaga claimed that in the 1940s the groups most associated with single motherhood were domestic workers, waitresses, and government employees. Women who worked before marriage, he argued, more frequently retained an attitude of self-sufficiency that women had not had in the past. This self-sufficiency destabilized marriage, "for it is well-known that a good part of family solidarity is anchored in the absolute economic dependence of women on their husbands." In the past, he reasoned, religious strictures had kept families together, but in the "modern" era this was no longer the case. Urbanization too was to blame, because "the rigid social control so characteristic of small towns" had ceased to restrict women's behavior.[23] So while Iturriaga praised Mexican economic development, he tended to blame the societal change wrought by modernization on women's individual choice to work outside the home.

Sociologists were not the only ones who concerned themselves with female independence and challenges to middle-class male authority. In 1942, Teresa de Cepeda published an article titled "The Woman Who Works" in *Excélsior*, wherein she documented the difficulties caused by women having to work, a problem she identified as unique to the middle class.[24] The typical middle-class Mexican girl, she wrote, had changed completely in the last twenty years: "The young aristocratic lady continues to do with her life what she has always done, and her customs and way of being have remained the same. By contrast, the middle-class girl has gained more courage, more responsibility, and a broader consciousness and sense of her obligations."[25] With the long hours that women worked, much of their socialization occurred in that space (see fig. 15). They had learned new ways of relating to men at work. Furthermore, work allowed women to forgo marriage if the opportunity did not present itself in truly favorable terms.

Cepeda celebrated the way the middle-class girl now lived a life more oriented around work and wage earning rather than around home life, but she also found this troubling. And, the ramifications for society were multiple. Working women did not need a large home that required attention and servants to govern. She did not overly concern herself with caring for furniture, plants, or meals. Middle-class women were no longer interested in large families, Cepeda argued. "Without even noticing, we are invaded, especially the middle class, by modernity." The exemplary middle-class family, she wrote, was that of the government employee. Such Mexican middle-class homes could easily compare to a humble home of employees in Texas or California, she wrote. More than cultural influences of one country or another, Cepeda warned, these are simply changing times, and not to be lamented. However, "in order that this active life that she now has not be something reprehensible, she must make another life, more intimate and self-reflective: a Christian life, marked by deep piety."[26]

Although some observers lamented the impact of work on middle-class women, others saw it as an opportunity. Guillermina Llach celebrated the way practices of class distinction had shifted, opening up more possibilities for women to work. She expressed her ideas in a radio address that appeared as an article titled "Women at the Office" in *IDEAS*, the magazine produced by the Atheneum of Mexican Women. Llach acknowledged that until only recently people had looked down on a young woman who worked, because that work was construed as a moral danger. The growing need for two incomes to support a middle-class lifestyle, however,

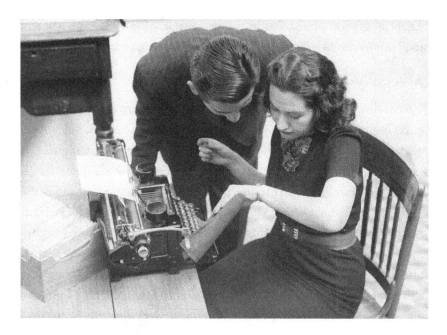

FIG. 15. A secretary in a government office, 1940s. SINAFO #164715. Reproduction authorized by the National Institute of Anthropology and History.

had led women to ignore the "naysayers." Llach identified office workers specifically as women who came from families where, in the past, they would have remained at home:

> The winds of misfortune meant that women had to leave the comforts of home, comforts cultivated from generation to generation, in order to contribute to supporting that home with the fruits of her labor. And yet, among people of a certain social category it was considered humiliating that a woman had to work outside of the home.[27]

The respectability and class identity of families had hinged on whether or not a woman worked outside the home. Such definitions of middle-class respectability had shifted, however, and now women frequently worked outside the home. It remained the task of women's advocates like Guillermina Llach to point to the structural factors that had led to women's increased workforce participation. A perspective like Llach's, which celebrated the beneficial aspects of changes in the perception of middle-class women, stood in contrast to portrayals of office workers that appeared in the movies.

On the Silver Screen and in Their Own Words

Female office workers were not central fixtures of Mexican cinema during the 1940s, but their appearances were telling. Mexican cinema's "Golden Age" celebrated self-sacrificing mothers and the bodies of sexy cabaret girls.[28] It was the era of Sara García and the films that began with *Cuando los hijos se van* (When children leave home, 1941) and its successors that shook the change out of the pockets of viewers willing to weep along with García as she suffered the trials of motherhood. García's trials, like those of other mothers in film during the 1940s, were private and domestic, even when infused with lessons in civic patriotism.[29] Teachers symbolized the mother figure and the nation in films like *Río escondido* (Hidden river, 1948). The 1940s was replete with female bodies for the viewer's pleasure. Dance-hall women who sacrificed their honor in order to raise chaste young ladies for future generations, as in *Salón México* (1948), were flanked by the exotic, hip-gyrating Tongolele in *Han matado a Tongolele* (They've killed Tongolele, 1948) and Ninón Sevilla in *Aventurera* (1949). In the midst of self-sacrificing mothers and cabaret girls, office workers took center stage in *Nosotras, las taquígrafas* (We shorthand typists, 1950), which, rather than reflecting the realities of office employment, echoed the concerns of sociologists and some journalist about the impact of working women on the family.

Nosotras, las taquígrafas, set in an unidentified government office, fits within the cultural current of films that explored modernity, celebrated love and motherhood confined to the domestic realm, and condemned women who worked outside its confines (fig. 16). Based on the eponymous book by Sarah Batiza Berkowitz, the screenplay was written by Alfonso Patiño Gómez. Emilio Gómez Muriel directed the film, which starred Alma Rosa Aguirre, David Silva, and Blanca de Castejón (see fig. 17). As the credits introduce the cast of characters, women punch a time clock and pause to check hair and lipstick before rushing off to work. María Eugenia, the main protagonist, enters the office to inquire about a job. As a part of the interview, she takes dictation and the audience enjoys a quick peek at her

FIG. 16. *Nosotras, las taquígrafas* movie poster, 1950. Courtesy of Steve Sando, Rancho Gordo New World Specialty Foods.

garters. María Eugenia cinches the job and is quickly introduced to the dictation pool, where women sit at desks, waiting to be called into the private office of a male licenciado. The impositions of work rhythms sit uncomfortably with female behavior rooted in the pursuit of marriage, as exemplified by women's competing with each other to take dictation for the more desirable men.

While the film begins with the world of work, it is largely a condemnation of the threats work poses to marriage and domesticity. The office provides the context for women to make decisions about whether to engage in illicit relationships or choose chastity and then marriage. At least two of María Eugenia's co-workers are having an affair. There are two couples: Elsa and licenciado Gálvez, and Berta and licenciado Ortíz. The latter couple has set up a *casa chica* (lit., "little house," but colloquially the home of a woman and a man who is married to someone else). María Eugenia, however, remains chaste. Her co-worker Elsa becomes pregnant by Gálvez. During the course of their courtship Gálvez has become engaged to a respectable young lady and refuses to marry Elsa. He offers her money to "take care" of the pregnancy. Elsa responds that "there are things in life that cannot be paid for with money," and runs out into the street. She considers stepping in front of a streetcar to kill herself, but upon seeing a little boy with his mother she changes her mind, only to wander into traffic, where she is hit by a bus. In representational terms, Elsa paid for the shame associated with having entered into the world of office work. There will be no single mothers in the film.

Meanwhile, back at the office, Ortíz's wife shoots and wounds María Eugenia, having mistaken her for the secretary with whom her husband is having an affair. The gossipy woman who tattled about the affair is only exposed after a hair-pulling brawl in the ladies room. For his part, Ortíz ends his relationship with Berta in order to stand by his wife, who has been detained by the police. Berta goes to the police to confess that she was Ortíz's lover, suggesting that she, and not the wife, should be held guilty. The penultimate scene is a chaste kiss between María Eugenia and David (a typewriter salesman), who will marry, now that he has earned a contract to sell typewriters to the government. Surrounded by the corrupting forces of office work, María Eugenia has proven her chastity and honorability.

FIG. 17. Alma Rosa Aguirre starred as María Eugenia in *Nosotras, las taquígrafas*. SINAFO #331173. Reproduction authorized by the National Institute of Anthropology and History.

The author of the book *Nosotras, las taquígrafas*, Sarah Batiza told quite a different story than the one that appeared in the film. Batiza, a graduate of the MLT, worked as an executive secretary in the Ministry of Finance.[30] *Nosotras, las taquígrafas* received a government-sponsored literary award in 1949.[31] Batiza went on to write several other books, including *Mis "yos" y Larry: Comedia de buen humor* (1958; My multiple selves and Larry: A light-hearted comedy), built on the premise of a secretary who enters into conversation with a man who, quite by accident, has stepped into her office to get out of the rain. The man subjects the secretary to incessant monologue, driven solely by his own psychological needs, and has no interest in an authentic conversation. All the while, the secretary thinks to herself about all the possible responses to the man's egotism, one of which is to kill him. Reviewers did not consider the book funny and panned its use of language as crude.[32]

In *Nosotras, las taquígrafas*, fiction and nonfiction seem to meld so that the novel is also a sharp social commentary on the ways women's position in the workforce subjects them to male privilege. The first-person narration in *Mis "yos" y Larry* and the first-person frame for *Nosotras, las taquígrafas* lend credibility to the events that unfold, and the fictional tone allowed the author to distance herself from the sort of behavior described in the novel. From the book's title to its last page, Batiza creates a "we" for *oficinistas* who, despite widely different class backgrounds, share a common condition. In an opening passage Batiza plays with the boundaries between biography and fiction when she writes, "I offer this book, my dear work colleague, in which I have summarized a series of observations relevant to our situation. It does not matter what your name is, or your age, or the social environment from which you come. You are, like me, a typist."[33]

Batiza's novel echoed 1940s sociological and popular commentary that associated female office workers with "a blurring of borders" of class identity. The government office as a place of work, for Batiza, included women from a wide range of class backgrounds, from the college educated to the daughter of a maid who grew up in a charitable government institution. The central character, María Eugenia, studied to be a secretary to expand her general knowledge, but not with the intention of actually working.

When her father died, she moved in with her sister and brother-in-law, who, while initially able to support her, fall on hard times. María Eugenia gets an office job to contribute to the household and to help support her sister's two sons. A letter of introduction from her brother-in-law to the head of the office helps her get her foot in the door. In contrast to María Eugenia, who would have preferred not to work, another office worker, Blanca is a university student and chooses office work to help pay for her studies and in the hopes of intellectual self-fulfillment.[34]

Although *Nosotras, las taquígrafas* appeared well after the culmination of the Revolution, Batiza construes her story as one of its legacies. Women who work in government offices are daughters of the Revolution, the product of a combination of economic hard times and women's responsibility for family. Bertha, from Torreón, comes from the provincial elite. Her family lost its land and hacienda in a government-sponsored land-redistribution program. Her family migrates to Mexico City, and she must work in order to help maintain their standard of living. Alejandra, another central character, is also from a well-to-do family that has fallen on hard times. Her father, after losing his business in Michoacán, loaded up the family on a second-class bus and moved to Mexico City. Yet another character, Miss González, lives off her measly salary and supports a "self-sacrificing and good mother" and four brothers, at the same time paying the mortgage on a humble little home. As the eldest daughter, Miss González first worked in a clothing store and then took night classes in stenography in hopes of improving her circumstances. As the narrator reflects, "life was like that for many empleadas."[35] The government office, as a place of work, gathered up women from a wide variety of circumstances, from the daughters of elite families fallen on hard times to those who work so that their mother can stay at home in order to raise her siblings. While sociologists of the time saw the "disintegration" of families, Batiza saw the centrality of women's labor in maintaining families in all of the forms they took.

Batiza represents the office as simultaneously factory-like and, as 1940s sociological commentary asserted, infused with middle-class culture. Invoking multiple class identities, she describes office workers as intellectual workers (*obreras del pensamiento*).[36] Batiza's depiction of offices as factory-like serves to emphasize women's exploitation. Women are called to work by the sound of a bell.[37] There is the pressure of being on time and the humiliation of punch cards. "No one likes work," says one of the women.[38] Batiza describes the work environment she would have preferred, one filled with sunlight and music, suggesting middle-class gentility. The women are educated, they are smart, they do their jobs well. They know how to take shorthand, type, file, and organize, and keep the men in the office happy so that the work at hand gets done. The office is portrayed as having an acculturating effect on working-class girls who manage to get an office job. Lupita, though an office worker herself, is the daughter of a servant. Having worked in an office, Lupita says, "I can't marry someone of my same category, now that I have known new worlds."[39] Office work has transformed her sense of her class identity.

Women who worked in offices, Batiza shows, came from a diversity of socioeconomic circumstances, but once employed there they shared a class position unique to women. The organization of work within offices subordinated women to men. Men's position in the workforce allows them to call on women to take dictation, to type up their thoughts, and to send them on errands. The women sit congregated in the dictation pool, a collection of desks in an open area of the office. The female section head coordinates the work, and when a licenciado calls for someone to take dictation, the woman goes to his private office. Jockeying for the favor of a handsome or powerful licenciado is an integral part of office politics. While men are distinguished by the title "licenciado" and referred to by surname, regardless of age or education, women are referred to as "señorita" and by first name. Women could not aspire to a promotion while men could.

In the novel, the subordination of women within the workplace is replicated in society. Women's limited access to higher education and their lower wages make them vulnerable to men, who are portrayed as of a better-off socioeconomic status. Men drive cars while women take public transportation. Men dine in fancy restaurants while women eat at home. Men purchase gifts for the women who work for them, including the nice clothes women "need" for work. This situation is made more difficult, according to Batiza, because of the large number of women looking for work, and employers who therefore can pay low wages. One office worker, Teté, uses a language of class exploitation to describe the gendered division of labor. Men are the bourgeoisie and women the proletariat, she says, both within the office and outside of it.[40] Teté was giving voice to the argument that empleada activists made during the late 1930s in the hopes of gaining recognition for an autonomous women's organization that would represent them vis-à-vis the state.

The privilege that men have over women, argues Blanca, manifests itself as an egotistical psychological need. In between typing up memoranda, the women debate whether or not they should placate men's need to feel superior to women and how much, given their need to keep their jobs, they might be able to resist doing so. Men, they come to agree, feel the need to be in a position of superiority over women, both intellectually and professionally. Men also seek to fulfill their psychological needs through the sexual conquest of women. The narrator, reinforcing the idea of women's economic and gender exploitation, concludes that it was those in most financial need who were most likely to fall to men's sexual advances. The office workers also decry men's tyranny over female bodies, telling women when to diet and how to dress, and exercising control over women's time and physical movement.[41] One woman adds that women are little better off than in days gone by when they were nothing more than parasites.

Batiza exposes how a woman's need to work denied her the status and respectability given to those who remained at home. Whereas in the movie María Eugenia is dating a typewriter salesman, in the book she is dating her coworker Gálvez. When she hears a rumor that he has a fiancée who belongs to an upper-class family from Guadalajara, described as "a nice girl," María Eugenia exclaims, "Do people think that, just because I am a typist, I am not?"[42] The revelation leads to a discussion of the way class status (being from a family with a respectable last name and from "society") is valued over education and merit.[43] Her exclamation is made in the context of a shift in middle-class respectability that, in the past, rested on a woman's presence in the home but is slowly (perhaps too slowly for María Eugenia) transforming to include women's work outside the home. The transition is not yet complete, though, and María Eugenia is stuck. Due largely to their work schedules, the narrator notes, typists only encounter men in a space where those men will not take them as serious marriage partners.

Somewhere between the hot pursuit of marriage and the threat of becoming an old maid, the one character who focuses on self-realization and companionship over marriage finds her way. When the story opens, we learn that Blanca thinks marriage is humiliating, especially because it implies taking money from a man.[44] Of all the women, she is the most cynical about men and provides a biting taxonomy of male predators in the office. It is only when she finds her own voice, and the capacity to write about her experiences and those of the women around her, that she opens up to an intimate relationship with licenciado Rivera, a co-worker. The relationship is described as a "complement" to her own aspirations and interests. This relationship, marked by camaraderie, emerges at the same moment that Blanca decides to type not only the words dictated to her but also her own thoughts and observations about the world of shorthand typists—perhaps the very book the reader holds in her hands. The possibility of equality between a man and a woman at work transforms that work into something pleasurable: "Not only did she feel a love for her work, but the very sound of the typewriter rang in her ears like celestial music."[45] The transformative nature of a relationship between a man and a woman marked by camaraderie coincides with a shift in the class associations of her work. The din produced by row upon row of typists recedes as Blanca, as an author, works to the music of the typewriter.

Batiza's treatment of motherhood distinguishes *Nosotras, las taquígrafas* from earlier discussions of women, work, and motherhood. At the turn of the century, female domesticity anchored middle-class identity, even for women who worked outside the home. During the 1920s, progressive women like María Ríos Cárdenas and Leonor Llach advanced the possibility that a mother might work outside the home if she needed to. Batiza introduces the idea that motherhood outside marriage is not only dignified but that it can be empowering. Rather than providing a prescriptive definition of motherhood, Batiza offers a portrayal of motherhood as a lived experience, with all its complexities. In one section of the book the narrator discusses two varieties of motherhood: "motherhood accepted as solely a reflection or consequence of love for a man . . . and the second, motherhood as an intimate and indestructible longing that emerges from a woman herself." The fundamental difference between the two types of motherhood is the difference between dependency and independence. A woman can define herself by the man who is the father of the child or by the energy and life force that comes from herself. Batiza writes: "Maternity, though a primordial and natural function, is considered a shameful affront. Isn't it worth asking: should woman love maternity independent of its cause? Should she love the child in the man? Should she love the man in the child? Or, should she love the child because it is of her own self?"[46] The remainder of the novel responds to these questions.

María Eugenia faces these questions when she becomes pregnant. Batiza puts every type of solution within María Eugenia's reach, including a proposal of marriage from yet another co-worker who offers to protect her public respectability. The young man with whom she became pregnant offers her money for an abortion, or to continue as his lover, both of which she rejects. María Eugenia also considers suicide, but instead chooses to become a single mother. "And that night the woman in María Eugenia who had loved, and for having done so had become a mother, died, leaving space for the emergence of the mother who waited anxiously to hold close to her heart the child who would dignify her existence."[47] While the film version eliminated the possibility of single motherhood as respectable, in the book single motherhood is a metaphor for women's autonomy and dignity. This celebration of single motherhood stands in stark contrast to sociological studies that collected data on divorce and cohabitation rates, shrinking family size, and women's growing disinclination to marry. Batiza does not counter angst about the family by portraying working women who want to marry and have children, but rather by bringing dignity to single motherhood.

Although Batiza's book provided a complex portrait of single motherhood and women's working lives, when her book was discussed in the newspapers the message shifted. Poet and journalist Margarita Paz Paredes reviewed the book for *El Nacional* in 1949. "All women have a mother inside them," she wrote, but she failed to mention that the protagonist has a child out of wedlock. Paz Paredes praised the book for its social commentary and for making people more aware of "a little-understood sector of the workforce." In her review she wrote, "Undoubtedly this novel is no simple hobby, or something that can be dismissed under the old concept of 'art for art's sake,' rather it puts forth a position: the dignity of the woman who works. And, specifically, the dignity of that sector considered the most frivolous: the shorthand typist."[48]

Like Blanca in her novel, Batiza used her education and the power of the written word to engage in personal and societal transformation. She was part of a decades-long history of office workers who wrote about their condition and contributed to new conceptions of women's relationship to work, domesticity, and motherhood. Batiza offered an economic, social, and sexual critique of the subjugation of women. She also imagined women who defined their self-worth independent of men. Batiza does not label any of the characters as feminist. As her title implies, however, she charts a collective female space and shared identity: a *nosotras*. Durring the 1940s that shared identity informed women's activism as they mobilized to address the challenge of balancing work and child care.

Women Mobilize for Child Care

Having examined a variety of ways that different genres represented work and motherhood, we will shift now to how female office workers mobilized to address the challenge of balancing these responsibilities. In contrast to the decade of the 1930s, during the 1940s office workers' activism shifted from the streets to union halls. By organizing within government worker unions, women successfully forced their employer to recognize their dual roles as mothers and workers. Nichole Sanders demonstrates that by 1940 women employed in the Ministry of Public Assistance had pressured policymakers to acknowledge the political expediency of working in partnership with women.[49] In order for the thousands of women in government offices to be able to work on issues of importance to policymakers, they had to address how to support working mothers. The fight for equal pay for equal work and respect for seniority had been recognized in the public-employee statute, and public employees took related grievances to the TFCA. Compliance with recognized rights continued to be an issue. The statute also provided for maternity leave, though it is not clear how frequently women availed themselves of this provision. In the first five years of cases presented to the TFCA, no one filed for the enforcement of maternity leave.

The fight for day care, however, continued. Government employees advocated for the rights of working mothers in the 1942 social security law, which called for day care, as well as insurance for illness and maternity, incapacitation, old age, and other eventualities. In contrast to U.S. and European social security laws, Mexican social security did not provide unemployment insurance, though employers were obliged to cover three months' wages plus one month for each year of employment to those who were laid off. The social security law was passed in 1942 but was not implemented until the following year due to employers' and workers' resistance. The FSTSE protested against wage deductions meant to pay for the social security system. On July 20, 1943, workers and employees demonstrated in the Zócalo. The government response led to violence and bloodshed that resulted, perhaps intentionally, in the withering away of resistance to social security deductions.[50] Obliged to pay into the social security fund, women hoped that their specific needs would be met. In a 1942 speech addressing the social security law, Otilia Zambrano, a high-level administrator in the Ministry of Public Education, called attention to the ways women's civil status informed their legal rights:

> What marks the distinctly advanced revolutionary character of the social security law is the legal concession of insurance benefits not only to the legitimate wife, but also to the concubine who has lived over five years of marital life with the insured individual. In this way, the new law leaves behind the absurd pseudo-moralist and antiquated dead-weight of the past, and situates things in the appropriate setting, in accordance with inevitable realities.[51]

Zambrano saw the social security law as addressing the contemporary reality of working women. Women also wrote to the president, as was the case with Guadalupe Olvera H., who worked in the Ministry of Public Assistance and asked that the president not forget the needs of single mothers, who, she argued, were often legally marginalized.[52]

Zambrano also fought for day care. Her story allows us to see how women who had been thwarted in the 1930s in their efforts to create an autonomous space to advance women's causes continued to fight within unions during the 1940s. In February 1940 the National Union of Education Workers (Sindicato Nacional de Trabajadores de la Educación, SNTE) offered Zambrano the position of secretary of women's affairs. Zambrano, who was then embroiled in the conflict between national and local branches of the union, and in her own labor dispute before the TFCA, turned down the position. In a letter she expressed concern that if she were to occupy the position it would appear as political favoritism and self-interest. Union section number 3, to which Zambrano belonged, was in dispute with the leader of the national union, Manuel González. The following April, Zambrano attended the 1940 STERM congress and presented women's workplace concerns. She wrote several pieces advocating for working mothers, including one titled "Care and Support for Women as Mothers."[53] Handwritten notes in the document's margins identify different people in attendance, each of whom would raise a different point: Zambrano, María Luisa Ross (also employed by the SEP), and a third unidentified individual.

In "Care and Support for Women as Mothers," Zambrano cogently argued for resources for mothers, regardless of their civil status. The way she constructed her arguments echoes the intellectual thought that had emerged out of female office workers' movement over the prior decade or more. "Mothers have been celebrated by poets," she began, "but little has been done for them." Zambrano was concerned for women who had children out of wedlock, "especially when to have a child outside marriage was considered an irreparable wrong, as if it were a huge sin. Fortunately, in our times, motherhood is respectable and respected as a noble state, without stingy prejudices, without stupid opinions." She praised the evolution of ideas about single mothers and pointed out that little had thus far been done to support them. Although "we ought to confess, with great satisfaction, that our revolutionary laws already provide protection for mothers," promises are not enough:

The rest promised to expectant mothers is not enough. In order to address poor prenatal conditions and high infant mortality rates, expectant mothers need sanitary living conditions, peace and quiet, adequate housing, and prenatal education. It is not much to ask for maternity homes to be established, where women who work, and those who are supported by workers, would find a convenient and warm place to receive their children.

Support for women ought to continue once the mother has given birth and returned to work, she argued, and day care should be a priority. Women should have the assurance that their children "have been attended to with care and diligence, that they have been fed, clothed, and have had a place to sleep."[54]

The SNTE again offered Zambrano the position of secretary of the women's section, which she accepted on June 28, 1940. Wasting no time, on July 5 she held a meeting for the women of her sector to discuss their needs and formulate an action plan. Scattered evidence, such a letter from 1949, shows that Zambrano wrote to the women employed at the National Institute for Anthropology and History and related offices to announce classes in cooking, regional dances, swimming, and nursing, as well as a new day care on Plaza Domingo and a discounted grocery warehouse. Aurora Reyes, a STERM member, was also an early advocate for day care for teachers and public employees and participated in the founding of two day-care centers, one at the Normal School and the other at the Alberto Tejeda School.[55]

Demands for child care and maternity insurance percolated up through the SNTE. In 1941, 1945, and 1947, women working in government offices succeeded in getting the SEP to set up day-care facilities. They requested funds to pay teachers and personnel to staff the day care and asked that the union pay for meals for the children. The day care, on the sixth floor of a building located at 21 Brazil Street, consisted of one large and four small rooms that housed the *encargada*, a social worker, four nannies (*niñeras*), and thirty-five children. In 1947 the SNTE made a successful request for an additional day care, with twenty-seven cradles and fifty mattresses. Beyond those served, they argued, there was demand for one hundred more spaces for the children of government employees, including administrative staff, service workers, and teachers. There also seemed to be a need for better working conditions for the day-care workers themselves, who rarely stayed on the job for long. In 1946 the Mexican Social Security Institute (est. 1943) established a day care for its employees as well.[56]

The FSTSE women's sector became involved as well. In November 1945, Deputy Ruffo Figueroa, secretary general of the FSTSE, and Rebecca Herrera, from the women's sector of the FSTSE, engaged in high-level conversations and persuaded ministers to provide day care in all government ministries and departments. Feminine Action "has been asking for this for a long time," Herrera reminded them.[57] President Ávila Camacho pledged his support. When the FSTSE followed up on the conversations, they were assured that progress was being made and were pointed to the Division of General Statistics, which had already begun construction of the day care that would be inaugurated in April 1946.

Day-care advocates took their cause to the press. Social worker Josefina Gaona wrote an article for *El Universal* in 1945 that argued, "Mexican women have the right to work and they have the right to be a mother." Gaona acknowledged that federal labor law had room for improvement but said that a lot would be accomplished by simply enforcing the law that already existed. In addition, she wrote, the Department of Labor needed to engage in extensive research into the situation of working women. The Ministry of Public Health also had work to do, she pointed out. To support women in their dual role as worker and mother, there would need to be day-care facilities, kindergartens, and homes for working women at or near the places where large numbers of women were employed. Ever vigilant, public employees also rallied around ensuring the quality of existing day-care facilities. In 1945 more than two thousand mothers, children in tow, protested the cost of day care at the eleven government-sponsored centers and held as responsible the director of child welfare, Dr. Daniel Martinez. The women allied with journalist Consuelo Uranga to petition for presidential intervention in the dispute.[58]

Day care fit within the intellectual and political program that public employees had developed over the course of several decades and informed the continued fight for suffrage. In anticipation of the election of Miguel Alemán as president, a crowd of five thousand women, many of them government workers, gathered on July 27, 1945, at Arena México. Among them were many who had been active in the women's and public-employee movements of the 1930s and had risen through union ranks. The following list shows that union affiliation continued to be central to their public presentation: Graciana Becerril (CTM); Rebeca Herrera (FSTSE); Aurora Fernández (CNC); Estela Jiménez Esponda (Communist Party); Celia Ramírez (the Federal District Women's League); and María Guadalupe Ramírez (the CNOP's popular sector).[59] While these women made public appearances out of duty, they used those appearances to strengthen their demand for the vote. At the same time, Becerril, along with other female leaders, published a program of activities for the 1946–52 presidential term that continued to try to hold the Revolution to its promises: "If the Revolution considers itself competent enough to build a well-organized future, it cannot permit that a large percentage of the population of the Republic, women, believe that the word 'justice' is the slogan for the desperate."

The platform for the 1946–52 presidential term included a declaration of principles that reiterated the need to acknowledge women's economic production and reproductive labor. Women's reproductive and economic production must, they argued, exist in harmony. "Our concrete objective," they wrote, "is that raising children be compatible with women's economic, scientific, and artistic activities."[60] Women, they claimed, were the best equipped to lead the work toward achieving their goals, and the platform called for parity in government administration. Furthermore, women should lead the Ministry of Public Education and the Ministry of Public Health. "Men cannot be the only ones to represent the species, because they are not the only ones to produce that species, and so women must be directly involved in the socioeconomic administration of society."[61] Drawing on the idea of women's moral authority, they called for the elimination of dishonest, unprofessional, and inefficient employees. They asked for the elimination of distinctions between married and unmarried women in state and federal legal codes. The Federal Labor Law and the Agrarian Code should be reformed to grant expanded rights and protections for women. Their demands also included resources for education, health and welfare services, housing, access

FIG. 18. Alumni gathering at the "Miguel Lerdo de Tejada" Commercial School for Young Ladies. Paula Nava, Amalia de Castillo Ledón, Leonor Llach, and Adelina Zendejas. Joaquín Cacho García, *Cifra de oro de la escuela "Lerdo" (1903–1953)* (Mexico City: La Escuela, 1953), 82.

to water, drainage, light, parks, and cooperatives. The advocacy of the many female government workers, including women like Leonor Llach, in favor of an expanded role in government and for support for working mothers was, in part, addressed as the result of government workers continuing the push within the space of unions (see fig. 18).

Day care rose to the level of a national priority within the FSTSE by the close of the decade. Between 1949 and 1953 the FSTSE built twelve day-care facilities for federal employees in Mexico City. Day care was offered in the Ministry of Finance, the Ministry of Communications and Public Works, the Ministry of National Economy, the Ministry of Hydraulic Resources (est. 1946), the Ministry of National Marine (est. 1940), the Department of the Federal District, the Agrarian Department, and the Supreme Court. In addition, two apartment buildings for government employees offered day care, one named "President Juárez" and the other "President Alemán." In all, more than a thousand children were taken in, cared for, and provided with food, medical attention, and preschool education.[62] Women who had been at the center of the 1930s government-employee and women's movements continued to be activists during the 1940s. The conservative political turn that is visible at the level of national politics, pro-business policy, and union power struggles should not lead us to assume that women's activism died out during the 1940s. The location of that activism shifted. During the 1940s sociologists celebrated modernity and fretted about the disintegration of the Mexican family. The tragedies of working women flashed across the silver screen. Movie viewers were treated to visions of smartly dressed secretaries and relished women's cattiness while admonitions against women working outside the home seemed to fall on deaf ears. Women's role in supporting the household, both working- and middle-class, was a fact of modern life.

Conclusion

From Angel to Office Worker shows how the transformation of women's waged labor led to new configurations of middle-class identity in Mexico. Rather than limiting the notion of the middle class solely to objective criteria (occupation, income bracket, consumer habits) or political engagement, I have explored at least two additional ways middle-class identity has been constructed. In other words, I have chosen to look for insight into Mexican notions of middle-class identity by focusing on the variety of ways historical actors invoked the term. At the turn of the century, Mexicans began to consider what options middle-class women had for work outside the home. They began to imagine female office workers as occupying a middle space. The *El Imparcial* articles on feminism in the year 1900, for example, situated female office workers between cigarreras and seamstresses on the one hand and doctors on the other. By the 1920s, observers regularly identified female office workers as middle class, though studies like that conducted by Jesús Silva Herzog suggest that many women, with the wages they earned, may have fallen outside the middle class in material terms. During the 1930s the number of women working in government offices continued to grow (their numbers outpaced the number of female teachers in 1938). There are indications, however, that the market had become saturated and commentators began to describe female office workers as middle class while they threw that status into doubt when referring to empleaditas (office girls) who aspired to a middle-class lifestyle. The simultaneous assertion and questioning of the middle-class identity of office workers persisted through the 1940s.

The construction of middle-class identity also occurred based on a shifting constellation of gender norms. Key components of middle-class identity can be traced back to nineteenth-century relations of production and reproduction that continued to shape that identity even as women's productive roles changed. In the 1890s, Mexico City residents began to speak of the need for middle-class women to work outside the home, and during the 1910s dutiful daughters were considered respectable when they entered the workforce to support their siblings. The wages earned by daughters allowed mothers to stay at home to raise younger children. During the 1920s a select group of women who themselves worked in government offices and had access to publishing venues continued to assert women's right to work and extended that right to mothers. Domesticity remained a powerful reference nevertheless. The 1930s debates over women's right to work in government offices often hinged on assumptions about whether domesticity and work were compatible for middle-class women. Critiques of women's consumer habits and frivolous purchases were one expression of this attitude. Office work continued to be associated with middle-class identity during the 1940s, and journalist Teresa de Cepeda summed up nicely people's perceptions when she wrote that middle-class girls had become less concerned with home and large families and had gained "a broader consciousness and sense of their obligations."[1] Women's entrance into office work provoked important shifts in middle-class identity, however the obligations of motherhood, both as a material commitment and as a social restriction, continued to inform middle-class identity for women.

The study of empleadas públicas poses questions about women's relationship to class identity. Government offices employed people from a wide range of socioeconomic backgrounds. Some women earned salaries that permitted a middle-class lifestyle, while many others earned working-class wages. Civil status, household formation, professional mobility, and the hazards of the national economy all played a role in women's living standards. The gendered nature of these factors meant women could have a different relationship to class identity than men. From journalistic reports in the early 1900s to government studies conducted in the 1920s and 1930s, observers noted the gap between female office workers' living standards and middle-class identity. Public discourse offered contradictory messages about the class identity of female office workers in particular. While some observers wrote of the "bureaucratic proletariat," others questioned the office workers' precarious relationship to the middle class, a class identity they seemed as likely to aspire to as to actually inhabit.

That female office workers could claim middle-class identity despite modest salaries is explained by the various forms of capital that women acquired simply by becoming office workers. Pierre Bourdieu identifies multiple forms of capital that work in concert to define class identity. In addition to economic capital, class is also defined by social, cultural, political, and symbolic capital.[2] Women who attended commercial schools and took jobs in government offices—even those who did not come from the middle class or earn middle-class wages—gained access to each of these forms of capital in ways that associated them with middle-class identity. Women who attended commercial schools became part of female networks of power that connected them to jobs, resources, and influence. They gained political capital through participation in official government campaigns, reform movements, and student politics. In addition to gaining practice in middle-class forms of political engagement as students, women exercised citizenship despite being denied the legal right to vote in federal elections (which they did not gain until 1953). These forms of capital shaped women's class identity in early twentieth-century Mexico and help us move beyond conceptions of class identity based only on the occupation of the male head of household.

One of the goals of this book is to bring the middle class into Mexican labor studies. We have a rich understanding of middle-class politics, consumption, and manners. We also know the history of professional occupations like nurse, social worker, and teacher.[3] Scholars have combined analysis of labor regimes and social history in ways that are instructive for the history of office work. Historians have argued that labor regimes, including worker acceptance of authority and hierarchy, shape worker experience and mobilization. We have seen that gender informs worker deference and defiance.[4] The approaches scholars have used to examine factory labor are also useful for understanding office work. The historical development of these different workplaces means that while factories and offices alike were shaped by workers' tacit acceptance of hierarchy, management authority, and rules at work, the moment at which resistance to such regimes developed was determined by factors unique to each work environment. The peak of government worker organizing came a decade after that of industrial workers. Resistance to authority was also different for women than it was for men. Whereas male government workers began organizing in the 1920s, female office workers developed a consciousness of themselves as workers during the 1920s and organized as such during the 1930s.

By considering the history of office workers within the context of labor history, we also see that female office workers developed a unique critique of the workplace. Occupational segregation of the workforce, women's lower earning capacity, and the culture of gender relations at work all positioned women in subordinate positions to men inside and outside of the office. From María Ríos Cárdenas's 1921 novel *Atavismo* to Sarah Batiza's *Nosotras, las taquígrafas* in 1950, women developed an increasingly detailed portrait of that subordination. At work, women reported to men, took orders from them, listened to their words, wrote them down, and compiled them in reports that they sent off in the mail or filed away. Sometimes women played the dual role of worker and lover. Many women, when they left the office at the end of the day, went out into society with a few coins in their pocket and mounting debts at the local dress shop. They encountered men from a position of socioeconomic subordination. Licenciados drove cars, purchased gifts for their secretaries, and invited young women from the typing pool out to lunch, but they married society girls. In the 1930s, activists repeatedly used the argument that women constituted a class unique in their relationship to production and reproduction. Because women constitute a class on their own, they argued, they merited a specific political sector for women. Party officials and government representatives did not agree.

Scholars have found that in some industries occupational segregation has limited women's capacity to successfully make labor demands. On the other hand, the concentration of women in specific jobs or industries has also been conducive to women's successful organizing. Between 1890 and 1910, female office workers in Mexico integrated into a male-dominated workplace, but their concentration in certain jobs and offices limited their capacity to establish networks. The rapid increase in the number of women in government offices during the 1920s contributed to a critical mass. However, occupational segregation alone, no matter how many workers we are talking about, does not lead to solidarity or to successful protest. Increasingly, women came to know each other and to recognize their shared experiences as they participated in school politics and cultural events and, once they were employed, by circulating through different government offices. During the 1920s clerical workers attended the growing number of women's conferences. Women also formed networks through participating on sports teams, in official government campaigns, and cultural events. Even the newspaper-sponsored competitions connected clerical workers to mid-level functionaries who sponsored their candidacy and to the co-workers who would vote women to the top of the list to star in a film. As with the working-class neighborhood residents studied by John Lear, street vendors studied by Mario Barbosa Cruz, or the coffee sorters in Veracruz studied by Heather Fowler-Salamini, overlapping worlds of work and community shaped people's daily lives, their sense of a common cause, and their efforts to exert control over working conditions.[5]

Public employees faced a particular set of legal parameters that shaped their work experiences and labor organizing. Government employees' unionization efforts followed a different trajectory than that of workers. Article 123 of the Constitution of 1917, argues Aurora Gómez-Galvarriato, crystallized gains already made by workers in the prior decade, and did not represent the height of worker organizing. In contrast, public employees, because they were not explicitly covered under Article 123, stepped up their activism to demand the same rights afforded to obreros. As early as the teacher strike in 1919 and throughout the 1920s, teachers and government workers were repeatedly told that as state employees they did not have the right to strike. This did not stop them from trying. Samuel León and Ignacio Marván argue that the 1931 Federal Labor Law "concluded a period of ambiguities in the realm of labor." For government employees, the passage of the law, and their exclusion from it, reiterated ambiguities regarding their rights and heightened and focused their struggle. The Federal Labor Law served as a catalyst for subsequent organizing of government workers, just as it did for the domestic workers studied by Mary Goldsmith Connelly. Unlike domestic workers, who were covered by the Federal Labor Law, government workers mobilized during the 1930s despite lacking a legal right to do so.[6]

Women in many countries have not always found organized labor supportive of their specific demands. As Annelise Orleck has shown for the United States, working women found limited support within the American Federation of Labor and thus allied with middle- and upper-class women interested in supporting the labor, educational, and cultural aspirations of working women.[7] In Mexico as well, when faced with less than a full welcome in organized labor, women turned to other women as allies. The Mexican Communist Party privileged class over gender, leading Elena Torres and Refugio García to create alternative organizations like the Mexican Feminist Commission. The Regional Confederation of Mexican Workers also had a mixed relationship with women, first declaring their support for women in 1919 and then making some attempts in the 1920s to integrate them into their ranks. Shortly thereafter, the Mexican Regional Labor Confederation actively discriminated against women workers to the benefit of men, in Mexico City as well as in Jalisco and Veracruz. Nor were women able to make their voices heard in the organizations formed by high-level functionaries, such as the National Confederation of Public Administration and the Mexican Association of Official Employees. Many turned to the women's conferences held during the 1920s, allying themselves with professional women, teachers, and other office workers. As María Teresa Fernández Aceves has shown for women in Jalisco, women in Mexico City also formed cross-class alliances.[8]

The history of the feminist movement in Mexico has been told as organizational and political history, but it is also labor history. Clerical workers filled the seats of congresses dedicated to women's issues throughout the 1920s because they found little space within the public-employee movement to voice their demands. As Sofía Villa de Buentello reported, the ranks of 1920s women's congresses were filled with secretaries, typists, and other office workers who sought equal pay for equal work, the consideration of women as head of household, and the elimination of barriers to professional advancement. Office workers also sought to ease their dual role as worker and mother. They argued that they too deserved the rights granted to obreras in Article 123 of the Constitution of 1917 and called for maternity leave. They advocated for day care. Their arguments for equality at work and for resources to support working mothers informed the broader feminist movement. As the public-employee movement picked up steam during the 1930s, women sought to shape any proposed legislation that might benefit their working conditions and argued for equal treatment for women regardless of civil status. Female government workers were so successful in their efforts to change working conditions that men joined in their efforts, as was the case with workers in the Ministry of Public Education.

Government employees were uniquely positioned to contribute to the women's movement. Their location within the government workforce, their social worlds and cultural activities, their salary reductions and required membership in the political party, and their virtually obligatory membership in employee unions all contributed to their capacity to mobilize for change. As a populist politician, President Cárdenas paid attention to women's demands for national suffrage. He also did so because female office workers had taken to the streets, left work to attend meetings, insisted on action on the part of high-level party and government functionaries, and captured the attention of the press. The ability of the Sole Front for Women's Rights to demand the attention of the president was based in part on the membership of visible female government employees and of rank-and-file clerical workers. The power of female office workers to mobilize may also help to explain resistance to women's suffrage. The most frequent argument put forth by opponents of women's suffrage was that women were Catholic and, therefore, reactionary.[9] At the same time, the mass mobilization of female government workers was also a significant concern to many government functionaries and politicians.

The history of empleada activism highlights the relationship between working-class and middle-class labor mobilization in Mexico, a theme that has been developed by María Teresa Fernández Aceves.[10] Working- and middle-class activism overlapped in ways practical, political, and rhetorical. The working-class labor movement served both as a source of experience and as inspiration for many government employees, including women. The young women who petitioned Señora Carmen Romero Rubio de Díaz for a teacher's assistant for their stenography class in 1900 located themselves within the working-class labor force. Their petition was a part of the practice of petitions of seamstresses and tobacco workers. During the 1920s, the heyday of labor mobilization, individuals like Elvira Trueba, Gudelia Gómez, and others came from the trenches of working-class labor mobilization—Trueba in the railway strikes, and Gómez in the Ericsson telephone conflicts. They learned about organizing through experience, and brought those skills to the government-employee labor movement. As activists during the 1930s, they met and collaborated with women like Otilia Zambrano, who came from a more solidly middle-class background. Zambrano had built professional networks at the "Miguel Lerdo de Tejada" Commercial School and, inspired by the "Madero generation" and the activism of teachers in the Ministry of Public Education, parlayed those professional ties and experiences to become a leader in the public-employee and women's rights movements.

The Mexican case provides insight into how class identity has shaped women's organizations. Mexican women clerical workers organized in greater numbers and to greater effect than in the United States. In the United States, as Sharon Strom argues, "the working-class connotations of unions, the hostility of most of the dominant unions to women, and the middle-class origins (or aspirations) of many clerical workers made unionism an unworkable strategy."[11] In Mexico clerical workers claimed middle-class status and respectability, but this did not necessarily mean they avoided unions. Government employees saw the heightened activism and growing power of the Mexican working class during the 1920s as a political opportunity.

Workers had made significant gains, and public-sector employees associated themselves enough with organized labor to secure the same rights. Labor activism opened doors for professional mobility for some women. For Mexican clerical workers, during the 1920s and 1930s union activism provided one path to better working conditions and improved chances of consolidating the economic basis for middle-class status. Through union activism, women had a platform to fight for equal pay for equal work, respect for seniority, and professional training that would allow them to move up the ranks. This is not to say that that they were fully successful. In the midst of the fight for day care in the 1940s, women still lamented the lack of enforcement of the right to maternity leave. Nor is it to say there were not divisions, class-based and political, within the ranks of organized government employees. The class differences between clerical workers and teachers, for example, caused tensions during the 1930s. Nevertheless, in comparison to women's movements in other countries, Mexico is unique in the power clerical workers exercised and the degree to which the federal government supported them.

To distinguish between middle-class women who mobilized for political rights and working women who made practical demands contributes to a false dichotomy that obfuscates the extent to which the Mexico City women's movement was a labor movement. The Mexico City women's movement was many things, and not only about work, but women's entrance into the public-sector workforce gave life to a feminist critique that sat at the heart of the women's movement. The conservative shift in government in the 1940s coincided with a conservative shift in cultural production and the portrayal of working women in film, sociological literature, and the press. At the same time, women who worked in government offices continued to write, and some, like Sarah Batiza, contributed to middle-class respectability for office workers. Batiza also contributed to dignifying the role of single mothers. During the 1940s women became adept at maneuvering within unions in order to press their demands, as was the case, for example, with day care. Public-employee activism on behalf of working mothers may have echoed a conservative message that emphasized motherhood, but it was also a success for working women who, since the 1890s, had sought to combine work and motherhood in ways that allowed them to claim middle-class identity.

From the women who may have identified as the *angel del hogar* in the late nineteenth century to those who willingly joined the burocracia femi- nina in the 1940s, office workers made crucial contributions to the Mexican women's movement. At the beginning of the period, work and feminism were so closely identified that observers labeled middle-class women's work- force participation as feminism. Women did not embrace feminism as an abstract idea to argue for special protections or equal rights. Rather, based on their experiences at work, they gave voice to a new female consciousness. Some called this feminism and others did not. Writing and literacy were the tools of the trade for clerical workers, and a select group published on women's changing social roles and their labor demands. As their numbers grew, rank-and-file clerical workers allied with women who, by the 1930s, had gained some authority within the bureaucratic structure. Together they empowered the feminist movement by leveraging their obligatory member- ship in the political party that ruled the workplace. Doubts about whether middle-class women should work outside of the home were replaced with the fight for day care so that they could fulfill their dual roles as worker and as mother. From activism in the streets in the 1930s to union halls in the 1940s, clerical workers developed a feminist critique of the socioeconomic underpinnings of women's subordination to men.

NOTES

ABBREVIATIONS

AGN	Archivo General de la Nación, Mexico City
AHPD	Archivo Histórico Porfirio Díaz, Mexico City
AHSCJN	Archivo Histórico de la Suprema Corte de Justicia de la Nación, Mexico City
AHSEP	Archivo Histórico de la Secretaría de Educación Pública, Mexico City
AHSS	Archivo Histórico de la Secretaría de Salubridad, Mexico City
ALR	Abelardo L. Rodríguez, Presidentes
AM	Antiguo Magisterio
BMLT	Biblioteca Miguel Lerdo de Tejada, Mexico City
CEHMOM	Centro de Estudios Históricos del Movimiento Obrero Mexicano
DE	Departamento Escolar
DESIC	Dirección de Enseñanza Superior e Investigación Científica
DETIC	Departamento de Escuelas Técnicas, Industriales y Comerciales
DGA	Dirección General de Administración, Secretaría de Gobernación Siglo XX
DGIPS	Dirección General de Investigaciones Políticas y Sociales, Secretaría de Gobernación Siglo XX
DT	Departamento del Trabajo
EPG	Emilio Portes Gil, Presidentes
INAH	Instituto Nacional de Antropología e Historia
IPBA	Instrucción Pública y Bellas Artes
JFCA	Junta Federal de Conciliación y Arbitraje
LCR	Lázaro Cárdenas del Ríos, Presidentes
MAC	Manuel Ávila Camacho, Presidentes
MAV	Miguel Alemán Valdés, Presidentes

OC	Obregón Calles, Presidentes
OZ	Otilia Zambrano, Archivos de Particulares
PAL	Propiedad Artística y Literaria
POR	Pascual Ortiz Rubio, Presidentes
RJIP	Ramo Justicia e Instruccion Pública
SEP	Secretaría de Educación Pública
TFCA	Tribunal Federal de Conciliación y Arbitraje

INTRODUCTION

1. Contemporary portrayals of middle-class women who work include G. Loaeza, *Las reinas de Polanco*; S. Loaeza, *Clases medias y política*; Gilbert, *Mexico's Middle Class*.

2. Until the twenty-first century, historians of Latin America, more interested in the rural and urban working classes, paid little attention to the middle class. See Jiménez, "Elision of the Middle Class." For historical studies of Mexican middle-class women in the domestic sphere, see Arrom, *The Women of Mexico City*, chapter 1; French, "Prostitutes and Guardian Angels." Middle-class women's presence in the home included income-generating activity; see Francois, *A Culture of Everyday Credit*, 6, 162–63, 187. There is a rich literature on female reformers; for Mexico see Sanders, *Gender and Welfare*. For Brazil, see Besse, *Restructuring Patriarchy*, 84–86, 147–49. For Argentina see Guy, *Women Build the Welfare State*. On female reformers in Chile, see Rosemblatt, *Gendered Compromises*, 240–58. There is an extensive literature on women in the teaching profession in Mexico. Studies that mention the class status of teachers include Galván Lafarga, *Soledad compartida*; Galván and López, *Entre imaginarios y utopías*; and Bazant, *Historia de la educación durante el Porfiriato*. For a review of multiple studies on female reformers in Latin America see Porter, "Women, Children and Welfare."

3. Arrom, *The Women of Mexico City*, 166; and French, *A Peaceful and Working People*, 63–85. For a discussion of respectability and domestic space, see Lipsett-Rivera, *Gender and the Negotiation of Daily Life in Mexico*, 65–66, 240. Female domesticity has been key to middle-class identity in many historical contexts. For Victorian Britain, see Langland, *Nobody's Angels*; and for Brazil, see Leite da Silva Dias, *Power and Everyday Life*. Leite da Silva Dias's attention to race adds depth to discussions of women's labor, respectability, and class distinction.

4. LaGreca, *Rewriting Womanhood*, 9–11, 43.

5. A rich literature on reading, education, and gender has developed. See Montero Sánchez, *La construcción simbólica de las identidades sociales*, 92–94; Infante Vargas, "De lectoras y redactoras," 183–94; Clark de Lara and Speckman Guerra, *La república de las letras*, 184, 190, 201; and Ramos Escandón, "Género e identidad femenina y nacional."

6. Shifts in the economic value of women's labor in the United States are discussed in Jensen, "Butter Making and Economic." The generational shift of artisans into clerical work in the United States is examined in DeVault, *Sons and Daughter of Labor*, 68, 97–99. On women's entrance into government jobs in the United States, see Sondik Aron, *Ladies and Gentlemen of the Civil Service*, 46–71, 102.

7. On the role of race and class in shaping women's workforce participation in Mexico, see Arrom, *The Women of Mexico City*, 157–58, 161; Pérez Toledo, *Trabajadores, espacio urbano, y sociabilidad*, 114–15; Pérez Toledo, "Trabajadores urbanos"; see also Pérez Toledo, "El trabajo femenino." Women's income-generating work at home is discussed in Francois, *A Culture of Everyday Credit*, 104–8. For discussions of how race and class shaped women's workforce participation in Brazil, see Lauderdale Graham, "Making the Private Public"; and Leite da Silva Dias, *Power and Everyday Life*, 71–75. The intersection of race, class and gender in conceptions of respectability in the United States is laid out in Higginbotham, "African-American Women's History."

8. Arrom, *The Women of Mexico City*, 166, 171. Teacher training education is discussed in Bazant, *Historia de la educación durante el Porfiriato*, 115, 13. Although women in religious life were often held up as the ideal of female seclusion, those women in fact played an active role in economic and political life, an argument made for Mexico by Chowning, "The Catholic Church and the Ladies of the Vela Perpetua"; Chowning, *Rebellious Nuns*; and for Peru, Burns, *Colonial Habits*. The ban on women's employment in government offices is mentioned in Arrom, *The Women of Mexico City*, 163.

9. Economic conditions during the Porfiriato are addressed in Katz, "Mexico," 63–65, 28–30. Chassen-López questions the validity of national statistics in "Cheaper Than Machines." Her study of Oaxaca found that women comprised 15 percent of agricultural *jornaleros* (day laborers) in 1907. Women were also landowners, wage laborers, sharecroppers, and communal landholders; see Rendón Gan, *Trabajo de hombres y trabajo de mujeres*, 109–11. A mere 1.3 percent of economically active women (compared to 72 percent of men) worked in agricultural production in 1895, and 8 percent (compared to 73 percent of men) in 1910. Immigration data are from Porter, *Working Women in Mexico City*, 6.

10. Porter, *Working Women in Mexico City*, 14. On women in the cigar and cigarette industry see Saloma Gutiérrez, "Las hijas del trabajo"; Saloma Gutiérrez, "Forjando la vida"; Camacho Morfín and Hernández, "La cigarrera El Buen Tono."

11. The changing status of teachers is discussed in Chaoul Pereyra, "Un aparato ortopédico para el magisterio"; Chaoul Pereyra, *Entre la esperanza de cambio*; González Jiménez, "De cómo y por qué"; and Vaughan, *The State, Education, and Social Class*.

12. Rendón and Salas, "La evolución del empleo en México."

13. Raphael, *Ley y orden*, 3, 38, 69–71, 104. A discussion of the historiography of public administration in Mexico appears in Sánchez González, "Origen y desarrollo."
14. Silverstone, "Office Work for Women."
15. In the mid-nineteenth-century U.S. a small number of women also worked as fiction writers. Data on women's employment in government offices are provided in Sondik Aron, *Ladies and Gentlemen of the Civil Service*, 3–6. The U.S. context is also discussed in Davies, *Woman's Place Is at the Typewriter*, 183. For a discussion of women in clerical work in France and England, see Sohn, "Los roles sexuales en Francia e Inglaterra"; Wishnia, *The Proletarianization of the Fonctionnaires*; Bachrach, *Dames Employées*; and Clark, *The Rise of Professional Women*. For Argentina see Queirolo, "Mujeres que trabajan"; and Barrancos, *Mujeres en la sociedad argentina*, 139–48, 201–7. For Germany see Kracauer, *The Salaried Masses*; and Adams, *Women Clerks in Wilhelmine Germany*. For the United States see Bennet, *Our Women*, chapter 5, "Salary-Earning Girls"; Davies, *Woman's Place Is at the Typewriter*, 183; Fine, *Souls of the Skyscraper*; Turk, "Labor's Pink-Collar Aristocracy"; Berebitsky, *Sex in the Office*. In China, women who worked in offices during the 1920s also violated norms of respectability; see Goodman, "The New Woman Commits Suicide."
16. Cuéllar, *La linterna mágica*, 65, 300. A writer and educator, Sierra (1848–1912) served on the Supreme Court in 1894, as minister of justice and public education, and as minister of public education and fine arts (1905–11). He was ambassador to Spain (1911–12) under Francisco I. Madero. Sierra, *Evolución política del pueblo mexicano*, 186. Dumas contextualizes Sierra's ideas on the middle class in *Justo Sierra y el México de su tiempo*, 298; see Iturriaga, *La estructura social y cultural de México*, 28. Based on national population census data, Keesing finds that public-sector employment grew from 26,311 (1895) to 127,843 (1930) to 204,804 (1950). See Keesing, "Structural Change Early in Development."
17. Reyes Esparza, *La burguesía mexicana*, 22.
18. On the urban middle class in Latin America see Johnson, *Political Change in Latin America*. S. Loaeza, *Clases medias y política*, 192. On middle-class Bonapartism during the 1930s see Shulgovski, *México en la encrucijada de la historia*. On middle-class participation in the National Confederation of Popular Organizations and its influence on urban planning, see Davis, *Urban Leviathan*; Bertaccini, *El régimen priísta*, chapter 3; Walker, *Waking from the Dream*, chapter 5; Reyes Rodríguez, *Clases medias y poder politico*.
19. Scholars who focus on political participation tend to define the Mexican middle class by membership in organizations. For Mexico, the National Confederation of Popular Organizations has been the organization most closely associated with the middle class. As a result, such studies use a definition of the middle class that includes a heterogeneous group of people that may include small business owners, street vendors, and government workers. Bertaccini, *El régimen priísta*, chapter 3; Reyes Rodríguez,

Clases medias y poder político. On the history of middle sectors in Mexico, see Mentz, *Movilidad social de sectores medios.* Leal defines the Porfirian middle class by occupation in "Las clases sociales en México." Iturriaga distinguishes between the independent middle class and the dependent middle class, with the latter made up of salaried employees, especially government employees. Iturriaga categorized artisans as middle class. Iturriaga, *La estructura social y cultural de México,* 28, 60. Iturriaga's definition of the middle class is refined in Dorantes, *El conflicto universitario en Guadalajara,* 30–36. See also Careaga, "Clases medias." On the middle-class identity of government workers in Peru, see Parker, *The Idea of the Middle Class,* 99, 101, 149; and in Brazil, Ownesby, *Intimate Ironies,* 54.

20. Government workers are mentioned in passing in Joseph and Nugent, *Everyday Forms of State Formation,* 115, 273, 289, 330. Scattered references to the role of the middle class in the Mexican revolution appear in Knight, *The Mexican Revolution,* 43–52, 62–69, 132, 251–79; and Gillingham and Smith, *Dictablanda,* 189.

21. Eineigel, "Revolutionary Promises Encounter Urban Realities"; Barbosa Cruz, "Los empleados públicos." Ervin classifies professionals as middle class although his analysis does not concern itself with whether those individuals self-identified as such. See Ervin, "The Formation of the Revolutionary Middle Class."

22. Public employees are mentioned in passing in Anguiano, *El estado y la política obrera,* 56–60, 83, 137–39; and León and Marván, *La clase obrera,* 285. For recent reviews of Mexican labor historiography, see Trujillo Bolio, "La reciente historiografía de la vida laboral"; and Gómez Galvarriato Freer, "Industrialización, empresas y trabajadores industriales."

23. Leal, *Del mutualismo al sindicalismo,* 13. In 1875 *El Socialista* mentions the Public Employee Mutual Aid Society led by Francisco Montero Collado, which criticized the government and was short-lived. See List Arzubide, *Apuntes para la prehistoria de la Revolución,* 31; Leal, *Del mutualismo,* 13. Employees in the Ministry of Foreign Relations established a mutual aid society and published a pamphlet in 1894. See "Sociedad mutualista de empleados," AGN, Colección de Folletería, caja 42, folleto no. 1092.

24. *Diario Oficial,* September 23, 1927, 8. On the history of the labor arbitration board, see Middlebrook, *The Paradox of Revolution;* Suarez-Potts, *The Making of Law.* In 1960 the Constitution was amended to address civil servants. In 1963 the Federal State Workers Law was passed. A detailed discussion of the evolution of civil service legislation appears in Pardo, "El servicio profesional de carrera en México."

25. See, e.g., Anguiano, *El estado y la política obrera,* 56–60, 83, 137–39; Córdova, *La política de masas del cardenismo;* Snodgrass, *Deference and Defiance in Monterrey;* Davis, *Urban Leviathan,* 87–90.

26. Tribunal Federal de Conciliación y Arbitraje, *Diario Oficial*, December 5, 1938, 1–11. The FNTE emerged from the ranks of obreros employed in government offices such as the National Printing Press, Pavement and Sidewalks, Sanitation and Public Transportation, and the National Cemetery.

27. Cobble, *The Other Women's Movement*.

28. Horowitz, "Rethinking Betty Friedan." Joanne Meyerowitz argues Friedan has influenced the historiography of women's roles in postwar U.S. and offers a reassessment in Meyerowitz, "Beyond the Feminine Mystique.

29. For an example of attempts to discredit feminism by characterizing it as foreign to Mexico, see Molina Enríquez, *Los grandes problemas nacionales*, 321. The history of the word *féminisme* appears in Offen, "Defining Feminism." According to Goldstein, Charles Fourier first used the word *feminisme* in 1837; see Goldstein, "Early Feminist Themes," 92. On the appearance of the word *feminista* in the Southern Cone, see Lavrin, *Women, Feminism, and Social Change*, 15.

30. Early use of the word *feminista* has been studied by Cano, "Feminismo" and Infante Vargas, "De lectoras y redactoras," 192. The word feminism was used as early as 1897 to describe changes in women's workforce participation in Mexico. See "227 Señoras; el trabajo de la mujer," *El Imparcial*, December 23, 1897, 1.

31. For a study of women's periodicals, see Infante Vargas, "De lectoras y redactoras," and Alvarado, "La prensa como alternativa educativa." For the importance of liberal philosophy on how families thought of women's social roles see Fernández Aceves, "Guadalajaran Women and the Construction of National Identity"; Fernández Aceves, *Mujeres en el cambio social*. On Catholic women's activism on behalf of women, see Olimón Nolasco, *Sofía del Valle*; Boylan, "Gendering the Faith"; Arrom, *Volunteering for a Cause*.

32. Lau Jaiven, "Mujeres, feminismo y sufragio"; Lau Jaiven, "Entre ambas fronteras"; Lau Jaiven and Zúñiga Elizalde, *El sufragio femenino en Mexico*; Cano, "México 1923"; Ramos Escandón, "Challenging Legal and Gender Constraints in México."

33. The classic treatment of women's activism during the 1930s is E. Tuñón Pablos, *Mujeres que se organizan*. See also González and Riquelme Alcántar, "El presidente Cárdenas y el sufragio femenino." On women's suffrage activism between 1940 and 1953, see E. Tuñón Pablos, *Por fin!*

34. Muncy, *Creating a Female Dominion*; Koven and Michel, "Womanly Duties," 107–8; Cobble, *The Other Women's Movement*, 27, 50–55. The Mexican Department of Labor hired female inspectors in 1914; see Porter, *Working Women*, 168–73.

35. Castañeda, "Introducción." The concept of *cultura escrita* is taken up in Fernández Aceves, "El álbum biográfico de Guadalupe Martínez Villanueva." For an example of an early Argentine female government employee whose writing was integral to her activism Argentine. See Peard, "Enchanted Edens and Nation-Making." Juana

Manso was one of the first women appointed to a government position, and Peard describes her as a feminist who, while known for her writing as a novelist, should also be noted for her contributions to nation-building.

36. Raphael, *Ley y orden*, 69–70. In the United States, private commercial schools opened in the 1880s, and by the turn of the century public secondary schools integrated commercial education into the curriculum. See Aron, *Ladies and Gentlemen of the Civil Service*, 59.

37. Sandoval, *Memoria que el Oficial Mayor*, 108–11. The School for Manual Arts and Trades for Women was, by the 1920s, renamed the School for Manual Arts and Trades for Young Ladies (*señoritas*). On the ESCA, see Lazarín Miranda, "Enseñanzas propias de su sexo," 258.

38. The name "Escuela Comercial 'Miguel Lerdo de Tejada' para Señoritas" raises the question as to how to translate *señorita*, a word with multiple cultural resonances. Here it is translated as "young lady" because it echoes the way the word was used in English in the same time period. *Señorita* is sometimes translated as "girl," though *niña* is unequivocally a female child or girl. Of course, what defines someone as a girl, a young lady, or a woman depends on the historical moment and cultural constructions of childhood and adulthood. This said, *señorita* is sometimes used to describe girls and young ladies. It is also used to describe women in a way that disregards their status, expertise, or age or is meant explicitly to belittle them. Through the 1930s professional women in their twenties and thirties might have been called *señoritas*. For a discussion of the use of the word *señorita* in the workplace see Porter, "De obreras y señoritas."

39. Labor historians generally define class by occupation and socioeconomic status. See Camarena Ocampo and Adelson, *Comunidad, cultura y vida social*; L. Gamboa, *La urdimbre y la trama*; Bortz, *Revolution within the Revolution*; Womack, *Posición estratégica obrera*. Lear considers how people move through an urban geography as integral to class identity, see *Workers, Neighbors, and Citizens*. The relevance of political agenda to class status in Brazil is examined in McCann, "Carlos Lacerda," and in Peru by Parker, *The Idea of the Middle Class*. Middle-class consumer habits in Brazil are analyzed in Owensby, *Intimate Ironies*; and in Mexico by Bunker and Macías-González, "Consumption and Material Culture."

40. On sexuality in the workplace in Colombia, see Farnsworth-Alvear, *Dulcinea in the Factory*; for Chile, see Hutchison, *Labors Appropriate to Their Sex*; and for a collection of essays on different Latin American countries, see James and French, *Gendered Worlds*. For a review of historical studies of working-class women in Mexico, see Porter and Fernández Aceves, "Introducción." In *Género en la encrucijada*, 15–23; and Porter, "Working Women in the Midst of Revolution."

41. Weinstein, "'They Don't Even Look Like Women Workers." 162. Weinstein writes: "Subjected to disparaging constructions of working-class women by the dominant

classes and by the men of their own putative social class, seen as tainted and degraded by the experience of wage work (and factory work in particular), working-class women's response was likely to be an assertion of their femininity and respectability through approximation/appropriation of the taste and styles associated with the middle-class woman." Enstad, *Ladies of Labor, Girls of Adventure*, 1–3, 93.

42. Kracauer, *The Salaried Masses*, 24. For a study of class identity of clerks in the United States, see Luskey, *On the Make*.

43. For an introduction to the literature on Bourdieu, see Grenfell, *Key Concepts*, 50, 73. Novels that portray the changing class status of women include Charlotte Brontë, *Jane Eyre* (1847); Edith Wharton, *The House of Mirth* (1905); Teresa de la Parra, *Ifigenia* (1924). On U.S. government workers, see Sondik Aron, *Ladies and Gentlemen of the Civil Service*, 9.

44. Adamovsky, "Usos de la idea de 'clase media' en Francia." By the same author see "Acerca de la relación Radicalismo argentino y la 'clase media.'" See also Wahrman, *Imagining the Middle Class*. Historians of clerical work in the United States have approached class in ways that acknowledge the blurring of boundaries between social classes in certain historical moments. Ileen DeVault shows how clerical workers and labor aristocracy intermingled, thus showing that class differences were somewhat fluid. Brian Luskey argues that male clerks held an unstable class position in the imagination of mid-nineteenth-century America. DeVault, *Sons and Daughter of Labor*; Luskey, *On the Make*, 16–20.

45. The cross-fertilization of ideas about women, work, and class identity may also be rooted in cross-class alliances among women that date back to the early twentieth century. For Mexico City, see Porter, *Working Women in Mexico City*, 95. On teacher-worker alliances in 1930s Guadalajara, see Fernández Aceves, "The Struggle between the *Metate* and the *Molinos de Nixtamal* in Guadalajara," 149. My discussion of subjectivities draws from Enstad, *Ladies of Labor*, 13.

1. "WOMEN OF THE MIDDLE CLASS NEED TO WORK"

1. Unless otherwise noted, all translations are mine. The title of this chapter is from "El trabajo de la mujer," *El Porvenir de Chihuahua*, reprinted in *La Convención Radical Obrera*, October 8, 1894, 2. *El Porvenir de Chihuahua* is mentioned in Peñafiel, *Anuario estadístico de la república méxicana*, 266. La Convención Radical was formed in 1875 and in 1888 became La Convención Radical Obrera. The newspaper of the same name was founded in 1886. The organization dissolved in 1903. See Leal, *Del mutualismo al sindicalismo*, 50–51.

2. Gutíerrez, *El mundo del trabajo*, 113, 137, 177.

3. On working conditions for artisans, see Leal, *Del mutualismo al sindicalismo*, 44–46. On women in the sewing and cigarette industries, see Porter, *Working*

Women in Mexico City, 77–90. On Mexican economic development during the Porfiriato, see Katz, "Mexico," 63–65.

4. On early feminist activism, see Soto, *Emergence of the Modern Mexican Woman*, 31–96.

5. Diocapo, "El trabajo de la mujer," *El Hijo del Trabajo*, October 21, 1883, 2. For additional newspaper reports on women and work see Villalobos Calderón, *Las obreras en el Porfiriato*, 61.

6. On anarchosyndicalists' ideas regarding women and work see Leal, *Del mutualismo al sindicalismo*, 34–35; and Hart, *Anarchism and the Mexican Working Class*, 54–55, 180. On women's questioning of female dependency in the United States see Vapnek, *Breadwinners*, 4–6, 121.

7. Thompson, "Artisans, Marginals, and Proletarians," 307–24.

8. Keesing, "Structural Change Early in Development."

9. Gómez-Galvarriato and Muscachio, "Un nuevo índice." On the impact of inflation and food shortages on Mexico City see Rodríguez Kuri, *La Revolución en la ciudad de México*, 141–77. The U.S. government collected information on inflation in Mexico. For Mexico City see Records of the Department of State, Roll 161, 812.50–3 and 812.50/14.

10. Arrom, *The Women of Mexico City*, 154–58, 161, 165.

11. Pérez Toledo, *Trabajadores, espacio urbano y sociabilidad*, chapter 5. Textile factories hired women as early as the 1840s, as analyzed in Ramos Escandón, *Industrialización, género y trabajo femenino*, 160, 193, 198, 225, 228–31.

12. Women took in laundry and pawned personal items to earn an income, as discussed in Francois, *A Culture of Everyday Credit*.

13. Arrom, *The Women of Mexico City*, 197.

14. Porter, *Working Women in Mexico City*, 19, 23–25, 35.

15. For report on wages for seamstresses, see "227 señoras: El trabajo de la mujer en México," *El Imparcial*, December 23, 1897, 1. *El Imparcial* had a history of reporting on the activities of artisans, see Leal, *Del mutualismo al sindicalismo*, 20. For more on seamstress working conditions, see Porter, *Working Women in Mexico City*, 87–90.

16. "Sociedad Mutualista Fraternal de Costureras," *La Convención Radical Obrera*, March 5, 1893, 2; Porter, *Working Women in Mexico City*, 89.

17. Galván de Terrazas, *La educación superior*, 16; Galván and López Pérez, *Entre imaginarios y utopías*, 13; Arredondo, *Obedecer, servir y resistir;* Bacant, *Historia de la educación durante el Porfiriato*, 133.

18. Cano, "Género y contrucción cultural."

19. On working conditions for teachers in Mexico City, see Chaoul Pereyra, "Un aparato ortopédico para el magisterio"; Chaoul, *Entre la esperanza de cambio*; Bazant, *Historia de la educación durante el Porfiriato*, 145; Alvarado, *La educación "superior" femenina*, 203, 253; Vaughan, *The State, Education, and Social Class*; and

González Jiménez, "De cómo y por qué." For working conditions outside Mexico City see Gútierrez Graseda, *Educar en tiempos de Don Porfirio*; and, Santibáñez Tijerina, "Enseñanza y recreación."

20. Teachers petitions, 1898, AGN, IPBA, caja 237, exp. 69.

21. "Para las damas: Porvenir de la mujer," *La Convención Radical Obrera*, April 22, 1894, 2–3, and May 6, 1894, 2, reprinted in CEHMOM, *La mujer en el movimiento obrero*, 91–94.

22. "El trabajo de la mujer" appeared in *El Porvenir de Chihuahua* and was reprinted in *La Convención Radical Obrera* on October 8, 1894, 2, reprinted in CEHMOM, *La mujer en el movimiento obrero*, 133–36.

23. Dore, "One Step Forward, Two Steps Back," 18.

24. García Peña, *El fracaso del amor*, 24, 37–38.

25. "El divorcio," *La Mujer: Semanario de la Escuela de Artes y Oficios para Mujeres*, May 22, 1880, 1.

26. Women themselves and observers of the "woman question" often used the phrase "moral and material suffering," as for example in "Reducción de salarios a las costureras," *El Periódico de las Señoras*, August 22, 1896, 5, reprinted in Rocha, *El álbum de la mujer*, 4:191–93. Quotes come from Concepción Gimeno de Flaquer, "La obrera mexicana," *El Álbum de la Mujer*, 1884, 3–5, reprinted in Rocha, *El álbum de la mujer*, 4:173–74, 173–74. María de la Concepción Gimeno de Flaquer (1850–1919) was born in Teruel, Spain, and moved to Madrid when she was twenty. In 1883 she moved to Mexico, where she lived for seven years. Gimeno de Flaquer was the director of and published in *El Álbum de la Mujer*. On Gimeno de Flaquer in Mexico, see Ramos Escandón, "Espacios viajeros e identidad femenina;" Ramos Escandón, "Imperial Eyes," 117–23; and Ramos Escandón, "Concepción Gimeno de Flaquer."

27. Levitan, "Redundancy."

28. México, Secretaría de Agricultura y Fomento, Dirección General de Estadística, *Tercer censo de la población de los Estados Unidos Mexicanos, verificado 27 de octubre 1910*, vol. 1, chaps. 1–4, 42, 57–58.

29. For reports on women in the United States, Ireland, and other European cities, Diocapo, "El trabajo de la mujer," *El Hijo del Trabajo*, October 21, 1883, 2; and, *Las Hijas del Anáhuac*, March 4, 1888, 160.

30. Diocapo, "El trabajo de la mujer," *El Hijo del Trabajo*, October 21, 1883, 2.

31. Aron, *Ladies and Gentlemen of the Civil Service*, 6.

32. Gimeno de Flaquer, "La obrera mexicana," 3–5, in Rocha, *El álbum de la mujer*, 4:173–74; Gimeno de Flaquer, *La mujer española*.

33. "El divorcio," *La Mujer: Semanario de la Escuela de Artes y Oficios para Mujeres*, March 22, 1885, vol. 1, no. 4, 1.

34. Elisa, "La mujer," *El Socialista*, April 18, 1886, 1, 2; and Elisa, "La mujer," *El Socialista*, July 4, 1886, 1.

35. Observers expressed concern about men and women working together in factories; see Porter, *Working Women in Mexico City*, 53–55.

36. Gamboa, *Todos somos iguales*, 230–34.

37. For a fuller discussion of the relationship between economic dependency and moral weakness, see Porter, *Working Women in Mexico City*, 71–73, 87, 93–94, 116–18.

38. Translated from the French newspaper *L'Estafille* by A. D. M., the article appeared in two installments in *La Convención Radical Obrera*, May 5, 1895, and October 23, 1887, 2.

39. Louis Büchner, "La bendición del trabajo," *El Socialista*, September 13, 1885, 1, 2, translated from German by J. F. Jens, reprinted in CEHMOM, *La mujer en el movimiento obrero*, 89–91. The author may be Luise Büchner, who wrote *Die Frau: Hinterlassene Aufsätze, Abhandlungen und Berichte zur Frauenfrage con Luise Büchner* (1878). On Büchner see Bank, *Women of Two Countries*, 175. For similar debates about women and work in Europe, see Morgan, *A Victorian Woman's Place*, 1.

40. Illades, *Hacia la república del trabajo*, 18–22.

41. Gútierrez, *El mundo del trabajo*, 19–26.

42. Leal, *Del mutualismo al sindicalismo*, 50.

43. "El trabajo de la mujer" appeared in *El Porvenir de Chihuahua* and was reprinted in *La Convención Radical Obrera* on October 8, 1894, 2; CEHMOM, *La mujer en el movimiento obrero*, 133–36. A similar discussion of the need for work options for middle-class women continued into the first decade of the twentieth century. See "Las mujeres de clase media deben trabajar," *El Imparcial*, February 22, 1900, 1.

44. "El trabajo honrado y el porvenir de la mujer," *La Convención Radical Obrera*, May 26, 1901, 2.

45. "La mujer: Ventajas que reporta el trabajo," *La Convención Radical Obrera*, August 23, 1903, 2–3.

46. Knight, *The Mexican Revolution*, 23. Limantour taught political economy at the ESCA.

47. Ríos Cárdenas, *La mujer mexicana es ciudadana*, 115. Luz Bonequi began to work in the Central Telegraph Office in 1884. See Trillo Tinoco, "La presencia de las mujeres en la internet," 16. Bonequi was enrolled in telegraphy classes at the National Preparatory School during the 1883–84 school year. See Alvarado, *La educación "superior" femenina*, 325. Writing in the 1940s, Amalia de Castillo Ledón (a public employee and women's rights activist) claimed that women first began to work for the government in 1895. Emmy Ibáñez, herself an early pioneer for women's rights, began to work in the Ministry of Finance and Public Credit in 1905. See Cano, *Amalia de Castillo Ledón*, 179.

48. "El trabajo honrado y el porvenir de la mujer," *La Convención Radical Obrera*, May 26, 1901, 2; Villalobos Calderón, *Las obreras en el Porfiriato*, 232.

49. Ríos Cárdenas, *La mujer mexicana es ciudadana*; González Jiménez, *Las maestras en México*, 115.

50. México, *Ley de ingresos y presupuesto de egresos del erario federal para el año fiscal que comienza el 1 de julio de 1905 y termina el 30 de junio de 1906* (Mexico City: Tipográfica de la Oficina Impresora de Estampillas, 1905), 53; México, *Ley de ingresos y presupuesto de egresos del erario federal para el año fiscal que comienza el 1 de julio de 1914 y termina el 30 de junio de 1915* (Mexico City: Tipográfica de la Oficina Impresora de Estampillas, 1914), 32, 235; Stampa, *Historia del correo en México*, 51–53. Moya Gútierrez, *Arquitectura, historia y poder*.

51. The Department of Labor reported in 1914 that women in government offices worked as typists, shorthand typists, scribes, calculators, taxidermists, and nurses; see "Informe," AGN, DT, caja 68, exp. 1, 1914. For a complete accounting of government hiring in the Post Office, see México, Secretaría de Hacienda y Crédito Público, *Ley de ingresos y presupuesto de egresos del tesoro federal*, 1880, 1884; México, Secretaría de Hacienda y Crédito Público, *Ley de ingresos y presupuesto de ingresos del tesoro federal*, 1891; México, Secretaría de Hacienda y Crédito Público, *Ley de ingresos y presupuesto de egresos del erario federal*, 1905; México, Secretaría de Hacienda y Crédito Público, *Ley de egresos y presupuesto de egresos del erario federal*, 1904, 1906, 1907, 1908, 1909, 1910, 1911, 1913, 1914; México, Secretaría de Hacienda y Crédito Público, *Presupuesto de egresos de la federación*, 1928; and México, Poder Ejecutivo Federal Departamento de Aprovisionamientos Generales, *Ley de ingresos y presupuesto de egresos del erario federal*, 1920.

52. Señorita Esther C. Quijas, AHSS, Personal, file 61-21, 1913; for similar examples of women working in unpaid positions, see files 58-1 and 71-12.

53. Señorita Esther C. Quijas, AHSS, Personal, file 61-21, and Adela de Galván Viuda de Gastellum, file 30-14.

54. México, Dirección General de Instrucción Primaria del Distrito y Territorios Federales, *La escuela mexicana*, 609–20. The value of public employee wages declined over the period 1895–1910, from .999 in 1885 to .874 in 1908, with the most precipitous decline beginning in 1900. See Colegio de México, *Estadísticas económicas del Porfiriato*, 152–53.

55. As a point of comparison, for the period 1900–1919 male sales clerks at El Palacio de Hierro department store began at 20 to 30 pesos a month, unskilled laborers earned 30 pesos a month, and skilled laborers might earn 60 pesos a month. Bunker, *Creating Mexican Consumer Culture*, 126.

56. Carmen González, AHSS, Personal, file 34-28, 1911; see also Señorita Concepción Lopez, file 43-15, 1909; and Josefina González, file 35-12, 1914.

57. Elena Llarios, AHSS, Personal, file 40-22.

58. Moreno-Brid and Ros, *Development and Growth*, 64; Gómez-Galvarriato and Muscachio, "Un nuevo índice." On public-employee real wages see Colegio de México, *Estadísticas económicas del Porfiriato*, 152–53.

59. Cost of Living Study, AGN, DT, caja 83, exp. 6, 1914.

60. For El Palacio de Hierro department store advertisements that include prices, see *El Demócrata*, October 28, 1914, 4. For a detailed history of the department store, see Bunker, *Creating Mexican Consumer Culture*.

61. For similar discussions in England, see J. D. Milne's *Industrial and Social Position of Women in the Middle and Lower Ranks* (1857). Milne advocated vocational training for women as a solution for women caught between poor working conditions in factories, on the one hand, and as governesses, on the other. Milne ultimately emphasized the primacy of middle-class women's obligations to domestic labor, but he also argued that it was necessary for women to enter the workforce in order to develop an interest in politics and society. Morgan, *A Victorian Woman's Place*, 43.

62. Arrom, *The Women of Mexico City*, 24, 29–30.

63. Infante Vargas, "De lectoras y redactoras."

64. During the 1880s the National Preparatory School offered clerical instruction to women; see Alvarado, *La educación "superior" femenina*, 325. Girls academies in Oaxaca and Michocán also began to offer commercial subjects, though the curriculum focused primarily on sewing, literacy, and mathematics; see López Pérez, *Educación, lectura y construcción de género*, 83–94.

65. México, Secretaría de Instrucción Pública y Bellas Artes, *Boletín de Instrucción Pública* 1 (January 1902): 481–83; Alvarado, *La educacción "superior" femenina*, 222. Bazant dates the establishment of the School for Manual Arts and Trades for Young Ladies in 1872; see *Historia de la educación durante el Porfiriato*, 118.

66. "Escuela de Artes y Oficios para Mujeres," *Boletín de la Sociedad de Geografía y Estadística de la República Mexicana* 5 (1880): 684–93. Alvarado states that the school opened with 508 students and that ten years later enrollments had doubled; see *La educación "superior" femenina*, 221–23.

67. During the Porfiriato women were most likely to study to become, in order of importance, teacher, midwife, and accountant (*corredora*); see Bazant, *Historia de la educación durante el Porfiriato*, 120–21, 254–58, 260, 266. On telegraphy classes at the School for Manual Arts and Trades and on the opening of the Telegraphy School, see México, Secretaría de Instrucción Pública y Bellas Artes, *Boletín de Instrucción Pública* 5 (1905): 462. On shifts in women's education more generally see Meneses Morales, *Tendencias educativas oficiales en México*.

68. The Lancasterian Method, named for Joseph Lancaster, began with Anglican missionary schools in Madras, India. The method relied on advanced students to

teach large numbers of students at the same time. The method spread to England, the United States, and Mexico. Lancasterian schools accepted large numbers of girls. See Tanck Estrada, "Las escuelas lancasterianas en la ciudad de México."

69. On Tagle Meza, see Wright de Kleinhans, "La emancipación de la mujer." Tagle Meza is listed as an instructor at the EAOM in 1880. *La Mujer*, July 1, 1880, 1. For her date of birth see Tovar Ramírez, *Mil quinientas mujeres*, 613–14. Six out of fourteen instructors were women, including Tagle Meza, who taught business math and accounting. Other subjects included sewing, embroidery, and artificial flower making. Another woman also served as assistant to the drawing and painting instructor. Tagle Meza married Tomás Eguilúz in 1882 and lived in Guanajuato. She died in childbirth at the age of thirty. Wright de Kleinhans, *Mujeres notables mexicanas*, 546; Cano, *Amalia de Castillo Ledón*, 79.

70. For more on the ESCA, see Bazant, *Historia de la educación durante el Porfiriato*, 254–58; D. Rafael Lozada, "Discurso inaugural del Prof. y Presidente H. de la Sociedad, D. Rafael Lozada," and Sr. Cruz D. Olivares, "El porvenir de la taquigrafía en México, Julio 2, 1901," in Centro Taquigráfico, *Conferencias*, 6–13, 24–29. Chavero was a distinguished historian, lawyer, and deputy. For more information on García Clavellina and Chavero, see Figueroa Doménech, *Guía general descriptiva*, 110, 472, 595, 610, 622–23, 642.

71. Lazarín Miranda, "Enseñanzas propias de su sexo"; Rodríguez and Krongold, *50 años de educación tecnológica*; Rodríguez, *ESCA*; Galván, "La educación técnica," 217; Lazarín Miranda, *La política para el desarrollo*; AGN, IPBA, caja 49, leg. 49, exp. 5, and leg. 47, exp. 87; Bazant, *Historia de la educación durante el Porfiriato*, 255, 262.

72. Letter from ESCA students to Carmen Romero Rubio de Díaz, January 1900, AHPD, folder 73, Cartas, Carmen Romero Rubio de Díaz; AGN, IPBA, caja 49, leg. 49, exp. 5, and leg. 47, exp. 87.

73. Letter from ESCA students to Carmen Romero Rubio de Díaz, January 1900.

74. On the women's tradition of petitioning other women for assistance, see Matabuena Peláez, *Algunos usos y conceptos de la fotografía*, 133; Porter, *Working Women in Mexico City*, 81, 162, 186.

75. Letter from ESCA students to Carmen Romero Rubio de Díaz, January 1900.

76. María Macaria, AGN, IPBA, caja 125-49, exp. 27, 1900, and caja 4, exp. 28, 1900. Antonio L. Olivera was named assistant in the shorthand and typing classes. The next year (1901) he was replaced temporarily by Enriqueta Ortiz. See Olivera, AGN, IPBA, caja 125-49, exp. 2, 1901. In 1905 two women and one man, in succession, filled his place, María Ángulo, Constanza Sánchez, and José Arechaga. See AGN, IPBA, caja 125-51, exp. 3. In 1905 there was a request to make them permanent. In 1915 Ángulo was named typing professor at the ESCA. The school implemented a degree in accounting (contador de comercio) in 1905. See León López, *El Instituto Politécnico Nacional*, 17.

77. "Informe leído por el C. Presidente de la República al abrirse el segundo período de sesiones del XX Congreso de la Unión, el 1 de abril de 1903," *Boletín de Instrucción Pública* 1 (1903): 625–27.

78. Lazarín Miranda, "Enseñanzas propias de su sexo," 258. A presidential decree on December 12, 1901, called for a commercial school for girls. There was a slight decline in federal investment in education between 1902 and 1904. On federal investment in education see Colegio de México, *Estadísticas económicas del Porfiriato*, 265, 294–95. The Commercial and Industrial School of Guadalajara opened in 1906. See Peregrina, *La Escuela Normal de Jalisco*, 11, 24–26, 50.

79. *Boletín de Instrucción Pública: Órgano de la Secretaría del Ramo* 4, no. 2 (January 10, 1905): 275–83.

80. "Adiciones y modificaciones á la Ley para la enseñanza comercial en el Distrito Federal" and "Informe rendido por el Director de la Escuela S. de Comercio y referente al año de 1905," *Boletín de Instrucción Pública* 5 (1905): 227–30, 235–37.

81. Solfeo is a pedagogical technique to teach sight reading of sheet music for singing, developed by the Englishwoman Sarah Ann Glover (1785–1867). MLT directors were Profa. Ma. Luisa de la Torre (1914–16), Profa. Elena Valensuela (1916–19), and Profa. Ma. Luisa de la Torre (1919–20).

82. Palacios and Pruneda, *Guía de la Secretaría de Instrucción Pública y Bellas Artes*, 22–24; AHSEP, *Escuela de Negocios, "Doctor Mora"; Información general* 9, no. 20 (Mexico City: Editorial Cultura, 1926).

83. Santoyo's employment record is located at Raquel Santoyo Halsey, 1891–1933, AHSEP, DETIC, caja 2317, exp. 120. Santoyo was a member of the Public Education Advisory Board (Consejo Superior de Educación Pública). See Alvarado, *La educación "superior" femenina*, 281. Breaking from the practice that directors live on school grounds, Santoyo lived at 64 Santa Teresa Street. She traveled with Carmen Krause de la Rosa Álvarez to Chicago and later to Paris to study commercial, industrial, and primary education. See "Gacetilla: A Europa," *Diario del Hogar*, June 30, 1906, 3; *Boletín de la Secretaría de Educación Pública* 7, no. 3 (March 1925): 121; Dumas, *Justo Sierra*, 183; "Informe rendido por la Srta. Raquel Santoyo y la Sra, Carmen Krause de Alvarez de la Rosa, acerca de la comisión que se les confirió en los Estados Unidos de América," *Boletín de Instrucción Pública: Órgano de la Secretaría del Ramo* (1904), 668–88; and *Boletín de Instrucción Pública: Órgano de la Secretaría del Ramo* (1907), 150.

84. R. Santoyo's remarks on the occasion of the first anniversary of the MLT, *Boletín de Instrucción Pública: Órgano de la Secretaría del Ramo* 3 (September 10, 1904): 861–67; Sierra, *Obras completas*, 326–30, 367–69. The newspaper often wrote about education as a marker of middle-class status; see, e.g., "Las personas decentes," *La Clase Media*, March 8, 1909, 2.

85. Schell shows how teachers and students subverted traditional gender norms in Schell, "Gender, Class, and Anxiety," 115.

86. "Informe de la excurción," *Boletín de la Universidad: Órgano del Departamento Universitario y de Bellas Artes* época IV, 3, no. 6 (August 1921): 346–47.

87. "La Escuela Miguel Lerdo de Tejada," *La Clase Media*, May 1, 1909, 1. The store opened in 1909.

88. R. Santoyo's remarks on the occasion of the first anniversary of the MLT, 861–67.

89. "La Escuela Primaria Comercial 'Miguel Lerdo de Tejada,'" *Boletín de la Educación*, September 1, 1914, 96–97.

90. R. Santoyo's remarks on the occasion of the first anniversary of the MLT, 865.

91. The school offered scholarships, and teachers sometimes made gifts to students in need. At times this caused tension among students. See "La cuestión de los obsequios en la Escuela Miguel Lerdo de Tejada," *El País*, June 13, 1908, 2.

92. *Escuela Comercial Miguel Lerdo de Tejada; Registro de diplomas*, 1906–1921, AHSEP; México, Dirección de Talleres Gráficos, "El movimiento educativo en México," *Informe de los trabajos realizados por la Dirección General de la Enseñanza Técnica en el periodo comprendido de 1 de diciembre de 1920 al 30 de junio de 1921* (Mexico City, 1922), 521.

93. Castañeda López and Rodríguez de Romo, *Pioneras de la medicina mexicana*, 204.

94. My discussion of rhetorical gestures builds on Mattingly, *Appropriate[ing] Dress*, 6–14.

95. In a tableau, elegantly dressed young women took the stage and struck a pose. Music and public speaking were popular subjects among women. Women's enrollments (1900): ESCA, 225; Conservatorio Nacional de Música y Declamación, 314; Escuela Normal para Profesoras, 599. Bazant, *Historia de la educación*, 262. On one teacher's use of public-speaking skills, see Bazant, *Laura Méndez de Cuenca*, 92. End-of-year ceremonies are described in Cacho García, *Cifra de oro de la Escuela "Lerdo,"* 107.

96. "La Escuela Miguel Lerdo de Tejada," *La Clase Media*, May 1, 1909, 1. The ministry bulletin also announced the event. See Bruno Martínez, "Fiesta en la Escuela 'Miguel Lerdo de Tejada,'" in México, Dirección General de Instrucción Primaria del Distrito y Territorios Federales, *La escuela mexicana*, 609–13.

97. "La señorita María Corona," *La Clase Media*, March 1, 1909, 3.

98. Raquel Santoyo, "De la Srita. Profesora Raquel Santoyo, Director de la Escuela 'Miguel Lerdo de Tejada,' dicho en la fiesta que allí se verificó el día 30 del ultimo mes de enero," in México, Dirección General de Instrucción Primaria del Distrito y Territorios Federales, *La escuela mexicana*, 615–20. Raquel Santoyo Halsey, 1891–1933, AHSEP, DETIC, caja 2317, exp. 120; "To Be Reorganized: American Methods Will Be

Adopted in Women's School," *Mexican Herald*, August 10, 1904, 8. At the time of the trip Krauze was teaching English at the MLT; "La directora de la Escuela Lerdo festejada por profesoras y alumnas," *El Imparcial*, July 29, 1908, 1. For report on Santoyo's travels to the United States and Europe, see México, Dirección General de Instrucción Primaria del Distrito y Territorios Federales, *La escuela mexicana* 8: 150–73.

99. "Gacetilla; A Europa," *Diario del Hogar*, June 30, 1906, 4. Santoyo was also absent from the school in 1914, when Ana Durán served as director. On Santoyo's absence see México, Dirección General de Instrucción Primaria del Distrito y Territorios Federales, *La escuela mexicana*, 301, 482–85. Durán taught accounting, often without pay. See AHSEP, DE, caja 7, exp. 35, and caja 6, exp. 26. She advocated for expanding commercial education for women in "La escuela primaria comercial 'Miguel Lerdo de Tejada,'" *Boletín de la Educación*, September 1, 1914, 96–99.

100. "Señorita Raquel Santoyo," *La Clase Media*, January 30, 1910, 2.

101. "La navidad de los niños pobres," *El Heraldo del Hogar*, December 31, 1909, 1. A large photograph of the event filled the front page.

102. Cano, "Feminismo." Sierra mused about what he described as "feminist" passengers aboard the ship on which he traveled. He drew the profile of a woman, writing "ugly" in the margins of his notes. Dumas, *Justo Sierra y el México de sus tiempos*, 32.

103. Infante Vargas, "De lectoras y redactoras," 192. Other early uses of the word include a 1906 zarzuela *El Congreso Feminista* showing at the Teatro Principal in Mexico City. See "Teatros," *El Imparcial*, March 20, 1906, 2.

104. "El concurso feminista," *El Imparcial*, April 1, 1905, 1. See also "Concurso de estenografía y mecanografía," *El Imparcial*, April 17, 1905, 1.

105. "El concurso de 'El Mundo Ilustrado,'" March 16, 1905, 1; "Juventud, belleza y trabajo: Significación social del concurso, El Mundo Ilustrado, "El concurso de estenografía y mecanografía," and "Semana alegre de tick-tack," all in *El Imparcial*, April 8, 1905, 1; "El concurso de hoy," *El Imparcial*, April 16, 1905, 1. For coverage of contests in subsequent years see "El concurso abierto por 'El Imparcial,'" *El Imparcial*, March 1, 1912, 6; "Mañana se cierran las inscripciones para el gran concurso feminista," *El Imparcial*, March 6, 1912, 7; "Un nuevo triunfo de la Oliver," *El Imparcial*, March 17, 1912, 12; "El concurso feminista y su significación," *El Imparcial*, April 11, 1912, 3; and, "Nuestros dos últimos concursos," *El Imparcial*, April 14, 1912, 7; "El segundo concurso feminists de taquigrafía y mecanografía," *El Imparcial*, April 14, 1912, 7; "Cerca de doscientas señoritas taquimecanógrafas tomaron parte ayer en el noble torneo que fue preparado por 'Excélsior,'" *Excélsior*, October 27, 1919, 1; "Enaltecimiento del trabajo femenino," *Excélsior*, February 6, 1921, 11.

106. "Las bellas mecanógrafas, vals lento," no. reg. 568, 1913, AGN, IPBA, PAL, caja 238, exp.17: 3–5.

107. "Concurso de mecanografía en la Secretaría de Gobernación," *El Imparcial*, April 16, 1913, 5.

108. Sesto, *El México de Porfirio Díaz*, 218–24.

109. "227 Señoras; el trabajo de la mujer," *El Imparcial*, December 23, 1897, 1. Prior to 1897 the word *feminist* was used to describe events outside of Mexico. See, e.g., "Los abogados femeninos en Bruselas," *Voz de México*, June 13, 1894, 3.

110. The three-part series appeared as "Femenismo y hogar," in *El Imparcial* on June 21, 1, 8, on June 23, 1908, 1, and on June 25, 1908, 1, 2.

111. Alvarado, *El siglo XIX ante el feminismo*, 16, 118. For a similar discussion of women and work, see Pavissich, *Mujer antigua y mujer moderna* (1910). For a similar definition of feminism as women working outside the home see V. Villalva, "El feminismo económico," *Excélsior*, April 9, 1917, 7.

112. Barreda's essay appears in M. Alvarado, *El siglo XIX ante el feminismo*, 117–18.

113. "Concurso feminista" *Semana Ilustrada*, March 13, 1912; and "Vencedoras del concurso feminista," *Semana Ilustrada*, March 20, 1912.

114. Gautreau, "La ilustracion semanal y el archivo Casasola."

115. *Semana Ilustrada* coverage of MLT ceremonies appears in Cacho García, *Cifra de oro de la Escuela "Lerdo,"* 107. MLT students appeared taking the podium at an event for those in battle; see "Para honrar los en campaña," *Semana Ilustrada*, April 24, 1912.

116. Coverage of typing contests includes "El feminismo de los millones," *Semana Illustrada*, March 24, 1911; "Concurso feminista de 'El Imparcial,'" *Semana Ilustrada*, March 31, 1912; and "El concurso feminista," *Semana Ilustrada*, May 1, 1912. Feminism was so closely associated with office workers that when Gildardo Gómez, deputy for Sonora, filed a complaint against an "empleada pública" who worked in the Post Office, the press reported "Un diputado que se declara enemigo del feminismo," *El Universal*, December 12, 1919, 5,

117. "De política y administración," *Semana Ilustrada*, March 13, 1912. A group of at least forty public employees went to President Francisco Madero's home to petition the passage of laws that would regulate their working conditions. Two women appear in the photograph. See *Semana Ilustrada*, October 13, 1991, cover.

118. Carlos Fernández Benedicto, "El espiritísmo está de moda," *Semana Ilustrada*, July 3, 1912.

119. Soto, *Emergence of the Modern Mexican Woman*, 33. The Admiradoras de Juárez (est. 1906) were examples of women's anti-Porfirio Díaz organizations. Members included Eulalia Guzmán, Hermila Galindo, and Luz Vera. Regeneración y Concordia (est. 1911) included Dolores Jiménez y Muro. Office workers and commercial school students who engaged in political action are reported in "Elías Amador to Srta. María A. González," *La Patria*, June 16, 1911, 3; "El mutualismo

feminista: Las alumnas de la escuela 'Miguel Lerdo,'" *El Imparcial*, April 11, 1910, 1. Post office workers petition reported in "Los empleados de la D. G. de Correos piden instrucción military," *El País*, May 1, 1914, 6. Thirty-seven MLT alumni organized to defend Santoyo from a public smear campaign; see "Las alumnas de la escuela 'Miguel Lerdo' desmienten á 'El Demócrata Mejicano,'" *El País*, September 16, 1911, 4; "Nuevas protestas contra Santín," *Diario del Hogar*, September 24, 1911, 5.

120. Arias Bernal, AHSEP, Personal Sobresaliente, A-4, 8. Born Mexico City, April 18, 1884 (Mexico City); died 1920 (Tlalpan). Arias Bernal began working in Mexico City public schools in February, 1904. She was hired as an assistant at the Escuela Superior #8 (1904); teacher for primary education at School for Manual Arts and Trades for Young Ladies (1905); interim teacher at the MLT (1905); and, assistant at the MLT (1907). Arias Bernal was let go from the MLT and thenrehired in 1909. Bernal later went on to the Normal School in Mexico City, where by 1914 she served as director. Along with Oliva Espinosa and María Luisa de la Torre (both teachers), Arias Bernal was invited to Veracruz while Huerta was in power. Bernal, as director of the Normal School, was a founder of the National Women's Confederation (Confederación Femenil Mexicana) on June 20, 1916. On women's organizing, see Kranzthor Shutz, "Mexican Women as They Are." For Arias Bernal on feminism, which she defines as a woman being able to support herself economically, see "Hagamos corazones y no cerebros," *El Demócrata*, October 26, 1914, 4.

121. Brinsmade and Rolland, *Mexican Problems*, 31.

122. Santoyo was let go as director of the MLT in August 1914 and was rehired in December of the same year. See Raquel Santoyo Halsey, 1891–1933, AHSEP, DETIC, caja 2317, exp. 120; *Mujeres mexicanas notables*, 60–61; Acosta, *Veinte mujeres*, 73. María Sandoval de Zarco, the first female lawyer in Mexico, taught business law at the MLT. See Cano, *Amalia de Castillo Ledón*, 200.

123. For biographical information on González see Rodríguez Campos, "Una mujer impresaria." Galindo published *La mujer moderna* (1915) and organized the First Feminist Congress in Yucatán in 1916. For biographical information on Galindo, see Orellana Trinidad, "'La mujer del porvenir.'"

124. Galindo advocated for women's right to work in government offices. See Galindo, "La mujer moderna," 10: "I have taken advantage of the brilliant historic opportunity that this epoch has presenteed by advocating... two very prominent tendencies: The Feminist Ideal... and the Idea of Revolutionary Reform." Her program sought first "to obtain for woman, without pretending that she should drop her labors that are inherent to the home, her intervention, slowly but progressively, in the political and administrative labors of Government." Translation from original.

125. "Toma gran incremento el feminismo: Millares de empleos públicos y particulares servidos por mujeres aptas y honradas," *Alianza*, February 1, 1914, 14.

126. Méndez de Cuenca, "El decantado feminismo." Foreign observers too noted the shift away from the practice of "seclusion" among the upper classes. See Kranzthor Shutz, "Mexican Women as They Are."

127. Early feminist organizing included a congress sponsored by Governor Francsico Múgica in Tabasco in 1915 and a congress sponsored by Governor Salvador Álvarado in Yucatán in 1916. See Julia Tuñón Pablos, *Women in Mexico*, 83–100; and Soto, *Emergence of the Modern Mexican Woman*, 160–62.

2. OFFICE WORK AND COMMERCIAL EDUCATION, 1920S

1. Statistics on strikes during the 1920s are in Tamayo, *La clase obrera*, 116–22. Street scene details come from newspaper reports of the Ericsson telephone operator strikes in the 1920s; see Porter, "De obreras y señoritas."

2. Stephen Haber argues that Mexican industry modernized during the Porfiriato and again in the late 1930s. Haber, *Industry and Underdevelopment* 116, 184–98. The impact of modernization on textile production and labor regimes is addressed in Gómez-Galvarriato, *Industry and Revolution*, 6–8, 21, 70. On the impact of mechanization on the coffee sorting industry, see Fowler-Salamini, *Working Women*, 9. New machinery was implemented in Mexico City cigar factories, to the detriment of the women who worked there; see Porter, *Working Women in Mexico City*, 111.

3. Alicia Alva, "La mujer en el trabajo," *El Nacional*, July 27, 1933. Elvira Vargas Rivera (1908–67) is known for her work as a journalist for *El Universal* and *El Nacional*. Romero Aveces, *La mujer en la historia de México*, 475–76.

4. Guerrero Orozco, "El Departamento de Contraloría."

5. México, *Nueva ley de secretarías de estado* (Mexico City: Imprenta de "El Diario Oficial," 1922). The law built on the *Ley de secretarías de estado*, December 1917. The seven ministries listed in the 1922 law were: Interior, Foreign Relations, Finance and Public Credit, War and Marine, Agriculture and Development, Communications and Public Works, and Industry, Commerce, and Labor. There was also a Ministry of the President, however it was not listed in any ministry laws until 1958. For a detailed discussion of the evolution of central government, including relevant legislation, see Blanco, *Empleo público*, 39–42.

6. México, Secretaría de Hacienda y Credito Publico, Comisión reorganizadora, 1927–1928, *Informe de sus labores*, 17, 63–64.

7. See Blanco, *Empleo publico*, Anexo estadístico, cuadro 7.

8. Alva, "La mujer en el trabajo." For government employees' working conditions during the 1920s, see Barbosa Cruz, "Los empleados públicos."

9. Gastón Roger, "Los escotes en las oficinas," *El Mundo*, August 8, 1923, 3.

10. Descriptive details in this paragraph come from figs. 8 and 10 and newspaper reports in notes 12 and 13 below. On sexuality in the U.S. workplace, see Berebitsky, *Sex in the Office*, chapter 2.

11. "Remington Noiseless," *El Universal Ilustrado*, April 28, 1928, 57. For criticism of women making noise at work, see "Más discreción en el trabajo," *El Mundo*, August 17, 1923, 3.

12. "Nuestro concurso de la empleada más apta," *El Mundo*, June 9, 1923, 1; "Nuestro concurso de la empleada más apta," *El Mundo*, June 30, 1, 2; "Reconquista del primer puesto: Consuelo Heredia," *El Mundo*, August 17, 1923, 4.

13. "Nuestro concurso de la empleada más apta," *El Mundo*, June 9, 1923, 1; "Nuestro concurso de la empleada más apta," *El Mundo*, June 30, 1923, 1, 2; "Reconquista del primer puesto: Consuelo Heredia," *El Mundo*, August 17, 1923, 4. Indicative of the turn to highlight women's advances in the workplace, the 1926 carnival queen was named "to honor women who work," in contrast to the older tradition of choosing a queen solely based on beauty. Ernestina Calles, the daughter of the president, won first place. See Collado Herrera, "El espejo de la élite social"; "El comité de las fiestas del centenario patrocina un concurso de taquimecanografía," *El Universal*, July 9, 1921, 9.

14. México, Secretaría de Hacienda y Crédito Público, Comisión Reorganizadora, 1927–1928, *Informe de sus labores*, 17, 63–64.

15. Jiménez Rueda, *Cándido cordero*, 28–31. The title translation is imperfect. Cándido is a man's name, and it plays on the word *candid*, or innocent; however, Innocent is an unusual name in English. *Cordero* is "lamb" and suggests someone who follows the herd. The alliteration is difficult to capture in English.

16. "Demócrata-AMEX Film Convoca a . . . ," *El Demócrata*, November 3, 1925, 7.

17. AGN, OZ, Correspondencia, caja 4, exp. 1, 1924–1932; "El Cristo de Oro," *El Universal Gráfico*, January 4, 1927, 15; and "Función en el Teatro Hidalgo a beneficio de los niños pobres," *El Universal Gráfico*, January 6, 1927, 10. On Sequeyro see Rashkin, *Women Filmmakers in Mexico*, 41; Rashkin, *The Stridentist Movement in Mexico*, 141.

18. "El reparto de premios a las vencedoras en nuestro concurso de taquimecanografía," *Excélsior*, January 3, 1921, 3; "Con una velada y un baile agasajará 'Excélsior' mañana por la noche a las señoritas que tomaron parte en el concurso de taquimecanografía," *Excélsior*, January 28, 1921, 7; "Festival que ofrece hoy 'Excélsior' en honor de las srtas. taquimecanografas," *Excélsior*, January 29, 1921, 9; "Con una brillante y significativa fiesta, premió 'Excélsior' a las señoritas que tomaron parte en su concurso de taquimecanografía," *Excélsior*, January 31, 1921, 7.

19. "Más discreción en el trabajo," *El Mundo*, August 17, 1923, 3; Gastón Roger, "Los escotes en las oficinas," *El Mundo*, August 8, 1923, 3.

20. "Por defender su reputación fue despedida una empleada," *Excélsior*, March 21, 1922, 8. Similar incidents occurred in private offices; see "La moralidad del Consejo de los FFCC," *Excélsior*, April 4, 1922, 1.

21. "La señorita Flirt," *El Universal*, February 19, 1922, 37. On the "Most Capable Empleada" contest, see "Nuestro concurso de la empleada más apta," *El Mundo*, June 9, 1923, 1; "Nuestro concurso de la empleada más apta," *El Mundo*, June 30, 1923, 1, 2; "Reconquista el primer puesto: Consuelo Heredia" *El Mundo*, August 17, 1923, 4.

22. Between 1914 and 1920 the Post Office grew from 1,570 to 1,627 employees. México, Poder Ejecutivo Federal Departamento de Aprovisionamientos Generales, *Ley de ingresos y presupuesto de egresos del erario federal para el año fiscal que comienza el 10 de enero y termina el 31 de diciembre de 1920*, 201–3.

23. Legislatura XXXIII—Año II—Período Ordinario, no. 40, jueves 26 de diciembre, 1929.

24. Jesús Silva Herzog (1892–1985), economist, historian, and politician, began his employment in the public sector in 1918 at the Department of Personnel, Statistics, and Archive. He then worked in the Ministry of the Interior (1919–25), the Ministry of Agriculture (1926–27), the Ministry of Finance and Public Credit's Department of Economic Library and Archives (1928), the Ministry of Foreign Relations (1929), Mexican National Railroads (1930–31), and the Ministry of Public Education (1932–33). In 1928 he helped found *Revista Mexicana de Economía* and the Mexican Institute of Economic Research. In 1937 he conducted a study of the oil industry that was used in the decision made by the Federal Arbitration Board and subsequently the Supreme Court. For more on Silvia Herzog's public-sector employment see his *Un estudio del costo de la vida*, 3–4.

25. Silva Herzog, *Un estudio del costo de la vida*, 27–29. For a discussion of the hazards of cost-of-living studies, see Bortz and Aguila, "Earning a Living."

26. Silva Herzog, *Un estudio del costo de la vida*, 25.

27. "New Women of Mexico Striving for Equality; American Suffragist the Model for Emancipation Program—Would First Stamp Out Ever-Recurrent Revolution, Then Fight for Economic Freedom," *New York Times*, March 2, 1924, 13.

28. Silva Herzog, *Un estudio del costo de la vida*, 25. Public employees in category B earned 105 pesos a month and spent 53 percent of their monthly income (56 pesos) on food and 14 percent (14.7 pesos) on housing. For Department of Labor cost-of-living and wage reports, see AGN, DT, caja 182, exps. 1, 11. Department of Labor inspectors pegged average wages at 1.50 to 2.50 pesos a day. The report estimates the cost of living in the Federal District as 2.52 pesos a day in 1920. Carpenters earned 3 pesos a day, and wages for sewing on an automatic sewing machine were 2.75 pesos a day. AGN, DT, caja 223, exps. 1–39, Jan.–April 1920.

29. Labor disputes often include long-term employment records. See, e.g., Otilia Sambrano [*sic*] Sánchez (Apoderado: Licenciado J. Jesús Castorena) vs. Minister of Public Education, for reinstatement, AGN, TFCA, 10: R75/939; and Gloria Barrena Campuzano vs. Minister of the Interior for the position of controller, AGN, TFCA, level 3, caja 111, exp. 882/941.

30. Guillermo Quintanar, "Investigación social obrera," *Universidad de México*, June 1, 1932, 189–97.

31. Crónicas de Lorely "El problema de las casas," *El Universal Gráfico*, March 13, 1924, 10.

32. Barbosa Cruz, "Los empleados públicos," 131–35. Eineigel, "Distinction, Culture, and Politics," 42, 78–94.

33. Blum, *Domestic Economies*, 73, 230–38.

34. "El engaño orilló a una pobre empleadita al suicidio," *Excélsior*, January 1, 1920, 9. For a fictional depiction of women's role in supporting family see Jiménez Rueda, *Cándido Cordero*, 33.

35. Schell, *Church and State Education*, 93.

36. On Vasconcelos's work as minister of public education, see Fell, *José Vasconcelos*; Marsiske, *La Universidad de México*, 133–35. For more on President Obregón's impact on Mexican schools, see Carranza Palacios, *100 años de educación en México*, 26; Puig Casauranc, *El esfuerzo educativo en México*; and Rockwell, "Schools of the Revolution."

37. Lazarín Miranda, *La política para el desarrollo*, 12, 25–26. The DETIC reported to the Department of Schools. For the regulations of the General Office of Technical Education, see *Boletín de la Universidad: Órgano del Departamento Universitario y de Bellas Artes* 2 (1921): 239–44.

38. Vaughan, *The State, Education, and Social Class*, 202–14; Torres Septién, *La educación privada en México*, 75, 151.

39. Mistral, *Lecturas para mujeres*, 8–9. There were those who hoped that technical education would not change women's "sweet" nature. See Máximo Silva, "La juventud escolar femenina," *Boletín de la Secretaría de Educación Pública*, no. 7 (1928): 26–28.

40. Schell, "Gender, Class, and Anxiety."

41. "Inscripciones," *Boletín de la Secretaría de Educación Pública* 1, no. 4 (primer semestre 1923): 487.

42. *Boletín de la Secretaría de Educación Pública* 1, no. 1 (May 1, 1922): 305.

43. "Inscripciones en la Escuela Comercial 'Miguel Lerdo de Tejada,'" *El Universal*, January 15, 1922, 14, and "Las mujeres que trabajan," *El Universal*, February 3, 1922, both reprinted in *Boletín de la Secretaría de Educación Pública* 1, no. 1 (May 1, 1922): 246. On enrollments, see also "Muchas inscripciones en la Escuela M. Lerdo de

Tejada," *Excélsior*, February 1, 1922, 5. On MLT student successes see also "Brillantes exámenes en la Escuela 'M. Lerdo de Tejada,'" *Excélsior*, December 5, 1922, 8.

44. Dolores Salcedo, AHSEP, AM, caja 299, exp. 11. Salcedo was born in Guadalajara on May 19, 1885. She graduated from the Jalisco Normal school in 1902. See Asociación de Maestros Egresados de la Escuela Normal de Jalisco, *La Escuela Normal de Jalisco*, 6. Salcedo replaced María Luisa de la Torre, who was director of the MLT from 1914 to 1916 and from 1919 to 1920; see "De la vida estudiantil," *Excélsior*, March 11, 1920, 12; "En honor de la Srita. Dolores Salcedo, directora de la Escuela Miguel Lerdo, hubo una simpática fiesta verificada ayer," *Excélsior*, March 19, 1921, 7. Elena Valensuela served as director of the MLT between 1916 and 1919.

45. "En honor de la Srita. Dolores Salcedo, Directora de la Escuela Miguel Lerdo de Tejada, hubo una simpática fiesta verificada ayer," *Excélsior*, March 19, 1921, 7; and, "Inscripciones en la Escuela Comercial 'Miguel Lerdo de Tejada,'" *El Universal*, January 15, 1922, 14.

46. Director Dolores Salcedo report on the MLT, AHSEP, DETIC, Escuelas Técnicas, 1925–1928, caja 18, exp. 97; and Escuela Miguel Lerdo de Tejada, *Reglamento para estimar el aprovechamiento de las alumnas*, 1922, located at AHSEP, Escuelas Técnicas, Subserie Miguel Lerdo de Tejada, caja 1, exp. 2.

47. AHSEP, DE, caja 8, exp.13, and *Boletín de la Secretaría de Educación Pública* 1, no. 2 (September 1, 1922): 93.

48. Personnel, AHSEP, Personal, caja 2368, exp. 37; AHSEP, DESIC, caja 5188, exp. 11. Technical education was free until 1924, when students were then charged. The money went directly to the schools until 1928, when it went to the Ministry of Finance and then, ideally, made it back to the schools.

49. *Boletín de la Universidad: Órgano del Departamento Universitario y de Bellas Artes* 3 (1921): 106–10.

50. The following speak to SEP intentions of preparing students for the new world of office work: Puig Casauranc, *El esfuerzo educativo de México*, 1:493; *Boletín de la Secretaría de Educación Pública* 9, no. 6 (June 1929): 59–62; "La educación técnica," *El País*, September 22, 1921, 2.

51. MLT curriculum, AHSEP, DETIC, caja 8, exp. 13, 1921; reprinted in *Boletín de la Secretaría de Educación Pública* 1, no. 3 (1922): 241.

52. Many schools carried the name Pitman. The "Isaac Pitman" Commercial School was a private school sponsored the Association of Shorthand Typists and Employees (Asociación de Taquígrafos y Empleados). Association of Shorthand Typists and Employees, AGN, DGA, 30.6/133/2, October 19, 1923.

53. Lazarín Miranda, *La política para el desarrollo*, 119–20; Cecilia Sandoval, "Archivo Histórico y Museo de la Escuela Bancaria y Comercial," January 22, 2015, https://

centrocien.wordpress.com/2015/01/22/archivo-historico-y-museo-de-la-escuela
-bancaria-y-comercial.

54. "Excesivas solicitudes de inscripción," *Excélsior*, January 21, 1922, in *Boletín de la Secretaría de Educación Pública* 1, no. 4 (1922): 201; Enrollments, AHSEP, DE, caja 9, exp. 10.

55. School for Shorthand Typists first-year enrollments (1922) were 396 women and 445 men, of whom 251 women and 134 men actually attended classes, most in night classes. *Boletín de la Secretaría de Educación Pública* 1, no. 1 (May 1, 1922): 205; 1, no. 3 (1922): 245; and 1, no. 4 (1923): 23.

56. *Boletín de la Secretaría de Instrucción Pública* 1, no. 3 (1922): 244; Manuel Centurión, "La Escuela Superior de Administración Pública," *Boletín de Informaciones de la Controlaría General de la Nación* 1, no. 4 (March–April 1925), reprinted in *Boletín de la Secretaría de Instrucción Pública* 1, no. 3 (1922): 442–58. Contradictory dates appear for the year the school was established. The *Boletín* states that the School for Advanced Study of Public Administration (Escuela Superior de Administración Pública; ESAP) was established in 1920 by a group of government employees in the Comptroller's office. Classes were offered in the former Normal School, the Law School, and the National High School annex. In 1926 the school acquired its own building and fell under the jurisdiction of the National University. Government employees enrolled at the ESAP squeezed three hours of classes into their workday. Classes included accounting, statistics, and stenography. The ESAP also offered basic education in mathematics and Spanish. Enrollment was free until 1927. Students ranged in age from eighteen to fifty-five, with an average age of thirty. Enrollments in 1923 were high, and classes in fiscal accounting alone enrolled 650 students. In 1929 the school had thirty-one paid instructors and seven additional instructors who worked for free. The school had a student association.

57. The Escuela Superior de Administración Pública began as the Escuela de Administración Pública, established by the Ministry of the Comptroller in 1922. Despite the enormous popularity of the school, which opened with seven hundred students, the ministry closed the school due to a lack of funds. After government employees enrolled in the school petitioned Comptroller General Luis Montes de Oca, reopened. It was moved to the National University for administrative and curricular oversight. The entire faculty was male. In 1927, 655 students took exams. Just for the degree of public accountant, the school enrolled 227 men and 97 women. Three of the 30 students listed on the 1925 honor roll were women who excelled in Spanish, general accounting (first year) and shorthand (second year). President Calles referred to the ESCA as a school "only for men." See Puig Casauranc, *El esfuerzo educativo de México*, 1:470, 481; Report, AHSEP, DETIC,

Serie Escuelas Técnicas, caja 16, exp. 1; and Félix F. Palavincini, *Boletín de la Secretaría de Educación Pública* 1, no. 4 (1923): 192.

58. *Boletín de la Secretaría de Educación Pública* 2, no. 5 (1923), 2, no. 6 (1923), and no. 5 (1924): 114. The Gabriela Mistral offered a two-year degree in shorthand typist. Puig Casauranc, *El esfuerzo educativo de México*, 1:522.

59. Calles, *Pensamiento político y social*; Marsiske, *La Universidad de México*, 133–35, 134.

60. For information on Pérez and his role in the oil industry, see *The Oil and Gas Journal: The Oil Investors Journal*, February 1, 1917, 26. In 1934 Pérez was president of the board for the newspaper *Excélsior*. González Marín, *Prensa y poder político*, 27; Abel R. Pérez, "Contra el alcoholismo," *El Universal*, July 7, 1929, cited in G. Pierce, "Sobering the Revolution: Anti-alcohol Campaign and the Process of State-Building, 1910–1940" (PhD diss., University of Arizona, 2008), 136. SEP goals for the ETIC are described in Puig Casauranc, *El esfuerzo educativo de México*, 1:487.

61. *Boletín de la Secretaría de Instrucción Pública* 3, no. 10 (March 1925): 278.

62. Report on the ETIC school, *Boletín de la Secretaría de Instrucción Pública* 3, no. 10 (March 1925): 278. Biographical information on Kraus de Álvarez de la Rosa is in Castañeda, *Amarres perros*. Carmen Kraus de Álvarez de la Rosa was the founder and first director of the National Industrial Elementary School for Girls, inaugurated in 1910 by Justo Sierra. She was Jorge Castañeda's great-grandmother. She died in Mexico City in 1967 at the age of ninety-five.

63. Report on the ETIC school, *Boletín de la Secretaría de Instrucción Pública* 3, no. 10 (March 1925): 178.

64. Report, 1928/1929," AHSEP, DETIC, Serie Escuelas Técnicas, caja 16, exp. 1.

65. Table comparing student registration, average attendance, and number of teachers, AHSEP, DETIC, caja 16, exp. 2.

66. Statistics for 1929, AHSEP, DETIC, caja, 16, exp. 2.

67. Report on school closures, AHSEP, DETIC, Escuelas Técnicas, caja 18, exp. 97, 1922–1928.

68. School closures are discussed in "Report on Technical Schools," ASEP, DETIC, Escuelas Técnicas, 18:97, 1925–1928; and Puig Casauranc, *El esfuerzo educativo*, 1:498–99. For enrollment data, see SEP, *Noticia estadística sobre la educación pública en México correspondiente al año de 1927* (Mexico City: Talleres Gráficos de la Nación, núm. 2, 1929), 688–89.

69. Government employee petition to the President, AGN, OC, exp. 227.731-C-18. The school offered degrees in office organization, library management, archiving, memorandum, and accounting, among other subjects.

70. Guzmán taught at the MLT until fired by President Huerta for her political activism, mentioned in Colón R., *Mujeres de México*, 132. Guzmán taught at

the Fournier School, the Normal School for Women, the Girls School, and the Valle Yaqui de Sonora Night School. In 1922 she was chief of the urban literacy campaign. She was director of the "Cuauhtémoc" Open Air School (1925), inspector of elementary schools (1926), part of the Monte Albán archaeological team (1931), chief of the Department of Elementary and Normal Schools (1932–33), and chief of the Department of Archaeology at the National Museum (1934). For additional biographical information on Guzmán see Chumacero, *Perfil y pensamiento de la mujer mexicana*, 87–90.

71. The literacy campaign is discussed in *Boletín de la Secretaría de Educación Pública* 1, no. 1 (1922): 3–7; and Fell, *José Vasconcelos*, 28. For a discussion of gender and class dynamics in Revolutionary Mexico, see S. Smith, *Gender and the Mexican Revolution*, 45–49. Lillian Estelle Fisher reported literacy campaign participation at six thousand men and women and two thousand students. See Fisher, "The Influence of the Present Mexican Revolution," 227.

72. The SEP called for women to participate in the anti-alcohol campaign in *Boletín de la Secretaría de Educación Pública* 8 (April 4, 1929): 143. On the long history of women's anti-alcohol reform in Mexico, see Muñiz, *Cuerpo, representación y poder*, 197; and Mitchell, "'Por la liberación de la mujer,'" 166. For a description of similar class dynamics in such reform movements in the United States, see L. D. Ginzberg, *Women and the Work of Benevolence*, 17–18.

73. Feminist newspapers promoted the anti-alcohol campaign. See "Un enemigo de la humanidad," *Mujer*, December 12, 1926, 10; "Sociedades mexicanas: La 'Federación de clubes de madres,'" *Mujer*, February 1, 1928, 12; and "Pro-campaña antialcohólica," *Mujer*, July 1, 1929, 14.

74. México, Secretaría de Educación Pública, *El pueblo contra el alcoholismo* (Mexico City: Secretaría de Educación Pública, 1929); Pedro M. Muro, *La campaña antialcohólica* (Mexico City: Secretaría de Educación Pública, 1929).

75. On changes in depictions of the female body during the 1920s, see Sluis, "Bataclanismo." The SEP and the press reported on women's engagement in physical exercise. See Report, 1928/1929, AHSEP, DETIC, Serie Escuelas Técnicas, caja 16, exp. 1; *Boletín de la Secretaría de Educación Pública* 1, no. 2 (1922): 93–94, 209; *Boletín de la Secretaría de Educación Pública* 7, no. 7 (1928): 177; "Festival de la Dirección de Cultura Estética," *El Universal*, July 21, 1921, 12; "Bailes de los estudiantes," *El Universal*, September 9, 1921, 2; "El festival de la Dirección de Cultura Estética," *El Universal*, July 21, 1921, 12.

76. *Boletín de la Secretaría de Educación Pública* 7, no. 8 (1929): 25; Economical Dress Competition, AHSEP, DETIC, Serie Escuelas Técnicas, caja 25, exps. 11, 12, 13; Report, department chief, Juan de Dios Bátiz, AHSEP, Subsecretaría de la SEP, DETIC; *Boletín de la Secretaría de Educación Pública* (1928): 280–82.

77. Economical Dress Competition, AHSEP, DETIC, Serie Escuelas Técnicas, caja 25, exps. 11, 12, 13.

78. For example, see "Los prejuicios que ocasiona el uso del tacón y del corset," *Mujer*, May 1, 1928, 3; "La mujer y la casa: Modas/lo que no debe hacerse/recetas," *Mujer*, December 1, 1927, 7.

79. "Digna actitud de las alumnas de la escuela 'Miguel Lerdo de Tejada,'" *Excélsior*, March 25, 1922, 6. The MLT student endorsement of the winning candidates Benito Flores and Rodriguez was printed in the newspaper. "Notas estudiantiles," *El Universal*, April 18, 1922, 2.

80. *Boletin de la Secretaría de Educación Pública* 7, no. 7 (July 1928): 177. On the film *False Modesty*, see Alanís, "Más que curar, prevenir"; "Falso Pudor," *O Paiz*, May 27, 1928, 1.

81. Report, 1928/1929, AHSEP, DETIC, Serie Escuelas Técnicas, caja 16, exp. 1. Employment records are located at Robles de Mendoza, 1921–1923, AHSEP, AM, Personal (Profesoras), caja 277, exp. 20; and expediente personal, Margarita Robles de Mendoza, Archivo Histórico de la Secretaría de Relaciones Exteriores, 24-6-92. Mendoza worked as an *oficial segundo* in the Ministry of Agriculture and Development (1914–15), as an English teacher at the School for Manual Arts and Vocations for Young Ladies (1920–21), as *oficial primera* in Customs (1923), and as *canciller de tercera* (1941–46), when she was promoted to *canciller de segunda*. She authored *La evolución de la mujer en México* (1931) and *Silbario de la ciudanía de la mujer* (1932). On her work as a journalist see Ibarra de Anda, *El periodismo en México*, 2:132.

82. Report on activities, MLT, 1928/29, AHSEP, DETIC, caja 16, exp 1.

83. "Una fiesta en la preparatoria en honor de Camila Quiroga," *El Universal*, February 5, 1922, 3. Actress Camila Passera de Quiroga was born in Chajarí, Entre Ríos, in 1896 and died in Buenos Aires in 1948. A tour in Spain and France in 1921 contributed to her fame. Two of her best-known performances were in *La Dama de las Camelias* and *El Abanico de Lady Windermere*. Students also organized Sunday events like one where they sang at a movie theater. See "Cultura Feminista," AHSEP, DETIC, Dirección de Cultura Estética, caja 25, exp. 6.

84. While the MLT continued to be a women's school during the 1920s, the ESCA was a coeducational school. In 1922 the ESCA enrolled 1,371 men and 467 women in various classes and degree programs. Women were predominantly enrolled in elective courses (225) and in the high school degree (102). *Boletín de la Secretaría de Educación Pública* 1, no. 3 (1922): 240. In 1929 the ESCA offered degrees in shorthand typing, accounting, and commercial accounting (the latter a five-year course of study). See *Boletín de la Secretaría de Educación Pública* 8, no. 1 (January 1929): 81.

85. AHSEP, DETIC, 8:15, October 2, 1923.

86. Trained as a lawyer, Zubaran Capmany served as a senator from Puebla, as the minister of the interior (1914–15), and as the minister of industry, commerce and labor (1920–22). Fabela, *Documentos históricos de la Revolución Mexicana*, document 119; Rafael Zubaran Capmany, "Escuela Mixta," *Coopera*, March 1927, 14.

87. Scholars have studied the role of gender dynamics in different work environments. See Fowler-Salamini, *Working Women*, 92–101; Fernández Aceves, "Once We Were Corn Grinders"; Olcott, "Miracle Workers"; Gauss, "Masculine Bonds and Modern Mothers"; Connelly, "Política, trabajo y género, 221–24"; Porter, *Working Women in Mexico City*, 127.

88. Vaughan, *Cultural Politics in Revolution*, 13, 16, 54.

3. WRITING AND ACTIVISM, 1920S

1. E. Tuñón Peblos, *¡Por fin*, 37. The history of suffrage in different states is told in Lau Jaiven and Zúñiga Elizalde, *El sufragio femenino en México*.

2. Buck, "El control de la natalidad"; Eriksen Persson, "Imágenes y representaciones femeninas," chapters 3 and 4.

3. Castañeda, "Introducción."

4. Cano, "México 1923"; Lau Jaiven, "Mujeres, feminismo y sufragio"; Lau, "Entre ambas fronteras."

5. For a discussion of literary depictions of gender norms see J. Tuñón Pablos, "Nueve escritoras, una revista y un escenario," 16–18. The novel of the Revolution tended to focus on rural Mexico. Important women writers include Nellie Campobello, who wrote *Cartucho* (1931) and *Las manos de mama* (1949). For criticism of the portrayal of women in the novel of the Revolution see Castillo, *Easy Women*, 162; and Linhard, *Fearless Women*, 106, 162–85. Rashkin does an in-depth analysis of depictions of women in Rashkin, *The Stridentist Movement in Mexico*, 133, 190. For a discussion of the contemporáneos, see Cuesta et al., *Los contemporáneous en "El Universal*," 208–10; "La Señorita Remington," *El Universal Ilustrado*, May 15, 1924, 27, 61 appears on pages, 208–20.

6. Zavala, *Becoming Modern, Becoming Tradition*, 4; Dorotinsky Alperstein, "Después de las utopías."

7. Women grew as a percentage of university students in the 1920s; see Cano, "La Escuela de Altos Estudios y la Facultad de Filosofía y Letras," 687. For a more thorough treatment of Ríos Cárdenas's literary work, see Ramos Escandón, "The Narrative Voice." On Rios Cárdenas's journalistic career, see Fisher, "The Influence of the Present Mexican Revolution." During the late 1920s Ríos Cárdenas allied herself with feminist organizations in Mexico City such as the Feminist Revolutionary Party (Partido Feminista Revolucionario). Macías, *Contra viento y marea*, 128. For

the record of Ríos Cárdenas's studies see María Ríos Cárdenas, Archivo Histórico de la Universidad Nacional Autónoma de México, Archivo General, Escuela Nacional de Altos Estudios, Historia escolar, 1920, exp. 19/221/32066; and María Ríos Cárdenas, Archivo Histórico de la Universidad Nacional Autónoma de México, Archivo General, Escuela Nacional de Medicina, Alumnos, 1915–1917, caja 62, exp. 262. For Ríos Cárdenas at the MLT, see AHSEP, DGA, caja D/131, exp. 62131.

8. New law published in four parts, *Diario Oficial*, May 26, July 14, August 3 and 31, 1928.

9. My discussion of how authors position themselves vis-à-vis their subjects draws on Steedman, *Past Tenses*. This was not the only time Ríos Cárdenas played with point of view and voice in her writing in order to tell a particular story. Twenty years later, in *La mujer mexicana es ciudadana*, she used the third person to write an organizational history of the Mexican women's movement. Use of the third person allowed her to include herself as a central player in that history, while not making the kind of claim to importance that writing in first person would have supposed.

10. Real Academia Española, http://www.rae.es/rae.html; Merriam-Webster, https://www.merriam-webster.com/dictionary/atavism.

11. Ríos Cárdenas, *Atavismo*, 1, 5–6. The 1924 film *Atavismo*, directed by Gustavo Sáenz de Sicilia, starred Ernesto García Cabral, Esther Carmona, and Manuel París and featured Adela Siqueyro (see Blum, *Domestic Economies*, 146, 235).

12. Ríos Cárdenas, *Atavismo*, 5–6.

13. Ríos Cárdenas, *Atavismo*, 8–9.

14. Ríos Cárdenas, *Atavismo*, 43–47, 51–53.

15. Approximately fourteen pages long, *Mujer* first appeared December 12, 1926, and ran as a monthly until December 1929. Subscriptions cost 10–15 centavos per issue, and a six-month subscription cost one peso.

16. Articles by Castillo Ledón include, "A los amantes de Talía: Adiós a la escena," *Mujer*, December 1, 1928, 12; "Dirección de Acción Cívica del Departamento del Distrito Federal," *Mujer*, June 1, 1929, 3–4; "El teatro, alto exponente de cultura," *Mujer*, December 1, 1929, 11. For Castillo Ledón's employment history, see Cano, *Amalia de Castillo Ledón*, 20–24. Other contributors to *Mujer* included public employee Esperanza Velázquez Bringas; see e.g., her "Trabajo de mujeres y de niños," *Mujer*, October 1, 1927, 8, 10.

17. Guillermina Llach, "La mujer y la casa: Recetas de cocina/Conocimientos útiles/Secretos de belleza/Aviso informative," *Mujer*, July 1, 1929, 6. Guillermina Llach also wrote "¿Porque los ojos tan azules?" *Mujer*, May 1, 1929, 8; and "Página literaria," *Mujer*, October 1, 1929, 8. See Esperanza Velázquez Bringas, "Trabajo de mujeres y de niños," *Mujer*, October 10, 1926, 8, 10.

18. Ríos Cárdenas, "Departamento de Salubridad Pública en México," *Mujer*, December 1, 1928, 4.

19. Sanders examines women's role in international children's congresses in the 1920s and women's influence as government employees on policy during the 1930s. Sanders, *Gender and Welfare*, 51, 136.

20. Rios Cárdenas, "Dos fases," *Mujer*, November 1, 1929, 7, 9. On the role of motherhood in the suffrage debate, see Buck, "El control de la natalidad." The role of the advertising industry in promoting motherhood has been studied by Hershfield, *Imagining the Chica Moderna*, chapter 3; and Eriksen Persson, "Imágenes y representaciones femeninas," chapters 3 and 4.

21. Rios Cárdenas, "Dos fases," 7, 9. See also her article "¿Debe permanecer la madre en el hogar?" *Mujer*, November 1, 1929, 14.

22. Rios Cárdenas, "En las gradas del deshonor," *Mujer*, May 1, 1929, 1. Ríos Cárdenas celebrated the wide range of jobs women occupied in "Profesiones femeninas," *Mujer*, March 1, 1929, 5.

23. "El progreso de la mujer en la República de Guatemala," *Mujer*, June 1, 1928, 8; Rebeca West, "Feminismo," *Mujer*, April 1, 1929, 6. Rebeca West (1892–1983) was a well-known British writer and feminist. See Norton, *Paradoxical Feminism*. On competition for government office work, see Ríos Cárdenas, "A los empleados cesantes," *Mujer*, April 1, 1929, 6.

24. "Más discreción en el trabajo," *El Mundo*, August 17, 1923, 3; Gastón Roger, "Los escotes en las oficinas," *El Mundo*, August 8, 1923, 3.

25. Sluis, "Bataclanismo!"

26. "Interesantes declaraciones del arzobispo en México," *El Universal Gráfico*, July 12, 1924, 2. For an excellent analysis of the attack on *pelonas*, see Rubenstein, "The War on 'Las Pelonas,'" 57–58. An example of a priest's critique of feminism can be found at Fray Xavier, "Pláticas Cuaresmales; Viernes Santo; del 'feminismo' actual," *El Universal*, April 2, 1920, 3. Though not identified by author, for a similar perspective see "A propósito del feminismo: Un poco de literatura filosófica," *El Universal*, February 19, 1922, 37.

27. Vasconcelos, *Memorias: Ulises Criollo, La Tormenta*, 630. *La Tormenta* was originally published in 1936, and the passage refers to the 1920s.

28. Villalba, *Mexican Calendar Girls*, 23.

29. Rios Cárdenas, "El uniforme," *Mujer*, November 1, 1928, 5, 12.

30. Leonor Llach described uniforms as turning women into no more than mozos (low-waged male labor). See Leonor Llach, "La situación de la mujer," *El Nacional*, December 11, 1933, 11. Newspaper clipping, Juan Zaravé, "Las empleadas dicen," *Rotafolio*, AGN, OZ, Correspondencia, caja 4, exp. 1, 1924–1932.

31. Boyer, *Becoming Campesino*, 5–15.

32. An employee plays a trick on a woman in the office in L. Saslavsky, "La Broma de la Señorita Fernández," *Mujer*, June 1, 1928, 6, 11. For a similar example, see Rios Cárdenas, "Esposa celosa, esposa engañada," *Mujer*, March 1, 1928, 3, 10.

33. Ríos Cárdenas, "En las gradas del dishonor," 5.

34. Quotation comes from Ríos Cárdenas, "Falta una cláusula en el código federal del trabajo," *Mujer*, August 1, 1929, 5. On Ríos Cárdenas's work typing up Article 90 of the Federal Labor Law, see "El Código Federal del Trabajo y la mujer," *Mujer*, December 1, 1929, 13–14. Additional reports on the proposed labor law include "En el segundo aniversario de Mujer/La convención patronal-obrera," *Mujer*, December 1, 1928, 5. For the final proposed law see México, Secretaría de Industria, Comercio y Trabajo, *Proyecto ley federal del trabajo*. Ríos Cárdenas contributed to activist networks by reporting on Elena Torres, "Feminismo internacional," *Mujer*, October 1, 1929, 12; on discussion of the civil code sponsored by the Cooperative of Women for Racial Uplift (Cooperativa Mujeres de la Raza), see "Feminismo internacional: En México," *Mujer*, August 1, 1928, 10; and on Sofía Villa de Buentello, "Feminismo internacional," *Mujer*, July 1, 1929, 12.

35. The minister of the interior is identified as an ally of women in government offices in "Feminismo internacional: En México," *Mujer*, December 1, 1928, 10.

36. Fondo Consejería Jurídica y de Servicios Legales; Sección Coordinación Jurídica; Serie: Asuntos migratorios; vol. 1: exp 215 (f. ext. 25/03/1889 I.F. Ext. 27/05/1930 T). According to migration records, Leonor Llach arrived at the Puerto de Veracruz on April 25, 1917. Her age, twenty-four, does not correspond with her birth date, listed as October 19, 1905 (exp. 12). The Llach family address was given as 264 Fresno Street. Jaime Llach Llagostera arrived in Veracruz on the *Antonio López* steamship on April 25, 1917 (registro 26 de Julio de 1930, exp. 9 13 fs.).

37. Death records list full names as Guillermina Luisa Llach Trevoux (b. 1903, d. April 17, 1995) and Leonor Josefa Amada Llach Trevoux (b. 1906, d. October 7, 1996). "México, Distrito Federal, Registro Civil, 1832–2005," database with images, *FamilySearch* (https://familysearch.org/ark:/61903/1:1:23KD-M2N), Leonor Josefa Amada Llach Trevoux, 07 Oct 1996; citing Death, Cuauhtémoc, Distrito Federal, Mexico, Archivo de Registro Civil de Distrito Federal (Distrito Federal Civil Registry Archives); FHL microfilm 2,244,899; and "México, Distrito Federal, Registro Civil, 1832–2005," database with images, *FamilySearch* (https://familysearch.org/ark:/61903/1:1:232N-TDG), Guillermina Luisa Leonor Llack [*sic*] Trevoux, 17 Apr 1995; citing Death, Cuauhtémoc, Distrito Federal, Mexico, Archivo de Registro Civil de Distrito Federal (Distrito Federal Civil Registry Archives); FHL microfilm 2,275,047.

38. Llach's employment record is located at AHSEP, Archivo de Concentración, prestamo, Leonor Llach Trevoux, G/131. Llach signed a petition as an employee in

the Department of Child Welfare in 1937; Letter from women in the Department of Child Welfare to President Lázaro Cárdenas, AGN, ALR, caja 831, exp. 544/1. Llach's name does not appear in the UNAM registry of graduates. Castañeda López and Rodríguez de Romo, *Pioneras de la medicina mexicana*. Llach worked as chief of the Department of Libraries in the 1960s. AHSEP, Archivo de Concentración, préstamo, Leonor Llach Trevoux. On women in higher education see Mazón, *Gender and the Modern Research University*.

39. García Rivas, *Historia de la literatura mexicana*, t. iv, 98 (Mexico City: Textos Universitarios, S.A., 1974), 398. Llach was an important figure in the world of librarians; see Morales Campos, *Forjadores e impulsores de la bibliotecología latinoamericana*, 263–65.

40. Leonor Llach, "La femeninidad y la cultura," *Elegancias*, March 3, 1926, 6.

41. L. Llach, "La femeninidad y la cultura," 6.

42. L. Llach, "La femeninidad y la cultura," 6.

43. L. Llach, "Influencia del medio en la prostitución," *Vida Femenina*, February 1935, 27.

44. Departamento de Salubridad Pública de México, "Higiene y salud: Ejercicio para conserver la esbeltez," *Mujer*, December 1, 1928, 4; J. de la Barrera y Vargas, "Importancia de la cultura moral en la mujer," *Mujer*, December 23, 1928, 11.

45. L. Llach, "Tiranías de la moda," *Alborada*, March 29, 1929, 6.

46. L. Llach, *Cuadros conocidos*, 20, 177–78.

47. L. Llach, "En defensa de las pelonas, por una que no lo es," *Elegancias*, June 1, 1925, 21. In contrast, the daughter of President Calles was proud to claim Mexico had flappers, "Mexico Has Flappers Says Señorita Calles," *Milwaukee Sentinel*, April 26, 1926, 4.

48. For the teacher strike in 1919, see Cano, "El mayo rojo de los maestros mexicanos."

49. The 1926 decisions states, "Labor.—Article 123 includes workers (obreros) and day laborers (jornaleros), as well as employees (empleados), and anyone in general who enters into a contract. (Orozco, Angel. Sent. De 30 de Julio de 1926. Tomo XIX, 209)." See Lastra y Villar, *Las leyes del trabajo*, 792–94. In 1927, the court found in (Mackeprang, Emilio. Sent. De 1927). The decision states, "Labor. —Sections XVII, XVIII and XX, article 123, state: first, workers have the right to strike; second, in the case of public services, the arbitration board must be informed of the date a strike will be declared; and third, all work conflicts must be resolved by an arbitration board and not the Ministry of Industry, Commerce, and Labor (December 10, 1927, vol. 21, 1457)." See Lastra y Villar, *Las leyes del trabajo*, 794–96.

50. Lastra y Villar, *Las leyes del trabajo*, 267 (Quiroz, J.M. Sent. De 23 de febrero de 1929. Tomo XXV, 918).

51. Rolland was a civil engineer, architect, and government employee. He published his proposals for local government reform. See Modesto Rolland, *El desastre*

municipal en la República Mexicana: La ciudad moderna, gobierno por comisión, gobierno por gerente, referendum, iniciativa, revocación, restricción del voto, servicio civil, impuestos (Mexico City, 1939); Brinsmade and Rolland, *Mexican Problems*, 29–31. The thirty-nine-hour work week included seven hours each weekday and four hours on Saturday. See also Guerrero, *Historia del servicio civil de carrera en México*, 380–400.

52. Solís Cámara, *Proyecto de ley del servicio civil: Incluyendo el establecimiento del Banco Mutualista de Empleados* (Mexico City: Porrúa, 1925). Pedro C. Solís Cámara served as a special delegate for the Ministry of Finance in 1920. See C. Ruíz Abreu and Jorge Abdo Francis, *El hombre del sureste: relación documental del archivo particular . . .*, vol. 1 (Mexico City: Universidad Juárez Autónoma de Tabasco/ Secretaría de Gobernación, Archivo General de la Nación, 2002), 136. He also served on the board of directors for the United Railroads of Yucatán. See Poor, *Poor's Manual of Railroads*, vol. 55 (New York: H.V. & H.W. Poor, 1922), 2065.

53. Guerrero, *Historia del servicio civil de carrera en México*, 360. A heterogeneous set of pension benefits were offered to public employees in some bureaucratic units. See Federación de Sindicatos de Trabajadores al Servicio del Estado, *Ley de pensiones civiles*, 7.

54. Barbosa Cruz, "Los empleados públicos, 1903–1931."

55. Letter to the Sub-minister of Finance, December 22, 1920, AGN, DGA, 4:6.00/18. The "Isaac Pitman" Commercial School was a private school sponsored the Association of Shorthand Typists and Employees (Asociación de Taquígrafos y Empleados). AGN, DGA, 30.6/133/2, October 19, 1923.

56. *Boletín de la Secretaría de Educación Pública* 1, no. 3 (1922): 47–49.

57. "Cinco mil señoritas empleadas serán despedidas," *El Gráfico Nacional*, August 9, 1921, 1.

58. "Mexico Cuts Salaries," *New York Times*, July 16, 1922, 14.

59. Membership of the 1920 organization overlaps with CNAP members, including Gregorio Cristiani and José Vasconcelos. The full list of the executive committee for the 1920 organization is in "La organización de los empleados públicos," *El Universal*, October 9, 1920, 4. CNAP membership and objectives are detailed in "La vigorosa acción social de la Confederación Nacional de la Administración Pública," 1922. For a discussion of the CNAP see Guerrero, *El funcionario, el diplomático, y el juez*, 453. In January 1921, Ingeniero Amado Aguirre presented a proposal to President Obregón to amend article 123 of the Constitution so that it did not recognize the right of public employees to strike but did ensure fair salaries. Adolfo de la Huerta called for the termination of the CNAP. See AGN, OC, 731.11, 1921; Iturriaga, *La estructura social y cultural de México*, 77.

60. Employee Day, AGN, OC, 256.805-E-52, 1922.

61. "Obregón Suspends Debt Agreement; New Loan Refused," *New York Times*, July 2, 1924, 1; "Bank Clerks Lose Fight in Mexico," *New York Times*, May 17, 1925, 17; "Mexico Drops 1,500 Employees," *New York Times*, June 1, 1925, 11. A 10 percent salary reduction had also been implemented in 1923. AGN, OC, 121.H-E-24; AGN, OC, 121.H-E-14; AGN, OC, 814.G-132. 1923.

62. Guerrero, *Historia del servicio civil de carrera en México*, 431–32. See also AGN, DGIPS, 30:53, May 10, May 16, 1924. Ministry of Finance employees were leaders in organizing the Asociación General de Empleados Federales y de Comercio de la República. With 350 in attendance, there is no mention of women. For newspaper coverage see *El Demócrata*, June 6, 1924. Participants included employees from the Ministry of Foreign Relations, Communications and Public Works, Charitable Works, Finance, and Agriculture and Development; and from the departments of Labor, Census and Equipo "POWERS," National Statistics, Administration, and Tax.

63. Minister of the National Mint, Francisco Valdés, to the President, AGN, DT, 722:1. 1924.

64. For mention of sanitation workers, see Blanco *Empleo público*, 41; and, Guerrero, *Historia del servicio civil de carrera en México*, 401; *Revista CROM*, year II, no. 36, August 15, 1926, 64; Guadarrama, *Los sindicatos y la política en México*, 64, 101–2, 179; *Boletín de la Secretaría de Educación Pública* 1, no. 3 (1922): 47–49. Coffee sorters in Veracruz initially were supported by the CROM. When women's labor demands were ignored by leadership they distanced themselves from the CROM and reorganized. See Fowler-Salamini, *Working Women*, chapter 3.

65. Cano, "México 1923"; Lau Jaiven, "Mujeres, feminismo y sufragio"; Lau, "Entre ambas fronteras."

66. Professional women were active in the child welfare movement during the 1920s. See Sanders, *Gender and Welfare*, chapter 1.

67. Evelyn Trent Roy (b. 1892 Salt Lake City, Utah–d. 1970 Auburn, California) was married to Manabedra Nath Roy. Both were important members of the communist community in Mexico. Trent is mentioned in Esperanza Tuñón Pablos, *Mujeres que se organizan*, 26. Elena Torres's work in support of the vasconcelista program allowed her to build practical experience and professional authority. Between October 28, 1921, and April 7, 1923, the government gave Elena Torres more than 1,000 pesos for the CFM. Torres lived at 107 Tlalpam Avenue, Churrubusco, Federal District. AGN, OC, exp. 605-F-3. C190. The CFM began as the Consejo Nacional de Mujeres on August 10, 1919, but because of internal conflict it was reorganized and renamed. For a more complete history of the CFM, see Lau Jaiven, "Mujeres, feminismo y sufragio." For newspaper coverage of the CFM, see "La mujer mexicana y el feminismo integral," *El Demócrata*, September 10, 1919,

3; "El 'Consejo Feminista Mexicano' aprobó ayer las bases de su plataforma," *El Demócrata*, November 17, 1919, 3.

68. CFM events included "Una agrupación feminista se ha dirigido a la Cámara," *El Demócrata*, November 4, 1920, 2; "Vida Social," *El Demócrata*, November 19, 1920, 2; "Fue gigantesca la manifestación obrera de ayer," *El Demócrata*, May 1, 1925, 1. A pamphlet containing family law, the civil code, and related laws from other countries could be purchased for 2 pesos. See "Libreria Editorial de la Viuda de Ch. Bouret, Avenida del 5 de mayo no. 45, Mexico, D.F. Ley de Relaciones Familiares," *El Demócrata*, November 4, 1920, 2.

69. "Una brillante conferencia feminista del Sr. Duplán en la preparatoria," *El Universal*, November 14, 1921, 8.

70. "Una brillante conferencia feminista," 8.

71. Lau Jaiven, "Entre ambas fronteras"; Cano, "México 1923." See also Sánchez Olvera, *El feminismo mexicano*. On the relationship between the Mexican congress organizers and the U.S. organizers and participants, see Threlkeld, *Pan American Women*, chapter 2.

72. *Primer congreso feminista de la liga panamericana de mujeres: Conclusiones y discurso de clausura* (Mexico City: Talleres Linotipografía "El Modelo," 1923); E. Tuñón Pablos, "La lucha de las mujeres en el cardenimso," 20. The government granted office workers the day off work to attend the conference.

73. Scholars describe Villa de Buentello as having a secondary education; see Ramos Escandón, "Desafiando el orden legal"; "Challenging Legal and Gender Constraints." For her reference to the economic causes of women's condition, see Villa de Buentello, *La mujer y la ley*, 98. See also Villa de Buentello, *Derechos civiles*.

74. Villa de Buentello to the president, AGN, OC, exp. 7-28-B-4. C219. Obregón asked the Departament of Libraries to read *La mujer y la ley* and offer their opinion.

75. Villa de Buentello to Mrs. Obregón, AGN, OC, exp. 7-28-B-4. C219; Villa de Buentello, *La verdad sobre el matrimonio*. María Claudia Tapia Monteverde (1888–1971) married Álvaro Obregón in 1916.

76. "New Women of Mexico Striving for Equality; American Suffragist the Model for Emancipation Program—Would First Stamp Out Ever-Recurrent Revolution, Then Fight for Economic Freedom," *New York Times*, March 2, 1924, 13.

77. "New Women of Mexico Striving for Equality," 13. For the date Villa de Buentello established the Cooperative Women's Union of Racial Pride, see Macías, *Contra viento y marea*, 108.

78. Esperanza Tuñón Pablos, *Mujeres que se organizan*, 26–27; Adelina Zendejas, "El movimiento femenil en México," *El Día*, June 17, 1975.

79. Ramos Escandón, "Desafiando el orden legal"; "Feminismo internacional," *Mujer*, July 1, 1929, 12.

80. "New Women of Mexico Striving for Equality," 13. The journalist described Villa de Buentello as "still beautiful at 40 (something unusual for Mexican women of the middle class)."

81. "New Women of Mexico Striving for Equality," 13. According to the article, women comprised 61,423 out of 286,782 merchants, salespeople, and clerks in 1910 and 80,173 out of 310,097 in 1921.

82. "Congreso Mujeres de la Raza," *El Demócrata*, July 6, 1925, 8.

83. "Congreso Mujeres de la Raza," 8. Palma Guillén, Catalina D'Erzell, and Elvia Carrillo Puerto also attended. Carrillo Puerto told the press she represented Yucatán.

84. Lau Jaiven, "Mujeres, feminismo, y sufragio," 82.

85. "Marruecos y China, temas a debate en el C. de mujeres," *El Universal*, July 12, 1925, 1.

86. The CFM meeting with Morones appears in "Hoy se inaugurará el primer . . . ," *El Demócrata*, July 5, 1925, 2.

87. The distinction between arguments based on difference and those based on demands for equality, see Buck, *The Meaning of the Women's Vote*, 73–74. Lau distinguishes between middle-class women (journalists, professionals, and teachers) who advocated for the vote and women who did not prioritize the vote (workers, peasants, and indigenous women). Office workers both advocated for the vote and made labor demands and joined the groups described by Lau, "Ciudad de México, 1917–1953," 16.

4. WOMEN AT WORK, 1930S

1. "La situación económica de la mujer," *Excélsior*, October 23, 1935, 10.

2. The numbers do not include teachers. Women were 22 percent of government workers in 1930, but this includes teachers. México, Dirección de Estadísticas, *Censo de funcionarios y empleados públicos, 30 de noviembre de 1930*, 1–8; México, Dirección de Pensiones Civiles de Retiro, *Tercer censo de empleados federales*, 4, 18–36.

3. Fowler-Salamini, *Working Women*; Fernández Aceves, "Once We Were Corn Grinders"; Olcott, "Miracle Workers"; Gauss, "Masculine Bonds and Modern Mothers"; Connelly, "Política, trabajo y género."

4. Blanco, *Empleo público*, 49–52; Schaeffer, *La administración pública mexicana*, 245; Guerrero Orozco, *Historia de la Secretaría de Gobernación*, 326.

5. Blanco, *Empleo público*, 52.

6. Creation of the Office of Stenographers, AGN, DGA, 109, VI/303/1933.

7. The 1930 census does not distinguish between job categories. The 1932 census indicates that in the Department of Health 48 percent of women occupied administrative positions; 5 percent occupied professional positions; 37 percent occupied sub-professional positions; 10 percent occupied service positions; and .3 percent were workers (obreros). México, Dirección de Estadísticas, *Censo de funcionarios*

y empleados públicos, 30 de noviembre de 1930, 58; México, Dirección de Pensiones Civiles de Retiro, *Segundo censo de empleados*, 37.

8. Ministry of Interior employees mentioned, AGN, DGIPS, cajas 1–3, exp. 2/30 (S-1) 24339, 1936–1941.

9. Based on census data, Keesing estimates that between 30,000 and 35,000 teachers were included in the 1930 federal population census. Keesing, "Structural Change Early in Development"; México, Dirección de Pensiones Civiles de Retiro, *Tercer censo de empleados federales*, 4, 36, 51.

10. The Ministry of Health Services (Salubridad y Asistencia) was led at the time by José Siurob, who supported women's suffrage and later played an important role in the CNOP, which was popular with women. José Siurob Ramíerz y Gutiérrez (b. 1886 in Querétaro, d. 1965 in Mexico City), a military doctor, served as governor of Querétaro (1915), Guanajuato (1915–16), and Quintana Roo territory (1928–31). Under President Cárdenas, Siurob served as chief of the Ministry of Public Health (1935–38; 1939–40) and of the Federal District Central Department (1938–39).

11. The 1938 census categorized workers by activities, breaking them down into *administrativo, educacional, especialista, judicial, obrero, profesional, servidumbre,* and *servicio exterior.* The census does not define these categories. Administration included a range of jobs, including typist and secretary, and those jobs varied in their responsibilities and pay. Women were roughly one-quarter to one-third of the total employees in the categories where they were most likely employed: *especialista* (36 percent), *servidumbre* (30 percent), and *administrativo* (23 percent). México, Dirección de Pensiones Civiles de Retiro, *Tercer censo de empleados federales*, 36; México, Dirección de Pensiones Civiles de Retiro, *Segundo censo de empleados*, 37.

12. Alva, "La mujer en el trabajo," 8.

13. Escudero Luján and García Torres, *Carolina Escudero Luján*, 147.

14. México, Dirección de Estadísticas, *Censo de funcionarios y empleados públicos, 30 de noviembre de 1930*, 50–51. The ratio of dependents per person is based on the number of men or women with dependents, not the total number of government employees.

15. México, Dirección de Estadísticas, *Censo de funcionarios y empleados públicos, 30 de noviembre de 1930*, 8, 12. The federal government was more likely to study those government employees who worked and resided in Mexico City. In 1930 women were 22 percent (28,816 men and 8,332 women) of government employees in the Federal District. According to Mendieta y Núñez, in 1935 the number of government employees in the Federal District had increased to 44,588. Mendieta y Núñez, *La administración pública en México*, 285.

16. México, Dirección de Estadísticas, *Censo de funcionarios y empleados públicos, 30 de noviembre de 1930*, 18–19.

17. "El trabajo femenino en las oficinas públicas," *El Nacional*, August 13, 1934, 8.

18. "Más de medio millón de mujeres hacen cabeza de casa en el país," *La Prensa*, June 7, 1936, 11.

19. México, Dirección de Pensiones Civiles de Retiro, *Tercer censo de empleados federales*, 36, 41, 50.

20. Occupational segregation and the impact on wages is discussed in Fowler-Salamini, *Working Women*, 83, 99–101, 110, 129; Gauss, "Working-Class Masculinity"; and Fernández Aceves, "The Struggle between the *Metate* and the *Molino de Nixtamal*."

21. Employees complain to President Ortiz Rubio regarding employees paid for more than one job, AGN, POR, exp. 86.3535-A, 30 de junio, 1931. The 1932 census of public employees attempted to document the frequency of individuals who held multiple jobs. See México, Dirección de Pensiones Civiles de Retiro, *Segundo censo de empleados federales*, 52.

22. Federal Tribunal cases frequently list position and salary and have the advantage of identifying the individual in the position. Wage data for shorthand typist, typist, secretary, clerk, controller, and archivist can be found in Gloria Barrena Campuzano vs. Minister of Interior, AGN, TFCA, caja 111, exp. 882/941; Narcisa Ascanio vs. Minister of National Marine, reinstatement, AGN, TFCA, caja 103, exp. 764/941; and Berta Escorcia Valencia vs. Minister of National Economy, claim for position of clerk rank 3, AGN, TFCA, caja 105, exp. 790/41. Cost-of-living studies include Bach and Reyna, "El nuevo índice"; and Bach, "Un estudio del costo de la vida."

23. The Department of Labor study is cited extensively in U.S. Department of State Records, "Minimum Wage Decisions throughout Mexico," prepared on behalf of the Department of Labor, 812.5041/85, SA5299408963, 1934, 6. According to the U.S. Department of State, the Mexican government planned to pay government workers the minimum wage. The plan did not apply to "salaried officials" who "are now being paid amply for their services." See "Minimum Wages for Public Servants of the Mexican Government," August 31, 1933, U.S. Department of State Records, SA5299357086.

24. Empleada letter to President Ortiz Rubio, AGN, POR, exp. 83.1414-A, April 6, 1931.

25. U.S. Department of State, American Consulate General, "Increase in Cost of Living in Mexico," 812.5041/85, SA5299396483, 1931, 2. The report draws from a report produced by the Bureau of Commerce, Department of Industry, Commerce, and Labor. For an in-depth study of department store culture, see Bunker, *Creating Mexican Consumer Culture*.

26. "El trabajo femenino en las oficinas públicas," *El Nacional*, August 13, 1934, 8. See also Gonzalo de la Parra, "Puntos de vista: Las mujeres que trabajan y los hombres que no trabajan," *El Nacional*, August 10, 1934, 9.

27. Silva Herzog, *Un estudio del costo de la vida*, 47–48. Silva Herzog deemed the cost-of-living study he conducted, discussed in chapter 2, to be valid for the 1930s.

México, Dirección de Estadísticas, *Censo de funcionarios y empleados públicos, 30 de noviembre de 1930*, 7, 47–48.

28. Silva Herzog, *Un estudio del costo de la vida*, 47–48.

29. Escudero Luján and García Torres, *Carolina Escudero Luján*, 154–57. Journalists for *El Nacional* reported that government jobs paid better than those in the private sector; see "Los mejores sueldos se pagan en las oficinas públicas federales, *El Nacional*, August 22, 1933, 1. Government-sponsored vacation activities appeared in the press; see, e.g., "Salió anoche la excursion para el estado de Michoacán," *El Nacional*, December 2, 1936, 1, 2. The outing mentioned was sponsored by the National Railroad Company. The stated purpose of the outing was to offer a diversion to the women who, throughout the year, worked in poorly lit offices. Twelve hundred employees took advantage of the opportunity. More than 90 percent of the people photographed for the newspaper article were women.

30. Silva Herzog, *Un estudio del costo de la vida*, 66, 68.

31. Employee letters to the President, AGN, ALR, exps. 10.104/77, 8.021/1, 13:130/6-2. Portes Gil, *Quince años de política mexicana*, 238. According to Carlos Tello, from 1929 to 1932 such deductions resulted in a 10–15 percent salary deduction. Tello, *Estado y desarrollo económico*, 147.

32. Both quotations in this paragraph appear in a letter from a group of public employees letter to the President, AGN, ALR, 8.021/1.

33. Araiza, *Historia del movimiento obrero mexicano*, 109, 113, 116–17.

34. Biography of Gudelia Gómez Rangel draws on newspaper reports. Adelina Zendejas (1909–93) refers to Gómez as a social worker in "La mujer en la vida política," *El Nacional*, March 22, 1947, 1, 4. Gómez's professional career is partially described in "El problema de la mujer que trabaja en cabarets," *El Nacional*, October 15, 1935, 1, 4; "Reunión de trabajadoras intelectuales de México," *El Nacional*, September 27, 1947, 2; "Está en México," *El Universal*, November 25, 1948, 18; and Porter, "De obreras y señoritas." Genaro Vicente Vásquez Quiroz (1892–1967) was governor of Oaxaca (1925–28), senator for Oaxaca (1930), and led the Department of Labor in 1935. For more on the Commission for the Investigation of Conditions for Women and Children, see "El problema de la mujer trabajadora," *El Nacional*, October 17, 1937, 8. The commission was also referred to as the office for the Protection of Women and Children; see "Alimentación de la mujer trabajadora," *El Nacional*, January 24, 1939, 8.

35. Trueba was born in Nanacamilpa, Tlaxcala, on October 30, 1899, to Don Tiburcio Delfino Trueba and Doña Guadalupe Coronel. Trueba served as general secretary of the Union of American Women and was in the Mexican Women's Front and the Mexican Coordinating Committee for Defense of the Fatherland. She died on February 14, 1993. See "Las niñas del 'Colegio Inglés' recibieron sus premios de

manos del Señor Gral. Benjamin J. Hill," *El Universal*, December 23, 1916, 1, 3. For reports on the 1921 railroad strike, see "Se prepara una huelga o una sublevación?" *El Demócrata*, April 14, 1921, 7. Trueba appears in a union conflict that went before the TFCA, as does Domingo Trueba, a lawyer (level C) in the legal section of the Nationalization Office, who may have been related. See Delegates to the second ordinary convention of the Ministry of the Interior Union vs. the National Union of Interior Workers (Executive Committee) for nullification of agreements made in the aforementioned convention, AGN, TFCA, caja 10, exp. 77/R/939.

36. Lorenzo, "Ayúdame que yo te ayudaré."

37. The government employee who secured a job for his daughter is mentioned in an interview with Rosa Margot conducted by Susie Porter, March 31, 2006. Rosal, *De taquígrafa a gran señora*; copyright registration for Rosal, AGN, PA.

38. "La situación social y económica de la mujer," *Excélsior*, October 23, 1935, 10. In a few instances a woman seeking employment would invoke ties that her husband had to the person being petitioned. See, e.g., Viuda de Alfonso Quintana to Pascual Ortiz Rubio, April 1931, AGN, POR, exp. 83:1414-A.

39. Government office jobs were advertised in the newspaper. See e.g., "Empleos, solicitudes y ofertas," *El Nacional*, November 2, 1938, 2.

40. Interview with Galvarriato conducted by Susie Porter and Aurora Gómez Galvarriato Freer, May 2006.

41. "¿Quieres ser empleada? Tribuna de la mujer. Crónicas de Lorely," *El Nacional*, February 23, 1939, 8.

42. María Ríos Cárdenas, "Costumbres que se Advierten en las oficinas," *El Nacional*, August, 22, 1932, 5; "Crónicas de Arlette. Abejas laboriosas.–Continuación," *Gráfico*, October 26, 1937, 12. Reyes de Govea's pseudonym is given in "Mexicanas ilustres de todos los tiempos," *La Prensa*, June 2, 1940, 11.

43. "Crónicas de Arlette. Abejas laboriosas.–Continuación," 12.

44. "Crónicas de Arlette. Abejas laboriosas.–Continuación," 12.

45. María Duarte, "Dos palabras a las taquígrafas," *Excélsior*, September 27, 1937, 10; I. Pitman, *Stenographic Sound-Hand*. Duarte was an advocate of women's workforce participation and a contributor to *Excélsior*.

46. On the Conciliation and Arbitration Board, see Suarez-Potts, *The Making of Law*. For history of the TFCA, see México, Tribunal de Arbitraje de los Trabajadores al Servicio de los Poderes de la Unión, *Primer informe anual de labores y tesis sustentadas*, 6, 10–11. José Guadalupe Zuno (1891–1980) was a lawyer and politician who served as governor of Jalisco from 1923 to 1926. President Cárdenas named him chief of the legal department and attorney general for the National Railroad Company of Mexico. He returned to Guadalajara in 1947 to teach.

47. Lastra y Villar, *Las leyes del trabajo*, 805.

48. The TFCA established administrative precedent with cases such as María de la Luz Rocha Rebolledo vs. Minister of Public Welfare for reinstatement, AGN, TFCA, caja 15, exp. 126/939; María Suazo Pérez vs. the Minister of Public Welfare for reinstatement, AGN, TFCA, caja 15, exp. 130/939; and Esperanza Medina Villa vs. Minister of Public Assistance for reinstatement, AGN, TFCA, caja 15, exp. 31/939.

49. For history of the professionalization of social work, see Sanders, *Gender and Welfare*, 119–25. Between 1901 and 1937 and again from 1938 to 1948, the number of economics degrees granted in Mexico increased twenty-fold. Iturriaga does not provide data on administrative degrees for the first period, but he counts 8,208 degrees given during the second period. See Iturriaga, *La estructura social y cultural de México*, 177–79. For nursing, see Torres-Barrera and Zambrano-Lizárraga, "Breve historia de la educación."

50. Ana Maytorena Iñigo Viuda de Villaseñor vs. Chief of the Department of Public Health for reinstatement as visiting nurse, AGN, TFCA, caja 187, exp. 2496/41.

51. Josefina Poulat Durán, Ana Mekler, Humberto González Angulo vs. Minister of National Economy, seniority violation, AGN, TFCA, caja 195, exp. 2708/941, 1941.

52. Carmen Aillaud Betanzos vs. Chief of the Department of the Federal District, seniority dispute, AGN, TFCA, caja 94, exp. R-28/940. Berta Escorcia Valencia complained that her training prepared her for a clerk position in Berta Escorcia Valencia vs. Minister of National Economy, claim to position of clerk rank 3, AGN, TFCA, caja 105, exp. 790/41.

53. México, Comisión Nacional de Escalafón, *Reglamento de escalafón*, 14–15. Administrative class 3 personnel included stenographers, telephone operators, and office heads.

54. See also Luz Emma Salgado vs. the Minister of the Interior, promotion and back wages, AGN, TFCA, caja 259, exp. 486/1941; and Aurora del Próo vs. the Ministry of the Interior, promotion to clerk rank 2, AGN, TFCA, 173836. 2651/41.

55. Julia Moreno Hurtado vs. Ministry of Agriculture and Development Seniority Board, seniority, AGN, TFCA, caja 122, exp. 1044/41; México, Tribunal de Arbitraje, *Primer informe*, 27–28.

56. For example, see Altagracia Cintra de Teresa vs. Minister of Communications and Public Works, promotion, AGN, TFCA, caja 44, exp. 28/R/940.

57. María Luisa Miranda Fragoso vs. Minister of Finance and Public Credit, reinstatement, AGN, TFCA, caja 4, exp. 34/R/39.

58. María Luisa Miranda Fragoso vs. Minister of Finance and Public Credit, reinstatement.

59. María Luisa Miranda Fragoso vs. Minister of Finance and Public Credit, reinstatement.

60. México, Tribunal de Arbitraje, *Primer informe*, 48–49.

61. "Seniority—General Definition of.—In accordance with Article 41, fraction I of the Workers Statute, seniority in each bureaucratic unit must consist of all of the employees in the unit. As a result, there is no legal reason not to authorize the promotion of a worker because said worker is not included in the budget for the dependency or office in the unit where the opening occurs. To define seniority by the Budget that governs the subdivision in which an individual is working is illegal, and prejudicial to the worker, whose opportunities for advancement would be structurally limited, and thus contrary to the letter and spirit of the aforementioned article 41." México, Tribunal de Arbitraje. *Primer informe*, 48–49. See original case at Felicidad J. López León vs. Minister of Finance and Public Credit, reinstatement, AGN, TFCA, caja 11, exp. 86/R/393.

62. Sara Flores Olguín vs. Minister of Finance, reinstatement AGN, TFCA, caja 94, exp. R-38/940.

63. Carmen Orlaineta Badillo vs. Minister of National Economy, promotion, AGN, TFCA, caja 13, exp. 101/R/939. The complete series of cases involving Orlaineta Badillo include Carmen Orlaineta Badillo vs. Minister of National Economy, hiring dispute, AGN, TFCA, caja 105, exp. 789/941; Carmen Orlaineta Badillo vs. Minister of National Economy, seniority violation, AGN, TFCA, caja 195, exp. 2705/941; Carmen Orlaineta Badillo vs. Minister of National Economy, nullification, AGN, TFCA, caja 281, exp. 827/942; and Carmen Orlaineta Badillo vs. Minister of Economy for lost wages, AGN, TFCA, caja 471, exp. 420/946.

64. Emma Emilia Otero vs. Minister of National Economy, firing, AGN, TFCA, caja 194, exp. 2671/941; Emma Otero Pablos vs. Minister of National Economy, nullification of hire as statistician level D, 1942, AGN, TFCA, caja 281, exp. 826/1942.

65. Junta Arbitral, Carmen Orlaineta and Emma Emilia Otero, for lack of discipline and disinclination to work, exp. 432/171/-14, included in Carmen Orlaineta Badillo vs. Minister of National Economy, hiring dispute, AGN, TFCA, caja 105, exp. 789/941.

66. Macías-González, "Masculine Friendships."

67. Knight, "The End of the Mexican Revolution?."

68. Josefina Poulat de Durán, Ana Mekler, y Humberto González Angulo vs. Minister of National Economy, AGN, TFCA, caja 54, exp. 113/R/1940.

69. Bertha Escorcia Valencia vs. Minister of National Economy, AGN, TFCA, caja 105, exp. 790/41; Altagracia Cintra de Teresa vs. Minister of Communications and Public Works, promotion, AGN, TFCA, caja 44, exp. 28/R/940; Sara Velázquez de García vs. Minister of Communications and Public Works, reinstatement as assistant clerk, level 2, March 12, 1940, AGN, TFCA, caja 161, exp. 1646/941. These findings complement Rocha's research on women veterans in public education. Rocha, *Los rostros de la rebeldía*.

70. México, Comisión Nacional de Escalafón, *Reglamento de escalafón*, 24–27.

1. Civera Cerecedo, "Crisis política y reforma educativa"; Vaughan, "El papel político"; Vázquez de Knaugth, "La educación socialista."

2. "Gran impulso a la enseñanza técnica al servicio de la juventud proletaria," *El Nacional*, 1935 (s/f), 8, from BMLT, Recortes, Educación Técnica.

3. León López, *El Instituto Politécnico Nacional*, 20–24; De la Rosa, "Características de la escuela socialista mexicana"; Civera, "La coeducación en la formación de maestros rurales"; Martínez Omaña, "La revolución entra a la escuela."

4. Calvillo and Ramírez Palacios, *Setenta años*," 88.

5. "Opiniones sin rumbo, por Nadie," *El Nacional*, October 30, 1931.

6. "Escuelas técnicas y no centros de recreo para las educandas," *El Universal*, April 1, 1932, 1, 4.

7. "Escuelas técnicas y no centros de recreo para las educandas," 1, 4.

8. Calvillo and Ramírez Palacios, *Setenta años*, 118, 156–58.

9. The schools Sor Juana Inés de la Cruz, Doctor Balmis, and Malinalxóchitl ceased to exist. AHSEP, DETIC, caja 5, exp. 25, 1932. See also *Memoria de la Secretaría de Educación Pública*, 1934, 172–73.

10. *Memoria de la Secretaría de Educación Pública*, 1935, 104; and *Memoria de la Secretaría de Educación Pública*, September 1937–August 1938, 213. Other sources gave the enrollments for ETIC of 17,981 in 1931 and 8,316 in 1935.

11. *Memoria de la Secretaría de Educación Pública*, September 1936–August 1937, 90.

12. *Memoria de la Secretaría de Educación Pública*, 1932, 373.

13. Erro Soler was born in Mexico City in 1897 and died in 1979. He studied civil engineering, accounting, and astronomy. As a professional educator and politician, he helped found the IPN and the Tonantzintla National Astrophysics Observatory, precursor to the National Institute of Astrophysics, Optics, and Electronics. While a student, he taught design at La Corregidora de Querétaro. Álvarez Lloveras, "Luis Enrique Erro Soler." León López, *El Instituto Politécnico Nacional*, 27–37.

14. León López, *El Instituto Politécnico Nacional*, 27–37.

15. *Memoria de la Secretaría de Educación Pública*, September 1936–August 1937, 92–93. Minister Bassols was forced to resign in May 1934 in the face of protest over his support of sex education.

16. René Rodríguez de la Rosa, AHSEP, Dirección General de Administración, caja 207, exp. 4342, 1922–1947. Rodríguez de la Rosa was born in 1898 to Zenaldo Rodríguez and Remigia de la Rosa in San Luís Potosí. During the 1930s she lived at Suiza Avenue, #8, Portales, General Anaya, Mexico City. For a recent biography of Rodríguez, see Guerrero Oliveros, *Renée Rodríguez de la Rosa*.

17. René Rodríguez de la Rosa, AHSEP, Dirección General de Administración, caja 207, exp. 4342, 1922–1947.
18. Juan de Dios Bátiz Soler was director of the DETIC from 1929 to 1931 and in 1935. León López, *Juan de Dios Bátiz*, 35. On the new direction taken by the DETIC see also "La enseñanza técnica tiene un nuevo plan," *El Nacional*, January 15, 1934, 2.
19. "La enseñanza técnica tiene un nuevo plan," 2.
20. "La enseñanza técnica tiene un nuevo plan," 2; Leonor Llach, "La Escuela Miguel Lerdo de Tejada," *El Nacional*, September 7, 1935, 2.
21. *Memoria de la Secretaría de Educación*, August 1935, 153.
22. *Memoria de la Secretaría de Educación*, August 1935, 145–49.
23. AHSEP, DETIC, caja 23, exp. 3. For more on Rodríguez Cabo see Sosenski and Sosenski, "En defensa de los niños y las mujeres"; Castañeda López and Rodríguez de Romo, *Las pioneras de la medicina mexicana*, 212. Rodríguez Cabo was born in Las Palmas, San Luís Potosí, on June 17, 1903. She received her degree as doctor and surgeon (*médico cirujano*) from the National School of Medicine in 1928. She had a long career that included extended service as a government employee.
24. "Conferencia sustentada por la Señorita González Ortega sobre el alcoholismo," AHSEP, DETIC, caja 23, exp. 15.
25. AHSEP, DETIC, caja 2367/v/000/-8, 1935.
26. AHSEP, DETIC, caja 18, exp. 67, 1938.
27. AHSEP, DETIC, caja 27, exp. 11, 1939.
28. AHSEP, DETIC, caja 23, exp. 6, 1939.
29. AHSEP, DETIC, caja 2368, exp. 42, 1935. For further examples of student activities see also AHSEP, DETIC, caja 2150, exp. 13, and caja 2150, exp. 16, 1926.
30. AHSEP, DETIC, caja 10, exp. 14, 1939.
31. María Ríos Cárdenas, "El aspecto intelectual de la mujer" *El Nacional*, May 27, 1932, 1.
32. María Ríos Cárdenas, "Nuestra campaña de mérito," *El Nacional*, May 27, 1932, 1.
33. AHSEP, Sección de Enseñanza Especial, Informe, 1937–1937. The editorial board included Professor Aurelia Barragán, chief of the Women's Industrial Sector; Professor Luz Luna de Ibarra, chief of administration; and editors Paula Nava and Miguel Huerta (both teachers). Contributors included Julia Nava de Ruisánchez, María Ríos Cárdenas, and Dolores Salcedo. AHSEP, AM, caja 70, Isaura Castillo, 1898–1954.
34. AHSEP, Investigaciones Científicas, 1951.
35. On women teachers and socialist education see Montes de Oca, "Las maestras socialistas" and "La educación en México."
36. AHSEP, DETIC, caja 2150, exp. 21, 1935.
37. On office workers' participation in sports see, e.g., "Festival deportivo en honor de 'el Nacional Revolucionario," *El Nacional*, September 22, 1931, 1; "Derrota al

'Comunicaciones," *El Nacional*, January 18, 1931, 6; and "Prorroga de inscripciones," *El Nacional*, July 4, 1932, 2.

38. *Centro Femenino de Estudios y Acción Social: Bases constitutivas y programa de acción* (Mexico City: Colegio Militar, 1939), AHSEP, Subsecretaría, caja 16, exp. 13, and caja 2376, exp. 43.

39. Articles mentioned in text appear in *Senda Nueva* 1, no. 3 (1936). In 1936 the cost of the magazine rose to 15 cents.

40. *Senda Nueva* 1, no. 3 (1936).

41. *Senda Nueva* 1, no. 4 (1936).

42. *Senda Nueva* 1, no. 4 (1936).

43. *Senda Nueva* 1, no. 3 (1936).

44. *Memoria de la Secretaría de Educación*, August 1935, 153.

45. AHSEP, Subsecretaría, caja 16, exp. 13, 1937, 1939; *Memoria de la Secretaría de Educación*, August 1935, 153. See also *Memoria de la Secretaría de Educación*, 1938, 163.

46. *Memoria de la Secretaría de Educación*, August 1935, 153. See also *Memoria de la Secretaría de Educación*, 1938, 163.

47. *Memoria de la Secretaría de Educación*, September 1936–August 1937, 92–93. This source states that in 1936 commercial schools were eliminated and replaced with vocational schools where the relatively quick degrees in shorthand typist and typist were overenrolled. The MLT officially became the Vocational School Number 4 in 1937, although the two names continued to be used interchangeably.

48. AHSEP, DETIC, Subsecretaria, caja 16, exp. 13, 1937, 1939.

49. AHSEP, DETIC, Subsecretaria, caja 16, exp. 13, 1937, 1939.

50. AHSEP, DETIC, Subsecretaria, caja 16, exp. 13, 1937, 1939.

51. AHSEP, DETIC, Subsecretaria, caja 16, exp. 13, 1937, 1939.

52. AHSEP, DETIC, Subsecretaría, caja 16, exp. 13, 1937, 1939.

53. AHSEP, DETIC, Subsecretaría caja 16, exp. 13, 1937, 1939.

54. AHSEP, DETIC, Subsecretaría caja 16, exp. 13, 1937, 1939.

55. The importance of private education is explored in Torres Septién, *La educación privada en México*, 75, 151, 179.

56. Forty-three percent of households used coal for cooking; 37 percent used a portable grill (anafre). Fifteen percent of families used aluminum or pewter cookware.

57. AHSEP, DETIC, Subsecretaría caja 16, exp. 13, 1937, 1939.

58. *El Nacional*, November 20, 1938, 16.

59. *El Nacional*, November 20, 1938, 16, and December 4, 1938, 8.

60. AHSEP, DETIC, Subsecretaría caja 16, exp. 13, 1937.

61. Rubenstein, "Theaters of Masculinity."

62. *El Nacional*, December 10, 1938, 6.

63. AHSEP, Subsecretaría de Educación Pública, Dirección General de Recursos Materiales y Servicios, Dirección de Servicios, caja, 16, exp. 18.

64. AHSEP, Subsecretaría de Educación Pública, Dirección General de Recursos Materiales y Servicios, Dirección de Servicios, caja 16, exp. 17.

65. On international tourism to Mexico see Berger, *The Development of Mexico's Tourism Industry*.

66. AHSEP, DETIC, caja 2150, exp. 36, 1935.

67. "Intenso movimiento de turismo en Hidalgo," *El Universal*, April 2, 1932, 8.

68. AHSEP, DETIC, caja 2312, exp. 89, 1936, 1938.

69. AHSEP, DETIC, caja 2312, exp. 89, 1936, 1938.

70. León López, *El Instituto Politécnico Nacional*, 20–24.

71. AHSEP, DETIC, caja 2151, caja 2863.

72. AHSEP, DETIC, caja 2376, exp. 43, 1935.

73. León López, *El Instituto Politécnico Nacional*, 28, 39–40.

74. *Memoria de la Secretaría de Educación Pública*, September 1936–August 1937, 75–180. Section III of the DETIC oversaw "Special Studies," which included women's pre-vocational schools, as well as the School for Sewing and Design, the School for Social Workers, and the School for Home Economics.

75. AHSEP, DETIC, caja 2135, exp. 24.

76. AHSEP, DETIC, Subseries, caja 2376, exp. 43.

77. AHSEP, DETIC, Subseries, caja 2376, exp. 43.

78. AHSEP, DETIC, caja 5181, exp. 35, and caja 5193, exp. 35, 1941.

79. Rene Rodríguez de la Rosa vs. Minister of Public Education, for reinstatement and unpaid wages, AGN, TFCA, caja 257, exp. 439/ 942; and Rene Rodríguez de la Rosa vs. Minister of Public Education, for reinstatement, AGN, TFCA, caja 265, exp. 580/942.

80. AHSCJN, Queja 114/43/Ac. México, Distrito Federal, Cuarta Sala, 6 de julio, 1943.

81. AHSEP, Dirección General de Administración, caja 207, exp. 4342, 1922–1947.

82. México, Secretaría de Educación Pública, Departamento de Enseñanza Técnica, Industrial y Comercial, *Memoria, 1937–1939*, 214–15, 238. Statistics are for the pre-vocational and Vocational Number 4.

83. Lazarín Miranda, *La política para el desarrollo*, 272; León López, *El Instituto Politécnico Nacional*, 49, 167.

84. Lazarín Miranda, *La política para el desarrollo*, 84.

85. The characterization of the 1930s as "dark years" for women's literary production appears in Robles, *La sombra fugitiva*, 223.

86. Gallo, *Mexican Modernity*, 67.

87. Castañeda, "Introducción."

88. The importance of the Athenaeum for women's literary production is explored in Lau Jaiven, "Expresiones políticas femeninas."

89. José Vasconcelos served as minister of public education from 1921 to 1924 and ran for president in 1929. Jaime Torres Bodet (1902–74) was an essayist, poet, diplomat, and public employee; among other posts, he served as minister of public education (1943–46, 1958–64), minister of foreign relations (1946–19), and Mexican ambassador to France (1954–58). Carlos Chávez (1899–1978) was a pianist, composer, teacher, and founder of the Mexican Symphonic Orchestra (est. 1928). When Chávez served as director of the National Institute of Fine Arts, Llach served as head of the administrative department. Llach served as the liaison between the SEP and Chávez while he toured outside the country. Llach and Chávez were drawn into a scandal surrounding the theft of a Diego Rivera painting in 1952. L. Llach, "El maestro Carrillo." Aguilar-Moreno and Cabrera, *Diego Rivera*, 100–101.

90. Llach's writing was praised in the press. One reviewer wrote: "Madame Sevigné would have asked for forgiveness from this young writer," see F. Ibarra de Anda, "Un nuevo libro de mujer," *El Nacional*, July 2, 1933, 23. The publication of *Cuadros conocidos* was announced in *La Familia para la Familia*, November 25, 1934, 8. Publications include Leonor Llach, "Una mujer honrada," *El Nacional Dominical*, May 29, 1932, 1; and "El suicidio," *El Informador*, June 5, 1932, 2.

91. Azuela, *Regina Landa*, 122.

92. Azuela, *Regina Landa*, 8, 19.

93. Azuela, *Regina Landa*, 107.

94. L. Llach, *Cuadros conocidos*, 161.

95. L. Llach, *Retratos de almas*, 66.

96. L. Llach, *Cuadros conocidos*, 67.

97. L. Llach, *Retratos de almas*, 47.

98. L. Llach, *Cuadros conocidos*, 178.

99. L. Llach, *Cuadros conocidos*, 175.

100. L. Llach, *Cuadros conocidos*, 40; L. Llach, *Retratos de almas*, 42.

101. For echoes of the phrase "poor but honorable" see L. Llach, *Cuadros conocidos*, 39, 50.

102. L. Llach, *Retratos de almas*, 49. Llach, in a defense of sex education for women, remarked that innocence is not beautiful, but tragic; see L. Llach, "La ética de la educación sexual," *El Nacional*, June 3, 1933, 3.

103. L. Llach, *Retratos de almas*, 96.

104. L. Llach, *Cuadros conocidos*, 30. Llach wrote an article on friendship between men and women in 1926. See "La vida feminina: Encuesta del día. ¿Cual es el hombre que la mujer prefiere para amigo?" *El Demócrata*, April 25, 1926. In contrast, María Ríos Cárdenas cautioned women that working in close company

with men not lead them to adopt the more vulgar aspects of male culture and language. See Ríos Cárdenas, "Costumbres que se advierten en las oficinas," *El Nacional*, August 22, 1932, 5.

105. L. Llach, *Cuadros conocidos*, 177.

106. L. Llach, "El seguro de la madre," 16–17. See, Llach's speech to the National Congress of Women Workers and Peasants in Guadalajara, "Defensa de la maternidad," *Crisol*, February 1, 1935, 75–80.

107. L. Llach, "Maternidad," 33–34.

108. For Llach's proposals to support mothers see L. Llach, "El seguro de la madre," 16–17.

109. L. Llach, "La mujer de ayer y la de hoy," 10–11.

6. OFFICE WORKERS ORGANIZE, 1930S

1. In the United States there was a debate over the right of married women to work and, therefore, over what Alice Kessler-Harris calls women's right to economic citizenship. The 1932 Economy Act, Section 213, called for the reduction in the number of civil service workers and first targeted married persons whose spouses were also employed by the federal government. Some sixteen hundred workers left either voluntarily or involuntarily, 75 percent of them women. A 1936 campaign targeted married women specifically for lay-offs. Hostility to married women working outside of the home declined as businesses needed workers. See Kessler-Harris, *In Pursuit of Equity*; Mink, *The Wages of Motherhood*; Ladd-Taylor, *Mother-Work*; Weiner, *From Working Girl to Working Mother*; Boris, "What about the Working of the Working Mother?" 104. According to Sondik Aron, the rule against hiring married women in government offices existed prior to the 1930s. Sondik Aron, *Ladies and Gentlemen of the Civil Service*, 52.

2. Historians have emphasized the divisions between the PNR party faithful and women who were more left-leaning. Such characterizations are not inaccurate, but should not overshadow how, for example, shared work experiences brought women together. Olcott, *Revolutionary Women*, 47–52. Evidence of connections between different generations of women activists that go beyond attendance at women's congresses include attendance at events from book publication events to funerals. Otilia and Esperanza Zambrano, Leonor Llach and others attended the funeral for Mathilde de P. Montoya; see "Necrológicas," *El Nacional*, January 30, 1939, 8.

3. Ríos Cárdenas, *La mujer mexicana es ciudadana*, 54.

4. "Fue inaugurado brillantemente el dia de ayer el Congreso Nacional de Obreras y Campesinas," *El Nacional*, October 4, 1931, 5. René Rodríguez de la Rosa, AHSEP, Dirección General de Administración, caja 207, exp. 4342, 1922–1947.

5. "Interesantes asuntos en el congreso de las mujeres," *El Universal*, October 4, 1931, 1, 8; "Desean las mujeres formar su organización independiente," *El Universal*, October 5, 1931, 1, 8; "El Congreso Nacional de Obreras y Campesinas," *El Nacional*, October 5, 1931, 1; "Voto para la mujer," *El Nacional*, October 6, 1931, 1; National Congress of Women Workers and Peasants, AGN, ALR, exp. 0676, 1933. See also Cano, "Las feministas en campaña."

6. Ríos Cárdenas, *La mujer mexicana es ciudadana*, 24–26. The Federal Labor Law was passed on August 18, 1931. Pardo, "El servicio profesional de carrera en México."

7. Esperanza Tuñón Pablos provides a discussion of the breadth of issues addressed at the congress in *Mujeres que se organizan*, 39–50. The call for maternity leave appears in "Las mujeres de México pugnan por la patria," *El Nacional*, October 7, 1931, 1.

8. "En la Secretaría de Educación no habará más ceses," *El Universal*, July 29, 1931, 9; "Los ceses en el Departamento Central," *El Nacional*, December 1, 1931, 8; "El día primero de enero, ocho mil empleados seran cesados automáticamente en México," *La Prensa* (San Antonio), 1931, 2; "Cesó el personal de todo un departamento," *El Universal*, January 1, 1932, 9; "Mas de ciento cincuenta empleados cesados en Guerra," *El Universal*, January 8, 1932, 9.

9. "La emancipación de la mujer se proclama," *El Nacional*, November 30, 1931, 8; AGN, POR, exp. 86:3535-A. June 1931. PNF leadership: president, Edelmira Rojas Vda. De Escudero; secretary general, Professor Josefina Garduño; secretary for minutes, Miss Maria Teresa Mangino; secretary for public relations, Professor Gumersinda Figueroa; secretary for the defense of government employees, A. Cabrera; secretary for the defense of commercial employees, Miss Carmen Crofts; secretary for unemployed women, Elena Aponte; secretary for the defense of the campesina, Virginia Gutierrez; press secretary, Trinidad Rosete; propaganda secretary, Ana María Bleker de Díaz Gutierrez.

10. President Emilio Portes Gil made the proposal in 1929; see AGN, EPG, exp.18-V-29-BPC.

11. "Las mujeres de México pugnan por la patria," *El Nacional*, October 7, 1931, 1; "La emancipación de la mujer se proclama," *El Nacional*, November 3, 8.

12. "La emancipación de la mujer se proclama," 8.

13. "La organización de la mujer en la lucha social," *El Nacional*, October 5, 1931, 1, 2, 8; "Se organizan las mujeres," *El Universal*, October 5, 1934, 1, 8; "Desean las mujeres formar su organización independiente," *El Universal*, October 5, 1, 8.

14. Enrique Pérez Arce served on the PNR leadership (1931–33) and went on to serve as governor of Sonora (1950–53). Just one example of the association of women with conservative Catholicism appeared in "El secreto de la influencia clerical está en el dominio que los curas tienen sobre las mujeres," *El Nacional*, November 5, 1934, 3.

15. The National Bloc of Revolutionary Women was established by Florinda Lazos León and Ana María Hernández. Lazos León had attended the 1925 Racial Uplift congress. "Una carta del Bloque de Mujeres Revolucionarias," *El Universal*, November 4, 1931, 4.

16. Ríos Cárdenas, *La mujer mexicana es ciudadana*, 55.

17. Fausto Bojórquez Castillo served as deputy of Campeche (1930–32). Wilfrido C. Cruz (Castillejos) was born on April 29, 1898, and died on August 26, 1948. From Oaxaca, Cruz studied law at UNAM. He served as a federal deputy from the state of Oaxaca, district 4 (1930–32), and as senator from the state of Oaxaca (1934–40); see Camp, *Mexican Political Biographies*, 235. According to Camp, Cruz supported women's suffrage. He was the author of several books, including *Oaxaca recóndita: Razas, idiomas, costumbres, leyendas y tradiciones del Estado de Oaxaca* (Mexico City: Linotipográficos Beatriz De Silva, 1946).

18. The debate appears in *Diario de Debates*, Legislatura XXXIV, año II, tomo III, número 31, efectuada el miercoles 9 de diciembre, 1931; and Legislatura XXXIV, año II, tomo III, número 32, efectuada el jueves 10 de diciembre, 1931.

19. *Diario de Debates*, Legislatura XXXIV, año II, tomo III, número 31, efectuada el miercoles 9 de diciembre, 1931; and Legislatura XXXIV, año II, tomo III, número 32, efectuada el jueves 10 de diciembre, 1931. For similar debates see over women's work, see *Diario Oficial*, February 7, 1931, 1–2. Some commentators confused women's right to work in government offices with the right to vote. See, e.g., "Las maravillas del sufragio," *El Universal*, November 19, 1931, 3; and Pablo de Góngora, "Si las mujeres mandasen," *El Universal*, November 17, 1931, 3, 6.

20. Esperanza Tuñón Pablos, *Mujeres que se organizan*, 39.

21. "Proclama dirigida al país ante la estación X.E.O. del PNR por la Señorita María Luisa Ocampo, Secretaria General del Círculo Relator del Consejo Organizador Nacional de Fomento Industrial y Agrícola que preside el Señor Licenciado Salvador Lira, la noche del 11 de los corrientes," *El Nacional*, May 13, 1933, 8, from BMLT, Recortes, Mujeres.

22. Blanca Lydia Trejo, "Se inauguró el Congreso Nacional de Obreras y Campesinas," *Excélsior*, November 26, 1933, 1, 3; "El comunismo se ha colado en el congreso feminil," *Excélsior*, November 27, 1933, 1. Similar arguments about the moralizing impact of women in government were put forward for the United States; see Baker, "The Domestification of Politics"; and Muncy, *Creating a Female Dominion*. For further information on Trejo see Esperanza Tuñón Pablos, *Mujeres que se organizan*, 41.

23. Congress program described in Ríos Cárdenas, *La mujer mexicana es ciudadana*, 60–65. Elvira Vargas is included in the list of congress speakers in "Mañana se inaugurá el congreso de obreros y campesinos," *El Nacional*, November 24, 1933,

7. For Vargas on working women, see Elvira Vargas, "Estudio de los problemas de trabajo que afectan a la mujer," *El Universal*, November 27, 1933, 2:1, and "El tostón diario," *El Nacional*, January 26, 1932, 5. The congress was front-page news; see "Igualdad política y civil solicitarán las mujeres," *El Nacional*, November 24, 1933, 1. For Uranga's position see "El comunismo se ha colado en el congreso femenil," *Excélsior*, November 27, 1933, 1; ""División en el congreso de mujeres obreros y campesinas," *El Universal*, November 28, 1933, 3, 8.

24. "Emancipación integral de las mujeres: Este interesante tema fue discutida en el congreso de obreras y campesinas," *El Nacional*, November 29, 1933, 5.

25. Leonor Llach later published her Guadalajara speech on motherhood, "Defensa de la maternidad," *Crisol*, February 1, 1935, 75–80. For more on the Third National Congress of Women Workers and Peasants, see Fernández Aceves, *Mujeres en el cambio social*, 212.

26. National Women's League platform, AGN, FLC, exp. 708/1.

27. Secretaría de Gobernación, *Acuerdo sobre la organización y funcionamiento del servicio civil*, in *Diario Oficial*, April 12, 1934. The agreement lasted until November 1934.

28. Civil service law proposal, AGN, ALR, exp. 562,1/106, exp. 130/6–7, and exp. 130/6–1.

29. Memorandum from the Bloque Revolucionario de Mujeres Mexicanas to presidential candidate Lázaro Cárdenas, 1934, AGN, ALR, exp. 16, 139/147.

30. "La mujer defiende enérgicamente a la mujer," *La Prensa*, August 2, 1934, 2, 14; for similar arguments, see also Pablo de Góngora, "Si las mujeres mandasen," *El Universal*, November 17, 1931, 3, 6.

31. María Ríos Cárdenas, "Afición a la empleomanía: Nuestro mál," *El Nacional*, August 6, 1934; Gonzalo de la Parra, "Puntos de vista: Las mujeres que trabajan y los hombres que no trabajan," *El Universal*, August 10, 1934, 9.

32. Ríos Cárdenas, "Afición a la empleomanía"; Leonor Llach, "Los ataques a las oficinistas," *La Prensa*, August 2, 1934, 11; *La Prensa*, August 5, 1934, 1; "Franco apoyo del PNR a las empleadas oficinistas," *El Nacional*, August 4, 1934, 1. To support Senator Carlos Rivas Palacios and his statements in support of female office workers, women organized a demonstration. See "Organizan una manifestación las empleadas," *El Nacional*, August 12, 1934, 4.

33. Gonzalo de la Parra, "Puntos de vista: Las mujeres que trabajan y los hombres que no trabajan," *El Nacional*, August 10, 1934, 9. Gonzalo de la Parra was the author of "La filiación política de los empleados federales," 41–46, and "Las once mil vírgenes," 157–60, both in his book *De como se hizo revolucionario un hombre de buena fé*.

34. "El trabajo feminino en las oficinas públicas," *El Nacional*, August 13, 1934, 3.

35. "Con risas catarinas y jubilosos paloteos, las nenas que trabajan en las oficinas públicas recibieron la noticia de que no seran removidas de sus cargos," *La Prensa*, August 5, 1934, 1, 3.

36. "Dan respuesta a una iniciativa las empleadas," *El Nacional*, September 13, 1935, 2. The protest was made by Angelina Gómez Serrano in name of the Bloc of Revolutionary Women. "Sesión de las empleadas en la SEP," *El Nacional*, October 2, 1935, 2. Luisa Rejón de Sotomayor presided over a meeting at Orientación Theater. See also María Ríos Cárdenas, "La mujer mexicana se organiza," *El Nacional*, September 1, 1935, 21.

37. U.S. feminists made arguments similar to that made by Zambrano; see Baker, "The Domestification of Politics," 620–47. Elvia Carrillo Puerto was from a prominent family in the Yucatán (her brother Felipe Carrillo Puerto served as governor of the state). She was a suffragist, activist, and member of several organizations, including the Feminist League of Yucatán and the Guidance League for Women's Action (of which she was a founder). In 1924 she ran for the Chamber of Deputies in San Luís Potosí. Though she won the seat, she was denied occupying it. Otilia Zambrano was an activist, suffragist, and longtime employee of the SEP. Her career is described in "Entrevista de hoy: Otilia Zambrano," *El Nacional*, December 6, 1938, 1, 4.

38. Ana Salado Alvarez frequently wrote articles on women and work for Mexico City newspapers. Ana Salado Alvarez, "Ya no hay quien disputa el derecho que tiene la mujer para trabajar," *La Prensa*, October 2, 1935, 11. Other articles that defended women's right to work in government offices include "Las mujeres que trabajan," *El Universal*, June 7, 1936, 1; and "Mas de medio millón de mujeres hacen cabeza de casa en el pais," *La Prensa*, June 7, 1936, 11. For data on government employee head of household, see México, Dirección de Pensiones Civiles de Retiro, *Tercer censo de empleados federales sujetos a la ley general de México*, 36, 41, 50.

39. *La Prensa* was initially oriented toward a popular audience and widespread distribution. It was characterized by a large format and tended toward police reports. Edited by the Companía Mexicana de Rotograbado, its slogan was "We publish what the rest are afraid to say." After being taken over by creditor San Rafael paper factory, and then by the government, in 1935 it was turned over to workers. From that time on, *La Prensa* tended to give President Cárdenas favorable treatment, see González Marín, *Prensa y poder politico*, 30–33.

40. "La situación social y económica de la mujer," *Excélsior*, October 23, 1935, 10; and *El Nacional*, October 6, 1935, 5. For the response of the Women's Action Guidance League (Liga Orientadora de la Acción Feminil) and a session held in the SEP offices, see Salado Alvarez, "Ya no hay quien disputa," 11.

41. Gonzalo de la Parra, "Puntos de vista: Las mujeres que trabajan y los hombres que no trabajan," *El Universal*, August 10, 1937, 9.

42. Juan de Dios Bojórquez, AGN, March 20, 1935.

43. Ríos Cárdenas, *La mujer mexicana es ciudadana*, 131.

44. Esperanza Tuñón Pablos, *Mujeres que se organizan*; Ramos Escandón, "La participación de la mujer en México."

45. In 1934 National Economy employees asked for the enforcement of Articles 37 and 60 of the Civil Service Law, which provided for overtime and severance pay. Blanco, *Empleo público*, 55. The papers reported that Ministry of Interior employees established a union in 1934, but they do not mention women, See "Los empleados de Hacienda constituyen un sindicato," *La Prensa*, April 13, 1943, 1. Women may also have participated in the September 6, 1935, establishment of the Workers Alliance, Department of Health (Alianza de Trabajadores de Salubridad), which later became the National Union of Workers in the Department of Health and Welfare (Sindicato Nacional de Trabajadores de Salubridad y Asistencia). "Congreso de trabajadores de Salubridad," *El Nacional*, October 27, 1937, 8. Llach attended the first National Congress on Health and Welfare, mentioned in *Gaceta médica*, April 4, 1946. Bazant, *Laura Méndez de Cuenca*, 413. Zambrano interview by Aurelio de los Reyes, December 4, 1974, Mexico City, Archivo de la Palabra, Instituto Mora, PHO/2/15, p. 15.

46. Guerrero, *Historia del servicio civil de carrera en México*, 363.

47. "Se rebelan las empleadas por los descuentos," *La Prensa*, April 23, 1936, 3, 23. For a discussion of the impact of wage deductions, see Anguiano, *El estado y la política obrera*, 36.

48. "Se impidió el mitin que trataban de celebrar ayer," *La Prensa*, April 24, 1936, 2, 6.

49. "Empleadas de la Federación" to President Cárdenas, AGN, LCR, exp. 831, 544/1.

50. "Empleadas de la Federación" to President Cárdenas.

51. Esperanza Balmaceda was featured in "La entrevista de hoy: Ezperanza Balmaceda," *El Nacional*, November 15, 1938, 1. Balmaceda translated books from English, including one by C. Gilbert Wrenn for secondary school students (*Sugestiones a los estudiantes de escuelas secundarias sobre la mejor forma de estudiar*, 1946). She wrote on a wide range of professional topics; see, e.g., *Guia de profesiones que ofrece a padres y a estudiantes una panorama de oportunidades educativas: escuelas, profesiones, estudios necesarios, tiempo requerido, requisitos de admisión, etc.* (Mexico City: E.D.I.A.S.A., 1940); and *Oportunidades educativas para alumnos que terminan la educación primaria* (Mexico City: Instituto Nacional de Pedagogía, 1961).

52. "El presidente no se opone a la organización de las mujeres en la lucha social," *La Prensa*, April 25, 1936, 3, 13; "El PNR sobre los derechos cívicos de la mujer," *El Nacional*, April 24, 1936, 1; México, Secretaría de Hacienda y Crédito Público, *México a través de los informes presidencial*, 77–88; letter signed by Elvia Carrillo Puerto and Esperanza F. G. de Santibañez, April 24, 1936, AGN, LCR, caja 24, exp. 111/1568, 1–14.

53. "El presidente no se opone a la organizacion de las mujeres en la lucha social," *La Prensa*, April 25, 1936, 3, 13. Portes Gil reports on the PNR position on women

in "El PNR sobre los derechos cívicos de la mujer, *El Nacional*, April 24, 1936, 1. Women voiced their discontent that the meeting was cancelled in "El gobierno ve con satifacción que las mujeres organizan," *El Nacional*, April 25, 1936, 2.

54. "Organización del elemento feminil en el seno del PNR: Las empleadas públicas tuvieron una junta con Portes Gil para definir su posición en la lucha social," *La Prensa*, May 9, 1936, 3, 6; and "Total organización del sector feminino," *El Nacional*, May 9, 1936, 1. On Portes Gil's reasons for not attending the meeting, see "Se impidió el mitin que trataban de celebrar ayer," *La Prensa*, April 24, 1936, 2, 6.

55. "Empleadas que serán cesadas en el gobierno por tomar parte de la agitación feminista, se les trata de eliminar en las oficinas públicas," *La Prensa*, April 26, 1936, 3, 22; "Los empleados públicos podrán organizarse," *La Prensa*, April 26, 1936, 1, 3.

56. "El PNR y las demandas de las empleadas," *El Nacional*, May 1, 1936.

57. "Sector feminino en organización," *Excélsior*, April 30, 1936; "Será organizado en forma seria el sector feminino que hace servicio oficial," *Excélsior*, May 1, 1936; "En favor de las empleadas," *El Universal*, May 1, 1936; "Las empleadas públicas van a tener iguales derechos que los empleados," *La Prensa*, May 1, 1936; "Las empleadas federales se agitan," *La Prensa*, May 7, 1936, 17; "El PNR y las demandas de las empleadas," *El Nacional*, May 1, 1936; Garrido, *El Partido de la Revolución institucionalizada*, between pp. 192 and 193; *El Nacional*, May 1, 1936, 1.

58. García's role is described in "Las empleadas públicas van a tener iguales derechos que los empleados," *La Prensa*, May 1, 1936, 3, 22; "Una convención de empleados," *La Prensa*, May 3, 1936. On García's role in the public-employee union movement, see Sindicato Nacional de Trabajadores de la Secretaría de Gobernación, *Historia del Sindicato Nacional de Trabajadores de la Secretaría de Gobernación*, 34–39. Members of the Ministry of the Interior union included Manuel Zatarain (Sección Administración), Inocencio Ramírez, Emma Salgado, Arcadio Ojeda, Alvira Palencia, Carolina Reyes, Adriana Moreno, María Reboulen, and Carlos Cruz Lara. For more information see "Delegates to the second ordinary convention of the Ministry of the Interior Union vs. the National Union of Ministry of the Interior Workers (executive committee), for nullification of agreements made at the aforementioned convention," AGN, TFCA, caja 10, exp. 77/R/939. Employment history and union activism are included in Thaís García vs. Minister of the Interior, for reinstatement, AGN, TFCA, caja 193, exp. 2652/941.

59. "Las empleadas no politiquean," *La Prensa*, May 8, 1936, 3, 23.

60. "Organización del elemento feminil en el seno del PNR," 3, 6.

61. "Las empleadas no politiquean," *La Prensa*, May 8, 1936, 3, 23; and "Las empleadas de Salubridad contra el alcoholismo," *El Nacional*, November 12, 1935, 1, 5. Llach was the first signatory on a letter to President Cárdenas congratulating him for his public support for women's suffrage. She was joined by eighty-eight other women

in the Department of Child Welfare. "Empleadas de la Federacion" to President
Cárdenas, AGN, LCR, exp. 831, 544/1.

62. "Las empleadas federales se agitan," *La Prensa*, May 7, 1936, 17; "Organización del
elemento feminil en el seno del PNR," 3, 6.

63. "Organización del elemento feminil en el seno del PNR," 3, 6; "Hay un gran alboroto
entre las empleadas de gobierno," *La Prensa*, May 10, 1936, 3; "Los empleados no
quieren el servicio civil," *La Prensa*, May 12, 1936, 3, 28.

64. "La agitada asamblea de las señoritas empleadas en la Secretaría de Educación,"
La Prensa, May 13, 2, 5.

65. "Opinan dos mujeres sobre la elección de su delegada al PNR," *La Prensa*, May 14,
1936, 12. Francisco R. Vila represented the cross office solidarity group, Francisco R.
Vila Jesus Moreno represented the Telegraph Office, and José Barriga represented
Communications and Public Works.

66. The organization that Rodríguez Cabo represented is not identified in the press.
"La ley del servicio civil y no las leyes del trabajo," *La Prensa*, May 15, 3, 4.

67. "Se organizan las empleadas del gobierno," *Excélsior*, May 21, 1936; and "Comité
ejecutivo de empleadas de gobierno," *El Universal*, May 21, 1936.

68. "Liberación de la mujer mexicana en todo el país," *El Nacional*, June 23, 1936;
"Programa de Organización Nacional Feminina de Empleadas Federales adherida
al PNR," *El Nacional*, August 25, 1936; "Amplia ayuda del PNR a las mujeres," *El
Nacional*, October 10, 1936. Refugio Rangel, Edelmira R. Viuda de Escudero, and
Aurora Fernández, as a part of the Cooperative for Mexican Women's Homes
(Pro Hogar de la Mujer Mexicana), proposed a bank for women who worked in
government offices in a letter May 7, 1935, AGN, LCR, caja 895, exp. 545.3/222.

69. "Empleadas de la Federación" to President Cárdenas, AGN, LCR, exp. 831, 544/1,
26. See also Portes Gil, *Quince años de política mexicana*, 513–14.

70. "Empleadas de la Federación" to President Cárdenas, AGN, LCR, exp. 831, 544/1, 26.

71. "El PNR da a la mujer participación en la dirección de sus organismos," *El Nacional*, October 6, 1937. The women's sector of the PNR continued to be closely
associated with female office workers. Sara Romero, former president of PNR
subcommittee no. 5, complained that when she had asked Lucina Villareal for a
committee membership card, Villareal had told her that the organization was for
female government workers only. Sara Romero, ex-president, PNR subcommittee
no. 5, to Lic. Barba Gonzalez, president of the PNR in the DF, December 4, 1937,
AGN, LCR, exp. 830, 544/1.

72. The U.S. Embassy reported on the president's strategy in United States Department
of State Records, SA5299415979, March 1938. On Cárdenas's strategy to contain
popular mobilization, see Garrido, *El Partido de la Revolución institucionalizada*,

317; Partido Revolucionario Institucional, *Historia*, 407–8; and León and Marván, *La clase obrera*, 295.

73. Middlebrook, *The Paradox of Revolution*, 93.

74. For President Cárdenas on a women's sector, see "Placemenes de las mujeres al H. Congreso," *El Nacional*, July 7, 1938; and Ríos Cárdenas, *La mujer mexicana es ciudadana*, 172–73. On the congress, see "El movimiento feminista y su progreso en la última etapa," *El Nacional*, May 27, 1938, 8. Mexico City representatives included Angela Garcia, Revolutionary Women's Center; Guadalupe Torres, "Flores Magón" Neighborhood Association; Elvira G. de Vidrio, "Macario Navarro" Neighborhood Association; Soledad Reyes, Revolutionary Women; Colonia 20 de noviembre; Modesta Ambriz, San Juanico Women's Center; and Luz Valdez, "Josefa Ortíz de Domínguez" Women's League.

75. FRITI, AGN, LCR, exp. 702.1/111, 1939. Cárdenas named Mathilde Rodríguez Cabo to head the Department of Social Welfare in the Department of the Federal District; see AGN, LCR, exp. 702.2/8589; and Enriqueta Tuñón Pablos, *Por fin!*, 52. From Veracruz, Mancisidor (1894–1956) followed Gonzalo Vázquez Vela to the SEP in 1935, where he worked until 1940. Also from Veracruz, Méndez was close with Adalberto Tejeda, see E. Ginzberg, *Revolutionary Ideology and Political Destiny*, 168, 177. Arellano Belloc, from San Luis Potosí, studied law at the UNAM and was instrumental in writing up the oil expropriation decree. Othón Díaz Melo (1904–67), from Oaxaca, first followed a religious vocation and then studied to be a teacher. In 1957 he established the Revolutionary Teachers Movement (Movimiento Revolucionario del Magisterio), later the National Coordinating Committee of Education Workers (Coordinadora Nacional de Trabajadores de la Educación). He was the author of numerous books, including *La montaña virgin* (1936).

76. FRITI, AGN, LCR, exp. 702.1/111, 1939. Membership is provided for only some of the organizations, including the School of Social Work (54 members in Mexico City), the Women's Social Studies Group (29), the Women's Revolutionary Institute (237), the Mexican Society of Women Lawyers (15), the National Social Workers Union (1,000), and the Midwife and Nurses Union (800). The Revolutionary Women's Institute (Instituto Revolucionario Feminino, est. July 1937), which included Concha Michel, Aurora Reyes, and Sara and Virginia Godínez, argued that while women might share common cause with workers, women constituted a distinct class based on their role in "reproduction of the human race." Selene de Dios Vallejo and Navarro Lara, "El feminismo como movimiento social."

77. The FRITI also included the "On the March" Group (20 Mexico City–based members), the Lawyers Socialist Front (157 Mexico City–based members), and the League of Revolutionary Writers and Artists (25 Mexico City–based members).

78. "Se inauguró ayer en Bellas Artes la sesión de los intelectuales," *La Prensa*, February 13, 1938, 3, 13. The photograph accompanying the article shows a crowd, more than two-thirds of which are women. Enriqueta de Parodi, "Un llamado a la mujer," *Crisol*, March 1, 1938, 25.

79. Letter dated February 23, 1938, from the Frente Revolucionarios de Trabajadores Intelectuales to C. President del Comite Ejecutivo Nacional del Partido Nacional Revolucionario, Lic. Silvano Barba Gonzalez, AGN, LCR, exp. 544.61/103.

80. "Programa de acción, estatutos y reglamentos del sector feminino del Frente Revolucionario Mexicano," signed by Elvia Carrillo Puerto, April 9, 1938, AGN, LCR, exp. 830.544/1, 1–14; and AGN, LCR, exp. 830, 544.61, exp. 103, pp. 355–60.

81. "La manifestación burocrática," *La Prensa*, February 11, 1938, 1; "Las mujeres burócratas montaron ayer guardias ante la campaña popular," *La Prensa*, February 16, 1938, 3, 4; "Amistad o guerra burócratas según escojan los cc. diputados," *La Prensa*, February 20, 1938, 1.

82. AGN, LCR, exp. 703.3/41.

83. Balmaceda request, AGN, LCR, exp. 830.544/1.

84. Office workers from the following government offices attended: Finance; Department of Labor; Juvenile Justice; Ministry of National Economy; Acción Feminina; Agrarian Department; Ministry of Communication and Public Works; Post, Telegraphy, and Roads; Interior; Public Education; the National Teacher's School; General Sanatorium; Public Health; and the Federation of State Workers Unions. Report on the "Special Meeting for Women," AGN, DGIPS, 30, exp. 20, February 1938. For further reports, see caja 68, exp. 4, 1938, and caja 79, exp. 1, 1938. Newspaper reports include "Conferencia especial de mujeres," *El Nacional*, February 17, 1938, 4; "Conferencia de Unificacion Feminina," *El Nacional*, February 19, 1938, 7.

85. Candidates included Adelina Zendejas, Concha Michel, María Rocha, Refugio García, Natividad Alvarez, Soledad Flores, Esther Chapa, and Elvira Trueba. AGN, DGIPS, caja 30, exp. 29, 1938, caja 68, exp. 4, 1938, and caja 79, exp. 1, 1938.

86. "Las mujeres burócratas montaron ayer guardias ante la campaña popular," *La Prensa*, February 16, 1938, 3, 4; "Amistad o guerra burócratas segun escojan los cc. diputados," *La Prensa*, February 20, 1938, 1.

87. Speakers named in the report include Otilia Zambrano, Adelina Zendejas, Angela Higueras, Ana María Hernandez, Refugio Guerrero, and Lucína Villarreal. AGN, DGIPS, caja 30, exp. 29, 1938, caja 68, exp. 4, 1938, and caja 79, exp. 1, 1938.

88. Report on CNOP gathering, AGN, DGIPS, caja 70, exp. 12. See also "Un cambio de impresiones con la CTM," February 11, 1938, 1, 8.

89. "Bases para el ingreso de la mujer en el partido," *El Nacional*, December 3, 1938, 1.

90. Partido Revolucionario Institucional, *Historia documental de la CNOP*, 1:38–49.

91. Esperanza Tuñón Pablos, *Mujeres que se organizen*, 139–40; Enriqueta Tuñón Pablos, *Por fin!*, 50; *La Voz de México*, March 8, 1939. The government spied on the women's section of the PRM's protest at the Chamber of Deputies. See AGN, DGIPS, caja 22, exp. 11, May 1939. On Jiménez Esponda, see "Señorita Estela Jiménez Esponda, secretaria de la seccion feminil del Sector Popular," *El Nacional*, August 31, 1939, 2.

92. The United States Embassy reported on Cárdenas's handling of the public-employee labor movement. See United States Department of State Records, SA5299415979. 812.504, November 16, 1938. Córdova states that Cárdenas proposed the FSTSE in June 1937. Córdova, *La política de masas*, 127. On the establishment of FSTSE see also Blanco, *Empleo público*, 50. FSTSE was led by Francisco Patiño Cruz (1938–40) and Cándido Jaramillo (1940–42). Camp, *Mexican Political Biographies*, 1300.

93. For a full list of unions that formed in the wake of the congress, see Federación de Sindicatos de Trabajadores al Servicio del Estado, *Breve historia de la FSTSE*, https://www.google.com/search?q=Federaci%C3%B3n+de+Sindicatos+de +Trabajadores+al+Servicio+del+Estado%2C+Breve+historia+de+la+FSTSE.& ie=utf-8&oe=utf-8. For the FSTSE declaration of loyalty to the government, see AGN, LCR, exp. 544.61/103; and Anguiano, *El estado y la política obrera*, 58–60. FSTSE had offices at 55 Lucerna Street.

94. "Diversas opiniones sobre el voto para las mujeres," *El Nacional*, November 20, 23, 1938, 8. For the interview with Leonor Conde, see "Sección de los trabajadores al servicio del estado," *El Nacional*, November 1, 1938, 8. Gómez was also interviewed in "Sección de los trabajadores al servicio del estado," *El Nacional*, November 13, 16, 1938, 2:2.

95. "Sección de los trabajadores al servicio del estado," *El Nacional*, November 2, 1938, 2; "Sección de los trabajadores al servicio del estado," *El Nacional*, November 3, 1938, 1, 7.

96. On FSTSE elections, see "Clausura de la convención de los empleados públicos," *El Nacional*, November 2, 1938, 1, 7. FSTSE negotiations with the National Con-federation of Veterans are reported in "Pacto firmado de solidaridad," *El Nacional*, January 11, 1941, 1, 7. Reports on Barrena's protests on the steps of the Chamber of Deputies include "Una manifestación hoy," *El Nacional*, September 8, 1939, 4; and "Federación de Sindicatos de Trabajadores al Servicio del Estado," *El Nacional*, February 14, 1939, 8. Barrena also engaged in service projects as in "Para mejorar a los niños autóctonos," *El Nacional*, November 17, 1938, 7.

97. "Manifestación feminil hoy," *El Nacional*, May 19, 1939, 1, 8.

98. "Un mitin de las mujeres por el voto," *El Nacional*, May 20, 1939, 8.

99. Telegrams to President Cárdenas, AGN, LCR, exp. 830.544/1. Many of the women who signed the telegrams were longtime empleada rights activists: Soledad Flores

(SEP), Thaís García (Gobernación), Licenciada Mercedes Martínez Montes (SEP), Refugio Rangel, Luz García Nuñez, Gudelia Gómez (Departamento del Trabajo), Leonor Llach (SEP), Elisa G. Flores, and Refugio Moreno Ruffo.

100. "La mujer organizada y el derecho de ciudanía," *Tesis* 1:12, June 30, 1939, 28–29. The *Tesis* article is addressed in H. M. Monteón and Riquelme Alcántar, "El presidente Cárdenas y el sufragio feminino."

101. While women lacked full citizenship and could not bring electoral pressure to bear on politicians, as Olcott points out, they nevertheless exerted pressure as employees of the government. Women, identifying themselves as government workers, continued to pressure Cárdenas for the vote. See "Empleadas de la Federación" to President Cárdenas, September 2, 1937, AGN, LCR, exp. 831, 544/1; Olcott, *Revolutionary Women*, 237.

7. WOMEN, WORK, AND MIDDLE-CLASS IDENTITY, 1940S

1. Rankin, *México, la patria!* 2, 210, 286; Niblo, *Mexico in the 1940s*.

2. Sanders, *Gender and Welfare*, 73.

3. Rendón Gan, *Trabajo de hombres y trabajo de mujeres*, 111; García, "Comparación de la información sobre subgrupos."

4. In 1940, 7.4 percent of women worked outside of the home. See México, Secretaría de la Economía Nacional, Dirección General de Estadistíca, *Sexto censo*, 28 For a discussion of women's workforce participation, see González Salazar, "La participación de la mujer," 111.

5. In the 1940 population census women were 24 percent of government employees (16,438 of 69,323). *Sexto censo de la población*, 28. According to the population censuses, in the Federal District the number of female government employees increased from 5,941 (1930) to 16,438 (1940), and the number of men increased from 38,552 (1930) to 52,885 (1940). In the Federal District the total number of government employees went from 44,493 (1930) to 69,323 (1940). According to Ernesto Lobato, drawing on statistics from the Ministry of Finance, the total number of government employees rose from 52,154 in 1933 to 130,953 in 1950. Lobato, "La burocracia mexicana."

6. Ferrer, December 30, 1940, AGN, MAC, 703.2/22.

7. Garrido to the president, January 4, 1941, AGN, MAC, 703.2/22. As during the 1930s, women again came to the defense of women's right to work in government offices. See, e.g., María del Socorro Hurtado, "En defensa de la mujer, *El Universal*, November 26, 1940, 9; María Engracia Roman, "Mujeres que trabajan," *Excélsior*, October, 1941, 4.

8. *Sexto censo de la población, 1940*, 28; México, Instituto Nacional de Estadística y Geografía e Informática, *100 años de censos de población*.

9. Basurto, *Cárdenas y el poder sindical*, 43–47, 97.

10. Iturriaga, *La estructura social y cultural*, 79.

11. On female government workers regarding salaries, see AGN, MAC, exp. 703.2/22. On dining halls, see Aguilar, "Cooking Modernity."

12. Trueba Urbina, *Legislación de emergencia*, 3–8, 45. The legislation provided for a wage increase for all workers except those working as domestic servants in private homes. After passing legislation for workers, the government did so for public employees, published in *Diario Oficial* on September 24, 1943.

13. Basurto, *Cárdenas y el poder sindical*, 97. On cost of living, see also México, Secretaría de Economía Nacional, *Memoria de la Secretaría de Economía Nacional*, 26. The study found that prices increased from a baseline of 100 in 1934 to 249.79 in 1943. On the increased cost of living in 1940s Mexico see also Rankin, *México, la patria!*, 210. On the NDR, see Moreno, *Yankee Don't Go Home!*, 34–36. Although the NDR was designed to benefit the public, it was not a state entity. See: amparo civil en revision 6191/48, in México, Suprema Corte de Justicia, Tercera Sala, Quínta época, *Semanario Judicial de la Federación*, tomo XCIX, 1373.

14. Basurto, *Cárdenas y el poder sindical*, 47; Moreno, *Yankee Don't Go Home!*, 32–37; Ochoa, *Feeding Mexico*, 14, 74. Medina, *Historia patria*, 219–20. See also *El Popular*, August 7, 8, 13, 30, 1943.

15. Antonio Armendariz, "Notas de México: Caminos para la mujer," *Excélsior*, November 24, 1943, 10.

16. Rendón Gan, *Trabajo de hombres y trabajo de mujeres*, 106–19.

17. Sodi de Pallares was born on November 18, 1903, to Carmen Pallares Portillo Demetrio Sodi Guergue, a lawyer who defended José de León Toral, who assassinated President Álvaro Obregón. She worked as a journalist and was the author of numerous books, including *Siluetas en papel* (1927); *Vidas y escenas burgesas* (1936); *Los cristeros y José de León Toral* (1936); *Historia del traje religioso* (1950); *Teodoro A. Dehesa: Una época y un hombre* (1959); and *Historia de una obra pía (el Hospital de Jesús en la historia de México)* (1956). See María Elena Sodi de Pallares, "El misérimo salario de las mujeres," *El Universal*, December 25, 1942, 9. Sodi de Pallares refers to the Comisión Reguladora de Comestibles.

18. The category "burocracia femenina" appears in Mendieta y Núñez, *La administración pública en México*, 283. For an introduction to Mendieta y Nuñez see Olvera Serrano, "La primera socialización intelectual de Lucío Mendieta y Núñez"; Zenteno, "Lucio Mendieta y Nuñez"; and Lobato, "La burocracia mexicana."

19. Mendieta y Núñez, *La administración pública en México*, 298. Mendieta y Núñez's discussion of class appears in *Las clases sociales*, 299–304. Mendieta y Núñez's discussion of women appears in *La administración pública en México*, 272, 283, 299–304.

20. Mendieta y Núñez, *Las clases sociales*, 148, 169–70.

21. Iturriaga, *La estructura social y cultural*. The Nacional Financiera, a state-run development bank, facilitated loans to private industry and promoted parastatals like PEMEX. José Ezequiel Iturriaga Sauco (b. April 20, 1914, d. February 18, 2011) assumed that the social class of an employed person indicated the class status of the entire family. Iturriaga, *La estructura social y cultural*, 25, 28, 60; Jorge Simmel, *Sociología*, vol. 1 (Buenos Aires: Espasa Calpe, S.A., 1939), 196–97.

22. Public employees (state and municipal): 1921, 63,074; 1930, 153,343; 1940, 191,588; and in 1950 approximately 250,000—nearly quadrupling in thirty years. Iturriaga, *La estructura social y cultural*, 58.

23. Iturriaga, *La estructura social y cultural*, 13–16, 22, 62–63. The information about the groups most associated with single motherhood appears in Iturriaga, *La estructura social y cultural*, 17.

24. Teresa de Cepeda, "La mujer que trabaja," *Excélsior*, September 6, 1942, 10.

25. De Cepeda, "La mujer que trabaja," 10.

26. De Cepeda, "La mujer que trabaja," 10.

27. Guillermina Llach, "La mujer en la oficina," transmitido por RADIO—SCOP, desde la Feria del Libro, en el programa de la editorial "IDEAS," November 9, 1944, and published in *IDEAS* 1944, 28–31.

28. Hirshfield and Maciel, *Mexico's Cinema*.

29. Several films presented the state as the savior of women. Emilio Fernández directed *Las abandonadas* (1945), in which masculine authority is reasserted as Pedro Armendáriz, representing the state, sweeps up one of the many young, unmarried mothers cast aside by society, played by Dolores del Rio. Del Río is dressed in one of the most expensive wardrobes (designed by Armando Valadez Peza) ever seen in Mexican film.

30. Born María Sarah Batiza Berkowitz in Mexico City on March 20, 1914, she died on June 2, 1981; Estate of Blanca Batiza Berckowitz de Rivera and Rodolfo Batiza Berckowitz. When Batiza crossed the border into the United States in January 1933, she said she was a twenty-two-year-old single stenographer. Her father had already passed away, and her mother, also named Sarah, lived in Calexico. When Sarah Batiza crossed again in 1947, she carried with her a letter of reference from El Palacio of Hierro, perhaps an employer; see http://interactive.ancestry.com.au/1082 /31343_B036717-03884/9090520?backurl=http%3a%2f%2fsearch.Ancestry.com .au%2fcgi-bin%2fsse.dll%3fgst%3d-6&ssrc=&backlabel=ReturnSearchResults. In 1947 Batiza lived at 268 Hamburgo Street, apartment 7. At age thirty-one she crossed the U.S.-Mexico border accompanied by her daughter, Blanca Batiza, whose age was not indicated; https://familysearch.org/ark:/61903/3:1:33S7-9RKK-7S3 ?i=2534&wc=M8R5-YNL%3A218842001%2C220927202%3Fcc%3D1923424 &cc=1923424.

31. "La nota cultural," *El Nacional*, March 2, 1950, 3–4. Batiza received the Certamen Cultural de Talleres Gráficos de la Nación in 1949.

32. Batiza published several more novels, including *Eso que se llama un niño* and *La araña ávara*. She also published stories that appeared in *El Magazine Dominical de El Universal*. See also Rangel and Portas, *Enciclopedia cinematográfica mexicana*.

33. Batiza, *Nosotras, las taquígrafas*, 9.

34. Batiza, *Nosotras, las taquígrafas*, 12, 40.

35. Batiza, *Nosotras, las taquígrafas*, 40–54, 98.

36. Batiza, *Nosotras, las taquígrafas*, 311.

37. Batiza, *Nosotras, las taquígrafas*, 59, 116–18.

38. Batiza, *Nosotras, las taquígrafas*,114.

39. Batiza, *Nosotras, las taquígrafas*, 46.

40. Batiza, *Nosotras, las taquígrafas*, 35–36, 203.

41. Batiza, *Nosotras, las taquígrafas*, 44, 90–92, 106–7, 116–17.

42. Batiza, *Nosotras, las taquígrafas*, 234.

43. Batiza, *Nosotras, las taquígrafas*, 22, 3436, 238.

44. Batiza, *Nosotras, las taquígrafas*, 32.

45. Batiza, *Nosotras, las taquígrafas*, 22, 260–61.

46. Batiza, *Nosotras, las taquígrafas*, 144, 154–57.

47. Batiza, *Nosotras, las taquígrafas*, 294–300.

48. The review appears in Margarita Pas Paredes, "*Mis Yos y Larry*," *El Nacional*, February 5, 1958, 11. The copyright for *Mis Yos y Larry* appeared in *Diario Oficial*, August 12, 1958, 3. Born Margarita Camacho Baquedano, Paz Paredes studied journalism at the Universidad Obrera and then at the Facultad de Filosofía y Letras, UNAM. She wrote *Sonaja* (1942) and went on to publish widely. She was a professor at the University of Toluca and the National Teaching School (Escuela Normal Superior de México). Pas wrote a poem for the fiftieth anniversary of the MLT and so may have been a graduate. See Cacho García, *Cifra de oro*, 70–71.

49. Sanders looks at women's role as social workers employed in government offices in *Gender and Welfare*, 3, 136.

50. For a description of the social security law and reaction to it, see Basurto, *La clase obrera*, 22–29; and Medina, *Historia patria*, 323. The law appeared in *Diario Oficial*, January 19, 1942. See also Instituto Mexicano de Seguro Social, *Código de seguridad social* (Mexico City: Instituto Mexicano de Seguro Social, 1947).

51. Zambrano, Social Security, AGN, OZ, December 31, 1942. For a discussion of the social security law, see Trueba Urbina and Trueba Barrera, *Legislación federal del trabajo burocrático*, 74.

52. Guadalupe Olvera H. to President Ávila Camacho, November 1945, AGN, MAC, 545.3/11.

53. Zambrano, "Care and Support for Women as Mothers," AGN, OZ, Correspondencia, caja 4, exp. 1. The other woman involved in strategizing how to present the case for working mothers may have been Aurora Reyes, who represented the STERM at the 1939 women's conference in Cuba. See Aguilar Urbán, *Aurora Reyes*, 37; Reyes, *Diccionario de escritores mexicanos, siglo XX* (Mexico City: Universidad Nacional Autónomo de México, 2004), 7:205.

54. Zambrano, "Care and Support for Women as Mothers," AGN, OZ, Correspondencia, caja 4, exp. 1. "Grandiose speeches, poetry, and verse dedicated to mothers must be translated into concrete resources. The Latin phrase has never been more appropriate: 'Facta non verba!'"

55. SNTE to Zambrano, June 28, 1940, AGN, OZ, Correspondencia, caja 4, exp. 1.

56. Day care for office and factory workers was introduced to Congress in 1939; see "Creación de un seguro de maternidad: Ha sido muy bien recibida la iniciativa del Diputado Alfonso F. Ramírez," *Excélsior*, May 5, 1939. On employees' request for day care, see AHSEP, Subsecretaria, "Guardería Infantil de la Secretaría," caja 9, exp. 2, 1941, 1947.

57. Ruffo and Herrera inquiry about day care, AGN, MAC, 545.3/11, November 1945.

58. Josefina Gaona, "La mujer trabajadora y sus problemas," *El Universal*, September 20, 1945, 9. Gaona was the author of *Trabajo social: Algunos problemas sociales de México* (Mexico City: Ariel, 1946), and *Introducción al estudio del trabajo social* (Mexico City: Editorial Cultura, 1951). Gaona is mentioned in Sanders, *Gender and Welfare*, 26, 122.

59. "Arena México," *El Nacional*, July 28, 1945, 4. The National Women's Alliance (Alianza Nacional Femenina brought together union and organizational leaders, AGN, MAC, 135.2/547, March 1945.

60. Becerril, *Programa y centros de actividad*, 4.

61. Becerril, *Programa y centros de actividad*, 6. See also Fernández Aceves, "Las políticas de género."

62. Federación de Sindicatos de Trabajadores al Servicio del Estado, *La F.S.T.S.E. en marcha*, 16–20. See also "Disciplina absoluta y mayor esfuerzo, pide a los burócratas su secretario general," *Novedades*, February 2, 1950; and "La Burocracia," *Excélsior*, June 19, 1950, 10.

CONCLUSION

1. Teresa de Cepeda, "La mujer que trabaja," *Excélsior*, September 6, 1942, 10. For references to middle-class politics in Mexico, see Introduction herein, notes 17–20 and 22. Middle-class consumer habits are discussed in Bunker, *Creating Mexican*

Consumer Culture, 127–33. Middle-class manners are discussed in Muñíz, *Cuerpo, representación y poder*, 23–24.

2. Grenfell, *Key Concepts*, 50, 73.

3. See, e.g., Cano, Gabriela. "Género y construcción cultural"; Bazant, *Laura Méndez de Cuenca*.

4. Bortz, *Revolution within the Revolution*, 59–73; Womack, *El trabajo en la Cervecería Moctezuma*, 16–17. Bortz explains occupational segregation of the workforce as resulting from Mexican cultural practices that identify women primarily with the home. On the role of norms of femininity in factory labor regimes see Fowler-Salamini, *Working Women*, 102, 117, 177; Snodgrass, *Deference and Defiance*, 75–78; Porter, *Working Women in Mexico City*, 128–32, 187; and Porter, "De obreras y señoritas." On the role of gender norms in factory labor regimes in Colombia see Farnsworth-Alvear, *Dulcinea in the Factory*.

5. Gauss, "Working-Class Masculinity"; Porter, *Working Women in Mexico City*, 18, 128–32, 155; Lear, *Workers, Neighbors, and Citizens*, 8; Barbosa Cruz, *El trabajo en la calle*, 30; Eineigel, "Revolutionary Promises Encounter Urban Realities." Women's ties through work and community are discussed in Fowler-Salamini, *Working Women*, 83–85.

6. Gómez-Galvarriato, *Industry and Revolution*, 148; León and Marván, *La clase obrera*, 9; Connelly, "Política, trabajo y género," 216.

7. Orleck, *Commen Sense and a Little Fire*, 296. On women's relationship with organized labor in the United States, see also Kessler-Harris, *Out to Work*, 152. Discussions of the relationship between women and organized labor in Mexico include Fowler-Salamini, *Working Women*, chapters 3 and 4; Fernández Aceves, "Once We Were Corn Grinders"; Lear, *Workers, Neighbors, and Citizens*, 348–50; Porter, *Working Women in Mexico City*, 110–14.

8. Fernández Aceves, "Once We Were Corn Grinders."

9. Enriqueta Tuñón Pablos, *¡Por fin*, 49, 113, 141, 278–80; Olcott, *Revolutionary Women in Postrevolutionary Mexico*, 28. Leonor Llach accepted the idea that women tended to be more conservative than men. The Revolution had failed women, she argued, and they had therefore turned to religion to deal with their problems. Leonor Llach, "La situación de la Mujer," *El Nacional*, December 11, 1933, 8.

10. Fernández-Aceves, "Once We Were Corn Grinders."

11. Strom, *Beyond the Typewriter*, 9.

BIBLIOGRAPHY

ARCHIVES

Archivo General de la Nación, Mexico City
    Archivos de Particulares
        Personas/Otilia Zambrano
    Departamento del Trabajo
    Colección de Folletería de los Siglos XIX y XX
    Instrucción Pública y Bellas Artes
        Instrucción Pública y Bellas Artes
        Propiedad Artística y Literaria
    Junta Federal de Conciliación y Arbitraje
    Justicia
        Justicia e Instruccion Pública
    Presidentes
        Miguel Alemán Valdés
        Manuel Ávila Camacho
        Lázaro Cárdenas del Río
        Álvaro Obregón-Plutarco Elías Calles
        Pascual Ortiz Rubio
        Emilio Portes Gil
        Abelardo L. Rodríguez
    Secretaría de Gobernación Siglo XX
        Dirección General de Administración
        Dirección General de Investigaciones Políticas y Sociales
    Tribunal Federal de Conciliación y Arbitraje
Archivo Histórico de la Secretaría de Educación Pública, Mexico City
    Antiguo Magisterio
    Departamento de Escuelas Técnicas, Industriales y Comerciales
    Departamento Escolar
    Dirección de Enseñanza Superior e Investigación Científica
    Dirección General de Administración
    Personal
Archivo Histórico de la Secretaría de Relaciones Exteriores, Mexico City

Archivo Histórico de la Secretaría de Salubridad, Mexico City
    Personal
Archivo Histórico de la Suprema Corte de Justicia de la Nación, Mexico City
Archivo Histórico de la Universidad Nacional Autónoma de México
    Archivo General
        Escuela Nacional de Altos Estudios
        Escuela Nacional de Medicina
Archivo Histórico Porfirio Díaz, Mexico City
Biblioteca Miguel Lerdo de Tejada, Mexico City
    Recortes

PUBLISHED WORKS

Acosta, Helia d.' *Veinte mujeres*. Mexico City: Editores Asociados, 1971.
Adamovsky, Ezequiel. "Acerca de la relación entre el Radicalismo argentino y la 'clase media' (una vez más)." *Hispanic American Historical Review* 89, no. 2 (2009): 209–51.
———. "Usos de la idea de 'clase media' en Francia: La imaginación social y geográfica en la formación de la sociedad burguesa." *Prohistoria* 13, no. 13 (Spring 2009): 9–29.
Adams, Carole Elizabeth. *Women Clerks in Wilhelmine Germany: Issues of Class and Gender*. Cambridge: Cambridge University Press, 1988.
Adams, Rachael. *Continental Divides: Remapping the Cultures of North America*. Chicago: University of Chicago Press, 2009.
Aguilar-Rodríguez, Sandra. "Cooking Modernity: Nutrition Policies, Class, and Gender in 1940s and 1950s Mexico." *The Americas* 64, no. 2 (October 2007): 177–205.
Aguilar-Moreno, Manuel, and Erika Cabrera. *Diego Rivera: A Biography*. Santa Barbara CA: Greenwood Biographies, 2011.
Aguilar Urbán, Margarita. *Aurora Reyes: Alma de Montaña*. Prologue by Alberto Híjar Serrano. Chihuahua: Instituto Chihuahuense de la Cultura, 2010.
Alanís, Mercedes. "Más que curar, prevenir: Surgimiento y primera etapa de los Centros de Higiene Infantil en la ciudad de México, 1922–1932." *História, Ciencia, Saúde Manguinhos* 22, no. 2 (April–June 2015): 391–409.
Albarrán, Elena Jackson. *Seen and Heard in Mexico: Children and Revolutionary Cultural Nationalism*. Lincoln: University of Nebraska Press, 2015.
Alvarado, María de Lourdes. *La educación "superior" femenina en el México del siglo XIX: Demanda social y reto gubernamental*. Mexico City: Universidad Nacional Autónoma de México, 2004.
———. "La prensa como alternativa educativa para las mujeres de principios de siglo XIX." In *Familia y educación en iberoamérica*, ed. Pilar Gonzalbo Aizpuru, 267–85. Mexico City: El Colegio de México, 2003.

——, comp. *El siglo XIX ante el feminismo: Una interpretación positivista*. Mexico City: Universidad Nacional Autónoma de México, Coordinación de Humanidades, Centro de Estudios Universitarios, 1991.

Álvarez Lloveras, Guadalupe. "Luis Enrique Erro Soler." *El Cronista Politécnico* 8, no. 32 (January–March 2007): 2–6.

Andreo, Juan, and Sara Beatriz Guardia, eds. *Historia de las mujeres en América Latina*. Murcia: Universidad de Murcia, 2002.

Anguiano, Arturo. *El estado y la política obrera del cardenismo*. Mexico City: Ediciones Era, 1986.

Araiza, José Luís. *Historia del movimiento obrero mexicano*. Mexico City: Editorial de la Casa del Obrero Mundial, 1964.

Arredondo, María Adelina. *Obedecer, servir y resistir: La educación de las mujeres en la historia de México*. Mexico City: Universidad Pedagógica Nacional/Porrúa, 2003.

Arrom, Silvia Marina. *Volunteering for a Cause: Gender, Faith and Charity in Mexico from the Reform to the Revolution*. Albuquerque: University of New Mexico Press, 2016.

——. *The Women of Mexico City, 1790–1857*. Stanford: Stanford University Press, 1985.

Asociación de Maestros Egresados de la Escuela Normal de Jalisco. *La Escuela Normal de Jalisco: Galeria de generaciones de maestros esgresados de ella, 1894–1958*. Guadalajara, 1958.

Azuela, Mariano. *Regina Landa*. Mexico City: Ediciones Botas, 1939.

Bach, Federico. "Un estudio del costo de la vida." *Trimestre Económico* 2, no. 5 (1935): 12–49.

Bach, Federico, and Margarita Reyna. "El nuevo índice de precios al mayoreo en la ciudad de México de la Secretaría de la Economía Nacional." *Trimestre Económico* 10, no. 37(1) (April–June 1943): 1–63.

Bachrach, Susan. *Dames Employées: The Feminization of Postal Work in Nineteenth Century France*. New York: Institute for Research in History, 1984.

Baker, Paula Baker. "The Domestification of Politics: Women and American Political Society, 1780–1920." *American Historical Review* 89 (June 1984): 620–47.

Bank, Michaela. *Women of Two Countries: German American Women, Women's Rights, and Nativism, 1848–1890*. New York: Berghahn, 2012.

Barbieri, Teresita de. *Movimientos feministas*. Mexico City: Universidad Nacional Autónoma de México, Coordinación de Humanidades, 1986.

Barbosa Cruz, Mario. "Empleados públicos en la Ciudad de México: Condiciones laborales y construcción de la administración pública (1903–1931)." In *Cuestión social, políticas sociales y construcción del estado social en América Latina, siglo XX*, ed. Mario Barbosa Cruz and Fernando J. Remedi, 129–50. Córdoba, Argentina: Centro de Estudios Históricos "Prof. Carlos S. A. Segreti"/Consejo Nacional de Investigaciones Científicas y Técnicas/Universidad Autónoma de México–Cuajimalpa, 2014.

———. "Los empleados públicos, 1903–1931." In *Los trabajadores de la Ciudad de México, 1860–1950: Textos en homenaje a Clara E. Lida*, ed. Carlos Illades and Mario Barbosa Cruz, 117–54. Mexico City: El Colegio de México/Universidad Autónoma Metropolitana, Cuajimalpa, 2013.

———. *El trabajo en las calles: Subsistencia y negociación política en la Ciudad de México a comienzos del siglo XX*. Mexico City: El Colegio de México/Universidad Autónoma de México–Cuajimalpa, 2008.

Barrancos, Dora. *Mujeres en la sociedad argentina: Una historia de cinco siglos*. Buenos Aires: Editorial Sudamericana, 2007.

Basurto, Jorge. *Cárdenas y el poder sindical*. Mexico City: Editores Era, 1983.

———. *La clase obrera en la historia de México: Del avilacamachismo al alemanismo (1940–1952)*. Mexico City: Siglo XXI Editores, 1984.

Batiza, Sarah. *La araña ávara*. Mexico City: Bruguera Mexicana, 1979.

———. *Eso que se llama un niño*. Mexico: Organización Editorial Novaro, 1968.

———. *Nosotras, las taquígrafas*. Mexico City: Editorial Stylo, 1950.

Bazant, Mílada. *Historia de la educación durante el Porfiriato*. Mexico City: Colegio de México, Centro de Estudios Históricos, 1993.

———. *Laura Méndez de Cuenca: Mujer indómita y moderna (1853–1928)*. Toluca, Estado de México: El Colegio Mexiquense, 2011.

Becerril, Graciana. *Programa y centros de actividad que la mujer mexicana se propone lograr dentro del plan general que regirá a la nación durante el periodo presidencial de los años de 1946–1952*. Mexico City, 1944.

Benítez Zenteno, Raúl. "Lucio Mendieta y Núñez: Sociólogo y fundador de instituciones." In *Precursores de la sociología moderna en México*, ed. Verónica Comero Medina and Alfredo Andrade Carreño, 13–34. Mexico City: Siglo XXI Editores, 2008.

Bennet, Arnold. *Our Women: Chapters on the Sex-Discord*. New York: George H. Doran, 1920.

Berebitsky, Julie. *Sex in the Office: A History of Gender, Power, and Desire*. New Haven: Yale University Press, 2012.

Berger, Dina. *The Development of Mexico's Tourism Industry: Pyramids by Day, Martinis by Night*. New York: Pallgrave Macmillan, 2006.

Bertaccini, Tiziana. *El régimen priísta frente a las clases medias, 1943–1964*. Mexico City: Consejo Nacional para la Cultura y las Artes, Dirección General de Publicaciones, 2009.

Besse, Susan. *Restructuring Patriarchy: The Modernization of Gender Inequality in Brazil, 1914–1940*. Chapel Hill: University of North Carolina Press, 1996.

Blanco, Mercedes. *Empleo público en la administración central mexicana: Evolución y tendencias (1920–1988)*. Mexico City: Centro de Investigaciónes y Estudios Superiores en Antropología Social, 1995.

———. "Trayectorias laborales y cambio generacional: Mujeres de sectores medios en la Ciudad de México." *Revista Mexicana de Sociología* 63, no. 2 (April–June 2001): 91–111.

Blum, Ann S. *Domestic Economies: Family, Work, and Welfare in Mexico City, 1884–1943*. Lincoln: University of Nebraska Press, 2009.

Boris, Eileen. "What about the Working of the Working Mother?" *Journal of Women's History* 5, no. 2 (Fall 1993): 104–9.

Bortz, Jeffrey. *Revolution within the Revolution: Cotton Textile Workers and the Mexican Labor Regime, 1910–1923*. Stanford: Stanford University Press, 2008.

Bortz, Jeffrey, and Marcos Aguila. "Earning a Living: A History of Real Wage Studies in Twentieth-Century Mexico." *Latin American Research Review* 41, no. 2 (2006): 112–38.

Boyer, Christopher R. *Becoming Campesinos: Politics, Identity, and Agrarian Struggle in Postrevolutionary Michoacán, 1920–1935*. Stanford: Stanford University Press, 2003.

Boylan, Kristina A. "Gendering the Faith and Altering the Nation: Mexican Catholic Women's Activism, 1917–1940." In *Sex in Revolution: Gender, Politics, and Power in Modern Mexico*, ed. Jocelyn Olcott, Mary Kay Vaughan, and Gabriela Cano, 199–222. Durham: Duke University Press, 2006.

Bringas, Guillermina, and David Mascareño. *Esbozo histórico de la prensa obrera en México*. Mexico City: Universidad Nacional Autónoma de México, 1988.

Brinsmade, Robert Bruce, and M. C. Rolland. *Mexican Problems*. New York: Latin American News Association, 1916.

Britton, John A. "Teacher Unionization and the Corporate State in Mexico, 1931–1945." *Hispanic American Historical Review* 59, no. 4 (November 1979): 674–90.

Buck, Sarah A. "El control de la natalidad y el día de la madre: Política feminista y reaccionaria en México, 1922–1923." *Signos Históricos* 5 (2001): 9–53.

———. "The Meaning of the Women's Vote in Mexico: 1917–1953." In *The Women's Revolution in Mexico, 1910–1953*, ed. Stephanie Mitchell and Patience A. Schell, 73–98. Lanham MD: Rowman and Littlefield.

———. "New Perspectives on Female Suffrage." *History Compass* 3 (2005). DOI: 10.1111/j.1478–0542.2005.00133.x.

Bugeda, Diego, and Juan Manuel Ramírez Vélez. *Mujeres insurgentes*. Mexico City: Siglo XXI Editores/Senado de la República, 2010.

Bunker, Steven B. *Creating Mexican Consumer Culture in the Age of Porfirio Díaz, 1876–1911*. Albuquerque: University of New Mexico Press, 2012.

Bunker, Steven B., and Víctor Macías-González. "Consumption and Material Culture in the Twentieth Century." In *Companion to Mexican History and Culture*, ed. William H. Beezley, 83–118. Chichester: Wiley-Blackwell, 2011.

Burns, Kathryn. *Colonial Habits: Convents and the Spiritual Economy of Cuzco, Peru*. Durham: Duke University Press, 1999.

Cacho García, Joaquín. *Cifra de oro de la escuela "Lerdo" (1903–1953)*. Mexico City: La Escuela, 1953.

Calles, Plutarco Elías. *Pensamiento político y social: Antología (1913–1936)* Mexico City: Fondo de Cultura Económica/Instituto de Estudios Históricos de la Revolución Mexicana/Fideicomiso Plutarco Elías Calles y Fernando Torreblanca, 1991.

Calvillo, Max, and Lourdes Rocío Ramírez Palacios. *Setenta años de historia del Instituto Nacional Politécnico*. Vol. 1. Mexico City: Instituto Nacional Politécnico, 2006.

Camacho Morfín, Thelma, and Hugo Pichardo Hernández. "La cigarrera El Buen Tono (1889–1920)." In *Poder público y poder privado: Gobiernos, empresarios y empresas, 1880–1980*, ed. María Eugenia Romero Ibarra, José Mario Contreras Valdés, and Jesús Méndez Reyes, 83–106. Mexico City: Universidad Nacional Autónoma de México, 2006.

Camarena Ocampo, Mario. *Jornaleros, tejedores y obreros: Historia social de los trabajadores de San Angel (1850–1930)*. Mexico City: Plaza y Valdés, 2001.

Camarena Ocampo, Mario, and S. Lief Adelson, eds. *Comunidad, cultura y vida social: Ensayos sobre la formación de la clase obrera*. Mexico City: Instituto Nacional de Antropología e Historia, 1991.

Camp, Roderic Ai. *Mexican Political Biographies, 1935–2009*. 4th ed. Austin: University of Texas Press, 2011.

Candina, Azun. *Por una vida digna y decorosa: Clase media y empleados públicos en el siglo XX chileno*. Santiago: Facultad de Filosofía y Humanidades/Universidad de Chile, 2009.

Cano, Gabriela, "Adelina Zendejas: Arquitecta de su memoria." *Debate Feminista* 8 (September 1993): 387–400.

———. *Amalia de Castillo Ledón: Mujer de letras, mujer de poder. Antología*. Mexico City: Consejo Nacional para la Cultura y las Artes, 2011.

———. "Ciudadanía y sufragio femenino: El discurso igualitario de Lázaro Cárdenas." In *Miradas feministas sobre las mexicanas del siglo XX*, ed. Marta Lamas, 151–90. Mexico City: Fondo de Cultura Económica, 2007.

———. "Debates en torno al sufragio y la ciudadanía de las mujeres en México." In *Historia de las mujeres en España y América Latina, del siglo XX a los umbrales del XXI*, ed. Isabel Morant Deusa, 535–51. Madrid: Cátedra, 2005–6.

———. "La Escuela de Altos Estudios y la Facultad de Filosofía y Letras, 1910–1929." In *Estudios y estudiantes de filosofía; De la Facultad de Artes a la Facultad de Filosofía y Letras (1551–1929)*, ed. Enrique González González, 541–72. Mexico City: Universidad Nacional Autónoma de México, Instituto de Investigaciones sobre la Universidad y la Educación, Facultad de Filosofía y Letras/El Colegio de Michoacán, 2008.

———. "Feminismo." In *Léxico de la política*, ed. Laura Baca Olamendi, Judit Boker-Liwerant, Fernando Castañeda, Isidro H. Cisneros, and Germán Pérez Fernández del Castillo, 242–47. Mexico City: Facultad Latinoamericana de Ciencias Sociales, Sede Académica de México, 2000.

———. "Las feministas en campaña: La primera mitad del siglo XX." *Debate Feminista* 2, no. 4 (1991): 269–92.

———. "Género y construcción cultural de las profesiones en el Porfiriato: Magisterio, medicina, jurisprudencia y odontología." *Historia y Grafía*, no. 14 (2000): 207–43.

———. "Más de un siglo de feminismo en México." *Debate Feminista* 7, no. 14 (1996): 345–60.

———. "El mayo rojo de los maestros mexicanos: La huelga magisterial de 1919 en la ciudad de México." Undergraduate thesis in history, Facultad de Filosofía y Letras, Universidad Nacional Autónoma de México, 1984.

———. "México 1923: Primer Congreso Feminista Panamericano." *Debate Feminista* 1 (March 1990): 303–18.

———. "Revolución, feminismo y ciudadanía en México (1915–1940)." In *Historia de las mujeres*, vol. 5, *El siglo XX: La nueva mujer*, ed. Georges Duby and Michelle Perrot, 685–96. Madrid: Taurus, 1993.

Careaga, Gabriel. "Clases medias." In *Léxico de la política*, ed. Laura Baca Olamendi, Judit Bokser-Liwerant, Fernando Castañeda, Isidro H. Cisneros, and Germán Pérez Fernández del Castillo, 58–63. Mexico City: Facultad Latinoamericana de Ciencias Sociales/Fondo de Cultura Económica, 2000.

Carranza Palacios, José Antonio. *100 años de educación en México, 1900–2000*. Mexico City: Limusa, 2012.

Carrera Stampa, Manuel. *Historia del correo en México*. Mexico City: Secretaría de Comunicaciones y Transportes, 1970.

Carrillo, Ana María. "Salud pública y poder en México durante el cardenismo, 1934–1940." *Dynamis: Acta Hispánica ad Medicinae Scientiarumque Historiam Illustrandam* 25 (2005): 145–78. http://www.raco.cat/index.php/Dynamis/article/view/114016/142473.

Castañeda, Carmen. "Introducción: Descubriendo la historia de la cultura escrita." *Cultura Escrita y Sociedad* 11 (December 2010): 9–14.

Castañeda, Jorge G. *Amarres perros: Una biografía*. Mexico City: Alfaguara, 2014.

Castañeda López, Gabriela, and Ana Cecilia Rodríguez de Romo. *Pioneras de la medicina mexicana en la UNAM: del Porfiriato al nuevo régimen, 1887–1936*. Mexico City: Ediciones Díaz de Santos, 2000.

Castillo, Debra. *Easy Women: Sex and Gender in Modern Mexican Fiction*. Minneapolis: University of Minnesota Press, 1998.

Centro de Estudios Históricos del Movimiento Obrero Mexicano. *La mujer en el movimiento obrero en el siglo XIX: Antología de prensa.* Mexico City: Centro de Estudios Históricos del Movimiento Obrero Mexicano, 1974.

Centro Taquigráfico. *Conferencias.* Mexico City: Centro Taquigráfico, 1901–6.

Chaoul Pereyra, María Eugenia. *Entre la esperanza de cambio y la continuidad de la vida: El espacio de las escuelas primarias nacionales en la Ciudad de México, 1891–1919.* Mexico City: Instituto de Investigaciones Dr. José Luis Mora/Consejo Nacional de Ciencia y Tecnología, 2014.

———. "Un aparato ortopédico para el magisterio: La Dirección General de Educación Primaria y los maestros en el Distrito Federal, 1896–1913." *Revista Secuencia* 95 (May–August 2016): 63–90.

Chassen-López, Francie. "Cheaper Than Machines: Women in Agriculture in Porfirian Oaxaca." In *Creating Spaces, Shaping Transitions: Women of the Mexican Countryside, 1850–1990,* ed. Mary Kay Vaughan and Heather Fowler-Salamini, 27–50. Tucson: University of Arizona Press, 1994.

Chowning, Margaret. "The Catholic Church and the Ladies of the Vela Perpetua: Gender and Devotional Change in Nineteenth-Century Mexico." *Past & Present* 221, no. 1 (November 2013): 197–237.

———. *Rebellious Nuns: The Troubled History of a Mexican Convent, 1752–1863.* New York: Oxford University Press, 2005.

Chumacero, Rosalia d'. *Perfil y pensamiento de la mujer mexicana.* Mexico City: Editores Mexicanos Unidos, 1974.

Civera Cerecedo, Alicia. "La coeducación en la formación de los maestros rurales en México (1934–1944)." *Revista Mexicana de Investigación Educativa* 11, no. 28 (2006): 269–91.

———. "Crisis política y reforma educativa, el Estado de México, 1934–1940." In *Escuela y sociedad en el periodo cardenista,* ed. Susana Quintanilla and Mary Kay Vaughan, 141–65. Mexico City: Fondo de Cultura Económica, 1997.

———. *La escuela como opción de vida: La formación de maestros normalistas rurales en México, 1921–1945.* Toluca, Estado de México: El Colegio Mexiquense, 2008.

Clark, Linda L. *The Rise of Professional Women in France: Gender and Public Administration since 1830.* Cambridge: Cambridge University Press, 2004.

Cobble, Dorothy Sue. *The Other Women's Movement: Workplace Justice and Social Rights in Modern America.* Princeton: Princeton University Press, 2005.

Colegio de México. *Estadísticas económicas del Porfiriato: Fuerza de trabajo y actividad económica por sectores.* Mexico City: El Colegio de México, 1964.

Collado Herrera, María del Carmen. "El espejo de la élite social (1920–1940)." In *Historia de la vida cotidiana en México,* vol. 5, pt. 1, *Siglo XX: Campo y ciudad,* ed. Pilar Gonzalbo Aizpuru and Aurelio de los Reyes, 89–125, Mexico City: El Colegio de México/ Fondo de Cultura Económica, 2006.

Colón R., Consuelo. *Mujeres de México*. Mexico City: Imprenta Gallarda, I.A. Franco, 1944.

Connelly, Mary Goldsmith. "Política, trabajo y género: La sindicalización de las y los trabajadores domésticos y el Estado mexicano." In *Orden social e identidad de género: México, siglos XIX y XX*, ed. María Teresa Fernández Aceves, Carmen Ramos Escandón, and Susie S. Porter, 215–46. Guadalajara: Universidad de Guadalajara/ Centro de Investigaciónes y Estudios Superiores en Antropología Social, 2006.

Contreras, Ariel José. *México 1940: Industrialización y crisis política. Estado y sociedad civil en las elecciones presidenciales*. Mexico City: Siglo XXI Editores, 1977.

Córdova, Arnaldo. *La política de masas del cardenismo*. Mexico City: Ediciones Era, 1974.

Cortina, Regina. "Gender and Power in the Teacher's Union of Mexico." *Mexican Studies/Estudios Mexicanos* 6, no. 2 (Summer 1990): 241–62.

Cuéllar, José Tomás. *La linterna mágica*. Mexico City: Ignacio Cumplido, 1871.

Cuesta, Jorge, Salvador Novo, Jaime Torres Bodet, and Xavier Villaurrutia. *Los contemporáneos en "El Universal."* Mexico City: Fondo de Cultura Económica, 2016.

Cuevas Perus, Marcos. "Clase media, poder, y mito en el México posrevolucionario: Una exploración." *Estudios Políticos* 20, no. 9 (May–August 2010): 105–29.

Davies, Margery W. *Woman's Place Is at the Typewriter: Office Work and Office Workers, 1870–1930*. Philadelphia: Temple University Press, 1982.

Davis, Diane E. *Urban Leviathan: Mexico City in the Twentieth Century*. Philadelphia: Temple University Press, 1994.

De la Rosa, Jesús. "Características de la escuela socialista mexicana." In *La educación socialista en México (1934–1945)*, ed. Gilberto Guevara Niebla, 121–33. Mexico City: El Caballito Ediciones, 1985.

Deslippe, Dennis. *Rights, Not Roses: Unions and the Rise of Working-Class Feminism, 1945–1980*. Urbana: University of Illinois Press, 2000.

DeVault, Ileen. *Sons and Daughter of Labor: Class and Clerical Work in Turn-of-the-Century Pittsburgh*. Ithaca: Cornell University Press, 1990.

Díaz, Ana Ivonne. "*El álbum de la mujer*: Periodismo femenino: El primer paso hacia la modernidad y la ciudanía." *Desacatos* 3 (2000): 107–14.

Dion, Michelle. "The Origins of Social Security during the Cárdenas and Ávila Camacho Administrations." *Mexican Studies/Estudios Mexicanos* 21, no. 1 (Winter 2005): 59–95.

Dios Vallejo, Delia Selene de, and María Esther Navarro Lara. "El feminismo como movimiento social." *Perspectiva de Género: Serie Género y Trabajo Social* 1 (2004): 23–56.

Domínguez, Julieta. *Funcionarias: Publicación conmemorativa del ideario político de la mujer XI aniversario de la reforma de los artículos 34 y 115*. Mexico City, 1963.

Dorantes, Alma. *El conflicto universitario en Guadalajara, 1933–1937*. Guadalajara: Secretaría de Cultura de Jalisco/Instituto Nacional de Antropología e Historia, 1993.

Dore, Elizabeth. "One Step Forward, Two Steps Back: Gender and the State in the Long Nineteenth Century." In *Hidden Histories of Gender and the State in Latin America*, ed. Elizabeth Dore and Maxine Molyneux, 3–32. Durham: Duke University Press, 2000.

Dorotinsky Alperstein, Deborah. "Después de las utopías, la nostalgia: El siglo XIX y su recepción en el siglo XX." *Anales del Instituto de Investigaciones Estéticas* 36, no. 105 (2014): 9–38.

Dumas, Claude. *Justo Sierra y el México de su tiempo, 1848–1912*. Mexico City: Universidad Nacional Autónoma de México, 1992.

Eineigel, Susanne Karin. "Distinction, Culture, and Politics in Mexico City's Middle Class, 1890–1940." PhD diss., University of Maryland, 2011.

———. "Revolutionary Promises Encounter Urban Realities for Mexico City's Middle Class, 1915–1928." In *The Making of the Middle Class: Toward a Transnational History*, ed. A. Ricardo López and Barbara Weinstein, 196–222. Durham: Duke University Press, 2012.

Enstad, Nan. *Ladies of Labor, Girls of Adventure: Working Women, Popular Culture, and Labor Politics at the Turn of the Twentieth Century*. New York: Columbia University Press, 1999.

Eriksen Persson, Ana Lorena. "Imágenes y representaciones femeninas: ¿Un problema entre la tradición y la modernidad? (1920–1934)." PhD thesis, Escuela Nacional de Antropología e Historia, 2013.

Ervin, Michael E. "The Formation of the Revolutionary Middle Class during the Mexican Revolution." In *The Making of the Middle Class: Toward a Transnational History*, ed. A. Ricardo López and Barbara Weinstein, 196–222. Durham: Duke University Press, 2012.

Escobar Toledo, Saúl. *Los trabajadores en el siglo XX: Sindicato, estado y sociedad en México, 1907–2004*. Mexico City: Sindicato de Trabajadores de la Universidad Nacional Autónoma de México, 2006.

Escudero Luján, Carolina, and Guadalupe García Torres. *Carolina Escudero Luján: Una mujer en la historia de México: Testimonio oral*. Morelia: Instituto Michoacano de Cultura, Centro de Estudios de la Revolución Mexicana "Lázaro Cárdenas," Archivo de Historia Oral, 1992.

Fabela, Isidro. *Documentos históricos de la Revolución Mexicana: Revolución y régimen constitucionalista*. Mexico City: Banco de México, 2013.

Farnsworth-Alvear, Ann. *Dulcinea in the Factory: Myths, Morals, Men, and Women in Colombia's Industrial Experiment, 1905–1960*. Durham: Duke University Press, 2000.

Federación de Sindicatos de Trabajadores al Servicio del Estado. *La F.S.T.S.E. en marcha: Realidades, no promesas, 1949–1953*. Mexico City, 1953.

————. *Ley de pensiones civiles*. Mexico City: Dirección de Pensiones Civiles, 1947.

Fell, Claude. *José Vasconcelos: Los años del águila, 1920–1925: Educación, cultura e iberoamericanismo en el México postrevolucionario*. Mexico City: Universidad Nacional Autónoma de México, 1989.

Fernández Aceves, María Teresa. "El álbum biográfico de Guadalupe Martínez Villanueva: Cultura oral y escrita en Guadalajara, 1920–1970." *Cultura Escrita y Sociedad* 11 (December 2010): 120–45.

————. "Guadalajaran Women and the Construction of National Identity." In *The Eagle and the Virgin: Nation and Cultural Revolution in Mexico, 1920–1940*, ed. Mary Kay Vaughan and Stephen Lewis, 297–313. Durham: Duke University Press, 2006.

————. "La lucha sobre el sufragio femenino en Jalisco, 1910–1958." *Ventana*, no. 19 (June 2004): 132–51.

————. *Mujeres en el cambio social en el siglo XX mexicano*. Mexico City: Centro de Investigaciones e Estudios Superiores de Antropología Social–Siglo XXI Editores, 2014.

————. "Once We Were Corn Grinders: Women and Labor in the Tortilla Industry of Guadalajara, 1920–1940." *International Labor and Working-Class History* 63 (Spring 2003): 81–101.

————. "Las políticas de género de la Confederación Nacional Campesina y el liderazgo de María Guadalupe Urzúa Flores, 1950–1960." In *Mexico in Transition: New Persectives on Mexican Agrarian History, Nineteenth and Twentieth Centuries/ México y sus transiciones: Reconsideraciones sobre la historia agraria mexicana, siglos XIX y XX*, ed. Antonio Escobar Ohmstede and Matthew Butler, 567–600. Mexico City: Centro de Investigaciónes y Estudios Superiores en Antropología Social/ University of Texas–Austin, 2013.

————. "The Struggle between the *Metate* and the *Molinos de Nixtamal* in Guadalajara, 1920–1940." In *Sex in Revolution: Gender, Politics, and Power in Modern Mexico*, ed. Jocelyn Olcott, Mary Kay Vaughan, and Gabriela Cano, 147–61. Durham: Duke University Press, 2006.

Figueroa Domenech, J. *Guía general descriptiva de la República Mexicana*. Vol. 1. Mexico City: Ramón de S.N. Araluce, 1899.

Fine, Lisa M. *The Souls of the Skyscraper: Female Clerical Workers in Chicago, 1870–1930*. Philadelphia: Temple University Press, 1999.

Fisher, Lillian Estelle. "The Influence of the Present Mexican Revolution upon the Status of Mexican Women." *Hispanic American Historical Review* 22 (February 1942): 211–28.

Fowler-Salamini, Heather. *Working Women, Entrepreneurs, and the Mexican Revolution: The Coffee Culture of Córdoba, Veracruz*. Lincoln: University of Nebraska Press, 2013.

Francois, Marie Eileen. *A Culture of Everyday Credit: Housekeeping, Pawnbroking, and Governance in Mexico City, 1750–1920*. Lincoln: University of Nebraska Press, 2006.

French, William. *A Peaceful and Working People: Manners, Morals, and Class Formation in Northern Mexico*. Albuquerque: University of New Mexico, 1996.

———. "Prostitutes and Guardian Angels: Women, Work, and the Family in Porfirian Mexico." *Hispanic American Historical Review* 72, no. 4 (1992): 529–53.

Gabin, Nancy. *Feminism in the Labor Movement: Women and the United Auto Workers, 1935–1975*. Ithaca: Cornell University Press, 1990.

Galindo, Hermila. "La mujer moderna." *Mexican Review* 2, no. 5 (1918): 10.

Gallo, Rubén. *Mexican Modernity: The Avant-Garde and the Technological Revolution*. Cambridge: Massachusetts Institute of Technology Press, 2005.

Galván de Terrazas, Luz Elena. *La educación superior de la mujer en México, 1876–1940*. Mexico City: Centro de Investigaciónes y Estudios Superiores en Antropología Social, 1984.

———. "La educación técnica: Ámbito de estudio en la historia de la educación." In María de los Ángeles Rodríguez, *50 años de educación tecnológica en México*, 57–72. Mexico City: Instituto Politécnico Nacional, 1988.

Galván Lafarga, Luz Elena. *Soledad compartida: Una historia de maestros, 1908–1910*. Mexico City: Centro de Investigaciones y Estudios Superiores en Antropología Social, 2010.

Galván Lafarga, Luz Elena, and Oresta López Pérez, eds. *Entre imaginarios y utopías: Historias de maestras*. Mexico City: Casa Chata/Universidad Nacional Autónoma de México Programa Universitario de Estudios de Género/Centro de Investigaciónes y Estudios Superiores en Antropología Social/El Colegio de San Luís Potosí, 2008.

Gamboa, Federico. *Todos somos iguales frente a las tentaciones: Una antología general*. Mexico City: Fondo de Cultura Económica/Fundación para las Letras Mexicanas/Universidad Nacional Autónoma de México, 2012.

Gamboa Ojeda, Leticia. *La urdimbre y la trama: Historia social de los obreros textiles de Atlixco, 1899–1924*. Mexico City: Fondo de Cultura Económica, 2001.

García, Brígida. "Comparación de la información sobre subgrupos de actividad económica de los censos de población de 1950 y 1970." *Demografía y Economía* 7, no. 2 (1973): 249–64.

García Díaz, Bernardo. *Textiles del valle de Orizaba (1880–1925): Cinco ensayos de historia sindical y social*. Xalapa, Ver.: Universidad Veracruzana, Centro de Investigaciones Históricas, 1990.

García Peña, Ana Lidia. "Continuidades y cambios en las relaciones de género en la familia, del Porfiriato a la Revolución Mexicana." In *Voces del antiguo régimen: Representaciones, sociedad y gobierno en México contemporáneo*, ed. Eduardo N. Mijangos Díaz and Marisa Pérez Domínguez, 311–42. Zamora, Mich.: Universidad Michoacana de San Nicolás de Hidalgo and Mexico City: Instituto Mora, 2009.

———. *El fracaso del amor: Género e individualismo en el siglo XIX mexicano*. Mexico City: El Colegio de México/Universidad Autónoma del Estado de México, 2006.

García Rivas, Heriberto. *Historia de la literatura mexicana, t. iv, siglo XX: 1951–1971*. Mexico City: Librería de Manuel Porrúa, 1974.

Garrido, Luis Javier. *El Partido de la revolución institucionalizada: La formación del nuevo estado en México (1928–1945)*. Mexico City: Siglo XXI Editores, 1982.

Gauss, Susan. "Masculine Bonds and Modern Mothers: The Rationalization of Gender in the Textile Industry in Puebla, 1940–1952." *International Labor and Working-Class History* 63 (2003): 63–80.

———. "Working-Class Masculinity and the Rationalized Sex: Gender and Industrial Modernization in the Textile Industry in Postrevolutionary Puebla." In *Sex in Revolution: Gender, Politics, and Power in Modern Mexico*, ed. Jocelyn Olcott, Mary Kay Vaughan, and Gabriela Cano, 181–96. Durham: Duke University Press, 2006.

Gautreau, Marion. "La Ilustración Semanal y el archivo Casasola: Una aproximación a la desmitificación de la fotografía de la Revolución Mexicana." *Cuicuilco* 14, no. 41 (September–December 2007): 113–42.

Gilbert, Dennis. *Mexico's Middle Class in the Neoliberal Era*. Tucson: University of Arizona Press, 2007.

Gillingham, Paul, and Benjamin Smith. *Dictablanda: Politics, Work, and Culture in Mexico, 1938–1968*. Durham: Duke University Press, 2014.

Gimeno de Flaquer, Concepción. *Madres de hombres célebres*. Mexico City: Tipografía de la Escuela Industrial de Huérfanos, 1884.

———. *La mujer española: Un estudio acerca de su educación y sus facultades*. Madrid: Imprenta y Librería de Miguel Guijarro, 1877.

Ginzberg, Eitan. *Revolutionary Ideology and Political Destiny, 1928–1934: Lázaro Cárdenas and Adalberto Tejeda*. Brighton: Sussex Academic e-Library, 2015.

Ginzberg, Lori D. *Women and the Work of Benevolence: Morality, Politics, and Class in the Nineteenth-Century United States*. New Haven: Yale University Press, 1990.

Goldstein, Leslie F. "Early Feminist Themes in French Utopian Socialism: The St.-Simonians and Fourier." *Journal of the History of Ideas* 43, no. 1 (January–March 1982): 91–108.

Gómez-Galvarriato, Aurora. *Industry and Revolution: Social and Economic Change in the Orizaba Valley, Mexico*. Cambridge: Harvard University Press, 2013.

Gómez-Galvarriato, Aurora, and Aldo Musacchio. "Un nuevo índice de precios para México, 1886–1929." *El Trimestre Económico* 67, no. 256 (January–March 2000): 47–91.

Gómez Galvarriato Freer, Aurora. "Industrialización, empresas y trabajadores industriales, del Porfiriato a la Revolución: La nueva historiografía." *Historia Mexicana* 52, no. 3 (January–March 2003): 773–804.

Gonzalbo Aizpuru, Pilar, ed. *Género, familia, y mentalidades en América Latina*. San Juan: Editorial de la Universidad de Puerto Rico, 1997.

González Jiménez, Rosa María. "De cómo y por qué las maestras llegaron a ser mayoría en las escuelas primarias de México, Distrito Federal." *Revista Mexicana de Investigación Educativa* 14, no. 42 (July–September 2009): 747–85.

———. *Las maestras en México: Re-cuento de una historia*. Mexico City: Universidad Pedagógica Nacional/Fundación Para la Cultura del Maestro, 2007.

González Marín, Silvia. "La imagen de la mujer latinoamericana en las revistas femeninas de la década de los trienta." In *America Llatína, ahir i avui: Cinquena Trobada Debat*, ed. Pilar García Jordá, 529–37. Barcelona: Universitat de Barcelona, 1996.

———. *Prensa y poder político: La elección presidencial de 1940 en la prensa Mexicana*. Mexico City: Siglo XXI Editores, 2006.

González Salazar, Gloria. "La participación de la mujer en la actividad laboral de México." In *La mujer en América Latina*, ed. María del Carmen Elu de Leñero, 105–35. Mexico City: Sep-Setentas, 1975.

Goodman, Bryna. "The New Woman Commits Suicide: The Press, Cultural Memory, and the New Republic." *Journal of Asian Studies* 64, no. 1 (2005): 67–101.

Greenwald, Maurine Weiner. "Working-Class Feminism ad the Family Wage Ideal: The Seattle Debate on Married Women's Right to Work, 1914–1920." *Journal of American History* 7, no. 1 (June 1989): 188–49.

Grenfell, Michael. *Pierre Bourdieu. Key Concepts*. New York: Routledge, 2014.

Guadarrama, Rocío. *Los sindicatos y la política en México: La CROM (1918–1928)*. Mexico City: Ediciones Era, 1981.

Guerrero, Omar. *El funcionario, el diplomático, y el juez: las experiencias en la formación profesional del servicio público en el mundo*. Mexico City: Universidad de Guanajuato/Instituto de Administración Pública de Guanajuato/Instituto Nacional de Administración Pública/ Plaza y Valdés Editores, 1998.

———. *Historia del servicio civil de carrera en México: Los protagonistas, las ideas, los testimonios*. Mexico City: Universidad Autónoma del Estado de México, Facultad de Ciencias Políticas y Sociales; Instituto de Administración Pública del Estado de México, 2011.

Guerrero Oliveros, Gabriela. *Renée Rodríguez de la Rosa: Fundadora de instituciones politécnicas*. Mexico City: Instituto Politécnico Nacional, 2005.

Guerrero Orozco, Omar. "El Departamento de Contraloría, 1917–1933." *Revista de Administración Pública* 57–58 (1984): 219–43.

———. *Historia de la Secretaría de Gobernación: De su origen al final del siglo XX*. Mexico City: Editorial Porrúa/Universidad Nacional Autónoma de México, 2011.

———. *Introducción a la administración pública*. Mexico City: Harper and Row Latinoamericana, 1985.

Gútierrez, Florencia. *El mundo del trabajo y el poder político: Integración, consenso y resistencia en la Ciudad de México a fines del siglo XIX*. Mexico City: El Colegio de México, 2011.

Gutiérrez Grageda, Blanca Estela. *Educar en tiempos de Don Porfirio: Querétaro, 1876–1911*. Querétaro, Que.: Universidad Autónoma de Querétaro, 2002.

Guy, Donna. *Women Build the Welfare State: Performing Charity and Creating Rights in Argentina, 1880–1950*. Durham: Duke University Press, 2009.

Haber, Stephen H. *Industry and Underdevelopment: The Industrialization of Mexico, 1890–1940*. Stanford: Stanford University Press, 1989.

Hart, John. *Anarchism and the Mexican Working Class, 1860–1931*. Austin: University of Texas Press, 1978.

Hartman Strom, Sharon. *Beyond the Typewriter: Gender, Class, and the Origins of Modern American Office Work, 1900–1930*. Urbana: University of Illinois Press, 1994.

Healy, Teresa. *Gendered Struggles against Globalisation in Mexico*. Burlington VT: Ashgate, 2008.

Hernández Carballido, Elvira. "La participación femenina en el periodismo nacional durante la Revolución Mexicana." PhD diss., Facultad de Ciencias Políticas y Sociales–Universidad Nacional Autónoma de México, México, 2003.

——. "La prensa femenina en México durante el siglo XIX." Licentiate thesis, Facultad de Ciencias Políticas y Sociales–Universidad Nacional Autónoma de México, México, 1986.

——. "Las primeras reporteras mexicanas: Magdalena Mondragón, Elvira Vargas y Esperanza Velásquez Bringas." Master's thesis, Facultad de Ciencias Políticas y Sociales–Universidad Nacional Autónoma de México, México, 1997.

Hershfield, Joanne. *Imagining the Chica Moderna: Women, Nation, and Visual Culture in Mexico, 1917–1936*. Durham: Duke University Press, 2008.

Higginbotham, Evelyn Brooks. "African-American Women's History and the Metalanguage of Race." *Signs* 17, no. 2 (Winter 1992): 251–74.

Hind, Emily. *Femmenism and the Mexican Woman Intellectual from Sor Juana to Poniatowska. BOOB LIT*. New York: Palgrave Macmillan, 2010.

Hirshfield, Joanne, and David R. Maciel. *Mexico's Cinema: A Century of Film and Filmmakers*. Lanham MD: Rowman and Littlefield, 1999.

Holcombe, Lee. *Victorian Ladies at Work: Middle-Class Working Women in England and Wales, 1850–1914*. Hamden CT: Archon Books, 1973.

Horowitz, Daniel. "Rethinking Betty Friedan and the *Feminine Mystique*: Labor Union Radicalism and Feminism in Cold War America." *American Quarterly* 48, no. 1 (1996): 1–42.

Hutchison, Elizabeth Quay. *Labors Appropriate to Their Sex: Gender, Labor, and Politics in Urban Chile, 1900–1930*. Durham: Duke University Press, 2001.

Ibarra de Anda, Fortino and Concepción de Villareal. *El periodismo en México*. Vol 2. Mexico City: Editorial Juventa, 1937.

Illades, Carlos. *Hacia la república del trabajo: La organización artesanal en la Ciudad de México, 1853–1876*. Mexico City: Universidad Autónoma Metropolitana, Iztapalapa/El Colegio de México, 1996.

Illades, Carlos, and Mario Barbosa Cruz. *Los trabajadores de la ciudad de México, 1860–1950: Textos en homenaje a Clara E. Lida*. Mexico City: El Colegio de México/ Universidad Autónoma Metropolitana, Cuajimalpa, 2013.

Infante Vargas, Lucrecia. "De lectoras y redactoras: Las publicaciones 'femeninas' en México durante el siglo XIX." In *La república de las letras: Asomos a la cultura escrita del México decimonónico*, vol. 2, ed. Belem Clark de Lara and Elisa Speckman, 69–105. Mexico City: Universidad Nacional Autónoma de México, 2005.

Iturriaga, José E. *La estructura social y cultural de México*. Mexico City: Fondo de Cultura, Económica, 1951.

James, Daniel, and John D. French. *The Gendered Worlds of Latin American Working Women: From Household and Factory to the Union Hall and Ballot Box*. Durham: Duke University Press, 1997.

Jensen, Joan M. "Butter Making and Economic Development in Mid-Atlantic Americas from 1750 to 1850." *SIGNS* 13, no. 4 (1988): 813–29.

Jiménez, Michael F. "The Elision of the Middle Class and Beyond: History, Politics, and Development Studies in Latin America's 'Short Twentieth Century." In *Colonial Legacies: The Problem of Persistence in Latin American History*, ed. Jeremy Adelman, 207–28. New York: Routledge, 1999.

Jiménez Rueda, Julio. *Cándido Cordero, empleado público: Farsa en tres actos*. Mexico City: Talleres Gráficos de la Nación, 1929.

Johnson, John J. *Political Change in Latin America: The Emergence of the Middle Sectors*. Stanford: Stanford University Press, 1958.

Joseph, Gilbert M., and Daniel Nugent, eds. *Everyday Forms of State Formation: Revolution and the Negotiation of Rule in Modern Mexico*. Durham: Duke University Press, 1994.

Kaplan, Temma. *Red City, Blue Period: Social Movements in Picasso's Barcelona*. Berkeley: University of California Press, 1993.

Katz, Friedrich. "Mexico: Restored Republic and Porfiriato, 1876–1910." In *The Cambridge History of Latin America*, ed. Leslie Bethell, 5:1–78. New York: Cambridge University Press, 1986.

Keesing, Donald B. "Structural Change Early in Development: Mexico's Changing Industrial and Occupational Structure from 1895 to 1950." *Journal of Economic History* 29, no. 4 (1969): 716–38.

Kessler-Harris, Alice. *In Pursuit of Equity: Women, Men, and the Quest for Economic Citizenship in 20th-Century America*. New York: Oxford University Press, 2001.

———. *Out to Work: A History of Wage-Earning Women in the United States*. Oxford: Oxford University Press, 1982.

———. "The Wages of Patriarchy: Some Thoughts about the Continuing Relevance of Class and Gender." *Labor* 3, no. 3 (2006): 7–21.

Knight, Alan. "The Character and Consequences of the Great Depression in Mexico." In *The Great Depression in Latin America*, ed. Alan Knight and Paul Drinoto, 213–45. Durham: Duke University Press, 2014.

———. *The Mexican Revolution*. Vol. 1, *Porfirians, Liberals, and Peasants*. Lincoln: University of Nebraska Press, 1986.

———. "The End of the Mexican Revolution? From Cárdenas to Avila Camacho, 1937–1941." In *Dictablanda: Politics, Work, and Culture in Mexico, 1938–1968*, ed. Paul Gillingham and Benjamin T. Smith, 47–68. Durham: Duke University Press, 2014.

———. "The Weight of the State in Modern Mexico." In *Studies in the Formation of the Nation-State in Latin America*, ed. James Dunkerley, 212–53. London: Institute of Latin American Studies, 2002.

Koven, Seth, and Sonya Michel. "Womanly Duties: Maternalist Politics and the Origins of Welfare States in France, Germany, Great Britain, and the United States, 1880–1920." *American Historical Review* 95, no. 4 (October, 1990): 1076–1108.

Kracauer, Siegfried. *The Salaried Masses: Duty and Distraction in Weimar Germany*. Trans. Quintin Hoare. London: Verso, 1998.

Kranzthor Shutz, Irene. "Mexican Women as They Are." *Mexican Review* 2, no. 8 (1918): 4–5.

Ladd-Taylor, Molly. *Mother-Work: Women, Child Welfare, and the State, 1890–1930*. Urbana: University of Illinois Press, 1994.

LaGreca, Nancy. *Rewriting Womanhood: Feminism, Subjectivity, and the Angel of the House in the Latin American Novel, 1887–1903*. University Park: Pennsylvania State University Press, 2009.

Langland, Elizabeth. *Nobody's Angels: Middle-Class Women and Domestic Ideology in Victorian Culture*. New York: Cornell University Press, 1995.

Lara y Pardo, Luis. *La prostitución en México*. Mexico City: Librería de la Viuda de Ch. Bouret, 1908.

Lastra y Villar, Alfonso. *Las leyes del trabajo de la República mexicana interpretadas por la Suprema Corte de Justicia de la Nación*. Mexico City, 1936.

Lau Jaiven, Ana. "Ciudad de México, 1917–1953." In *El sufragio femenino en México: Voto en los estados (1917–1965)*, ed. Ana Lau Jaiven and Mercedes Zúñiga Elizalde, 15–48. Hermosillo, Sonora: El Colegio de Sonora, 2013.

———. "Cuando hablan las mujeres." In *Debates en torno a una metodología feminista*, ed. Eli Bartra, 185–97. Mexico City: Universidad Nacional Autónoma de México, Xochimilco, Programa Universitario de Estudios de Género, 2002.

———. "Entre ambas fronteras: La búsqueda de la igualdad de derechos para las mujeres." *Política y Cultura*, no. 31 (Spring 2009): 235–55.

———. "Expresiones políticas femeninas en el México del siglo XX: El Ateneo Mexicano de Mujeres y la Alianza de Mujeres de México (1934–1953)." In *Orden social e identidad de género: México, siglos XIX y XX*, ed. María Teresa Fernández Aceves, Carmen Ramos Escandón, and Susie S. Porter, 93–124. Guadalajara: Universidad de Guadalajara/Centro de Investigaciónes y Estudios Superiores en Antropología Social, 2006.

———. "Mujeres, feminismo y sufragio en los años veinte." In *Un fantasma recorre el siglo: Luchas feministas en México, 1910–2010*, ed. Gisela Espinosa Damián and Ana Lau Jaiven, 59–94. Mexico City: Universidad Autónoma Metropolitana, Xochimilco, Ciencias Sociales y Historia, Departamento de Relaciones Sociales, 2011.

———. *La nueva ola del feminismo en México*. Mexico City: Planeta, 1987.

Lau Jaiven, Ana, and Carmen Ramos-Escandón. *Mujeres y revolución, 1900–1917*. Mexico City: Instituto Nacional de Estudios Históricos de la Revolución Mexicana, 1993.

Lavrin, Asunción. *Women, Feminism, and Social Change in Argentina, Chile, and Uruguay, 1890–1940*. Lincoln: University of Nebraska Press, 1995.

Lauderdale Graham, Sandra. "Making the Private Public: A Brazilian Perspective." *Journal of Women's History* 15, no. 1 (2003): 28–42.

Lazarín Miranda, Federico. "Enzeñanzas propias de su sexo: La educación técnica de la mujer, 1871–1932." In *Obedecer, servir y resistir: La educación de las mujeres en la historia de México*, ed. María Adelina Arredondo, 249–78. Mexico City: Universidad Pedagógica Nacional/Miguel Ángel Porrúa, 2003.

———. *La política para el desarrollo: Las escuelas técnicas industriales y comerciales en la ciudad de México, 1920–1932*. Mexico City: Universidad Autónoma Metropolitana, Unidad Iztapalapa, División de Ciencias Sociales y Humanidades, Departamento de Filosofía, 1996.

Leal, Juan Felipe. "Las clases sociales en México: 1880–1910." *Revista Mexicana de Ciencia Política* 17, no. 65 (July–September 1971): 44–57.

———. *Del mutualismo al sindicalismo en México: 1843–1910*. Mexico City: El Caballito, 1991.

Lear, John Robert. *Workers, Neighbors, and Citizens: The Revolution in Mexico City, 1910–1917*. Lincoln: University of Nebraska Press, 2001.

Ledón, Luis Castillo. *El Museo Nacional de Arqueología, Historia y Etnografía, 1825–1925: Reseña histórica escrita para la celebración de su primer centenario*. Mexico City: Talleres Gráficos del Museo Nacional de Arqueología, Historia y Etnografía, 1924.

Leite da Silva Dias, Maria Odila. *Power and Everyday Life: The Lives of Working Women in Nineteenth-Century Brazil*. New Brunswick: Rutgers University Press, 1995.

León, Samuel, and Ignacio Marván. *La clase obrera en la historia de México: En el cardenismo, 1934–1940*. Mexico City: Siglo XXI Editores, 1985.

León López, Enrique. *El Instituto Politécnico Nacional: Origen y evolución histórica*. Mexico City: Secretaría de Educación Pública, 1975.

———. *Juan de Dios Bátiz: Breve historia de su vida*. Mexico City: Instituto Politécnico Nacional, Dirección de Bibliotecas y Publicaciones, 1991.

Lerner, Victoria. "Historia de la reforma educativa, 1933–1945." *Historia Mexicana* 29, no. 1 (July–September 1979): 91–132.

Levitan, Kathrin. "Redundancy, the 'Surplus Women' Problem, and the British Census, 1851–1861." *Women's History Review* 17, no. 3 (July 2008): 359–76.

Linhard, Tabea Alexa. *Fearless Women in the Mexican Revolution and the Spanish Civil War*. Columbia: University of Missouri Press, 2005.

Lipsett-Rivera, Sonya. *Gender and the Negotiation of Daily Life in Mexico, 1750–1856*. Lincoln: University of Nebraska Press, 2012.

List Arzubide, Armando. *Apuntes para la prehistoria de la Revolución*. Mexico City, 1958.

Llach Trevoux, Guillermina. *Belisario Domínguez: Momentos culminantes de su vida*. Mexico City: F. Trillas, 1963.

———. "Patronato para reos libertados." Master's thesis, Universidad Nacional Autónoma de México, 1946.

Llach Trevoux, Leonor. *Cuadros conocidos (cuentos)*. Mexico City: Editorial Cvltvra, 1933.

———. "El maestro Carrillo." *Horizonte*, Guadalajara 8, no. 44 (1965): 20–21.

———. "Maternidad." *Vida Femenina* 5, no. 50 (1937): 33–34.

———. "La mujer de ayer y la de hoy." *Vida Femenina* 6, no. 68 (1939): 10–11.

———. *Retratos de almas*. Mexico City: La Impresora, S. Turanzas del Valle, 1939.

———. "El seguro de la madre." *Vida Femenina* 3, no. 35 (1936): 16–17.

Loaeza, Guadalupe. *Las niñas bien*. Mexico City: Aguilar, León y Cal Editores, 1993.

———. *Las reinas de Polanco*. Mexico City: Oceano Exprés, 2012.

Loaeza, Soledad. *Clases medias y política en México: La querella escolar, 1959–1963*. Mexico City: El Colegio de México, 1988.

Lobato, Ernesto. "La burocracia mexicana." *Revista Económica*, October 1951, 307–12.

Lomas, Clara. "Transborder Discourse: The Articulation of Gender in the Borderlands in the Early Twentieth Century." *Frontiers: A Journal of Women's Studies* 24, nos. 2–3 (June–September 2003): 51–74.

Lomnitz, Claudio, ed. *Vicios públicos, virtudes privadas: La corrupción en México* Mexico City: Centro de Investigaciónes y Estudios Superiores en Antropología Social/ Porrúa, 2000.

López Pérez, Oresta. *La educación, lectura y construcción de género en la Academia de niñas de Morelia (1886–1915)*. Mexico City: Universidad Autónoma de México/Programa de Estudios de Género/El Colegio de San Luís Potosí, 2016.

Lorenzo, María Dolores. "'Ayúdame que yo te ayudaré': La política laboral en el Banco Oriental de México (1900–1915)." *Secuencias: Revista de Historia y Ciencias Sociales*, no. 64 (January–April 2006): 31–48.

Luskey, Brian P. *On the Make: Clerks and the Quest for Capital in Nineteenth-Century America*. New York: New York University Press, 2011.

Macías, Anna. *Contra viento y marea: El movimiento feminista en México hasta 1940*. Mexico City: Programa Universitario de Estudios de Género, 2002.

Macías-González, Víctor Manuel. "Masculine Friendships, Sentiment, and Homoerotics in Nineteenth-Century Mexico: The Correspondence of José María Calderón y Tapia, 1820s–1850s." *Journal of the History of Sexuality* 16, no. 3 (September 2007): 416–35.

Marsiske, Renate. *La Universidad de México: Un recorrido histórico de la época colonial al presente*. Mexico City: Universidad Nacional Autónoma de México, 2001.

Martínez Omaña, María Concepción. "La Revolución entra a la escuela: Recuerdos, imágenes y vivencias de la educación socialista en México/Revolution in the Schools: Memories, Images, and Experiences of Socialist Education in Mexico." *Revista Mexicana de Historia de la Educación* 3, no. 5 (2015): 27–46.

Matabuena Peláez, Teresa. *Algunos usos y conceptos de la fotografía en el Porfiriato*. Mexico City: Universidad Iberoamericana, 1991.

Mattingly, Carol. *Appropriate[ing] Dress: Women's Rhetorical Style in Nineteenth-Century America*. Carbondale: Southern Illinois University Press, 2002.

Mazón, Patricia M. *Gender and the Modern Research University: The Admission of Women to German Higher Education, 1865–1914*. Stanford: Stanford University Press, 2003.

McCann, Bryan. "Carlos Lacerda: The Rise and Fall of a Middle-Class Populist in 1950s Brazil." *Hispanic American Historical Review* 83, no. 4 (2003): 661–96.

Medina, Luis. *Historia de la Revolución Mexicana, 1940–1952: Del cardenismo al avilacamachismo*. Mexico City: El Colegio de México, 1978.

Melero, Pilar. *Mythological Constructs of Mexican Femininity*. New York: Palgrave Macmillan, 2015.

Méndez de Cuenca, Laura. "El decantado feminismo." In *Laura Méndez de Cuenca: Una antología general*, ed. Pablo Mora, 252–55. Mexico City: Biblioteca Americana, Fondo de Cultura Económica, 2006.

Mendieta y Núñez, Lucio. *La administración pública en México*. Mexico City: Imprenta Universitaria, 1943.

———. *Las clases sociales*. Mexico City: Universidad Nacional, 1947.

Meneses Morales, Ernesto. *Tendencias educativas oficiales en México, 1821–1911: La problemática de la educación mexicana en el siglo XIX y principios del XX*. Mexico City: Centro de Estudios Educativos/Universidad Iberoamericana, 1998.

Mentz, Brígida Von. *Movilidad social de sectores medios: Una retrospectiva histórica (siglos XVII al XX)*. Mexico City: Centro de Investigaciónes y Estudios Superiores en Antropología Social/Miguel Ángel Porrúa, 2003.

México, Comisión Mixta de Escalafón. *Reglamento de escalafón para los empleados de base*. Mexico City: Secretaría de Hacienda y Crédito Público, 1945.

México, Comisión Nacional de Escalafón. *Reglamento de escalafón*. Mexico City: Departamento de Divulgación, 1948.

México, Dirección de Estadísticas. *Censo de funcionarios y empleados públicos, 30 de noviembre de 1930*. Mexico City: Talleres Gráficos de la Nación, 1934.

México, Dirección de Pensiones Civiles de Retiro, Departamento de Estadística. *Segundo censo de empleados sujetos a la ley general de pensiones civiles de retiro, 1932*. Mexico City: Imprenta Franco Elizondo hermanos, 1933.

———. *Tercer censo de empleados federales, sujetos a la ley general de pensiones civiles de retiro, 1938*. Mexico City: Imprenta M. L. Sánchez, 1939.

México, Dirección General de Instrucción Primaria del Distrito y Territorios Federales. *La escuela mexicana: Órgano de la Dirección General de Instrucción Primaria del Distrito y Territorios*. Vol. 5. Mexico City: Tipografía Económica, 1908.

México, Instituto Nacional de Estadística, Geografía e Informática. *100 años de censos de población: Estados Unidos Mexicanos*. Aguascalientes: Instituto Nacional de Estadística, Geografía e Informática, 1996.

México, Poder Ejecutivo Federal, Departamento de Aprovisionamientos Generales. *Ley de ingresos y presupuesto de egresos del erario federal para el año fiscal que comienza el 10 de enero y termina el 31 de diciembre de 1920*. Mexico City: Dirección de Talleres Gráficos, 1919.

México, Secretaría de Agricultura y Fomento, Dirección de Estadística. *Tercer censo de la población de los Estados Unidos Mexicanos, verificado el 27 de octubre de 1910*. Mexico City: Oficina Impresora de la Secretaría de Hacienda, Departamento de Fomento, 1918.

México, Secretaría de Economía Nacional. Memoria de la Secretaría de Economía Nacional, septiembre 1942–agosto 1943. Mexico City: Secretaría de Economía Nacional, 1943.

México, Secretaría de la Economía Nacional, Dirección General de Estadística. *Sexto censo de la población, 1940*. Mexico City, 1943.

México, Secretaría de Educación Pública, Departamento de Enseñanza Técnica, Industrial y Comercial. *Memoria, 1937–1939*. Vol. 1. Mexico City: Talleres Gráficos de la Nación, 1938.

México, Secretaría de Gobernación, Departamento de Prevención Social. *Ley de prevención social*. Mexico City, 1934.

México, Secretaría de Hacienda y Crédito Público. *Ley de ingresos y presupuesto de egresos del erario federal*. Mexico City: Imprenta del Gobierno Federal, 1905.

——. *Ley de ingresos y presupuesto de egresos del erario federal*. Mexico City: Tipografía de la Oficina Impresora de Estampillas, Palacio Nacional, 1904, 1907, 1906, 1908, 1909, 1910, 1911, 1913, 1914.

——. *Ley de ingresos y presupuesto de egresos del tesoro federal*. Mexico City: Imprenta de I. Cumplido, 1880, 1884.

——. *Ley de ingresos y presupuesto de egresos del tesoro federal*. Mexico City: Imprenta del Gobierno Federal en el Ex-Arzobispado, 1891.

——. *México a través de los informes presidenciales: La administración pública tomo IV*. Mexico City: Secretaría de Hacienda y Crédito Público and Secretaría de la Presidencia, 1976.

——. *Presupuesto de egresos de la federación*. Mexico City: Talleres Gráficos de la Nación, 1928.

México, Secretaría de Hacienda y Credito Publico, Comisión Reorganizadora, 1927–1928. *Informe de sus labores*. Mexico City: Secretaría de Hacienda y Crédito Público, 1928.

México, Secretaría de Industria, Comercio y Trabajo. *Proyecto de ley federal del trabajo*. Mexico City: Talleres Gráficos de la Nación, 1931.

México, Secretaría de Justicia e Instrucción Pública. *Memoria*. Mexico City: Secretaría de Justicia e Instrucción Pública, 1895.

México, Secretaría del Trabajo y Previsión Social. *Evolución histórica de la Secretaría del Trabajo y Previsión Social*. Mexico City: Imprenta Talleres Gráficos de la Nación, 1957.

México, Suprema Corte de Justicia de la Nación. *Reglamento de escalafón de los funcionarios, empleados y trabajadores que dependen directamente de la Suprema Corte de Justicia de la Nación*. Mexico City, 1942.

México, Tribunal de Arbitraje de los Trabajadores al Servicio de los Poderes de la Unión. *Primer informe anual de labores y tesis sustentadas hasta junio de 1940*. Mexico City, 1940.

México, Unión Sindical de Trabajadores del Museo Nacional. *Estatutos de la Unión Sindical de Trabajadores del Museo Nacional*. Mexico City, 1936.

Meyerowitz, Joanne. "Beyond the Feminine Mystique: A Reassessment of Postwar Mass Culture, 1946–1958." *Journal of American History* 79, no. 4 (March 1993): 1455–82.

Middlebrook, Kevin. *The Paradox of Revolution: Labor, the State, and Authoritarianism in Mexico*. Baltimore: Johns Hopkins University Press, 1995.

Milne, J. D. *Industrial and Social Position of Women in the Middle and Lower Ranks*. London: Chapman and Hall, 1857.

Mink, Gwendolyn. *The Wages of Motherhood: Inequality in the Welfare State, 1917–1942*. Ithaca: Cornell University Press, 1995.

Mistral, Gabriela. *Lecturas para mujeres destinadas a la eseñanza del lenguaje*. Mexico City: Escuela Hogar Gabriela Mistral, 1924.

Mitchell, Stephanie. "'Por la liberación de la mujer': Women and the Anti-Alcohol Campaign." In *The Women's Revolution in Mexico*, ed. Stephanie Mitchell and Patience Schell, 165–85. Lanham MD: Rowman and Littlefield, 2007.

Molina Enríquez, Andrés. *Los grandes problemas nacionales*. Mexico City: Imprenta de A. Carranza e hijos, 1909.

Monteón González, Humberto, and Gabriela María Luisa Riquelme Alcántar. "El presidente Cárdenas y el sufragio femenino." *Espiral* 13, no. 38 (January–April 2007): 81–209.

Montero Sánchez, Susana. *La construcción simbólica de las identidades sociales: Un análisis a través de la literatura mexicana del siglo XIX*. Mexico City: Programa Universitario de Estudios de Género/Centro Coordinador y Difusor de Estudios Latinoamericanos/Plaza y Valdés, 2002.

Montes de Oca Navas, Elvia. "La educación en México: Los libros oficiales de lectura editados durante el gobierno de Lázaro Cárdenas, 1934–1940." *Perfiles Educativos* 29, no. 117 (July–September 2007): 111–30.

———. "Las maestras socialistas en el Estado de México, 1934–1940." *Sociológica* 17, no. 48 (January–April 2002): 185–212.

Mora, José María Luis. "Discurso sobre los perniciosos efectos de la empleomanía." In *Obras sueltas*, 167–82. Mexico City: Universidad Nacional Autónoma de México, 1963.

Morales Campos, Estela. *Forjadores e impulsores de la bibliotecología latinoamericana*. Mexico City: Universidad Nacional Autónoma de México, Centro Universitario de Investigaciones Bibliotecológicas, Dirección General de Bibliotecas, 2006.

Morales Moreno, Luis Gerardo. *Orígenes de la museología mexicana: Fuentes para el estudio histórico del Museo Nacional, 1780–1940*. Mexico City: Universidad Iberoamericana, Departamento de Historia, 1994.

Morales Paulín, Carlos A. *Derecho burocrático*. Mexico City: Porrúa, 1995.

Moreno, Julio. *Yankee Don't Go Home! Mexican Nationalism, American Business Culture, and the Shaping of Modern Mexico, 1920–1950*. Chapel Hill: University of North Carolina, 2003.

Moreno-Brid, Juan Carlos, and Jaime Ros. *Development and Growth in the Mexican Economy: A Historical Perspective*. New York: Oxford University Press, 2009.

Morgan, Simon. *A Victorian Woman's Place: Public Culture in the Nineteenth Century*. New York: Tauris Academic Studies, 2007.

Morton, Ward. *Woman Suffrage in Mexico*. Gainesville: University of Florida Press, 1962.

Moya Gútierrez, Arnaldo. *Arquitectura, historia y poder bajo el régimen de Porfirio Díaz: Ciudad de México, 1876–1911*. Mexico City: Dirección General de Publicaciones del Consejo Nacional para la Cultura y las Artes, 2012.

Mujeres mexicanas notables. Mexico City: Cámara de Diputados, Donceles y Allende, 1975.

Mummert, Gail, and Luis Alfonso Ramírez. *Rehaciendo las diferencias: Identidades de género en Michoacán*. Zamora, Mich.: El Colegio de Michoacán/Universidad Autónoma de Yucatán, 1998.

Muncy, Robyn. *Creating a Female Dominion in American Reform, 1890–1935*. New York: Oxford University Press, 1994.

Munguía Escamilla, Estela. "Experiencias de lucha magisterial en Puebla de los años veintes." In *De la filantropía a la rebelión: Mujeres en los movimientos sociales de finales del siglo XIX al siglo XX*, ed. Gloria Arminda Tirado Villegas, 75–91. Puebla: Benemérita Universidad Autónoma de Puebla, Vicerrectoría de Investigación y Estudios de Posgrado, Cuerpo Académico de Estudios Históricos, 2008.

Muñiz, Elsa. *Cuerpo, representación y poder: México en los albores de la reconstrucción nacional, 1920–1934*. Mexico City: Universidad Autónoma Metropolitana, Azcapotzalco/Miguel Ángel Porrúa, 2002.

Nari, Marcela M. A. *Políticas de maternidad y maternalismo político: Buenos Aires, 1890–1940*. Buenos Aires: Biblos, 2004.

Niblo, Steven. *Mexico in the 1940s: Modernity, Politics, and Corruption*. Wilmington DE: Scholarly Resources, 1999.

Nordhoff, Charles. *La ciencia política al alcance de los jóvenes, obra escrita en inglés por Charles Nordhoff, traducida al castellano y arreglada á las instituciones y al carácter del pueblo máximo por el Lic. Eduardo Ruiz, dedicada a los colegios y escuelas de la República editada por J. V. Villada*. Mexico City: Imprenta Callejón de Santa Clara, 1885.

Norton, Ann V. *Paradoxical Feminism: The Novels of Rebecca West*. Lanham MD: Rowman and Littlefield, 2000.

Ochoa, Enrique C. *Feeding Mexico: The Political Uses of Food since 1910*. Wilmington DE: Scholarly Resources, 2000.

Offen, Karen. "Defining Feminism: A Comparative Historical Approach." *Signs* 14, no. 1 (Autumn 1988): 119–57.

Okión Solano, Verónica. *Cuca García (1889–1973): Por las causas de las mujeres y la Revolución*. Prologue by Mary Kay Vaughan. Zamora, Mich.: El Colegio de Michoacán/Centro de Investigaciones y Estudios de Género de la Universidad Nacional Autónoma de México/El Colegio de San Luís, 2016.

Olcott, Jocelyn. "Miracle Workers: Gender and State Mediation among Textile and Garment Workers in Mexico's Transition to Industrial Development." *International Labor and Working-Class History* 63, no.1 (2003): 45–62.

———. *Revolutionary Women in Postrevolutionary Mexico*. Durham: Duke University Press, 2005.

Olimón Nolasco, Miguel. *Sofía del Valle: Una mexicana universal*. Mexico City: Instituto Nacional de las Mujeres, 2009.

Olivé Negrete, Julio César, and Augusto Urteaga Castro-Pozo. *INAH: Una historia*. Mexico City: Instituto Nacional de Antropología e Historia, 1988.

Olvera Serrano, Margarita. "La primera socialización intelectual de Lucío Mendieta y Núñez." *Sociológica* 14, no. 39 (1999): 91–122.

Orellana Trinidad, Laura. "'La mujer del porvenir': Raíces intelectuales y alcances del pensamiento feminista de Hermila Galindo, 1915–1919." *Signos Históricos*, no. 5 (January–June 2001): 109–37.

Orleck, Annelise. *Common Sense and a Little Fire: Women and Working-Class Politics in the United States, 1900–1965*. Chapel Hill: University of North Carolina Press, 1995.

Owensby, Brian P. *Intimate Ironies: Modernity and the Making of Middle-Class Lives in Brazil*. Stanford: Stanford University Press, 1999.

Palacios, Juan, and Alfonso Pruneda. *Guía de la Secretaría de Instrucción Pública y Bellas Artes*. Mexico City: M.L. Sánchez, 1910.

Parcero, María de la Luz. *Condiciones de la mujer en México durante el siglo XIX*. Mexico City: Instituto Nacional de Antropología e Historia, 1992.

Pardo, María del Carmen. "El servicio profesional de carrera en México: De la tradición al cambio." *Foro Internacional* 45, no. 4 (2005): 599–634.

Parker, D. S. *The Idea of the Middle Class: White-Collar Workers and Peruvian Society, 1900–1950*. University Park: Pennsylvania State University Press, 1998.

Parra, Gonzalo de la. *De como se hizo revolucionario un hombre de buena fé*. Mexico City, 1915.

Partido Revolucionario Institucional. *Historia documental de la CNOP*. Vol. 1, *1943–1959*. Mexico City: Instituto de Capacitación Política, CNOP, 1984.

Pavissich, Antonio. *Mujer antigua y mujer moderna*. Madrid: Saturnino Calleja, 1910.

Peard, Julyan G. "Enchanted Edens and Nation-Making: Juana Manso, Education, Women and Trans-American Encounters in Nineteenth-Century Argentina." *Journal of Latin American Studies* 40, no. 3 (2008): 453–82.

Peña Doria, Olga Martha. *Catalina D'Erzell: Pionera del feminismo literario mexicano del siglo XX*. Guadalajara: Universidad de Guadalajara, 2000.

Peñafiel, Antonio. *Anuario estadístico de la República Mexicana*. Mexico City: Oficina Tipográfica de la Secretaría de Fomento, 1901.

Peniche Rivero, Piedad. "El movimiento feminista de Elvia Carrillo Puerto y las igualadas: Un liderazgo cultural en Yucatán." In *Dos mujeres fuera de serie: Elvia Carillo Puerto y Felipa Poot*, ed. Piedad Peniche Rivero and Kathleen R. Martín, 15–69. Mérida, Yucatán: Instituto de la Cultura de Yucatán, 2007.

Peregrina, Angélica. "La carrera magisterial: Una opción para las mujeres de Guadalajara (1900–1925)." *Revista Electrónica Sinéctica*, no. 28 (February–July 2006): 17–27.

———. *La Escuela Normal de Jalisco en su centenario (1892–1992)*. Guadalajara: El Colegio de Jalisco, 1992.

Pérez Toledo, Sonia. *Trabajadores, espacio urbano y sociabilidad en la Ciudad de México, 1790–1867*. Mexico City: Miguel Ángel de Porrúa/Universidad Autónoma Metropolitana, Iztapalapa, 2011.

———. "Trabajadores urbanos, empleo y control en la Ciudad de México." In *Trabajo, ocio y coacción: Trabajadores urbanos en México y Guatemala en el siglo XIX*, ed. Clara E. Lida and Sonia Pérez Toldeo, 157–96. Mexico City: Universidad Autónoma Metropolitana/Miguel Ángel Porrúa, 2001.

———. "El trabajo femenino en la Ciudad de México a mediados del siglo XIX." *Signos Históricos*, no. 10 (July–December 2003): 81–114.

Pierce, Gretchen Kristine. "Sobering the Revolution: Anti-alcohol Campaigns and the Process of State-Building, 1910–1940." PhD diss., University of Arizona, 2008.

Pitman, Isaac. *Stenographic Sound-Hand*. London: Samuel Bagster, 1837.

Pitman, Thea. "Identidad nacional y feminismo en el periodismo de mujeres: El caso de Elvira Vargas." *Literatura Mexicana* 18, no. 1 (2007): 131–43.

Poor, Henry V. *Poor's Manual of Railroads*. Vol. 55. New York: H. V. & H. W. Poor, 1922.

Poot Herrera, Sara. "Primicias feministas y amistades literarias." In *Nueve escritoras mexicanas nacidas en la primera mitad del siglo XX, y una revista*, ed. Elena Urrutia, 36–78. Mexico City: Instituto Nacional de las Mujeres/El Colegio de México, 2006.

Porter, Susie S. "De obreros y señoritas: Culturas de trabajo en la ciudad de México en la compañía Ericsson, en la década de 1920." In *Género en la encrucijada de la historia cultural y social*, ed. Susie S. Porter and María Teresa Fernández Aceves, 179–210. Zamora, Mich.: El Colegio de Michoacán/Centro de Investigaciónes y Estudios Superiores en Antropología Social, 2015.

———. *Mujeres y trabajo: Condiciones materiales y discursos públicos en la ciudad de México, 1879–1931*. Zamora, Mich.: El Colegio de Michoacán, 2008.

———. "Women, Children and Welfare in Latin American History." *Journal of Women's History* 25, no. 3 (Fall 2013): 212–20.

———. *Working Women in Mexico City: Material Conditions and Public Discourses, 1879–1931*. Tucson: University of Arizona Press, 2003.

———. "Working Women in the Mexican Revolution." In *Oxford Research Encyclopedias: Latin American History*, ed. William Beezley. New York: Oxford University Press, 2016). DOI: 10.1093/acrefore/9780199366439.013.16.

Porter, Susie, and María Teresa Fernández Aveces. "Introducción." In *Género en la encrucijada de la historia cultural y social*, ed. Susie S. Porter and María Teresa

Fernández Aceves, 9–31. Zamora, Mich.: El Colegio de Michoacán/Centro de Investigaciónes y Estudios Superiores en Antropología Social, 2015.

Portes Gil, Emilio. *Quince años de política mexicana: Prólogo del lic. Alfonso Teja Zabre.* Mexico City: Ediciones Botas, 1954.

Pratt, Mary Louise. "Mi cigarro, mi Singer, y la Revolución Mexicana: La danza ciudadana de Nellie Campobello." *Cadernos Pagu* 22 (2004): 151–84.

Puig Casauranc, José Manuel. *El esfuerzo educativo en México: La obra del gobierno federal en el Ramo de Educación Pública durante al administración del Presidente Plutarco Elías Calles (1924–1928). Memoria analítico-crítica de la organización actual de la Secretaría de Educación Pública, sus éxitos, sus francasos, los derroteros que la experiencia señala.* Vol. 1. Mexico City: Secretaría de Educación Pública, 1928.

Queirolo, Graciela. "Mujeres que trabajan: Una revisión historiográfica del trabajo femenino en la ciudad de Buenos Aires (1890–1940)." *Novo Topo: Revista de Historia y Pensamiento Crítico*, no. 3 (September 2006): 29–49.

Quintanilla, Susana. "El debate intelectual acerca de la educación socialista." In *Escuela y sociedad en el periodo cardenista*, ed. Susana Quintanilla and Mary Kay Vaughan, 47–75. Mexico City: Fondo de Cultura Económica, 1999.

Quirarte, Vicente. "Introducción." In *Los contemporáneos en "El Universal,"* by Jorge Cuesta, Salvador Novo, Jaime Torres Bodet, and Xavier Villaurrutia, 11–36. Mexico City: Fondo de Cultura Económica, 2016.

Ramos Escandón, Carmen. "Challenging Legal and Gender Constraints in México: Sofía Villa de Buentello's Criticism of Family Legislation, 1917–1927." In *The Women's Revolution in Mexico, 1910–1953*, ed. Stephanie Mitchel and Patience A. Schell, 53–71. Lanham MD: Roman and Littlefield, 2007.

———. "Concepción Gimeno de Flaquer: Identidad nacional y femenina en México, 1880–1900." *Arenal* 8, no. 2 (2001): 365–78.

———. "Desafiando el orden legal y las limitaciones en las conductas de género en México. La crítica de Sofía Villa de Buentello a la legislación familiar, 1917–1927." *La Aljaba: Revista de Estudios de Género* 7 (2002): 79–102.

———. "Espacios viajeros e identidad femenina en el México de fin de siècle: *El Álbum de la Mujer* de Concepción Gimeno, 1883–1890." *Frentes avanzados*, March 22, 2006. Editoras Mayte Díez y Luz Congosto. Internet.

———. "Género e identidad femenina y nacional en *El Álbum de la Mujer* de Concepción Gimeno de Flaquer." In *La República de las letras: Asomos a la cultura escrita del México decimonónico*, vol. 2, ed. Belem Clark de Lara and Elisa Speckman, 195–208. Mexico City: Universidad Nacional Autónoma de México, 2005.

———. "Imperial Eyes, Gendered Views: Concepción Gimeno Re-writes the Aztecas at the End of the Nineteenth Century." In *Women and the Colonial Gaze*, ed. T. L. Hunt and M. R. Lessard, 117–23. New York: New York University Press, 2002.

———. *Industrialización, género y trabajo femenino en el sector textil mexicano: El obraje, la fábrica y la compañía industrial.* Mexico City: Centro de Investigaciónes y Estudios Superiores en Antropología Social, 2004.

———. "Metiéndose en la *bola*: Mujeres y política en la Revolución Mexicana, o el esfuerzo por tener voz ciudadana." *Sólo Historia*, no. 8 (April–June 2000): 4–8.

———. "Mujeres trabajadoras en el México porfiriano: Género e ideología del trabajo feminino, 1876–1911." *La Revista Europea de Estudios Latinoamericanos y del Caribe* 48 (June 1990): 27–44.

———. "Mujer y poder en el cardenismo: El debate por el sufragio." *Boletín Virtual del Centro de Estudios de Historia de la Mujer en América Latina* 5, no. 54 (2004).

———. "The Narrative Voice in María Ríos Cárdenas's *La mujer mexicana es ciudadana.*" In *Disciplines on the Line: Feminist Research on Spanish, Latin American and U.S. Latina Women*, ed. Anne J. Cruz, Rosalie Hernández-Pecoraro, and Joyce Tolliver, 167–87. Newark DE: Juan de la Cuesta Editores, 2003.

———. "La participación de la mujer en México: Del fusil al voto, 1915–1955." *Boletín Latinoamericanista* 44 (1994): 155–69.

———. "Women's Movements, Feminism, and Mexican Politics." In *The Women's Movement in Latin America: Participation and Democracy*, ed. Jane S. Jaquette, 199–221. Boulder: Westview Press, 1994.

Rangel, Ricardo E., and Rafael E. Portas. *Enciclopedia cinematográfica mexicana, 1897–1955.* Mexico City: Publicaciones Cinematográficas, 1955.

Rankin, Monica A. *México, la patria! Propaganda and Production during World War II.* Lincoln: University of Nebraska Press, 2009.

Raphael, Lutz. *Ley y orden: Dominación mediante la administración en el siglo XIX.* Madrid: Siglo XXI, 2008.

Rashkin, Elissa J. *The Stridentist Movement in Mexico: The Avante-Garde and Cultural Change in the 1920s.* Lanham MD: Lexington Books, 2009.

———. *Women Filmmakers in Mexico: The Country of Which We Dream.* Austin: University of Texas Press, 2001.

Rendón, MaríaTeresa, and Carlos Salas. "La evolución del empleo en México, 1895–1980." *Estudios Demográficos y Urbanos* 2, no. 2 (May–August 1987): 189–230.

Rendón Gan, Teresa. *Trabajo de hombres y trabajo de mujeres en el México del siglo XX* Mexico CIty: Universidad Nacional Autónoma de México/Programa de Estudios de Género, 2003.

Reyes Esparza, Ramiro. *La burguesía mexicana: Cuatro ensayos.* Mexico City: Editorial Nuestro Tiempo, 1973.

Reyes Rodríguez, Andrés. *Clases medias y poder político en Aguascalientes.* Aguascalientes: Universidad Autónoma de Aguascalientes, 2016.

Reyna, José Luis, and Raúl Trejo Delarbre. *La clase obrera en la historia de México: De Adolfo Ruiz Cortines a Adolfo López Mateos (1952–1964)*. Mexico City: Siglo XXI Editores, 1981.

Ríos Cárdenas, María. *Atavismo*. Mexico City: Tipografía "La Bética," 1922.

———. *La mujer mexicana es ciudadana: Historia, con fisonomía de una novela de costumbres, 1930–época–1940*. Mexico City: A. del Bosque, 1942.

Robles, Martha. *La sombra fugitiva*. Vols. 1 and 2. Mexico City: Universidad Nacional Autónoma de México, Instituto de Investigaciones Filológicas, Centros de Estudios Literarios, 1985.

Robles de Mendoza, Margarita. *La evolución de la mujer en México*. Mexico City: Imprenta Galas, 1931.

———. *Silbario de la ciudanía de la mujer*. Mexico City: Talleres Tipográficos del Gobierno, 1932.

Rocha, Martha Eva, ed. *El álbum de la mujer: Antología ilustrada de las mexicanas*. Vol. 4, *El Porfiriato y la Revolución*. Mexico City: Instituto Nacional de Antropología e Historia, 1991.

———. "The Faces of Rebellion: From Revolutionaries to Veterans in Nationalist Mexico." In *The Women's Revolution in Mexico, 1910–1953*, ed. Patience Schell and Stephanie Mitchell, 15–35. Lanham MD: Rowman and Littlefield, 2007.

———. *Los rostros de la rebeldía: Veteranas de la Revolución Mexicana, 1910–1939*. Mexico City: Secretaría de Cultura /Instituto Nacional de Estudios Históricos de las Revoluciones de México/Instituto Nacional de Antropología e Historia, 2016.

Rockwell, Elsie. "Reforma constitucional y controversias locales: La educación socialista en Tlaxcala, 1935–1936." In *Escuela y sociedad en el periodo cardenista*, ed. Susana Quintanilla and Mary Kay Vaughan, 196–228. Mexico City: Fondo de Cultura Económica, 1999.

———. "Schools of the Revoution: Enacting and Contesting State Forms in Tlaxcala, 1910–1930." In *Everyday Forms of State Formation: Revolution and the Negotiation of Rule in Modern Mexico*, ed. Gilbert M. Joseph and Daniel Nugent, 170–208. Durham: Duke University Press, 1994.

Rodríguez, María de los Ángeles. *ESCA: Pionera de la enseñanza comercial, contable y administrativa en América*. Mexico City: Instituto Politécnico Nacional, 1995.

Rodríguez, María de los Ángeles, and Max Krongold, eds. *50 años de educación tecnológica en México*. Mexico City: Instituto Politécnico Nacional, 1988.

Rodriguez Cabo, Mathilde. *La mujer y la Revolución: Conferencia dictada en el Frente Socialista de Abogados*. Mexico City: Frente Socialista de Abogados, 1937.

Rodríguez Campos, Patricia. "Una mujer impresaria de principios de siglo." *Sincronías* 5, no. 17 (Winter 2000): n.p.

Rodríguez Kuri, Ariel. *La Revolución en la Ciudad de México, 1911–1922*. Mexico City: El Colegio de México, Centro de Estudios Históricos, 2010.

Romero Aceves, Ricardo. *La mujer en la historia de México*. Mexico City: Costa-Amic Editores, 1982.

Rosal, Alicia de. *De taquígrafa a gran señora*. Mexico City: Galatea, 1946.

Rosemblatt, Karin Alejandra. *Gendered Compromises: Political Cultures and the State in Chile, 1920–1950*. Chapel Hill: University of North Carolina, 2000.

Rubenstein, Anne. "Theaters of Masculinity: Moviegoing and Male Roles in Mexico before 1960." In *Masculinity and Sexuality in Modern Mexico*, ed. Víctor Macías-González and Anne Rubenstein, 132–54. Albuquerque: University of New Mexico Press, 2012.

———. "The War on 'Las Pelonas': Modern Women and Their Enemies, Mexico City, 1924." In *Sex in Revolution: Gender, Politics, and Power in Modern Mexico*, ed. Jocelyn Olcott, Mary Kay Vaughan, and Gabriela Cano, 57–80. Durham: Duke University Press, 2006.

Ruíz Abreu, Carlos, and Jorge Abdo Francis. *El hombre del sureste: relación documental del archivo particular . . .* Vol. 1. Mexico City: Universidad Juárez Autónoma de Tabasco/Secretaría de Gobernación, Archivo General de la Nación, 2002.

Saloma Gutiérrez, Ana María. "Forjando la vida: Dichas y desdichas de las obreras de las fábricas cigarreras del Porfiriato." *Dimensión Antropológica* 18 (January–April 2000): 28–52.

———. "Las hijas del trabajo: Fabricantes cigarreras de la Ciudad de México en el siglo XIX." PhD thesis, Escuela Nacional de Antropología e Historia, 2001.

Sánchez González, José Juan. *La administración pública en México en el siglo XX*. Mexico City: Instituto Nacional de Administración Pública, 2010.

———. "Origen y desarrollo del estudio de la administración pública en México." *Convergencia* 16, no. 49 (2009): 37–72.

Sánchez Olvera, Alma Rosa. *El feminismo mexicano ante el movimiento urbano popular: Dos expresiones de lucha de género (1970–1985)*. Mexico City: Escuela Nacional de Estudios Profesionales Acatlán/Universidad Nacional Autónoma de México/ Plaza y Valdés, 2002.

Sanders, Nichole. *Gender and Welfare in Mexico: The Consolidation of a Postrevolutionary State*. University Park: Pennsylvania State University Press, 2011.

Sandoval, José María. *Memoria que el Oficial Mayor encargado de la Secretaría de Estado y del Despacho de Gobernación presenta al séptimo Congreso Constitucional*. Mexico City: Imprenta del Gobierno en Palacio, 1847.

Santibáñez Tijerina, Blanca Esthela. "Enseñanza y recreación: Imágenes femeninas en la sociedad tlaxcalteca porfirista." In *De la filantropía a la rebelión: Mujeres en los movimientos sociales de fines del siglo XIX al siglo XX*, ed. Gloria Arminda

Tirado Villegas, 61–73. Puebla: Benemérita Universidad Autónoma de Puebla, Vicerrectoría de Investigación y Estudios de Posgrado, Cuerpo Académico de Estudios Históricos, 2008.

Schaeffer, Wendell Karl Gordon. *La administración pública mexicana*. Mexico City: Instituto Nacional de Estudios Históricos de la Revolución Mexicana, 2003.

Schell, Patience A. *Church and State Education in Revolutionary Mexico City*. Tucson: University of Arizona Press, 2003.

———. "Gender, Class, and Anxiety at the Gabriela Mistral Vocational School, Revolutionary Mexico City." In *Sex in Revolution: Gender, Politics, and Power in Modern Mexico*, ed. Jocelyn Olcott, Mary Kay Vaughan, and Gabriela Cano, 112–26. Durham: Duke University Press, 2006.

Semo, Enrique. *Historia mexicana: Economía y lucha de clases*. 3rd ed. Mexico City: Editorial Era, 1984.

Sesto, Julio. *El México de Porfirio Díaz: (hombres y cosas). Estudio sobre el desenvolvimiento general de la República Méxicana después de diez años de permanencia en ella. Observaciones hechas en el terreno oficial y particular*. Valencia: F. Sempere y Compañía, 1910.

Shulgovski, Anatol. *México en la encrucijada de la historia*. Mexico City: Ediciones de Cultura Popular, 1968.

Sierra, Justo. *La evolución política del pueblo mexicano*. Mexico City: Universidad Nacional Autónoma de México, 1957.

———. *Obras completas: La educación nacional: Artículos, actuaciones y documentos*. Vol. 8. Ed. Agustín Yáñez. Mexico City: Universidad Nacional Autónoma de México, 1948.

Silva Herzog, Jesús. *Un estudio del costo de la vida en México*. Mexico City: Editorial Cvltvra, 1931.

Silverstone, Rosalie. "Office Work for Women: An Historical Overview." *Business History* 18 (1976): 98–110.

Sindicato Nacional de Trabajadores de la Secretaría de Gobernación (México). *Historia del Sindicato Nacional de la Secretaría de Gobernación: 50 aniversario, 1937–1986*. Mexico City: El Sindicato, 1986.

Sluis, Ageeth. "Bataclanismo! Or How Female Deco Bodies Transformed Post-Revolutionary Mexico City." *Americas* 66, no. 4 (2010): 469–99.

———. *Deco Body, Deco City: Female Spectacle and Modernity in Mexico City, 1900–1939*. Lincoln: University of Nebraska Press, 2016.

Smith, Benjamin, and Paul Gillingham, eds. *Dictablanda: Politics, Work, and Culture in Mexico, 1938–1968*. Durham: Duke University Press, 2014.

Smith, Stephanie J. *Gender and the Mexican Revolution: Yucatán Women and the Realities of Patriarchy*. Chapel Hill: University of North Carolina Press, 2009.

Snodgrass, Michael. *Deference and Defiance in Monterrey: Workers, Paternalism, and Revolution in Mexico, 1890–1950*. Cambridge: Cambridge University Press, 2003.

Sohn, Anne-Marie. "Los roles sexuales en Francia e Inglaterra: Una transición suave." In *Historia de las mujeres en occidente*, vol. 5, *El siglo XX*, ed. George Duby, Michelle Perrot, Mary Nash, Marco Aurelio Galmarini, and Thébaud Françoise, 127–57. Madrid: Taurus, 2003.

Sondik Aron, Cindy. *Ladies and Gentlemen of the Civil Service: Middle-Class Workers in Victorian America*. Oxford: Oxford University Press, 1987.

Sosenski, Susana, and Gregorio Sosenski. "En defensa de los niños y las mujeres: Un acercamiento a la vida de la psiquiatra Mathilde Rodríguez Cabo." *Salud Mental* 33, no. 1 (2010): 1–10.

Soto, Shirlene. *Emergence of the Modern Mexican Woman: Her Participation in Revolution and Struggle for Equality, 1910–1940*. Denver: Arden Press, 1990.

Steedman, Carolyn. *Past Tenses: Essays on Writing, Autobiography and History*. London: Rivers Oram Press, 1992.

Suarez-Potts, William. *The Making of Law: The Supreme Court and Labor Legislation in Mexico, 1875–1931*. Stanford: Stanford University Press 2012.

Tamayo, Jaime. *La clase obrera en la historia de México: El interinato de Adolfo de la Huerta y el gobierno de Álvaro Obregón (1920–1924)*. Mexico City: Siglo XXI Editores/Instituto de Investigaciones Sociales, Universidad Nacional Autónoma de México, 1987.

Tanck Estrada, Dorothy. "Las escuelas lancasterianas en la Ciudad de México: 1822–1842." *Historia Mexicana* 22, no. 4 (April–June 1973): 494–513.

Tello Macías, Carlos. *Estado y desarrollo económico: México, 1920–2006*. Mexico City: Universidad Nacional Autónoma de México, 2007.

Thompson, Lanny. "Artisans, Marginals, and Proletarians: The Households of the Popular Classes in Mexico City, 1876–1950." In *Five Centuries of Mexican History/Cinco siglos de historia de México*, ed. Virginia Guedea and Jaime Rodríguez, 2:76–137. Mexico City: Instituto de Investigaciones Dr. José María Luis Mora, 1992.

Threlkeld, Megan. *Pan American Women: U.S. Internationalists and Revolutionary Mexico*. Philadelphia: University of Pennsylvania Press, 2014.

Torres-Barrera, Sara, and Elvia Zambrano-Lizárraga. "Breve historia de la educación de la enfermería en México." *Revista de Enfermería Instituto Mexicano de Seguro Social* 18, no. 2 (2010): 105–10.

Torres San Martín, Patricia, and Eduardo de la Vega. *Adela Sequeyro*. Guadalajara: Universidad de Guadalajara, 1997.

Torres Septién, Valentina. *La educación privada en México, 1903–1976*. Mexico City: El Colegio de México/ Universidad Iberoamericana, 1997.

Tossounian, Cecilia. "Women's Associations and the Emergence of the Social State: Protection for Mothers and Children in Buenos Aires, 1920–1940." *Journal of Latin American Studies* 45, no. 2 (2013): 297–324.

Tovar Ramírez, Aurora. *Mil quinientas mujeres en nuestra conciencia colectiva: Catálogo de mujeres de México*. Mexico City: Documentación y Estudio de Mujeres, 1996.

Trillo Tinoco, Flor Elisa. "La presencia de las mujeres en la internet." Thesis for the degree of librarian, Universidad Nacional Autónoma de México, Facultad de Filosofía y Letras, 2004.

Trueba Urbina, Alberto. *Legislación de emergencia sobre el salario insuficiente (concordada y comentada)*. Mexico City: Talleres Gráficos, 1943.

Trueba Urbina, Alberto, and Jorge Trueba Barrera. *Legislación federal del trabajo buro-crático: Comentarios y jurisprudencia*. Mexico City: Editorial Porrúa, 1964.

Trujillo Bolio, Mario. "La reciente historiografía de la vida laboral en la sociedad novo-hispana y en el México decimonónico." *Iztapalapa: Revista de Ciencias Sociales y Humanidades* 1, no. 66 (2009): 165–84.

Tuñón Pablos, Enriqueta. "Amalia Castillo Ledón: Una feminista en un mundo de hombres, 1929–1953." In *De espacios domésticos y mundos públicos: El siglo de las mujeres en México*, ed. Martha Eva Rocha, Anna Rivera Carbó, Enriqueta Tuñón Pablos, Lilia Venegas Arroyo, 71–94. Mexico City: Instituto Nacional de Antropología e Historia, 2010.

——. *¡Por fin . . .—Ya podemos elegir y ser electas!: el sufragio femenino en México, 1935–1953*. Mexico City: Plaza y Valdés, 2002.

Tuñón Pablos, Esperanza. "El Frente Único Pro Derechos de la Mujer, 1935–1938." *Fem* 8, no. 30 (1983): 21–23.

——. "La lucha de las mujeres en el cardenismo." Master's thesis, Universidad Nacional Autónoma de México, 1985.

——. *Mujeres que se organizan: El Frente Único Pro Derechos de la Mujer, 1935–1938*. Mexico City: Editorial Miguel Ángel Porrúa, 1992.

Tuñón Pablos, Julia. "Nueve escritoras, una revista y un escenario: Cuando se junta la oportunidad con el talento." In *Nueve escritoras mexicanas nacidas en la primera mitad del siglo XX, y una revista*, ed. Elena Urrutia, 3–32. Mexico City: Instituto Nacional de las Mujeres/El Colegio de México, 2006.

——. *Women in Mexico: A Past Unveiled*. Trans. Alan Hynd. Austin: University of Texas Press, 1999.

Turk, Katherine. "Labor's Pink-Collar Aristocracy: The National Secretaries Asso-ciation's Encounters with Feminism in the Age of Automation." *Labor* 11, no. 2 (2014): 85–109.

van der Klein, Marian, Rebecca Jo Plant, Nichole Sanders, and Lori R. Weintrob, eds. *Maternalism Reconsidered: Motherhood, Welfare and Social Policy in the Twentieth Century*. New York: Berghahn Books, 2012.

Vapnek, Lara. *Breadwinners: Working Women and Economic Independence, 1865–1920*. Urbana: University of Illinois Press, 2009.

Vasconcelos, José. *Memorias: Ulises Criollo, La Tormenta*. Mexico City: Fondo de Cultura Económica, 1982.

Vaughan, Mary Kay. *Cultural Politics in Revolution: Teachers, Peasants, and Schools in Mexico, 1930–1940*. Tucson: University of Arizona Press, 1997.

———. "El papel político de los maestros federales durante la época de Cárdenas: Sonora y Puebla." In *Escuela y sociedad en el periodo cardenista*, ed. Susana Quintanilla and Mary Kay Vaughan, 166–95. Mexico City: Fondo de Cultura Económica, 1997.

———. *The State, Education, and Social Class in Mexico, 1880–1928*. DeKalb: Northern Illinois Press, 1982.

Vaughan, Mary Kay, and Stephen E. Lewis, eds. *The Virgin and the Eagle*. Durham: Duke University Press, 2006.

Vázquez de Knaugth, Josefina Zoraida. "La educación socialista de los años treinta." *Historia Mexicana* 18, no. 3 (January–March 1969): 408–23.

Villa de Buentello, Sofia. *Derechos civiles de la mujer y ley de relaciones familiares*. Mexico City: Imprenta Franco-Mexicana, S.A., 1923.

———. *La mujer y la ley: Pequeña parte tomada de la obra en preparación titulada "¡La Esclava se levanta!": Estudio importantísimo para la mujer que desee su emancipación y para el hombre amante del bien y de la justicia*. Mexico City: Talleres de la Imprenta Franco Mexicana, 1921.

———. *La verdad sobre el matrimonio . . . estudio importantísimo sobre la triste condición de la mujer en el matrimonio*. Mexico City: Talleres de la Imprenta Franco Mexicana, 1923.

Villalba, Angela. *Mexican Calendar Girls: Golden Age of Calendar Art, 1930–1960*. San Francisco: Chronicle Books, 2006.

Villalobos Calderón, Liborio. *Las obreras en el Porfiriato*. Mexico City: Universidad Autónoma Metropolitana, Xochimilco/Plaza y Valdés, 2002.

Wacquant, Löic J. D. "Making Class: The Middle Class(es) in Social Theory and Social Structure." In *Bringing Class Back In: Contemporary and Historical Perspectives*, ed. Scott G. McNall, Rhonda F. Levine, and Rick Fantasia, 39–64. Boulder: Westview Press, 1991.

Wahrman, Dror. *Imagining the Middle Class: The Political Representation of Class in Britain, 1780–1840*. New York: Cambridge University Press, 1995.

Walker, Louise. *Waking from the Dream: Mexico's Middle Class after 1968*. Stanford: Stanford University Press, 2013.

Weiner, Lynn. *From Working Girl to Working Mother: The Female Labor Force in the United States, 1820–1980*. Chapel Hill: University of North Carolina, 1985.

Weinstein, Barbara. "'They Don't Even Look Like Women Workers': Femininity and Class in Twentieth-Century Latin America." *International Labor and Working-Class History* 69, no. 1 (2006): 161–76.

Wishnia, Judith. *The Proletarianization of the Fonctionnaires: Civil Service Workers and the Labor Movement under the Third Republic*. Baton Rouge: Louisiana State University Press, 1990.

Womack, John, Jr. *Posición estratégica obrera: Hacia una nueva historia de los movimientos obreros*. Mexico City: Fondo de Cultura Económica, 2008.

——— . *El trabajo en la Cervecería Moctezuma, 1908*. Mexico City: El Colegio de México/Fideicomiso Historia de las Américas/H. Congreso del Estado de Veracruz, LXII Legislatura, 2012.

Wright de Kleinhans, Laureana. "La emancipación de la mujer por medio del estudio." *La Mujer Mexicana*, 1905. Reprinted in *El álbum de la mujer*, vol. 4, *El Porfiriato y la Revolución*, ed. Martha Eva Rocha and Enriqueta Tuñón, 214–21. Mexico City: Instituto Nacional de Antropología e Historia, 1991.

——— . *Mujeres notables mexicanas*. Mexico City: Tipografía Económica, 1910.

Zapata, Francisco. "Condición de vida y conciencia obrera de las trabajadoras de la Volkswagen de México." In *Historia y cultura obrera*, ed. Victoria Novelo, 188–221. Mexico City: Centro de Investigaciónes y Estudios Superiores en Antropología Social/Instituto Mora, 1999.

Zavala, Adriana. *Becoming Modern, Becoming Tradition: Women, Gender, and Representation in Mexico*. University Park: Penn State University Press, 2009.

INDEX

Acción Cívica. *See* Civic Action

Acción Feminina. *See* Feminine Action

Action Group (Ministry of Public Education), 188–89

Aguirre, Alma Rosa, 210, 213

Aguirre Berlanga, Manuel, 32

Alas (newspaper), 97

Alborada (newspaper), 97

El Álbum de la Mujer (newspaper), 24, 248n26

alcohol, campaign against, 81–86, 93, 149

Alemán Valdés, Miguel, 203, 224, 226

Alessio Robles, Miguel, 103

Alianza (newspaper), 58

Alliance of Workers of the Ministry of Public Education, 188

Alva, Alicia, 63, 116–19

Alvarez, Cholita, 187

Alvarez, Concepción, 47

"angel of the home," 1–2, 20–21, 58, 238

Angulo, María, 109

Arellano Belloc, Francisco, 192

Arias Bernal, María, 57, 257n120

Arlette. *See* Reyes de Govea, María Aurelia (Arlette)

artisans, 2–3, 7–8, 19–22, 28–29, 40, 71, 151–53, 242n19

Asociación Mexicana de Empleados Oficiales. *See* Mexican Association of Official Employees

atavism, 90–92, 232

Atavismo (Ríos Cárdenas), 90–92, 232

Athenaeum of Mexican Women, 160, 192

Aventurera (Alberto Gout, 1949), 210

Ávila Camacho, Manuel, 201–3, 224

Azuela, Mariano, 161

Balmaceda, Esperanza, 184–87, 192–94

Barreda, Horacio, 55–56

Barrena Campuzano, Gloria, 196–97

Batiza Berckowitz, Sarah, 210–20, 232, 237, 300n30

Becerril, Graciana, 225–26

Berrueco, Manuel, 43

Best, Gustavo, 188

Bloque Nacional de Mujeres Revolucionarias. *See* National Bloc of Revolutionary Women

Bojórquez Castillo, Fausto, 172–73

Boletín (Ministry of Public Education), 45

Bravo Adams, Caridad, 179

Brindis, Fidelia, 109

Büchner, Lois, 28, 249n39

budget: federal, 32, 68, 102, 120, 123, 132–34, 157, 190, 197; education, 72, 79, 102, 142, 144,

bureaucracy, 4–6, 12, 20, 32, 62–67, 199, 201

"burocracia feminina," 238

Calles, Ernestine, 99–100

Calles, Plutarco Elías, 57, 63, 79, 108, 263

campesinos, 25, 68, 95–96, 110, 191, 194

Commercial Education, 72–73, 78–83, 142–51, 155–57

government ministries: Communications and Public Works, 112–20, 130, 136, 185, 188–89, 226; Feminine Action, 189–92, 224; Finance and Public Credit, 41, 49, 64, 102–3, 112–18, 125, 133–35, 182, 189, 214, 226; Health, 125, 130, 182; Hydraulic Resources, 226; Industry, Commerce, and Labor, 85, 103, 109, 112, 114; National Economy, 8, 112, 117, 121, 124, 130, 131, 135, 138, 182, 188, 226; National Marine, 226; National Mint, 104; Public Assistance, 112, 118, 200, 220, 221; Public Education, 45, 72, 109, 112–18, 130, 142, 159, 179, 182–88, 197, 221, 225, 235–36; Public Instruction and Fine Arts, 40

government offices: Central Telegraph, 31, 188; Federal Attorney General, 112, 114; General Office for Statistics, 63; High Commission on Health, 34; Migration, 186, 202; National Statistics, 63, 68, 112–17, 136; Post, 32–37, 57, 67–71; Social Welfare, 190, 196; Stenographers, 113

Government Press Union, 104

Guerrero, Silvestre, 187

Guzmán, Eulalia, 57, 80, 108

Han matado a Tongolele (Gavaldón), 210

Hay, Eduardo, 5

Hernández, Ana María, 175

Herrera, Rebeca, 224–25

Las Hijas del Anáhuac (periodical), 11, 81

El Hijo del Trabajo (newspaper), 25

El Hogar (periodical), 97

honor, 23, 27–28, 41–42, 49, 58, 96, 128, 161–63, 210, 212

Horizontes (periodical), 97

household: economy, 19, 22, 152–54; female head of, 34, 67–72, 106, 117–23, 179, 235; women's role in, 2, 67–72, 93, 117–23, 177, 204, 215, 231

Huerta, Victoriano, 57

Huerta, Adolfo de la, 72, 180

Ibáñez, Emmy, 34, 55

Ideas (periodical), 97, 208

El Imparcial (newspaper), 23, 51–58, 229

independence, 8, 24, 39, 55, 91, 94, 128, 207, 219

inequality, 88, 90, 150, 214–20, 225

Instituto Nacional de Antropología e Historia. See National Institute for Anthropology and History

International League of Iberian and Hispanic-American Women, 108, 192

Iturriaga, José E., 6, 204, 206–7

Jiménez Esponda, Estela, 195–97, 225

Jiménez Rueda, Julio, 66

José María Morelos Party, 175

Jóvenes Revolucionarios. See Young Revolutionaries

Knights of Columbus, 170

Kraus de Álvarez de la Rosa, Carmen, 78, 144

law (regulating government offices), 63

Law, Federal Labor (1931), 8, 96, 107, 109, 11, 168–74, 182–88, 224–25, 234

League of Women Voters (United States), 106

motherhood: advocates for, 164, 172, 222; and class, 15, 18, 87–88, 230, 237; in film, 200, 210; invoked to limit women's rights, 18, 98; single, 34, 67–72, 106, 117–23, 179, 207, 218–20, 235; and work, 10, 12, 126, 172–73

Múgica, Francisco, 81, 119

La Mujer (periodical), 106

Mujer (periodical), 61, 93–97

La Mujer (periodical), 24

Mujeres Libres. *See* Free Women

El Mundo (newspaper), 65–67, 94

mutual aid societies: artisans, 8, 28–30; cigarette workers, 28–30; empleadas, 171; Gran Círculo de Obreros, 45–49; MLT students, 57; National Confederation of Public Administration, 102–3, 234; public employees, 8, 182, 234n23; Sociedad Leona Vicario, 29; Sociedad Josefa Ortíz de Domínguez, 29; Workers Congress, 22–30

El Nacional (newspaper), 97, 120, 124, 126, 148, 161, 174, 176–78, 180, 194–95, 219

Nacional Distribuidora y Reguladora. *See* National Distributor and Regulator

Nacional Financiera. *See* Mexican Development Bank

Narváez, Rosa, 109

National Alliance of Women, 193

National Bloc of Revolutionary Women, 172–78

National Confederation of Popular Organizations, 191–95, 225

National Confederation of Public Administration, 102–3, 234

National Confederation of Veterans, 196

National Congress of Women Workers and Peasants. *See* congresses (women)

National Distributor and Regulator, 203–4

National Feminist Party, 170–71

National Institute for Anthropology and History, 223

National Organizing Board of National Industrial and Agricultural Development, 173

National Peasant Confederation, 191–95, 225

National Revolutionary Party (PNR), 123, 126, 168, 169–73, 176, 179–94

National Social Workers Union, 192

National Union of Education Workers, 222

National Women's League (Union of Women of the Americas, UMA), 175

National Women's Organization (PNR-affiliated), 189, 198

Nava de Ruisánchez, Julia, 106, 150

neighborhoods: Condesa, 71, 78; Cuauhtémoc, 71; Guerrero, 71, 178, 187; Peralvillo, 71; Roma, 71, 78, 92; Santa María de la Ribera, 71, 97, 154, 178

newspapers and periodicals. See *Alas; Alborada; El Álbum de la Mujer; Alianza; La Clase Media; La Convención Radical Obrera; Coopera; Crisol; El Demócrata; Diario del Hogar; Elegancias; Excélsior; Las Hijas del Anáhuac; El Hijo del Trabajo; El Hogar; Horizontes; Ideas; El Imparcial; Mujer; La Mujer; La Mujer; El Mundo; El Nacional; New York Times; La Prensa; Revista Positivista; La Semana Ilustrada; El Semanario de las Señoritas Mejicanas; Senda Nueva; El Socialista;*

professionalization, 12, 102, 111, 128–39
proletariat, 103, 150, 173, 217, 231
prostitution, 99, 128, 190, 205
public employees. *See* employees, public
Puig Casauranc, José Manuel, 72–77

Que en paz descanse (1962–2018), xii
Quesada, José Vicente, 188

radio address, 173, 208
Ramírez, Celia, 225
Ramírez, María Guadalupe, 225
Ramírez Garrido, Domingo José, 105
Rangel, Refugio, 189
Regina Landa (Azuela), 161
Regional Confederation of Mexican
    Workers, 104, 234
Retratos de Almas (Llach), 160, 162
Revista Positivista (periodical), 55
Revolutionary Action, 189
Revolutionary Front of Intellectual
    Workers, 192–94
Revolutionary Youth, 178–80
Reyes, Aurora, 223
Reyes de Govea, María Aurelia
    (Arlette), 127–28
Reyes Spíndola, Rafael, 51
Río escondido (Fernández), 210
Ríos Cárdenas, María, 32, 61, 81–110, 127,
    148, 169, 172, 176, 218, 232. See also
    Atavismo; Mujer
Rivas Palacio, Carlos, 176, 183–85
Robles de Mendoza, Margarita, 184
Rocha, María, 183
Rodríguez, Abelardo L., 123, 175, 182
Rodríguez, Luís L., 183
Rodríguez, Nita, 185
Rodríguez Cabo, Eva, 184, 188
Rodríguez Cabo, Matilde, 147, 192

Rodríguez de la Rosa, René, 146, 159, 169
Roger, Gastón, 66
Rojas de Escudero, Edelmira, 170
Rolland, Modesto C., 101
Romero Rubio de Díaz, Carmen, 14,
    41, 236
Rondero, Luz, 184
Rosal, Alicia de, 125
Ross, María Luisa, 109, 222

Salado Álvarez, Ana, 179
salaries. *See* wages
Salcedo, Dolores, 75–76, 83–85
Salón México (dance hall), 122
Salón México (film) (Fernández), 210
Santoyo, Raquel, 34, 43–45, 49–53,
    146, 148
school enrollment, 42, 49, 73–79, 89,
    142–45, 153, 158
school organizations: Miguel Lerdo de
    Tejada Commercial School, 57; "Fra-
    ternity" Women's Society (ESCA), 84;
    Student Federation (DETIC), 82–83
schools: Academy for Secondary
    Education and Languages Night
    School (formerly Benito Juárez),
    40; Adalberto Tejeda School, 223;
    Advanced Studies, 89; Advanced Study
    of Public Administration, 77; Banking
    and Commerce, 77; British School
    for Young Ladies, 76; Business and
    Administration School for Advanced
    Study, 14, 40–43, 74, 84, 102, 107,
    109, 145, 157; El Colegio Teresiano,
    109; Dr. Mora Commercial, 43, 74,
    79, 80; Gabriela Mistral, 73–80, 144;
    Industrial Night School Centers for
    Popular Culture, 77; for Manual Arts
    and Trades for Women, 13, 24, 26, 40,

To order or obtain more information on these or other University of Nebraska Press titles, visit nebraskapress.unl.edu.

CPSIA information can be obtained
at www.ICGtesting.com
Printed in the USA
LVHW032248160721
692960LV00006B/482